Grammar Dimensions

Book Three

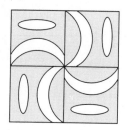

Grammar Dimensions
Book Three
Form, Meaning, and Use

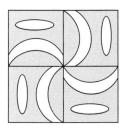

Stephen H. Thewlis

American Language Institute
San Francisco State University

Heinle & Heinle Publishers
A Division of Wadsworth, Inc.
Boston, Massachusetts 02116 U.S.A

Photo Credits:

Photos on page 1, page 15 (top middle, top right, bottom middle), page 67, page 121, and pa
are courtesy of Pat Martin. Top middle photo on page 15 was taken at FlightStar, Champaign, I
photo on page 15 was taken at Interior Galleries by Carter's, Champaign, IL; and photo on page
courtesy of Dr. Jan Colton.

Photos on page 2 (top) and page 107 appear courtesy of H. Armstrong Roberts.

Photo on page 2 (bottom) appears courtesy of NASA.

Photos on page 15 (top left, bottom left, and bottom right) appear courtesy of AP/Wide World

Photo on page 32 appears courtesy of Tennessee Wildlife Resources Agency.

Photo of Nazca Lines on page 46 appears courtesy of Paul Beals.

Photo of Stonehenge on page 46 appears courtesy of Robbie Edwards.

Photo on page 174 appears courtesy of Jessamine Santory.

Photo on page 181 appears courtesy of Florida Department of Natural Resources.

Photo on page 252 is United Nations Photo #123535, by Siceloff.

Photo on page 281 appears courtesy of Illinois Department of Transportation.

Photos on page 286 appear courtesy of Allen Bragdon.

Photo on page 339 appears courtesy of Sue Walton and Alan Thewlis.

The publication of the Grammar Dimensions series
was directed by the members of the Heinle & Heinle
ESL Publishing Team:

David Lee, Editorial Director
Susan Mraz, Marketing Manager
Lisa McLaughlin, Production Editor
Nancy Mann, Developmental Editor

Also participating in the publication of this program were:

Publisher: Stan Galek
Editorial Production Manager: Elizabeth Holthaus
Assistant Editor: Kenneth Mattsson
Manufacturing Coordinator: Mary Beth Lynch
Full Service Production/Design: Publication Services, Inc.
Cover Designer: Martucci Studio
Cover Artist: Susan Johnson

ISBN 0-8384-3970-5

10 9 8 7 6 5 4 3 2 1

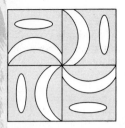

Table of Contents

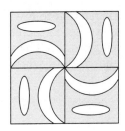

Preface to *Grammar Dimensions: Form, Meaning, and Use*

To the Teacher

ABOUT THE SERIES

With the recent emphasis on communication, the teaching of grammar has often been downplayed, or even overlooked entirely. Although one would not want to argue the goal of having students be able to communicate successfully, it is important to recognize that a major means to this end is to teach students to use grammatical structures. Some grammatical structures may be acquired naturally without instruction, but it is assumed by the creators of this series that explicit focus on the troublesome aspects of English will facilitate and accelerate their acquisition. The teaching needs to be done, however, in such a way that the interdependence of grammar and communication is appreciated.

In this regard, it is crucial to recognize that the use of grammatical structures involves more than having students achieve formal accuracy. Students must be able to use the structures meaningfully and appropriately as well. This series, therefore, takes into account all three dimensions of language: syntax/morphology (form), semantics (meaning), and pragmatics (use). The relevant facts about the **form, meaning,** and **use** of English grammatical structures were compiled into a comprehensive scope and sequence and distributed across a four-book series. Where the grammatical system is complex (e.g., the verb-tense system) or the structure complicated (e.g., the passive voice), it is revisited in each book in the series. Nevertheless, each book is free-standing and may be used independently of the others in the series if the student or program needs warrant.

Another way in which the interdependence of grammar and communication is stressed is that students first encounter every structure in a meaningful context where their attention is not immediately drawn to its formal properties. Each treatment of a grammatical structure concludes with students being given the opportunity to use the structure in communicative activities. The point of the series is not to teach grammar as static knowledge, but to have students use it in the dynamic process of communication. In this way grammar might better be thought of as a skill, rather than as an area of knowledge.

It is my hope that this book will provide teachers with the means to create, along with their students, learning opportunities that are tailored to learners' needs, are enjoyable, and will maximize everyone's learning.

ABOUT THE BOOK

This book deals with grammatical structures that ESL/EFL students often find challenging, such as the use of infinitives and gerunds. It also employs a discourse orientation when dealing with structures such as verb tenses and articles. Units that share certain features have been clustered together. No more than three or four units are clustered at one time, however, in order to provide for some variety of focus. As the units have been designed to stand independently, It is possible for a syllabus to be constructed that follows a different order of structures than the one presented in the book. It is also not expected that there will be sufficient time to deal with all the matieral that has been introduced here within a single course. Teachers are encouraged to see the book as a resource from which they can select units or parts of units which best meet student needs.

Unit Organization

TASKS

One way in which to identify student needs is to use the **Tasks**, which open each unit as a pre-test. Learner engagement in the Tasks may show that students have already learned what they need to know about a certain structure, in which case the unit can be skipped entirely. Or it may be possible, from examining students' performance, to pinpoint precisely where the students need to work. For any given structure, the learning challenge presented by the three dimensions of language is not equal. Some structures present more of a form-based challenge to learners; for others, the long-term challenge is to learn what the structures mean or when to use them. The type and degree of challenge varies according to the inherent complexity of the structure itself and the particular language background and level of English proficiency of the students.

FOCUS BOXES

Relevant facts about the form, meaning, and use of the structure are presented in **Focus Boxes** following the Task. Teachers can work their way systematically through a given unit or can pick and choose from among the Focus Boxes those points on which they feel students specifically need to concentrate.

EXERCISES

From a pedagogical perspective, it is helpful to think of grammar as a skill to be developed. Thus, in this book, **Exercises** have been provided to accompany each Focus Box. Certain of the Exercises may be done individually, others with students working in pairs or in small groups. Some of the Exercises can be done in class, others assigned as homework. Students' learning styles and the learning challenge they are working on will help teachers determine the most effective way to have students use the Exercises. (The Instructor's Manual should be consulted also for helpful hints in this regard.)

ACTIVITIES

At the end of each unit are a series of **Activities** that help students realize the communicative value of the grammar they are learning and that offer them further practice in using the grammar to convey meaning. Teachers or students may select the Activities from which they believe they would derive the most benefit and enjoyment. Student performance on these Activities can be used as a post-test as well. Teachers should not expect perfect performance at this point, however. Often there is a delayed effect in learning anything, and even some temporary backsliding in student performance as new material is introduced.

OTHER COMPONENTS

An **Instructor's Manual** is available for this book. The Manual contains answers to the Exercise questions and grammatical notes where pertinent. The Manual also further discusses the theory underlying the series and "walks a teacher through" a typical unit, suggesting ways in which the various components of the unit might be used and supplemented in the classroom.

A student **Workbook** also accompanies this book. It provides additional exercises to support the material presented in this text. Many of the workbook exercises are specially designed to help students prepare for the TOEFL (Test of English as a Foreign Language).

To the Student

All grammar structures have a form, a meaning, and a use. We can show this with a pie chart:

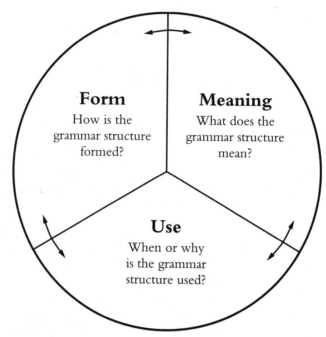

Often you will find that you know the answer to one or more of these questions, but not to all of them, for a particular grammar structure. This book has been written to help you learn answers to these questions for the major grammar structures of English. More importantly, it gives you practice with the answers so that you can develop your ability to use English grammar structures accurately, meaningfully, and appropriately.

At the beginning of each unit, you will be asked to work on a task. The task will introduce you to the grammar structures to be studied in the unit. However, it is not important at this point that you think about grammar. You should just do the task as well as you can.

In the next section of the unit are focus boxes and exercises. You will see that the boxes are labeled with **FORM, MEANING, USE,** or a combination of these, corresponding to the three parts of the pie chart. In each focus box is information that answers one or more of the questions in the pie. Along with the focus box are exercises that should help you put into practice what you have studied.

The last section of each unit contains communicative activities. Hopefully, you will enjoy doing these and at the same time receive further practice using the grammar structures in meaningful ways.

By working on the task, studying the focus boxes, doing the exercises, and engaging in the activities, you will develop greater knowledge of English grammar and skill in using it. I also believe you will enjoy the learning experience along the way.

Diane Larsen-Freeman

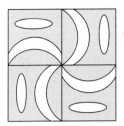

Acknowledgments

Series Director Acknowledgments

As with any project this ambitious, a number of people have made important contributions. I need to thank my students in the MAT Program at the School for International Training and audiences worldwide for listening to me talk about my ideas for reconciling the teaching of grammar with communicative language teaching. Their feedback and questions have been invaluable in the evolution of my thinking. One student, Anna Mussman, should be singled out for her helpful comments on the manuscript that she was able to provide based on her years of English teaching. A number of other anonymous teacher reviewers have also had a formative role in the development of the series. I hope they derive some satisfaction in seeing that their concerns were addressed wherever possible. In addition, Marianne Celce-Murcia not only helped with the original scope and sequence of the series, but also provided valuable guidance throughout its evolution.

I feel extremely grateful, as well, for the professionalism of the authors, who had to put into practice the ideas behind this series. Their commitment to the project, patience with its organic nature, and willingness to keep at it are all much appreciated. I insisted that the authors be practicing ESL teachers. I believe the series has benefited from this decision, but I am also cognizant of the demands it has put on the authors' lives these past few years.

Finally, I must acknowledge the support of the Heinle and Heinle "team." This project was "inherited" by Heinle and Heinle during its formative stage. To Dave Lee, Susan Mraz, Lisa McLaughlin, and especially Susan Maguire, who never stopped believing in this project, I am indeed thankful. And to Nancy Mann, who helped the belief become a reality, I am very grateful.

Author Acknowledgments

To H. Douglas Brown, who pushed me into publishing. To my colleagues at the American Language Institute, who covered my bippy while I did it. To Diane (Sine qua non) Larsen-Freeman, for her guidance and direction in the development of the series, her great patience and flexibility, and her ability to find ways of keeping me busy and involved during the entire course of the project. To Nancy Mann for her extraordinarily sensitive perspective. To the teachers and students of the American Language Institute, who piloted the materials and made enormously helpful comments—especially Beth Erickson and Jennifer Schmidt.

To the reviewers of the manuscript, Janet Goodwin (UCLA), Patricia Brennecke (Harvard University), Corey Mass (Miami-Dade Community College), Paul E. Munsell (Michigan State University), Michael Calderado (Passaic Community College), Marlene Gross (Concordia College), Joseph Dunwoody (San Antonio College), Jack Ramsay (American University), and to Rita Silver, who class tested the manuscript at Boston University.

To the people, real and imaginary, who appear in these pages. And most especially to Michael Mercil, for his love, support, and patience all through this long, long sojourn in Grammarland.

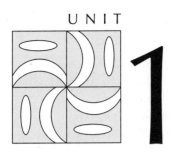

UNIT

1

An Overview of the English Verb System 1:
Time Frame and Moment of Focus

Task

The twentieth century has seen the entire world undergo the most rapid social and technological upheavals in the history of the planet. Until this century, most people could count on living in a world that was very much like the world in which their grandparents grew up. They could be sure that the lives of their grandchildren would not be substantially different from their own. But the twentieth century has changed all that. The world of your grandparents is completely different from your own. The world of your grandchildren will be even more different.

- Explore some of these social and technological changes by examining the following information about the life of a typical American college student, as compared to his grandfather's life, and to the kind of life that his granddaughter can look forward to.

Think and Write

- Use the information about these three people to write a short paragraph about each of them that describes their world and their activities.

BOB SCHILLING—STUDENT

born: 1970

family: two brothers and one sister, living with mother; parents divorced; Bob lives in a college dorm

occupation: currently a sophomore, studying biology, plans to be a doctor

regular activities: school, part-time job in the library, time with girlfriend, visiting family some weekends and during school vacations

hobbies or favorite sports: basketball, skiing, computers, music, TV

visits to foreign countries: Mexico (once), Canada (twice)

special skills or abilities: computers, university chorus

probable activity at this moment: studying for biology midterm

ROBERT SCHILLING—GRANDFATHER

born: 1915 **died:** 1987
family: five brothers, four sisters; only one sister and brother survived childhood; father died of tuberculosis when Robert was 14 years old.
occupation: factory worker, never finished high school
regular activities: job (12-hour days), helping mother, family life
hobbies or favorite sport: radio, baseball (on factory team), church
visits to foreign countries: none
special skills or abilities: baseball, playing harmonica
probable activity when Bob was born: working at the factory

• Use what you know about current trends to estimate how the life of Bob's granddaughter will be different from Bob's or Robert's. Fill in some information and then write a paragraph describing her world and activities.

ROBERTA CHONG-DAVIS—GRANDDAUGHTER

born: 2030

family:_____

occupation:_____

regular activities:_____

_____

hobbies or favorite sport:_____

_____

visits to foreign countries or planets:_____

_____

special skills or abilities:_____

_____

probable activity 100 years from today:_____

_____

Discuss

- Compare what you have written with two or three other students. Discuss these questions:
  - What predictions did you make about the future of technological and social change? What were the similarities and differences between what you expect to take place in the next century and what other students expect?
  - Decide on the three most significant effects of rapid social change. Base your decisions on what you have written and predicted.
- Present the results of your discussion to the rest of the class.

Focus 1

FORM ● MEANING

Overview of the English Verb System

FORM
MEANING

- The verb system of English is rather simple. Once you understand how all the tenses fit together, it is easy to choose the correct tense for the meaning you are trying to convey.
- The word *tense* refers to the **form** a verb takes, which is based on two things, **Time Frame** and **Aspect**:
  - **Time Frame** tells whether a verb refers to now, or some particular time in the past or the future.
  - **Aspect** tells how the verb is related to that time. There are four kinds of aspect, each one having its own basic meaning:

Aspect	Meaning
simple	**at** that time
progressive	**in progress during** that time
perfect	**before** that time
perfect progressive	**in progress during and before** that time

- Combining Time Frame and Aspect creates 12 possible combinations of forms. These forms are **tenses**, and the name of each tense tells which Time Frame and which Aspect is being used: simple past tense, present perfect, future progressive, and so on.

3

ASPECT→ TIME FRAME↓	Simple	Progressive	Perfect	Perfect Progressive
Present	study/ studies give/ gives	am/ is/ are studying am/is/are giving	has/ have studied has/have given	has/ have been studying has/have been giving
Past	studied gave	was/ were studying was/were giving	had studied had given	had been studying had been giving
Future	will study will give	will be studying will be giving	will have studied will have given	will have been studying will have been giving

Focus 2

FORM ● MEANING ● USE

Identifying the Basic Time Frame

FORM
MEANING
USE

- Uses of the three basic time frames in English vary. The different forms and uses are listed in Charts 1-1 to 1-3.
  - Use the **Present Time Frame** to talk about general relationships. Most scientific and technical writing is in Present Time. Anything that is related to the present moment is also expressed in Present Time, so newspaper headlines, news stories, spoken conversations, jokes, and informal narratives are often in Present Time Frame.
  - Use the **Past Time Frame** to talk about things that are not directly connected to the present moment. Most fiction, historical accounts, and factual descriptions of past events are in Past Time Frame.
  - Use the **Future Time Frame** for anything that is scheduled to happen or predicted for the future.
- Identifying the correct time frame is the first step in deciding which tense to use. The second step is to choose from the tenses within that time frame.

Chart 1–1   Present Time Frame

Form	Meaning	Use	Example
SIMPLE PRESENT *I/ you/ we/ they +* simple form of verb *he/ she/ it + -s* form of verb	now	• general relationships and timeless truths	**(a)** Time **changes** the way people live.
		• permanent states	**(b)** Bob **likes** being away from home.
		• habitual and recurring actions	**(c)** Bob **works** in the library every afternoon.
PRESENT PROGRESSIVE *am/ is/ are +* present participle (verb + *-ing*)	already in progress now	• actions in progress	**(d)** Bob **is studying** for a midterm at this moment.
		• repetition or duration	**(e)** Bob **is taking** a biology class this semester.
		• temporary states and actions	**(f)** Bob's brother **is living** with his father for the summer.
		• uncompleted actions	**(g)** He **is** still **looking** for a cheap apartment.
PRESENT PERFECT *have/ has +* past participle (verb + *-ed* or 3rd form of irregular verbs)	in the past but related in some way to the present	• past events related to the present by time.	**(h)** Bob **has visited** Canada twice, so he won't join the tour to Quebec.
		• past events related to the present by logical relationship	**(i)** Bob **has gotten** very good at the computer, so he doesn't need to take another class.
PRESENT PERFECT PROGRESSIVE *have/ has +* verb + present participle (verb + *-ing*)	until and often including the present	• repeated and/or continuous actions	**(j)** Bob **has been spending** his weekends at home since he started living in the dorm.
			(k) Bob **has been singing** in a chorus ever since he was in high school.

Chart 1–2   Past Time Frame

Form	Meaning	Use	Example
SIMPLE PAST verb + -*ed* or irregular past form	at a certain time in the past	• states or general relationships that were true in the past	**(a)** Tuberculosis **was** a common cause of death 50 years ago.
		• habitual or recurrent actions that took place in the past	**(b)** Robert Schilling **worked** 12 hours a day for low wages.
		• specific events that took place in the past	**(c)** Robert Schilling **went** to work in a factory at age 14.
PAST PROGRESSIVE *was/ were* + present participle (verb + -*ing*)	in progress at a certain time in the past.	• interrupted actions	**(d)** Robert **was studying** in high school when his father died.
		• repeated actions and actions over time	**(e)** Robert **was** always **trying** to get promotions at the factory.
PAST PERFECT *had* past participle (verb + -*ed* or 3rd form of irregular verb)	before a certain time in the past.	• actions or states that took place before other events in the past	**(f)** His father **had been dead** for several weeks when Robert quit school and started working to help his mother.
PAST PERFECT PROGRESSIVE *had been* + present participle (verb + -*ing*)	until a certain time in the past.	• continuous vs. repeated actions	**(g)** Robert **had been working** for 12 hours when the foreman told him to go home.
		• uncompleted vs. completed actions	**(h)** Robert **had been hoping** to complete school when he had to find a factory job to help his family.

Chart 1–3 Future Time Frame

Form	Meaning	Use	Example
SIMPLE PRESENT	already scheduled or expected in the future	• schedules	**(a)** The plane **leaves** at 6:30 tomorrow.
PRESENT PROGRESSIVE		• definite future plans	**(b)** I **am spending** next summer in France.
SIMPLE FUTURE one-word modal (*will/might* etc.) or phrasal modal (*am/is/are* + *going to*) + simple verb	at a certain time in the future	• predictions about the future	**(c)** Roberta **is going to take** a vacation on the moon.
			(d) She **will** probably **get** there by space shuttle, and she **might stay** on an observation platform.
FUTURE PROGRESSIVE modal + *be* + verb + *-ing*	in progress at a certain time in the future	• events happening at the same time as other future events	**(e)** 100 years from now Roberta **will be** living on the moon.
FUTURE PERFECT modal + *have* + past participle (verb + *-ed* or 3rd form of irregular verb)	before a certain time in the future	• events happening before other future events	**(f)** Scientists **will have visited** the moon long before tourists will be able to.
FUTURE PERFECT PROGRESSIVE modal + *have* + *been* + verb + *-ing*	up until a certain time in the future	• repeated and/or continuous actions	**(g)** When Roberta retires on Earth she will probably not be used to the earth's level of gravity because she **will have been living** on the moon for several years.

• Notice here that two tenses (simple present and present progressive) associated with the present time frame can be used to talk about future plans or scheduled events.

7

Exercise 1

Identify the time frame for each of these passages. Is it Present Time, Past Time, or Future Time?

1. (a) Mac had a terrible headache. (b) His tongue was dry, and his eyes were burning. (c) He had been sneezing constantly for nearly an hour. (d) He hated springtime. (e) For most people, spring meant flowers and sunshine, but for Mac it meant hay fever.

2. (a) I really don't know what to do for vacation. (b) My vacation starts in three weeks, and (c) I'm trying to decide what to do. (d) I've been to Hawaii and New York. (e) It's too early in the year to go camping in the mountains. (f) I've been working hard at the office, and I really need a break. (g) I've saved enough money to have a really nice trip. (h) I just can't decide where to go or what to do.

3. (a) The people of ancient Greece and ancient India were not strangers to each other. (b) For many generations, there had been regular trade and commerce between the two regions. (c) Alexander the Great had known of the great wealth of the lands of the East before he decided to expand his empire.

4. (a) The changing world climate will mean changes in food production. (b) Scientists think that summers throughout North America will become much hotter and drier than they are now. (c) Crops that require a lot of water will be less economical to grow. (d) Society will have to develop different energy sources, since hydroelectric power may not be abundant, and (e) fossil fuels, such as coal and oil, may have become depleted by the end of the next century.

5. (a) Social Darwinism was a popular theory of the nineteenth century. (b) It compared social and economic development with biological evolution. (c) According to this theory, competition between rich people and poor people was unavoidable. (d) The poor were like dinosaurs who were dying out because they had lost the battle for survival—economic survival.

6. (a) Scientific research often has an important social impact. (c) In recent years, scientists have discovered that Vitamin B can prevent certain kinds of childhood blindness. (d) As a result, programs have been established that provide education and dietary supplements to children in developing countries.

7. (a) Scientists are developing more effective drugs to help deal with mental illness. (b) Many forms of insanity actually result from a chemical imbalance in the brain. (c) Experimental drugs are proving to be useful in a number of cases. (d) Although some doctors worry about the ethics of requiring people to take drugs for the rest of their lives, (e) these new drugs have apparently helped many people in significant ways.

Exercise 2

In the passages above, underline each complete verb (the verb plus any auxiliary—*have, do, be*, etc.—that shows the tense of the verb) and name the tense of each verb.

Exercise 3

Use the example sentences in the charts to help you decide what tense you should be looking for in order to complete the following exercise. Look at the passages in Exercise 1. (This exercise will help you remember and apply the information given in the verb tense charts on pages 5, 6, 7.)

1. From the sentences that refer to Present Time, identify at least one example of a verb phrase that is being used to express
   a. a timeless truth; *6a, b , 7 b,d*
   b. a past event or situation that is related to the present; *2d, f, g , 6. e,d   7c*
   c. an action still in progress; *2c, f 7a,c*
   d. a general relationship; *2 e, f*
   e. a state that is true now. *2 g f h*
2. From the sentences that refer to Future Time, identify at least one example of a verb phrase that is being used to express
   a. an event that is already scheduled to take place in the future; *2 b*
   b. an event or state that is predicted for the future; *4 a, b, e, d, e*
   c. an event that will be taking place until and including a specific future time. *4e*
3. From the sentences that refer to Past Time, identify at least one example of a verb phrase that is being used to express
   a. a general statement; *1d ,e ,3a , 5a bcd*
   b. a continuous or repeated action that happened in the past; *1 c, 5d*
   c. an action or state that took place before other events in the past; *1e, 3bc, 5d*
   d. an action that took place at a specific time in the past. *1a, b, 3 c*

Focus 3

USE

Changing Time Frame within a Given Passage

USE

- Sometimes an author changes the time frame within a given passage if there is
  - movement from general statement to specific example:

    There **are** many examples in history of increasing military power causing a declining standard of living. Rome **was** unable to maintain both its army and the welfare of its population. Great Britain **declined** steadily from its leading position in the early part of this century. America's attempt to be a world leader **has resulted** in a huge national debt and a shocking standard of living for the rapidly growing number of poor people.

- an important contrast in time signaled by a clear marker:

One hundred years ago the life expectancy in the United States was about 65. **Nowadays** it has increased by an average of ten years. **In the next century**, if current trends continue, people should be able to live until their nineties. Interestingly enough, however, **one hundred years ago** the number of people who were over 100 was less than one percent of the population. That figure has not changed substantially **even today**. Scientists expect that we will not be able to extend life much more than is currently possible, in spite of medical advances.

- a statement of general truth that "interrupts" the text:

I saw an old lady yesterday. **You don't see her kind much anymore**. She was wearing a black shawl and she was carrying an umbrella. **Most old ladies I know don't carry umbrellas, and slacks are more common than shawls.** As she walked down the street, I thought about how much life has changed since she was my age.

Exercise 4

Mark the following passages with a slash (/) to show where the time frame changes. The first one has been done for you as an example.

1. My brother called me up yesterday. / I always know he needs to borrow money when he calls, because I never hear from him at any other time. / We spoke about this and that for a few minutes. He asked about my job and my family. We talked about his problems with his boss. / These are typical topics before he finally asks for a loan. / This phone call was no exception. He needed $50 "until payday." / Somehow, when payday comes he never remembers to pay back the loan.

2. I'll be really happy when the summer is over. I don't like hot weather, and I can't stand mosquitoes. There's a lot of both of those things in the summer. Last summer I tried to escape by going on a trip to Alaska. The heat wasn't bad, but the mosquitoes were terrible! Next year I think I'll consider a vacation in Tierra del Fuego. I understand it's really cold there in July.

3. For more than 50 years, scientists around the world have used a single means of measuring the strength (or magnitude) of earthquakes. The Richter scale was developed by Charles Richter in 1935. It was designed so scientists could compare the intensity of earthquakes in different parts of the world. It was designed to measure intensity in earthquakes, not damage. This is because a less powerful earthquake in a heavily populated area can cause more damage than a stronger earthquake in an unpopulated area.

4. Every year archaeologists and anthropologists find out more information about how the Western Hemisphere was settled. By examining burial sites and learning about the linguistic relationships between various languages, researchers have established some basic facts about how and when man first came to the New World. Native Americans (or "Indians," as they came to be known) inhabited North America in several "waves" of migration. The first wave was at least 15,000 years ago. The most recent wave probably ended with the retreat of the glaciers at the end of the last Ice Age. Although there is still disagreement among experts as to exactly when and how many "waves" actually occurred, most researchers agree that there were at least three and perhaps as many as five separate migrations.

Exercise 5

Analyze each change of time frame that you found in Exercise 4. What reason did the author have for changing the time frame? There may be more than one reason.

Exercise 6

Underline the complete verb (verb plus auxiliaries) in the passages in Exercise 4 and name the tense of each verb phrase.

Focus 4

MEANING

Identifying the Moment of Focus

MEANING

- Determining the *moment of focus* is the next step in choosing the correct tense.
  - For Present Time, the moment of focus is always **now** (the moment of speaking or writing), and all ideas are expressed in relation to it.
  - For Past Time or Future Time, the moment of focus is usually a particular specified time. We can use the word *then* to refer to the moment of focus in these time frames.
- The moment of focus can be a point of time or a period of time.

Point of Time	Period of Time
(a) One dark midnight, on December 25, 1871, there was an amazing sight.	**(c) During the fourteenth century,** several outbreaks of bubonic plague decimated the population of Europe, and caused widespread social changes.
(b) On February 28, 2050, Roberta Chong-Davis will be 20 years old.	**(d) In the coming years,** there may be big changes in health care in the United States.

- The moment of focus can be explicitly stated or implied.

Stated Explicitly	Implied from a Context
(e) Yesterday I saw an amazing sight. **(f) When I was a child,** I was afraid of the dark. **(g)** Jeff had dinner **before he left for the opera.**	**(h) Ancient Mayans** had a very advanced knowledge of mathematics. **(i) My grandfather** was born in England.

- The same moment of focus can refer to several sentences, or it can change from sentence to sentence.

Same Moment of Focus	Changing Moment of Focus
(j) When the earthquake struck, Jeff was still in his office. He had been trying to finish a project. Suddenly the building began to sway, and the bookshelf in his office tipped over.	**(k) When Jeff first moved** to San Francisco, he had never eaten Chinese food. **By the time he met Matt**, however, he was going out for Chinese food almost every weekend.

Exercise 7

Identify the moment of focus in the following passages. There may be only one, or it may change from sentence to sentence. Is it explicitly stated or implied? Is it a point of time or a period of time?

1. I had an interesting experience yesterday afternoon. I was walking from my house to the grocery store when I saw someone I had gone to high school with.
2. The moment Peter heard that John F. Kennedy had been assassinated was one that he would never forget. He was a junior in high school. He was studying in the school library at the time.
3. The Imperial City of Rome was badly damaged by fire during the first century A.D. It was widely believed that the Emperor Nero played a violin while the city burned to the ground.
4. During the last years of his life, Wolfgang Amadeus Mozart was virtually penniless. In spite of his fame as a composer, he was forced to borrow from friends, and to move frequently, since he was unable to pay his rent.
5. When John first arrives in Paris, he's going to stay with a local French teacher and his family. Once he is able to speak French well enough, he will probably find a small apartment of his own.
6. What will you bring to the party? I hear we'll be playing games. I hope there will be dancing as well!

Exercise 8

Underline each complete verb (verb plus auxiliaries) in the passages in Exercise 7 and name the tense of each verb.

Activities

Activity 1

Rewrite the paragraphs you wrote for the Task at the beginning of this unit, this time writing about your own life and that of your grandfather and granddaughter. Identify the Time Frame for each paragraph and make sure that you are only using tenses that are appropriate for that particular Time Frame.

Activity 2

Work with a partner. Describe a typical day in your life. Tell your partner about the things you do, where you go, and how you typically spend your time. Mention at least five regular activities.

- Next, describe a typical day in your life five years ago. Mention at least five activities that you did on a regular basis.
- Your partner should use this information to decide what three things in your life have changed the most in the last five years, and report this information to the rest of the class. Make a similar report to the class about the changes in your partner's life.

Activity 3

Congratulations! You've just won a million dollars in a contest. BUT ... you have to spend all the money in a single week, AND ... you can't spend more than $50,000 for any single purchase. (In other words, you can't just buy a million-dollar house. You have to make at least 20 separate purchases.) If you don't spend it all, you won't get any of it. What are your plans? In a brief essay, or in an oral presentation, answer this question: How you will spend the money?

- It's the end of the week. You managed to make the required number of purchases. How did you spend your money? Change the verb tenses of your essay or presentation in order to explain to the contest judges the answer to this question: How did you spend the money?

Activity 4

Look at the front page of the newspaper. Find three examples of each of the three frames of reference. They may be in the same article or three different articles.

Activity 5

How are you progressing in English?

Think and Write

- Describe how your ability to communicate in English has changed since you began your studies. What kinds of things were you able to accomplish a year ago and what can you do now that is different?

    EXAMPLES: A year ago I couldn't understand spoken English very well. My listening comprehension has improved a lot. I understand most things people say to me.

    A year ago I needed to use a dictionary for almost every word. Now my vocabulary in much larger.

- Think of at least three areas in which your skills have improved. Write sentences describing those things under the column marked *accomplishments*.

- Next, describe some things that you still can't do but want to be able to do when you have finished this course. Think of at least three things you can't or don't do now but want to be able to do by the end of this course.

    EXAMPLES: I don't talk to my friends on the telephone because I have a hard time understanding them. I want to be able to talk on the telephone.

    I can't pass the TOEFL. My scores on Part 2 are a little low. I want to get a good score on the TOEFL.

    Write sentences describing those skills under the column marked *goals*.

Discuss

- Compare your accomplishments and goals to those of some other people in the class. Identify the group's two or three most common accomplishments (things you can do in English) and the group's two or three most common goals. As a group, devise three to five *strategies* for increasing your language abilities and achieving your goals.

- Present your common accomplishments, goals, and your list of strategies to the rest of the class.

Accomplishments	Goals	Strategies
1.	1.	1.
2.	2.	2.
3.	3.	3.

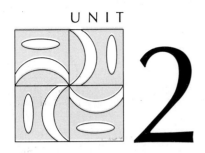

UNIT

2

An Overview of the English Verb System 2:

Aspect

Task

An old Chinese saying states that "a picture is worth a thousand words." Following are some photographs that have appeared recently in newspapers and magazines. With a partner, discuss each of these pictures and together write sentences that describe them. Your sentences should answer these questions.

What has just happened? Why do you think so?
What is happening now? Why do you think so?
What is going to happen next? Why do you think so?

After describing all the pictures, compare your descriptions with those of two other pairs of students. Do you all agree? Did you use the same verb tenses in your descriptions?

• Report any interesting similarities and differences in interpretation or description to the rest of the class.

15

Focus 1

Aspect

MEANING

- After determining the correct time frame and moment of focus you wish to use to describe an event or situation, it is necessary to express how every verb within that time frame is related to the moment of focus. We use **aspect** to show this relationship. *Aspect* is **the additional information** that a particular tense contains about the relation of that verb to the moment of focus. There are four kinds of aspect, and each one has a basic meaning:

Aspect	Meaning
simple	at that time
progressive	in progress during that time
perfect	before that time
perfect progressive	in progress during and before that time

- *Aspect* can also be used to describe whether an action
  - happens just once, or continuously or repeatedly:
    - **(a)** The protester **disrupted** the politician's speech.
    - **(b)** Protesters **have been disrupting** politicians' speeches as long as politicians **have been making them**.
  - is still happening or is completed:
    - **(c)** The police **are arresting** the demonstrator, but perhaps she'll escape.
    - **(d)** The police **have arrested** the demonstrator, so she won't be able to escape.
  - is temporary or permanent:
    - **(e)** Shopkeepers **are storing** some of their breakable merchandise on the floor until the threat of earthquake aftershocks has passed.
    - **(f)** Shopkeepers in earthquake areas **store** expensive, breakable merchandise on the lower shelves, in order to lessen the possibility of damage.

- By understanding how aspect gives additional information in all three time frames, you can more easily choose the correct tense to express your ideas.

Exercise 1

Each of these paragraphs has a single moment of focus, which has been underlined. Identify all the other verb phrases in the paragraph. What is the relation of all the other verbs to the moment of focus? Do they happen before, after, or at the same time as the moment of focus? How is this relation indicated? Discuss your ideas with a partner and present them to the rest of the class.

1. By the time John gets on Flight 53 to Paris the day after tomorrow, he will have accomplished a great deal in a relatively short period of time. He will have moved out of the apartment where he has been living for the last couple of years. He will have said some long, sad good-byes. He will certainly be thinking about all the friends he will no longer see every day.

2. When the earthquake hit San Francisco in 1989, Jeff was still at his office. He had been trying to finish a project. He had been working on it for over a week, and he was almost done. He was just making some final adjustments when the building started to move. When the quake started, he quickly got under his desk. He was glad that he had once read an article on what to do in earthquakes. He had studied the article rather carefully, and as a result, he knew exactly what to do. As soon as things started falling off the shelves, Jeff dove for cover.

3. Denise is quite a stylish dresser. She thinks that it is important to be neat and well-groomed, and she always wants to look her best. Every morning before she leaves for work, she looks at herself in the mirror. She checks to make sure that she has combed her hair and hasn't put her makeup on too heavily. She makes sure that she is wearing colors that go nicely with the clothes she is wearing. She checks to see that her slip isn't showing, and if her stockings are straight. She makes sure that the shoes she has chosen match the color of her dress and her overcoat. She likes feeling confident and attractive, and feels that taking an extra minute in front of the mirror is worth the time.

Focus 2

USE

Simple Tenses

USE

- Simple tenses (simple present, simple past, and simple future) contain no additional aspect markers. Use simple tenses
  - to express general ideas, relationships, and truths:
    - **(a)** Social psychology **is** the study of the factors that **influence** group behavior.
    - **(b)** The people of ancient Rome **spoke** Latin.
    - **(c)** A criminal **will always return** to the scene of the crime.
  - to describe habitual or recurrent actions:
    - **(d)** Denise always **checks** her appearance in the mirror before she leaves for work.
    - **(e)** James Fenimore Cooper **wrote** for three hours every day except Sunday.
    - **(f)** People **will travel** to the moon by spaceship at the end of the next century.
  - to identify time frame or moment of focus:
    - **(g)** Scientists **believe** that they have identified the cause of AIDS.
    - **(h)** When Alexander the Great **decided** to conquer Asia, he had already heard many stories about the great riches there.
    - **(i)** Mary **will visit** John while he is studying in France.

17

Focus 3

Progressive Aspect

FORM
USE

- The progressive tenses (present progressive, past progressive, and future progressive) are of the form *be* + verb + *ing*. You can add progressive aspect to a basic time to describe
  - actions already in progress as opposed to actions that happen at or after the moment of focus:

Moment of Focus	Implied Meaning
(a) When I **left** the room the students **were studying**.	They were studying **before** I left.
(b) When I **left** the room, the students **laughed**.	They laughed **after** I left.
(c) Other people **are always waiting** when Jeff **gets** to the bus stop.	They're already waiting **before** he gets there.
(d) Jeff **reads** the morning paper when he **gets** to the bus stop.	He reads his paper **after** he gets there.

  - actions that happen at the moment of focus as opposed to habitual actions:
    - **(e)** I **teach** English (habitual action), but I'**m not teaching** now (action at the moment of focus).
    - **(f)** John **studied** in France for a year (habitual action), but he **wasn't studying** last Bastille Day (action at the moment of focus).
  - temporary situations as opposed to permanent states:
    - **(g)** Mary still **lives** with her parents (permanent), but she's **staying** with friends while her parents are away (temporary).
  - a period of time as opposed to a point of time:
    - **(h)** Last night I **spoke** (point of time) to my son about the problems he **was having** with his classes this semester (period of time).
    - **(i)** I **was speaking** to my son (period of time) when I **remembered** (point of time) that I **had** (point of time) a meeting downtown.
  - repeated actions:
    - **(j)** Those students **are always asking** questions.
  - uncompleted actions:
    - **(k)** John is still **working** to perfect his French accent.
  - actions rather than states:
    - **(l)** The coach **feels** (state) that Biff should do another exercise, but Biff **is feeling** his muscles (action) and **checking** his form (action).

Exercise 2

Decide what additional information the progressive aspect communicates in the following sentences. There may be more than one possible reason why the progressive aspect is used:

a) action happening at the moment of focus

b) temporary situation rather than permanent

c) period of time rather than point of time

d) repeated actions

e) uncompleted action

f) action rather than state

1. John **was reading** a book when I saw him. a , e
2. He **is studying** for an examination now. a , e
3. Don't call him after 10:00 because he **will be sleeping**. a , c e
4. They **were selling** candy from house to house yesterday afternoon. d
5. Whenever I see John, he **is** always **reading** a book. a , d
6. I **will be visiting** friends all over the country during the summer. c , d
7. I thought John was sleeping, but in fact he **was thinking** about a solution to his problem, so I didn't interrupt him. c , e , f
8. He **was living** with his cousin for a while. b
9. I **am having** trouble with this assignment. a , b
10. I **will be staying** at the Bates Motel during the conference. b , c
11. I **am trying** to explain this, so please pay attention. a , e

Exercise 3

Decide whether to use **simple** or **progressive aspect** in the following sentences. Both choices may be correct, so prepare to explain why you chose the form you did.

1. Please turn down the radio. I _____ (study) for a test.

2. Jeff _____ (read) the newspaper when the phone rang.

3. I'm afraid those students might _____ (get) in trouble with immigration because they_____ (work) without official permission.

4. I still _____ (not study) as much as my parents want me to.

5. Rebecca _____ (speak) Russian. I wonder where she learned it?

6. Columbus _____ (look) for a shorter route to Asia when he _____ (discover) the New World by mistake.

7. When Columbus _____ (reach) Cuba, he _____ (thought) it was India.

8. I _____ (try) to explain the problem. Please pay attention.

9. I _____ (study) in the library, when I _____ (hear) the news about Kennedy's assassination.

10. Jack will probably_____ (sleep), if you wait until midnight to call him.

Focus 4

USE

Perfect Aspect

USE

- Perfect tenses (present perfect, past perfect, and future perfect) are of the forms *have* + past participle (verb + *-ed* or the third form of an irregular verb). Perfect aspect is used for **related situations** in which two verbs are involved. The basic meaning of perfect aspect is that the event that the verb describes happens before and continues to influence the moment of focus. We do not use perfect aspect to connect unrelated events.
- Use perfect aspect for events that
  - happen before as opposed to after the moment of focus:

	Implied Meaning
(a) He **had finished** the project when I **talked** to him.	The project was finished before I talked to him.
(b) He **finished** the project when I talked to him.	I talked to him first, and then he finished the project.

  - are true now as opposed to being no longer true:

	Implied Meaning
(c) Robert Schilling **has worked** in a factory for 35 years.	He still works there.
(d) Robert Schilling **worked** in a factory for 35 years.	He doesn't work there anymore.

• are related to the moment of focus and not separate ideas:

Reason for the Action	Two Separate Actions
(e) I **have already seen** that movie, **so** I won't join you tonight.	**(f)** I **saw** an interesting movie **last night**, but **tonight** I have to stay home and do homework.

• are completed or not completed:

Completed	Incomplete
(g) We can go to the movies as soon as you **have cleaned** the kitchen	**(h)** We can go to the movies even though you **haven't cleaned** the kitchen.

Exercise 4

Determine what additional information the perfect aspect communicates in the following sentences. There may be more than one kind of information.

a) happens before the moment of focus

b) true now rather than no longer true

c) related to the moment of focus

d) completed or not completed

1. Please don't take my plate. I **haven't finished** my dessert. ~~c~~ d inc
2. You are too late; the doctor **has just left** the office. d comp. a.
3. He **had forgotten** to leave a key, so we couldn't get into the office. a.
4. She **will already have left** before you receive her farewell letter. d comp. a.
5. I've **done** my homework for tomorrow. d comp.
6. Biff **hadn't even finished** high school when he joined the Army. inc a
7. The teacher **has canceled** the test, so you won't need to study tonight. a.
8. It **has rained** every January for the last ten years, so I don't think it's a good idea to plan a picnic. ᴜ<

Exercise 5

Decide whether to use **perfect** or **simple aspect** in the following sentences.

1. John _____ (say) good-bye to his classmates at school, when he started his final packing for his trip.

2. Jonas Salk _____ (conduct) many unsuccessful experiments when his efforts finally resulted in the discovery of a vaccine for polio.

3. The United States _____ (have) the same form of government for more than 200 years.

4. Bob _____ (visit) Mexico five times so far. He really likes traveling there.

5. When Bambang _____ (come) to the United States, he never _____ (be) away from his parents for more than a few days.

6. By the time Roberta Chong-Davis is 50 years old, she will probably _____ (travel) to the moon several times.

7. I _____ (not sleep) well since those noisy people moved into the apartment next door.

8. Columbus _____ (completed) three voyages to islands in the Caribbean when he _____ (realize) that the islands _____ (not be) part of India.

9. We _____ (live) in this house since 1968.

10. Lucy _____ (study) very hard for the TOEFL, so I hope she passes!

Focus 5

Perfect Progressive Aspect

USE

- Perfect progressive tenses (present perfect progressive, past perfect progressive, and future perfect progressive) are of the form *have + been + verb + ing*.
  Use perfect progressive aspect to describe
  - uncompleted as opposed to completed actions:
    - **(a)** Jeff **has been working** on that project all day. He still **hasn't finished** it.
    - **(b)** Jeff **has worked** on that project for three hours. Now he can do something else.
  - continuous processes as opposed to repeated actions:
    - **(c)** You **have been talking constantly for the last hour.** Please give someone else a chance to say something.
    - **(d)** I **have talked** to him **several times** about his lack of effort.

Exercise 6

Determine what additional information the perfect progressive aspect communicates in the following sentences. Does it indicate that the verb is

(a) uncompleted rather than completed;

(b) continuous rather than repeated?

1. Scientists **have been looking** for a cure for AIDS since the disease first appeared in 1981. a , b
2. Jonas Salk **had been searching** for a polio vaccine for more than ten years before he finally succeeded. a , b
3. By the time we finally get to the ticket window, we **will have been waiting** for over an hour. a, b,
4. I **have been trying** all day to reach her by telephone, but the line is still busy!
5. We **have been learning** about the verb system of English.

Exercise 7

Decide whether these sentences should use **perfect** or **perfect progressive aspect**. More than one answer may be correct.

1. It _____ (rain) ever since we got here. I wish it would stop.

2. He _____ (work) on that virus for nearly a year before he realized that nothing could destroy it.

3. I'm very pleased. I _____ (find) the article I read about in your paper.

4. Lately John _____ (find) life without Mary more and more difficult.

5. Joyce _____ (cook) all afternoon. I hope the food will be as delicious as it smells.

6. Bill _____ (look) for his car keys for over an hour, when he realized that he _____ (leave) them in the car.

7. I _____ (try) to solve the problem for over an hour. I give up!

8. Next January 31, Jeff and Matt _____ (live) together as roommates for five years.

9. The Girl Scouts _____ (come) to the house to sell cookies every year since I _____ (move) there.

10. I _____ (try) to reach him several times by phone without success.

Exercise 8

Write the appropriate form of the verbs in the following paragraph.

I had an "interesting" time last Friday. My roommate (we call him Louis, the dancing fool) (1) _____ (have) a dance party last Friday night. I (2) _____ (work) that night, so I (3) _____ (not get) home until 10:00. By the time I (4) _____ (get) there, everyone (5) _____ (start) dancing. I (6) _____ (hear) the music when I (7) _____ (pull) up in my car outside the apartment. When I (8) _____ (walk) into the room, everybody (9) _____ (shout) "Welcome home!" because I (10) _____ (just arrive), but they (11) _____ (keep dancing), so I (12) _____ (go) into the kitchen to find something to drink. There (13) _____ (be) several other people in the kitchen. I (14) _____ (can tell) that they (15) _____ (dance) for some time, because they (16) _____ (sit) by an open window, and their clothes

(17) _____ (be) damp with perspiration. We (18) _____ (chat) and (19) _____ (laugh) for a while. Just when I (20) _____ (be) about ready to start dancing myself, there (21) _____ (be) a knock at the door. I (22) _____ (go) to answer it, and (23) _____ (discover) a policeman standing in the hall. Apparently another neighbor (24) _____ (complain) about the noise, and the policeman (25) _____ (tell) us to turn the music down. We (26) _____ (obey), of course. Although the party (27) _____ (get) a little quieter, we still (28) _____ (have) just as much fun. I (29) _____ (be) somewhat surprised that anyone (30) _____ (complain), because I (31) _____ (think) all the other neighbors (32) _____ (be invited) and (33) _____ (dance) with the rest of us.

Exercise 9

Rewrite the paragraph in Exercise 8 in a Present Time Frame. Keep the time relations between the verbs the same by maintaining the same aspect differences as in the model paragraph.

Every Friday night **has been** the same since I got my new roommate, Louis the "dancing fool." My roommate **has** a dance party every Friday night. I **am working** nights these days, so . . . .

Exercise 10

Rewrite the paragraph in Exercise 8 in a Future Time Frame. Keep the time relations between the verbs the same by maintaining the same aspect differences as in the model paragraph.

My roommate (we call him Louis, the dancing fool) **is going to have** a dance party next Friday night, and I think I know exactly what's **going to happen**. **I'll be working** that night, so . . . .

Exercise 11

Complete these sentences with real information. Compare your answers with other students in the class. Did you use the same verb forms?

1. Until I came to this country, I . . . .
2. I often think about my problems when . . . .
3. I had never seen . . . before I . . . .

4. The next time I see my family, they . . . .
5. I am usually unhappy if . . . .
6. When I was growing up, I . . . .
7. I have been studying English since I . . . .
8. Lately I . . . .
9. Once I have completed my education, I . . . .
10. I have never . . . , but I plan to do it someday.

Exercise 12

Determine the probable reasons for the following situations. Make sure you use an appropriate time frame in your answer. Compare your answers with those of a partner. Who has a more plausible explanation? Did you use the same tenses to describe the reasons?

> **EXAMPLE:** The window was broken. The TV was missing.
> *A thief had broken into the house.*
> The students are quiet. They're listening carefully.
> *They're taking a listening comprehension test.*

1. A young woman was crying. She had been looking at a picture.
2. John's waiting at the airport. He's looking at his watch.
3. Rebecca will be smiling. Her parents will congratulate her.
4. The men have been digging holes. They are looking at an old map.
5. A woman was shouting happily. She had just received an envelope in the mail.
6. Bill studies every night. He sends applications to universities.
7. The old man wears ragged clothes. He doesn't have enough to eat.
8. The fire fighters ran to the firetruck. They drove quickly to the house.

Exercise 13

Discuss the possible difference in meaning between these groups of sentences with a partner. Add appropriate adverbs to help clarify meaning. Compare your ideas to those of other students in the class.

1. I live by myself.
   I'm living by myself.
2. I have lived by myself.
   I have been living by myself.
3. He has paid the money.
   He has been paying the money.
4. I studied when he left.
   I was studying when he left.
   I had studied when he left.
5. Robert Schilling worked in a factory.
   Robert Schilling has worked in a factory.
6. I studied for an hour.
   I have been studying for an hour.

Activities

Activity 1

Revise your descriptions of the pictures in the Task by using Past Time Frame. Start your descriptions, "When this picture was taken . . . ."

Activity 2

Bring in three to five photographs from the newspaper that you think are interesting. Make a brief presentation about these photos to the rest of the class. Describe what is happening, what has happened, and what is going to happen. Give three reasons why you think the photo is interesting.

Activity 3

Describe a routine that you typically follow. Then describe one time when you did not follow that routine, and tell what happened. For example, perhaps you usually take the bus to school. What time do you get there? What are people on the bus doing when you get on? What happened on the day when you decided to walk to school because the bus was late, or on the day when your classmate offered to take you for a ride in his cousin's brand-new car?

Activity 4

Give a short presentation about two famous people—one who is living and one who is no longer living. Identify three or four accomplishments that these individuals are famous for. What tenses will you use to describe the person who is living? What tenses will you use for the person who is deceased?

UNIT

3

Adverbials

Task

"Six Universal Questions" are taught to students of journalism. Many editors feel that any news story can be reported by asking just six questions: *who, what, when, where, why,* and *how.* Editors say that you can summarize all basic information about people and events by asking and answering those six basic questions.

- Scan the newspaper for three short articles that interest you. Possibilities include current events, stories (local or international), human interest stories, or features. Summarize the important information in each story by writing *wh-questions* and answers. Write as many questions and answers as you need to in order to summarize all the important information.

- Give your list of *wh-questions* (but *not* the answers) to a partner. Your partner should try to reconstruct the article by writing a short paragraph based on your questions. Do the same with your partner's questions.

- Do the same thing with the second article. But this time do not include any of your *who* or *what* questions. Only give your partner the *where, when, how,* and *why* questions. Your partner should again try to reconstruct the story based on your questions.

- Give your partner only the *who* and *what* questions with the third article. Follow the same procedure.

- Compare the three reconstructions. What information is missing from the second or third paragraphs? Which set of questions, *who/what* or *where/when/why/how,* provided the most complete information?

- Report your experience to the rest of the class.

Focus 1

FORM ● MEANING

Overview of Adverbials in English

FORM
MEANING

- Adverbials communicate a great deal of important information because we use adverbials to answer many *wh-questions*. In order to recognize and use adverbials correctly it is necessary to understand both their meaning and their grammatical form.

Meaning	Grammatical Form
WHERE: place (position, direction) WHEN: time HOW LONG: duration HOW OFTEN: frequency HOW: manner HOW MUCH: degree WHY: cause and effect reason and result	adverbs: *now, there, quickly, often, completely* adverbial phrases: *at noon, from Japan, with care, for fun, because of the problem, by quitting, in order to learn English, to find some money* adverbial clauses: *after I finish school, because he needed money, so that he left the party.*

Exercise 1

"Jeopardy" is a popular American TV quiz show. Contestants on "Jeopardy" choose answers, and they must provide the question for that particular answer. What questions can you ask that would get the following answers? Make up a question for each numbered answer and compare your questions to those of your classmates.

> **EXAMPLES:** **now** *When are we going to study adverbials?*
> **by studying** *How can I get a good score on the TOEFL?*
> **since 1985** *How long have you been studying English?*

1. now
2. here
3. quickly
4. often
5. carefully
6. in 1990
7. since 1985
8. until 1995
9. at noon
10. from Japan
11. for fun
12. because of the TOEFL
13. by studying
14. in order to learn English
15. to find a good job
16. after I finish school
17. because he needs money
18. until he passes the TOEFL
19. as long as I am a student
20. so he can buy books

29

The first step to understanding and using adverbials correctly is to identify their meaning and their form. This chart summarizes common adverbial forms and meaning.

COMMON ADVERBIALS

Meaning		Form		
		Adverbs	Adverbial Phrases	Adverbial Clauses
WHERE?	PLACE— POSITION Where do you live? DIRECTION Where are you going?	here/there downtown/home everywhere	in the dormitory on Main Street at the office beside/next to between/among above/below to/from out of/into through/along/ across	(a) I live **where Matt does.**
WHEN?	TIME—WHEN When will you finish the assignment? When did they leave for Florida?	now/then forever/always recently yesterday last year next week two years ago a week from today	in 1985 on Tuesday at 3:00 after lunch during vacation	(b) I'll do it **when I have time.** (c) I left **after John arrived.** (d) Nero fiddled **while Rome burned.**
HOW LONG?	TIME— DURATION How long has he been working? How many years have you been studying English?	forever	for hours from 12:00 to 2:00 since 1937 until Saturday	(e) Peter has worked there **since he first moved to the city.** (f) He will keep working... ...**as long as he has a job.** ...**until he is finished.** ...**while the boss is watching.**

Meaning		Form		
		Adverbs	Adverbial Phrases	Adverbial Clauses
HOW OFTEN?	FREQUENCY How often do you write your family? Do you ever write your family?	every night once a week often/ usually/ sometimes	on many occasions from time to time at regular intervals	(g) He goes to the movies... ...**whenever he has a chance.** ...**as often as he can.**
HOW?	MANNER/ MEANS How does John behave in formal situations? How can I get to Carnegie Hall?	quickly/well/ cleverly manually electronically	with considerable care, in a graceful fashion, like an expert with a knife by practicing through practice	(h) John did the homework **as carefully as he could.** (i) John behaves **as if he were afraid of his own shadow.**
HOW MUCH?	DEGREE How busy was the office yesterday? How much does it cost?	really completely rather too/very/enough	to a large/small extent too much/many to do busy enough to do more _____/-er than	(j) He talks **so quickly that nobody can understand him.** (k) This is **such a** serious problem **that productivity is decreasing.**
WHY?	PURPOSE AND REASON Why did you go to the bank?	thus	for some money (In order) to + verb because of	(l) I went to the bank... **so (that) I could get some cash, because I needed money.**
	CAUSE AND EFFECT What will happen if I push this button?	consequently then thus so	from as a result of	(m) If you do that, **(then) you'll get in trouble.**

Exercise 2

This exercise will help you become familiar with the chart on the previous pages. If necessary look at the categories and examples listed there to help you decide where each adverbial belongs. Answer the following questions for each underlined adverbial structure in the news article.

1. Which *wh-question* word would you use to ask a question about this information?
2. What grammatical form is it—adverb, adverbial phrase, or adverbial clause?
3. Which meaning category is it in—place, time, manner, degree, or cause and effect?

The first three have been done for you as examples:

EXAMPLES: 1. *HOW; adverb; manner*
 2. *WHERE; adverbial phrase; place*
 3. *WHEN; adverbial clause; time*

BIZARRE ATTACK BY WILD PIGS ON RAMPAGE

Buttonwillow, GA

Mary Morris is a lucky woman. She is resting (1) comfortably (2) at her Buttonwillow home (3) after doctors released her from Buttonwillow Hospital earlier this afternoon. Early this morning she was involved in one of the strangest automobile mishaps in local history. Her car was attacked by a herd of wild pigs.

"I was driving on a dirt road (4) along the river, (5) just as I always do" she told reporters in an impromptu news conference (6) at the hospital, (7) "when I hit a muddy patch of road. I got out of the car (8) to try to push it out of the mud. All of a sudden a herd of pigs came out of the bushes and attacked me. There were (9) so many of them that I was completely surrounded. I was able to get back into the car and I scared them away (10) by blowing the horn. But I sat there (11) for several hours (12) before I felt safe (13) enough to leave the car and go looking (14) for some help." Ms. Morris was treated for gashes on her legs and shock. She was given a tetanus shot, and released later in the day. Scientists are (15) a little puzzled as to why the pigs might have attacked in the first place. Animal psychologist, Dr. Lassie Kumholm suggested that it may have been (16) because one of the females in the herd could have just given birth near where the car got stuck. Pigs are known to be (17) quite aggressive (18) if their young are threatened. The herd of wild pigs is a well-known nuisance in the area, and have (19) frequently caused minor damage, but this is the first time they have been known to actually attack humans. Local property owners have submitted several petitions to county officials (20) to complain about the problem.

32

Exercise 3

Answer the following questions for each of the underlined adverbial forms in these news articles:

1. Which *wh-question* word would you use to ask a question about this information?
2. Decide on the grammatical form (adverb, adverbial phrase, or adverbial clause) and category of meaning (place, time, manner, degree, or cause and effect).
3. Put the number of the structure in the appropriate square on the blank adverb grid on the next page. The first three have been done for you as examples.

CHRISTMAS COUP IN SURINAM
Elections Promised

Paramaribo, Surinam

An army-led coup (1) <u>on Christmas Eve</u> toppled the two-year-old civilian government of Surinam. The coup was carried off (2) <u>without a single shot being fired</u>, and (3) <u>by today</u> normal holiday activity had resumed in the capital, Paramaribo.

Ivan Graanoogst, leader of the country's military police, announced that elections would be held (4) <u>within 100 days</u>. Graanoogst acknowledged being the leader of the coup, and served as the "official voice" (5) <u>to announce the coup</u> (6) <u>on national television</u>, but the real leader is widely believed to be Army Chief Desi Bouterse. Bouterse was the dictator of the former Dutch Colony (7) <u>from 1980 to 1988</u> and commander of the Armed Forces (8) <u>since then</u>. Bouterse announced his own resignation from the Army (9) <u>earlier in the day</u>, but is reportedly still in charge of the troops.

Both the United States and Dutch governments (10) <u>vigorously</u> condemned the takeover. Bouterse carried out a similar coup (11) <u>in 1980</u>, which toppled a previously-elected government.

AIDS ACTIVIST SUCCUMBS

Oakland, CA

Roosevelt Williams, a well-known educator and AIDS activist in Alameda County, died (12) <u>peacefully</u> on August 27 (13) <u>from complications caused by AIDS</u>. He was one of the world's longest-surviving AIDS patients.

(14) <u>From when he was first diagnosed in 1980</u>, Williams successfully combatted the disease (15) <u>for nearly ten years</u>. (16) <u>Whenever he had the opportunity</u>, he appeared in schools, churches, and (17) <u>on radio and television</u> (18) <u>to argue</u> (19) <u>as persuasively as he could</u> for more education, support, and understanding for people with AIDS. His efforts were (20) <u>so successful that a number of private organizations set up free treatment programs for the public</u>. Memorial services will be held (21) <u>in a number of area churches</u> (22) <u>on Sunday</u>.

Meaning		Form		
		Adverbs	Adverbial Phrases	Adverbial Clauses
WHERE	PLACE			
WHEN	TIME— WHEN		1, 3	
HOW LONG	TIME— DURATION			
HOW OFTEN	FREQUENCY			
HOW	MANNER		2	
HOW MUCH	DEGREE			
WHY	PURPOSE AND REASON			
	CAUSE AND EFFECT			

Focus 2

FORM

Position of Adverbials

FORM

- In English, adverbial information *usually* appears in this basic order:

how often frequency	VERB PHRASE (verb + object)	how manner	where place	when time	why cause and effect
I sometimes	lift weights	vigorously	at the gym	after work	to combat stress.

Exercise 4

Identify the verb phrases and the adverbials for each of the numbered sentences in this passage. Write them in the appropriate column in the grid on the next page. The first two sentences have been done for you. Are there any sentences in which the adverbials do not follow the basic order listed above? Which sentences? What is the order?

Biff Bicep and Gladstone Gulp are close friends. (1)They're always trying to change the way they look because neither one is very pleased with his appearance, (2)but they go about it differently.

Biff Bicep is a serious bodybuilder. (3)He tries to increase the size of his muscles by lifting weights at a gym near his house. (4)He usually goes there at the same time every day. (5)He drinks special vitamin supplements to gain weight, and (6)works out vigorously twice a day— in the morning and in the afternoon. (7)He usually starts out on an exercise bike to warm up his muscles. Then he moves on to his exercises. (8)He exercises his upper body on Mondays, Wednesdays, and Fridays. (9)On Tuesdays, Thursdays, and Saturdays, he does exercises to develop the muscles of his lower body. (10)He never works out on Sundays, so his muscles can have a chance to rest.

Gladstone Gulp is a serious dieter. (11)He always seems to be trying to lose weight by going on special weight-reducing diets whenever he feels too heavy. (12)He usually drinks a special diet drink at breakfast and lunch. (13)Sometimes he doesn't eat anything after breakfast in order to save a few calories. (14)He also tries not to snack between meals. (15)As a result, he is usually really hungry when he gets home, and (16)so he often goes directly to the kitchen to find something to eat. Although he is a serious dieter, he's not a terribly successful one. (17)He has never permanently lost more than a few pounds. (18)He's always looking for a magic way to lose weight without having to diet or exercise.

How Often (Frequency)	VERB PHRASE	How (Manner)	Where (Place)	When (Time)	Why (Cause and Effect)
1. always	are trying to change the way they look				because neither one is very pleased with his appearance
2.	go about it	differently			
3.					
4.					
5.					
6.					
7.					
8.					
9.					
10.					
11.					
12.					
13.					
14.					
15.					
16.					
17.					
18.					

Focus 3

Position and Movement of Adverbs

- Adverbs usually appear in this order: frequency, manner, place, time. However, order can vary, especially when there is more than one adverbial in the clause.

HOW OFTEN: Adverbs of Frequency	
usual position: **(a)** Gladstone **often goes** on strange diets. **(b)** He **has never lost** more than a few pounds.	Adverbs of frequency usually come before the verb and after the auxiliary.
also possible: **(c)** Gladstone **goes** on strange diets **often**.	Affirmative adverbs of frequency (except *always*) can also come after the verb phrase (verb + object);
not possible: **(d)** NOT: Gladstone **goes often** on strange diets **(e)** NOT: He **has lost** more than a few pounds **never**.	Negative adverbs (*never, seldom,* etc.) cannot.

HOW: Adverbs of Manner/Means	
usual position: **(f)** He diets **faithfully**. **(g)** He has tried to lose weight **electronically**.	Adverbs of manner or means usually come after the verb, especially if there are no other adverbials in the sentence.
also possible: **(h)** He **rigorously** avoids sweets.	They can also come before the verb if there is no auxiliary.
not possible: **(i)** NOT: He has tried **electronically** to lose weight. **(j)** AWKWARD: He has **electronically** tried to lose weight.	

37

• WHERE & WHEN: Adverbs of Place and Time	
usual position: (k) Denise sells stocks and bonds **downtown.** (l) Gladstone lost 50 pounds **recently**.	Adverbs of time and place usually come after the verb phrase.
also possible: (m) He **recently** lost 50 pounds. **not possible:** (n) NOT: She **downtown** sells stocks and bonds. (o) NOT: He **yesterday** lost 50 pounds.	Some indefinite adverbs of time (*recently, not long ago,* etc.) can come before the verb.

Exercise 5

Add the given adverbials to each sentence. More than one position may be possible, so be ready to explain why you put the adverbial where you did.

> **EXAMPLE:** He gains back the lost weight. (quickly) (usually)
>
> *He usually gains the lost weight back quickly.*
> *Usually he quickly gains back the lost weight.*

1. Gladstone Gulp goes on a new diet. (every few months)(because he feels heavy)
2. He uses diet pills. (regularly)(to increase his metabolism)
3. He rides an exercise bicycle. (infrequently) (very hard) (to use up calories)
4. He trades diet plans. (with his friend Biff) (sometimes)
5. He reads about every new diet. (in magazines)(carefully)(whenever he can)
6. He doesn't follow their directions. (carefully) (always)
7. He drinks a special vitamin supplement. (usually) (to make sure he gets proper nutrition)

Exercise 6

Interview a classmate and find out something that he or she does

1. every day
2. carefully
3. very well
4. before bedtime
5. outdoors
6. occasionally

7. better than anyone else in his or her family
8. automatically
9. with considerable difficulty
10. after class

Write complete sentences about these activities and report them to the rest of the class.

Focus 4

FORM

Position and Order of Adverbial Phrases

FORM

- Adverbial phrases usually come after the verb phrase and other one-word adverbs. They also follow the general order of manner, place, time, and cause and effect. When more than one adverbial phrase occur in a clause, the order is variable but follows these general principles:
  - Shorter adverbials usually come before longer adverbials:
    (a) He exercises **vigorously, as if his life depended on it.**
    (b) NOT: He exercises **as if his life depended on it vigorously.**
  - When there are two adverbials of the same kind, the more specific adverbial always comes first:
    (c) Many people frequently eat dinner **in neighborhood restaurants in Toronto.**
    (d) NOT: Many people frequently eat dinner **in Toronto in neighborhood restaurants.**
  - It is unusual to have more than two or three adverbials after the verb phrase. If there are several adverbials, then one is usually moved to the beginning of the sentence:
    (e) AWKWARD: He washes his car carefully in the driveway with a special soap once a week.
    (f) BETTER: Once a week, he carefully washes his car in the driveway with a special soap.

39

Exercise 7

Identify the meaning and form of the underlined adverbials in the numbered sentences in the following article. Tell why you think they appear in the order that they do. Several reasons may be possible, so compare your ideas with those of a partner. The first two sentences have been done for you.

EXAMPLE: 1. (a) *place, adverbial phrase* (b) *place, adverbial phrase*
(c) *time, adverb*
Reasons: (a) *comes before* (b) *because it is more specific. Indefinite time adverbs can come before the main verb.*
2. (a) *frequency, adverb* (b) *reason, adverbial phrase*
Reasons: *Frequency adverbs come before the verb, reason adverbials come after the verb.*

STUDY FINDS EXERCISE PATTERNS LINKED TO MOTIVATION, PERSONALITY

Madison, Wisconsin

(1) Graduate students conducting research (a)<u>in the Exercise Physiology Program</u> (b)<u>at the University of Wisconsin</u> have (c)<u>recently</u> found some interesting connections between people's personalities and why, when, and how they choose to exercise.

There appear to be two broad "types" of amateur athletes. Type A athletes are those who use exercise to "rev up" for increased competition both on and off the playing field. (2) Type B athletes (a)<u>usually</u> tend to use exercise to "cool out," (b)<u>as a way to decrease stress</u>. There are some interesting connections between these two different kinds of people and their preferred time, place, and means of exercise.

Researchers found that preferred time for exercise depends on type of personality. (3) Most Type A people do some form of extremely vigorous exercise (a)<u>in the early morning</u> (b)<u>before work</u> (c)<u>every day,</u> (d)<u>to invigorate their bodies.</u> (4) Type B people, on the other hand, (a)<u>generally</u> don't like to exercise (b)<u>very vigorously</u> (c)<u>before the middle of the day.</u> (5) Consequently, they (a)<u>usually</u> prefer to exercise (b)<u>after work</u> (c)<u>for relaxation</u> rather than invigoration.

People's favorite kinds of exercise and how hard they play also depend on personality and motivation. Type A people play as hard as they work. (6) They (a)<u>usually</u> prefer to pursue highly competitive sports (b)<u>most of the time,</u> such as tennis or racquetball, (c)<u>to encourage their maximum performance.</u> Even in individual sports such as jogging or weightlifting, they tend to be extremely competitive. (7) As a rule, they work out (a)<u>regularly</u> (b)<u>with a partner or as part of a team,</u> (8) because they (a)<u>constantly</u> have to perform (b)<u>better than their partner</u> (c)<u>in order to feel</u> <u>satisfied</u>. Having someone to compete with generally makes Type A people more conscientious about their exercise routine.

(9) Type B people, on the other hand, (a)<u>usually</u> prefer to work out (b)<u>by themselves.</u> (10) They prefer noncompetitive activities such as walking, tai-chi, or yoga, and exercise (a)<u>on a regular basis</u> (b)<u>as a form of meditation or relaxation</u>, rather than competition. (11) If they do participate in team sports, it is (a)<u>almost always</u> (b)<u>just for fun.</u> Type B athletes rarely even keep score.

Personality even seems to be linked to where people like to exercise. (12) Type B people (a)<u>usually</u> prefer to work out (b)<u>at a gym</u> (c)<u>near their homes,</u> (d)<u>as a means of relaxation</u> (13) (a)<u>As a rule</u>, Type A people prefer to exercise (b)<u>vigorously,</u> (c)<u>near their offices</u> (d)<u>just before work or during lunch.</u>

USE

Putting Adverbials at the Beginning of a Sentence

USE

- Most adverbials can also appear at the beginning of a clause or sentence
  - if there are several other adverbs or adverbial phrases, or if the object in the verb phrase is very long:
    - **(a) Once a week** he carefully washes his car in the driveway with a special soap.
    - **(b) In the suitcase,** he found an extra wool sweater that had been knitted by his grandmother.
    - **(c)** NOT: He found a extra wool sweater that had been knitted by his grandmother **in the suitcase.**
  - in order to emphasize adverbial information:
    - **(d) Carefully and slowly** John carried the heavy tray of fragile glasses to the table.
- You can place most adverbials at the beginning of the sentence without making other changes in word order. But negative adverbs of frequency (*never, seldom, rarely*) and certain adverbial phrases of degree require a question (or inverted) word order when they are put at the beginning of the sentence.

Normal Position	Emphatic Position
(e) Gladstone **seldom loses** more than a few pounds.	**(f) Seldom does** Gladstone lose more than a few pounds.
(g) Mary Morris was so frightened that she stayed in her car for several hours.	**(h) So frightened was Mary Morris** that she stayed in her car for several hours.

- We also put adverbials at the beginning of a sentence to indicate the relationship between sentences. We can use any adverbial we have studied in this unit:
  - **(i)** WHERE: John has a beautiful new apartment. **Along one wall** there are big windows with a marvelous view.
  - **(j)** WHEN: Matt was born in 1965. **In 1980,** he moved to San Francisco.
  - **(k)** WHY: John became fluent in French. **Consequently,** he was able to get a job with a company that exports computer parts to West Africa.
- We also use *sentence adverbials* to indicate these relationships:
  - **(l)** Type A people favor vigorous competitive exercise. **However,** Type B people seem to prefer more relaxing physical activities. **In fact,** some Type A athletes don't think Type B activities such as yoga or walking should be considered athletic activity at all.

  Sentence adverbs don't really give *wh-question* information. Instead, they show how different sentences relate to each other within a paragraph or a longer text. We study these kinds of adverbials in more detail in Unit 13.

Focus 6

Position of Adverbial Clauses

FORM

- Most adverbial clauses appear after the main clause, but many also come before the main clause. If an adverbial clause appears before the main clause, it may indicate that the writer wishes to
  - emphasize the adverbial clause:
    - **(a)** **As if it were the easiest thing in the world,** Mary did a backward somersault and sailed off across the ice.
    - **(b)** **As soon as John got to the airport,** he began to have second thoughts about going to France.
  - establish a context that applies to several sentences:
    - **(c)** **Until Jeff moved to San Francisco,** he had never seen the ocean. He had never been to a disco or eaten Chinese food. He had never even fallen in love.
    - **(d)** **Whenever John thought about Mary,** he began to feel guilty. He would imagine her sitting sadly at home, all by herself, writing him long letters. Meanwhile, he was spending his time in lively cafes, talking about philosophy and art with beautiful women, sipping espresso and smoking strong-smelling cigarettes.
  - express a logical or chronological relationship that suggests a particular order between the two sentences:
    - **(e)** I usually read the paper **before** I take a shower.
    - **(f)** **After** I read the paper, I usually take a shower.
    - **(g)** **If** you wash the dishes, **then** I'll dry them and put them away.
- Some adverbials generally appear either before or after the main clause.
  - Conditionals appear with the adverbial (*if*) clause before the main clause. If the adverbial clause follows the main clause, it is to emphasize the result, rather than to express a simple conditional relationship:
    - **(h)** You'll get in trouble if you don't watch out!
  - Adverbial clauses of place do not normally appear before the main clause, although this is sometimes possible in statements about a general truth:
    - **(i)** I shop where John shops.
    - **(j)** **AWKWARD:** Where John shops, I shop.
    - **(k)** **Wherever** he goes, John makes new friends and has wonderful adventures.

- Adverbial clauses of result with *so that* do not usually precede the main clause:

   (l) John worked all summer **so (that) he would have enough money.**

   (m) AWKWARD: **So that he would have enough money,** John worked all summer.

- Punctuation of adverbial clauses depends on their position in a sentence. Adverbial clauses appearing before the main clause are followed by a comma. Adverbial clauses appearing after the main clause require no extra punctuation.

   (n) I ate lunch **after I took the examination.**

   (o) **After I took the examination,** I ate lunch.

   (p) **Since you don't have much money,** I'll pay for dinner.

   (q) I'll pay for dinner **since you don't have much money.**

Exercise 8

Determine whether the adverbial clause in these sentences appears before or after the main clause. Why do you think the author chose to put the adverbial forms where they are?

1. Because some people enjoy vigorous exercise, they tend to pursue sports that "rev up" their bodies.

2. On the other hand, some people practice noncompetitive sports because for them exercise is a means of relaxation.

3. People want to lose weight because they want to feel and look better.

4. Because Mary Morris may have stopped her car too close to a newborn piglet, she became the victim of a bizarre attack.

5. When Ivan Graanoogst appeared yesterday on the national TV, he announced to the public that the Army had taken control of the government of Surinam.

6. Although Graanoogst announced that he had led the coup, the real leader is widely believed to be Army Chief Desi Bouterse.

7. Bouterse had been serving as commander of the Armed Forces when he permitted the return of civilian rule in 1988.

8. Roosevelt Williams spoke frequently on radio and television about his disease so that the public would become aware of the need for more support and understanding for people with AIDS.

9. Ever since he had first been diagnosed with AIDS in 1980, he spent more than ten years fighting the disease.

43

Activities

Activity 1

Introduce yourself or another student to the rest of the class by providing some basic information. Here are some suggested topics:

WHO: name, family background

WHAT: hobbies, special interests, plans for the future

WHERE: home town, current living situation

WHEN: date of birth, date of arrival in this country, date of expected completion of English studies

HOW LONG: length of time in this country, amount of previous English study

HOW OFTEN: regular activities, hobbies

HOW MUCH: special skills, abilities, and interests

WHY: reasons and goals for studying English, joining this class, leaving home

Activity 2

In the Task for this unit, you scanned the newspaper for articles of interest. That involved reading headlines to determine quickly what the article was about. Newspaper headlines represent a special kind of English. They typically focus on providing information about **who** and **what** and omit a lot of important grammatical information. For example, the headline **BABY FOUND IN BUS STATION** might appear as this complete sentence "A baby has been found in the bus station."

- Test how well you know the basic sentence elements of English by "translating" these headlines into complete sentences.
  - STOCK MARKET CRASHES
  - U.S. POPULATION MOVING WEST
  - NEW BUDGET TERMED "DISASTER"
  - PRESIDENT VISITS ASIA
  - U.S. TO PROTEST GILL NETS
  - POPE TO VISIT CHINA
  - DROUGHT EXPECTED TO WORSEN
  - NEW PLAN TO IMPROVE TRANSIT SERVICES
  - TEST SCORES IMPROVING IN PUBLIC SCHOOLS
  - LINK FOUND BETWEEN DIET AND HEART DISEASE
  - CANCER REPORTED INCREASING
  - MAJOR GROWTH IN FOREIGN STUDENTS IN U.S.
  - BIG KREMLIN SHAKE-UP

Activity 3

It seems that only two kinds of people inhabit the world: morning people (who do their best work early in the day) and night people (who are sleepy in the morning, and most productive in the late afternoon or even late at night). Most people have a strong connection between **when** they do something and **how** they do it.

- Use this grid to find out whether you (or a partner) are more of a "morning person" or a "night person." Describe **how** you (or a partner) do each of the listed activities (how accurately, how well, how energetically, etc.) at the particular time listed. Some examples have been provided.

WHEN: Time	Early morning	After lunch	Late at night
WHAT: Activities strenuous physical activity	HOW: slowly	well, but not if he's hungry	easily, but it keeps him awake
complex mathematical calculations			
creative writing, thinking or daydreaming			
reading for pleasure or enjoyment			
reading for information or for work or school			
social activity and conversation			
making presentations to other people			

Activity 4

In English, we use the term "ulterior motives" to describe a situation when a person has a bad reason for doing a good thing. For example, if your real reason for helping a friend who is in trouble is because you want that person to lend you money later, your motive may make your "good" action a bad one.

- In a small group, discuss the following situations. For each situation, identify some "pure motives"—potential reasons for doing the action that would make it a good or generous act—and some "ulterior motives"—potential reasons that would make the act a bad or selfish one.

    loaning someone money

    not telling a friend some bad news

    letting someone else take advantage of a lucky opportunity

    being friendly and obedient to a rich relative

    working harder than anyone else at your job

- Based on your discussion, decide whether people's actions should be judged by what they do (their actions) or why they do it (their motivations). Present your opinion and your reasons to the rest of the class.

Passive Verbs

Task

Certain structures around the world have extremely mysterious origins. Many people think their existence is proof that the Earth has been visited by people from other planets, because these structures were built in ways that cannot be fully explained. Two of the most famous Great Mysteries, Stonehenge and the Nazca Lines, have some very interesting things in common.

> **Stonehenge** is a circle of huge, upright stones that stand miles away from anything else in the middle of a plain in southern England. Nobody knows for sure how the stones got there, or what their exact purpose was.

> **The Nazca Lines** are a group of enormous pictures drawn in the desert of Western Peru, that can only be seen from an airplane. They were made by removing a layer of rocks to expose a layer of lighter soil underneath. Nobody knows why they are there, or how people were able to design such exact images which they themselves were unable see.

- Read the information on the next page and decide whether or not you think that such mysterious places are, in fact, proof that the Earth has been visited by beings from outer space.
- In a small group, discuss this information and try to come up with explanations for the three unanswered questions that all Great Mysteries share. Use any other information you know about these places to decide whether or not they are proof that the Earth has been visited by beings from some other planet.
- Present your ideas to the rest of the class.

The Unanswered Questions of Stonehenge and the Nazca Lines

How were they constructed? No theory has been able to account for these puzzling features:

Stonehenge

- The giant stones were transported from a great distance. Their place of origin is unknown. The stones show no signs of being cut from quarries.
- The stones are too heavy to be lifted upright, or to be placed on top of each other.
- There weren't enough people in prehistoric Britain to undertake such a gigantic project.
- The stones are placed in a very precise relation to each other. The distances between them are accurate to the millimeter.

The Nazca Lines

- The arrangements can only be seen from the air. They cannot be seen by anyone on the ground. They weren't even discovered until people started flying over the area in the 1930s.
- There isn't enough water in the region where the lines are found to support the work force that would be required to undertake such a large-scale project. It is one of the driest places on earth.
- The designs are very precise. One image is a perfect spiral, accurate to the millimeter.

Why were they constructed? There are some conflicting indications of their function:

Stonehenge

- It seems to be aligned to certain constellations.
- It seems to have some connection with the position of the sun at the equinox and solstice.
- It may have had some connection with human sacrifices.

The Nazca Lines

- They seem to have some kind of mathematical significance.
- Some represent abstract geometrical designs.
- Some represent flowers and animals that are not found anywhere near the location of the lines.
- Some designs have a resemblance to symbols that are used to direct modern-day aircraft.

When were they constructed? No one knows exactly how old they really are.

Stonehenge

- It was already a mystery when the Romans occupied Britain in the first century B.C.
- There is no historical record of its construction.

The Nazca Lines

- They weren't discovered until people started flying over the area in airplanes.
- They predate Inca civilization by at least 2,000 years.

Focus 1

Review of Passive Forms

FORM

- Most verbs can have both an active and a passive form. You can form all passive verbs in the same way: *be* + **past participle**

Active	Passive
(a) People first **discovered** the Nazca lines from the air.	**(b)** The Nazca Lines **were discovered** from air.
(c) People **didn't discover** them until the 1930s.	**(d)** They **weren't discovered** until the 1930s.

- The auxiliary *be* contains all information about:

Singular	Plural
(e) Stonehenge **is constructed** of rocks that came from many miles away.	**(f)** The Nazca Lines **were made** by removing soil and rocks to expose the different-colored soil underneath.

Affirmative	Negative
(g) Stonehenge **was constructed** long before Britain **was invaded** by the armies of Rome.	**(h)** The Nazca Lines **weren't discovered** until the 1930s because they **couldn't be seen** by people on the ground.

Time Frame

(i) Mysterious structures **are found** in a number of places in the world.

(j) The Nazca Lines **were discovered** only about 60 years ago.

(k) Perhaps the reasons for their existence **will be discovered** with further research.

Progressive or Perfect Aspect

(l) While Stonehenge **was being built**, the civilizations of Greece and Rome were still in their infancy.

(m) The origins and purposes of the Nazca Lines **have been debated** ever since the lines were discovered.

(n) By the time the government took steps to protect the Nazca Lines from further destruction, some of them **had been obliterated** almost completely by sightseers and souvenir hunters.

Modal Information

(o) The Nazca Lines **may be destroyed** if further preservation efforts are not undertaken.

(p) Preservation efforts for all such mysterious structures **ought to be undertaken** without delay.

(q) Stonehenge **might have been used** to predict astronomical events.

Exercise 1

Change these active verb forms to their passive counterparts. Be sure to maintain all aspectual information.

> **EXAMPLE:** is studying—*is being studied*
> has forgotten—*has been forgotten*
> gave—*was/were given*

1. is making
2. had left
3. built
4. produces

5. can read
6. will send
7. was planning
8. might have needed

Exercise 2

Change these passive verb forms to their active counterparts.

1. is being constructed
2. had been forgotten
3. was established
4. is manufactured

5. can be obtained
6. will be required
7. were being duplicated
8. might have been discovered

Exercise 3

Make up an original sentence for each of the passive verb forms you produced in Exercise 1 and transformed in Exercise 2.

Exercise 4

Restate these active sentences as passive sentences. Change the subject of the active sentence into an adverb of place.

> **EXAMPLE:** The Chinese **invented** gunpowder.
> *Gunpowder **was invented** in China.*

1. Pakistanis speak Urdu, Punjabi, Sindhi, Baluchi, Pashtu, and English.
2. The Tadjiks of Afghanistan have mined lapis lazuli for centuries.
3. The French consider snails a great delicacy.
4. People throughout Asia eat rice.
5. Australians consume more beer per capita than in any other country.
6. Ancient Egyptians worshiped cats.
7. The Japanese have developed a new system of high-resolution television.
8. Americans invented the games of baseball and basketball.

Exercise 5

Working with a partner, make up five additional passive sentences about products or accomplishments of a national or cultural group that you are familiar with.

Focus 2

MEANING

Agent versus Recipient

MEANING

- Two linguistic terms are important in understanding passive verbs and when to use them: *agent* and *recipient*. The *agent* refers to the doer of the action. The *recipient* refers to the receiver of the action.

<table>
<tr><td colspan="4">In active sentences the agent is the grammatical subject of the sentence; the recipient is the grammatical object:</td></tr>
<tr><td>FORM:</td><td>subject</td><td>active verb</td><td>object</td></tr>
<tr><td>MEANING:</td><td>agent</td><td>action</td><td>recipient</td></tr>
<tr><td>EXAMPLE:</td><td>(a) John</td><td>found</td><td>a wallet with a lot of money in it outside the office.</td></tr>
</table>

<table>
<tr><td colspan="4">In passive sentences, the recipient is the grammatical subject. The agent is very often omitted, but when it is mentioned, it occurs in a prepositional phrase with by.</td></tr>
<tr><td>FORM:</td><td>subject</td><td>passive verb</td><td>(by + NP)</td></tr>
<tr><td>MEANING:</td><td>recipient</td><td>action</td><td>(agent)</td></tr>
<tr><td>EXAMPLE:</td><td>(b) A wallet with a lot of money in it</td><td>was found out-side the office.</td><td></td></tr>
<tr><td></td><td>(c) The wallet</td><td>was found</td><td>by an employee who promptly notified the po-lice.</td></tr>
</table>

Exercise 6

For each of these sentences, identify the agent and the recipient. Tell what the grammatical function (subject, object) is.

> **EXAMPLE:** John misses Mary a great deal.
>
> *agent: John, recipient: Mary, subject: John, object: Mary*

1. This painting was done by my grandfather over 60 years ago.
2. Romans constructed an elaborate system of aqueducts to bring water to the city.
3. We were told by our teacher that we are not having a test next Monday after all.
4. Don't all students love grammar?
5. French is spoken by many government officials throughout West Africa.
6. Denise can't stand Peter's easygoing attitude about work.

Exercise 7

Underline the passive constructions in the following passage. For each passive that you can find, mark the recipient with *R*. If the agent is mentioned, mark it with *A*. The first sentence has been done as an example.

(1)The (R) Nazca Lines <u>were not discovered</u> until the 1930s, when (R) they <u>were first noticed</u> by airplane (A) pilots flying over Peru's Atacama Desert. (2)They consist of huge pictures, several kilometers in size, that were drawn in the desert. (3)They depict such things such as birds, spiders, and abstract geometrical designs. (4)These pictures were made more than 3,000 years ago by removing stones and dirt over large areas to expose the different-colored soil beneath.

(5)The amazing thing about the Nazca Lines is that none of these pictures can be seen by people on the ground. (6)They are so huge that they can only be seen from a great height. (7)The pictures were constructed with incredible precision. (8)Exactly how such precise measurements were made still hasn't been satisfactorily explained. (9)It seems impossible that the primitive construction techniques that existed 3,000 years ago could have been used to create such gigantic, perfectly constructed designs.

(10)Who made these gigantic pictures and why? (11)Were they intended to be used as offerings for the gods, as some people have suggested? (12)Or, as others believe, were they created as "direction signs" for visitors from other planets? (13)No one knows. (14) One thing is known: The reasons for and methods of construction have been obliterated with time, but the pictures have been preserved for at least 2,000–and maybe even 3,000–years!

Focus 3

The *Get* Passive

FORM
USE

- In spoken or informal English, you can use *get* instead of *be* as the passive auxiliary.

  (a) John rides to work with a neighbor who works nearby. He **is** picked up at the bus stop every morning. John **gets** dropped off in front of his office. He **should be getting picked up** in a few minutes.

- Questions and negatives require *do* if the verb phrase does not contain a form of *be* or a modal auxiliary.

  (b) **Did** John **get** picked up yesterday? He **didn't get** dropped off at the usual place. He **might not have gotten picked up** by his usual person.

- Using *get* in passive sentences

  - is more common with animate subjects:

    (c) Kennedy **was** elected President in 1960.

    (d) Kennedy **got** elected President in 1960.

    (e) The hospital **was built** in the 1930s.

    (f) NOT: The hospital **got built** in the 1930s.

  - often implies that the subject was actively involved in a process.

    (g) Nancy **was** hit by a car.

    (h) Nancy **got** hit by a car.

    (i) Jeff **was** born in Kansas.

    (j) NOT: Jeff **got** born in Kansas.

  - emphasizes the process rather than the state:

    (k) They hope to **get married** next Saturday.

    (l) They **have been married** since 1941.

  - is more common in informal contexts:

    (m) Did you hear the news? Bob **got** arrested!

  - often occurs in situations that have undesirable results:

    (n) What a terrible day! My car **got** towed, and my dog **got** taken to the pound.

Exercise 8

Decide whether *be* or *get* is a more suitable auxiliary in these sentences. There may be more than one correct answer, so prepare to explain why you chose the answer that you did.

1. The Nazca Lines _____ discovered in the 1930s.

2. My camera _____ damaged yesterday. It will have to _____ repaired before the picnic next week so I can take pictures.

3. New medicines are _____ developed that show great promise in fighting cancer.

4. John's car _____ damaged, so he had to take public transportation.

5. That's really dangerous. If you _____ hurt, don't blame me.

6. Scott _____ arrested on his way home from the football game.

7. I don't think John and Mary will ever _____ married. They're too different.

8. Don't put that fish in the same aquarium with the others. It might _____ eaten by the larger ones.

Focus 4

USE

Special Cases

USE

- Certain verbs may not have active or passive forms:
  - Some active verbs do not have passive forms.
    - **(a)** The rocks of Stonehenge **weigh** several tons each.
    - **(b)** The Nazca Lines **consist of** huge pictures that can only be seen from a great height.
    - **(c)** Some scientists think these pictures **had** a ceremonial function.
    - **(d)** Their true purpose and function **have vanished** under the sands of the Atacama Desert.
  - Some passive verbs do not have active forms, or have different meanings in active and passive.
    - **(e)** Jeff **was born** in Kansas.
    - **(f)** NOT: Jeff's mother **bore** him in Kansas.
    - **(g)** The Nazca Lines **are located** (exist) in the Atacama desert of Peru.
    - **(h)** They **located** (found) the Atacama Desert on a map.

Focus 5

Choosing Passive versus Active
USE

- Sentences usually require passive verbs instead of active verbs
  - if the agent is unknown, unimportant, or obvious from the context:
    - **(a)** Jan's purse was stolen from her locker at school. (agent unknown)
    - **(b)** The new library was finished about a year ago. (agent unimportant)
    - **(c)** I had an accident yesterday. My car was destroyed. (agent obvious from context)
  - to emphasize the recipient:
    - **(d)** **Matt** was injured slightly in the earthquake, but **Jeff** was OK.
  - to connect ideas in different clauses more clearly:
    - **(e)** Archaeologists would like to excavate the Nazca Lines, **if this can be done** without damaging them further.
  - to make generic explanations, statements, and announcements:
    - **(f)** The present perfect tense *is used* to describe actions in the past that are related to the present in some way.
    - **(g)** Passengers *are asked* to refrain from smoking.
    - **(h)** The audience *will be encouraged* to participate.
    - **(i)** Something *should be done* about the drug problem.

Exercise 9

Why do you think the author used passive verbs in these sentences?

1. No one is permitted to enter the laboratory while the experiment is being conducted.
2. Mary arrived late for the field trip, and got left behind.
3. These pictures were taken on our trip to Japan.
4. Reagan was first elected President in 1980.
5. There is a lot of controversy about the Nazca Lines, especially about why they were built and how they were constructed.
6. They weren't even noticed until people started flying over the area in planes.
7. Was it John's brother who got arrested at the demonstration?
8. The house was broken into while the family was away.
9. By the time the Romans arrived in Britain, the origin and purpose of Stonehenge had already been forgotten.
10. We'll take the apartment if it can be cleaned thoroughly before we move in.

Exercise 10

Identify the passive verb phrases in the following passage. Decide why the author chose to use passive constructions.

(1)In most societies, social minorities are often discriminated against by society as a whole. (2)People may be discriminated against on the basis of their race, religion, ethnic or cultural background, sexual preference, or even the language that they speak in their homes. (3)Such minority groups may not be allowed to use the same facilities as the general population, or have the same rights or legal protections. (4)For example, in some countries women are not allowed to drive cars or work in jobs where they face the public. (5)In other countries, people of certain ethnic backgrounds are not allowed to enter national universities, or conduct business in a particular language, or even wear certain colors of clothing. (6)But in many societies, this discrimination is being eliminated—at least in terms of legal and governmental policies.

(7)The United States, for example, has made a great deal of progress in eliminating some areas of discrimination against its social minorities. (8)But these changes have not come quickly or easily. (9)As recently as the 1950s blacks and whites were not allowed to get married in many southern states. (10)They were forced to use separate drinking fountains, rest rooms, and even schools and libraries. (11)However, as a result of active protest and political demonstration, such discriminatory laws were changed, and segregation based on race is no longer permitted. (12)People with physical disabilities were also forced to resort to demonstrations in order to gain access to basic public facilities such as rest rooms, movie theaters, or public transportation systems, and their efforts have resulted in new laws that require all public buildings in the United States to be wheelchair accessible.

(13)But other battles are still being fought. (14)Women have made considerable gains in American society, but they are still paid less than men for the same kinds of work. (15)Gay people are still confronted with enormous legal and social discrimination. (16)They are not allowed to serve in the Army or join organizations like the Boy Scouts; in many places they can be fired from their jobs if employers learn of their sexual orientation, and they do not have the same kind of basic legal protection for family relationships and community property rights that the rest of society takes for granted. (17)Conditions for all minorities in the United States seem to be improving, although it will be a long time before social attitudes catch up with the progress that has been made in legal protections.

Focus 6

USE

Passive Verbs
with a Stated Agent

USE

- Because we use passive verbs most often when the agent is unknown or unimportant, we usually omit agents (*by* + noun phrase) in passive sentences. However, it is common to state the agents of passive verbs if
  - the agent gives us more information:
    - **(a)** My car was struck **by a hit-and-run driver** last night.
    - **(b)** Many important scientific discoveries have been made **by women.**

- the agent is too important to omit:
  - **(c)** Radioactivity, for example, was discovered **by Madame Curie,** and has played a central role in the development of modern physics.
- the agent is surprising or unexpected:
  - **(d)** This music was written **by a computer.**
  - **(e)** That picture looks as if it were painted **by a drunken monkey.**

Exercise 11

Delete the agents in these sentences if it can be done without significant loss of information.

EXAMPLES: That symphony was written by a composer in the nineteenth century.

That symphony was written in the nineteenth century.

That symphony was written by an Armenian composer.

(Agent cannot be deleted.)

1. The Nazca Lines were constructed by an unknown civilization approximately 2,000 years ago.
2. The lesson was assigned by the teacher for next week.
3. This picture was painted by Picasso when Picasso was 12 years old.
4. My briefcase got taken by someone, but it was found and turned in to the Lost and Found Office by someone in my English class.
5. Many foreign students don't need scholarships because they are being supported by friends or relatives.
6. I would never guess that these poems were translated by children.

Focus 7

MEANING ● USE

Change-of-State Verbs

MEANING
USE

- Many verbs appear in active sentences without expressing the agent. Most of these verbs describe changes of state. Even though the subject obviously doesn't do the action, you can use active rather than passive forms.
  - **(a) (active)** Somebody or something **broke** the window.
  - **(b) (passive)** The window **was broken** into a million pieces.
  - **(c) (change of state)** The window **broke** into a million pieces.
  - **(d)** Most stores **open** at 10:00.
  - **(e)** Wholesale prices **have increased**, and real wages **have declined** over the past decade.

- You can use change-of-state verbs in active form
  - for dramatic narration:
    (f) Suddenly the window **shattered** into a million pieces.
  - when the most important information is not the verb:
    (g) The concert begins **at 8:00.**
    (h) The library closes **in 15 minutes.**
    (i) The mirror shattered **into a million tiny pieces.**
  - when there is no single identifiable agent, or the agent is unknown or unimportant:
    (j) The standard of living of the average American worker **has decreased** steadily since the beginning of the Reagan years.
    (k) The demonstration quickly **developed** into a serious confrontation with the police.
  - when the subject is one that can change without an apparent agent:
    (l) The **bubble** burst.
    (m) **Clouds** gathered over the mountains.

Exercise 12

Decide whether to use active or passive forms in the following sentences and write the correct form in the space provided. There may be more than one correct choice.

(1) A study _____ (release) recently about the economic changes that _____ (take place) during the time that Ronald Reagan was President of the United States. (2) The assertion that Reagan's economic policies benefited more than just the richest portion of the population _____ (disprove) in this report. (3) In the 1980s, the difference between the income of the richest 5% of American families and the rest of the country _____ (widen) to the biggest difference since 1947. (4) While the incomes of the richest 5% of American families _____ (increase), the incomes of most other Americans _____ (decrease), once adjustments _____ (make) for inflation. (5) For example, in 1987 the average wages of a male high school graduate with five years of work experience _____ (drop) to 18% below the level that the same kind of workers _____ (earn) in 1979. (6) In terms of real wages, such workers are making the same amount of money that they made in 1963. (7) In other words, while the actual incomes of the richest 5% of the country _____ (rise) by 15–20%, the poorest 25% found that their real wages _____ (decline) by 10%.

Exercise 13

Decide whether to use active or passive forms in the following sentences and write the correct form in the space provided. There may be more than one correct choice.

(1)The age of pyramid-building in Egypt _____ (begin) about 2900 B.C. (2)The great pyramids _____ (intend) to serve as burial vaults for the Pharaohs, as the hereditary kings of Egypt _____ (call). (3)Construction on the largest pyramid _____ (start) around 2800 B.C. for Khufu, the King of the Fourth Dynasty, or Cheops, as he _____ (refer to) in Greek historical accounts. (4)It _____ (measure) 482 feet high and 755 feet long. (5)The Pyramids as a group _____ (comprise) one of the Seven Wonders of the Ancient World. (6)The other six Wonders no longer _____ (stand), and modern archaeologists _____ (know) of them only through the accounts that _____ (write) at the time they still _____ (exist).

Exercise 14

Decide whether to use active or passive forms in the following sentences and write the correct form in the space provided. There may be more than one correct choice.

(1)The Taj Mahal in Agra, India, _____ (build) for the Moghul Emperor Shah Jahan. (2)It _____ (design) to _____ (serve) as a tomb for his beloved wife. (3)Many people _____ (consider) the Taj to be the most beautiful building in the world. (4)The entire structure _____ (make) of white marble and semiprecious stones. (5)Shah Jahan originally _____ (intend) for a second Taj to _____ (locate) across the river from the first one. (6)The second Taj was supposed to _____ (copy) the original Taj in every detail except one: (7)The second Taj, which Shah Jahan _____ (plan) as his own tomb, was supposed to _____ (consist) of black marble and semiprecious stones, instead of the same white marble that _____ (use) for the first Taj. (8)Shah Jahan _____ (imprison) by his own son, and _____ (die) before he _____ (get) a chance to _____ (implement) his plan. (9)His vision of two twin Taj Mahals, one white and one black, never _____ (realize).

Exercise 15

Decide whether to use active or passive forms in the following sentences and write the correct form in the space provided. There may be more than one correct choice.

(1)Gene-splicing is _____ (develop) as a new technique that may _____ (revolutionize) medical treatment in the next century. (2)Although the technique is still in an experimental stage, it is _____ (emerge) as a important development in both immunization and treatment. (3)In a few years, we may be able to _____ (immunize) easily against a whole number of dangerous viral diseases. (4)Here is how the technique will _____ (work). (5)Genes of dangerous viruses will_____ (split), and portions of the virus DNA will _____ (attach) to other harmless cells, such as blood cells or bone marrow cells. (6)When these altered cells _____ (inject) into the body, they will be able to _____ (reproduce) in sufficient quantities so that an immune reaction will _____ (occur) without letting the body _____ (expose) to the actual, dangerous virus. (7)The harmless cells will _____ (appear) so similar to the virus cells that the immune system will_____ (produce) various antibodies against these artificial cells. (8)These antibodies will also _____ (attack) the real virus cells, because the chromosome structures of the two kinds of cells will _____ (seem) nearly identical to the antibodies. (9)This technique will _____ (enable) scientists to make vaccines against a whole variety of diseases that are presently too virulent to _____ (use) to produce vaccines for human use.

Activities

Activity 1

Write a report on the history of a famous structure or public monument. Pick one of these examples or choose one of your own:

The Eiffel Tower	The Imperial Palace in Tokyo
The Golden Gate Bridge	The Temple of Heaven in Beijing
The Statue of Liberty	The Chunnel
Angkor Wat	The Sidney Opera House
The Parthenon	
The Empire State Building	

Include facts about its design, construction, and function, and be sure to provide information on why it is famous.

Activity 2

The article in Exercise 10 discussed discrimination against social minorities in the United States. Share your ideas and opinions about discrimination with other students in the class.

- First, discuss examples of other minorities that you are familiar with, and describe the discrimination that they face. These minorities could be

  ethnic minorities: Koreans in Japan, Turks in Germany, Arabs in France, Chinese in Southeast Asia, Palestinians in Israel, Indians in Fiji, Aborigines in Australia. Virtually every country has some identifiable ethnic minority.

  social minorities: gay people, people with physical disabilities, people with certain political beliefs, people with certain physical characteristics (fat people, short people, left-handed people).

  religious minorities: Jews in Eastern Europe, Hindus in Sri Lanka, Shi'ite Muslims in Afghanistan, Sunni Muslims in Iran, Catholics in Northern Ireland

- Next, discuss whether there are situations in which legal or social discrimination can ever be justified. Why or why not? Report the results of your discussion to the rest of the class. Report the things your entire group agreed on and the things that caused considerable disagreement. Report any interesting cultural patterns that you learned from the discussion.

Activity 3

Have you ever had a day that was so unlucky it made you wish that you had never even gotten out of bed? What happened? Was it unlucky because of what happened to you or because of something you did? Were you the "agent" or the "recipient" in your unlucky events? Write a paragraph that describes what happened on that day.

Activity 4

Find out how one or more of these common items are manufactured. If you prefer, you can talk about some other item you are familiar with. Report your findings to the rest of the class.

glass	rope
molasses	porcelain
beer	plywood
silicon chips	paper

Activity 5

In the Task, you examined information about two mysterious places to decide whether they offered proof that the Earth has been visited by beings from other planets. Do you believe in flying saucers, UFO's and visitors from outer space?

- Prepare a debate between people who believe that such things are possible and people who don't. Each side should present reasons and specific examples to support their opinions.

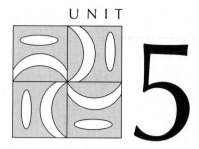

UNIT

5

One-Word
and Phrasal Modals

Task

Each year about 600,000 people become naturalized citizens of the United States. In addition to legal immigration, several thousand people enter the country illegally by overstaying tourist visas, entering on student visas and then dropping out of school to work, or even sneaking across the border into the country at night. For all immigrants, both legal and illegal, the move to their new country involves considerable hardship and difficulty. For some, it even involves serious physical danger. Many people risk their lives to seek a new life, because they hope it will be an improvement over their old one.

- Why do people decide to leave the country they were born in and go to live permanently in a new country? Make a list of five to eight reasons that you think might convince someone to emigrate to another country. Here are some examples:

   They can't make enough money to feed their families.
   They aren't allowed to practice their religion.
   They have to serve in the army for a long time.
   They are supposed to do what their parents want them to do.

- Now make a list of five to eight difficulties people face when they move to a new country. Here are some examples:

   They have to learn a new language.
   They are not able to forget their old customs.
   Their children do not grow up the way they did.
   They are supposed to take low-paying jobs because they cannot speak the language well.

- Write a paragraph that examines the advantages and disadvantages of emigrating to a new country.

Focus 1

Overview of Modals: One-Word and Phrasal Modals

USE

- There are two kinds of modal auxiliaries: one-word modals and phrasal modals.

ONE-WORD MODALS	PHRASAL MODALS
can/could	*be able to*
may/might	*be allowed to*
will/would	*be going to*
shall/should	*ought to/be supposed to/had better*
must	*have to, have got to*

- The English language most commonly employs one-word modals in basic social interactions, such as

requests:

(a) **Would** you help me? **May** I have some cheese? **Can** you turn down the radio?

offers:

(b) **Shall** I open a window?

invitations:

(c) **Can** you come to my party? **Would** you join us for dinner?

suggestions:

(d) We **could** have Chinese food tonight. We **might** try the Hong Kong Café.

complaints:

(e) **Must** you play that music so loud?

(f) Of course, we all knew that you **wouldn't** be on time!

- **Phrasal modals** are phrases that have many of the same meanings and applications as one-word modals. Common modal meanings and the one-word and phrasal modals we use to express those meanings are listed on the next two pages.

Common meanings that are communicated by modal auxiliaries:

Meaning	One-Word Modals	Examples	Phrasal Modals	Examples
necessity	*must/mustn't*	**(a)** We **must** leave before 5:00. **(b)** We **mustn't** be late.	*have to*	**(c)** You **have to** get another job if you want extra money.
			have got to	**(d)** You've **got to** stop spending so much money.
			be to	**(e)** You **are to** report to the office at once.
permission	*may* *can/ can't*	**(f)** **May** I come in? **(g)** You **can't** smoke here.	*be allowed to*	**(h)** You're **allowed to** bring a friend.
advisability/ obligation	*should/ shouldn't*	**(i)** Victor **should** study every day. **(j)** He **shouldn't** speak Spanish at home.	*ought to*	**(k)** You **ought to** do your homework every night.
			had better/ had better not	**(l)** You **had better** start working harder, if you want to pass this class.
			be supposed to	**(m)** You're **supposed to** do your homework every night.

Meaning	One-Word Modals	Examples	Phrasal Modals	Examples
ability	*can/ can't*	**(n)** I **can** ride a bicycle, but I **can't** swim.	*be able to*	**(o)** Jack **isn't able to** come to the phone.
future activity	all modals	**(p)** Roberta Chong-Davis **will** probably **be** living on the moon.	*be going to*	**(q)** I'm **going to** spend a month in France before I start my new job.
			be about to	**(r)** I'm **about to** leave for the airport.
			be to	**(s)** I'm **to** begin in six weeks.
inferences See Unit 21	all modals	**(t)** I **should** arrive arrive next Tuesday, but John **might** come the day before. **(v)** It **must** be raining, the streets are wet.	*have to* *have got to*	**(u)** Denise **has to be** really sick because she didn't come in today. **(w)** Bob **has got to be** the thief. No one else had a key to the cash box.

Focus 2

Multiple Meanings for a Single Modal

MEANING

- One modal form can have several possible meanings or uses. The first step in understanding modals is to make sure you know which meaning a modal is conveying.

Form	Meaning
(a) Victor **can** speak Spanish. He's **able to** express his ideas fluently.	He knows how to speak Spanish. (ability)
(b) But he **can't** speak Spanish in his English class, because he **isn't allowed to** speak anything but English.	It is not permitted. (permission)
(c) That **can't** be easy, because speaking a new language all the time **has to** be difficult!	It is not possible. There is no other possibility. (inference)

Exercise 1

How did the writer use the modal in each of these sentences? Is it expressing a social interaction (request, invitation, suggestion, etc.), necessity, permission, advice, ability, future prediction, or inference?

1. Can I ask you a question?
2. Can you speak Spanish?
3. Will you open the door?
4. Will the office be open tomorrow?
5. I can't hear you.
6. You shouldn't smoke; it's bad for your health.
7. You can't smoke here; it's a church.
8. Must you leave the window open? It's really cold outside.
9. You really should see a doctor.
10. The doctor should be ready to see you in just a minute.
11. I may be late tonight.
12. May I speak to Dr. Fleming?
13. You walked 20 miles today? You must be tired!
14. I'm interested in buying that car, but it could be too expensive.
15. Could you pass the butter?

Exercise 2

Write a sentence with a one-word modal that describes these ideas:

EXAMPLE: an activity to avoid if you want to be healthy
You should avoid foods that are high in fat.

1. a daily responsibility
2. the best way to keep in touch with friends who are far away
3. advice for a lazy student
4. something you know how to do well
5. a possible event or occurrence next year
6. something that is against school regulations
7. something you don't know how to do

Exercise 3

Restate the ideas you wrote about in Exercise 2 by using phrasal instead of one-word modals. What meanings can't you express with phrasal modals?

EXAMPLE: *You ought to avoid foods that are high in fat.*

Exercise 4

Underline the modals in this paragraph. Identify the meaning of each modal (permission, necessity, etc.).

(1)I'm not looking forward to this afternoon, because I have to go to the dentist. (2)I have a broken tooth, and I can't eat anything tough. (3)I'm supposed to be there at three o'clock, and I mustn't be more than five minutes late, or they'll cancel my appointment. (4)So I guess I had better leave plenty of time to get there. (5)The bus is supposed to come every ten minutes, but it's often late.

(6)I know that I ought to go to the dentist more often, but I really don't like to. (7)She's going to tell me that I have to take better care of my teeth. (8)I know I'm supposed to brush my teeth after every meal, but sometimes I just can't find the time. (9)After my appointment, I won't be able to eat anything for six hours, and I'm not supposed to eat anything for three hours before my appointment either. (10)I know I'm going to be hungry tonight!

Focus 3

Using Phrasal Modals to Introduce a Topic

USE

- You can use phrasal modals instead of one-word modals to introduce a topic. The initial statement often occurs with a phrasal modal, and subsequent sentences use one-word modals.

  (a) I **have to go** to the dentist today. I **must** get several fillings and possibly a root canal.

  (b) I **ought to** leave now if I want to be on time, because we **shouldn't** keep the dentist waiting.

  (c) Elizabeth **isn't going to** have much time to get ready for the dance. **She'll** be late if she spends too long getting ready.

Focus 4

USE

Combining Modal Meanings

USE

- You can use phrasal modals to combine two modal meanings in the same verb phrase because two one-word modals cannot be combined.

  (a) A teacher **must be able** to explain things clearly.

  (b) NOT: She **must can** explain things clearly.

  - We can combine a one-word and a phrasal modal:

    (c) Poor people **shouldn't have to** pay the same taxes as rich people.

    (d) I **may be able to** get some extra tickets.

  - We can also combine two phrasal modals:

    (e) A firefighter **has to be able to** carry at least 250 pounds.

    (f) You **ought to be able to** speak French if you want a job in Paris.

    (g) I'm **going to have to** leave in a minute.

Exercise 5

What modal meanings do the following sentences express?

> **EXAMPLES:** Don't leave the cheese anywhere that the dog is going to be able to reach. *future activity, ability*
>
> People ought to be allowed to read any book they want. *advisability, permission*

1. You're going to have to leave soon.
2. If Peter has another beer, he's not going to be able to drive.
3. The management isn't going to allow anyone to go backstage.
4. Most people have to be able to get a full night's sleep in order to be alert.
5. Horses have got to be allowed to exercise sufficiently if they are to stay healthy.
6. Some people feel that anyone who wants to become an American citizen ought to be able to speak English.
7. Children under 16 years old aren't supposed to be allowed to work without their parents' permission.
8. You don't have to be able to swim in order to enjoy the beach.

Exercise 6

Combine the modal meanings given:

> **EXAMPLE:** You *might be allowed to* bring a guest. (possibility, permission)

A. Use a one-word and phrasal modal combination:

1. I _____ speak with the doctor. (necessity, permission)

2. Dogs _____ ride on buses. (advisability, permission)

3. Students _____ speak English in class. (advisability, necessity)

B. Use two phrasal modals:

4. A fireman _____ carry at least 250 pounds. (necessity, ability)

5. I _____ (not) come to your party. (future, ability)

6. In order for plants to be healthy, they _____ grow freely. (necessity, ability)

7. You _____ speak French if you want a job in Paris. (advisability, ability)

Focus 5

Informality

USE

- Some phrasal modals are **more informal** than one-word modals. They are extremely common in conversation.

Meaning/Form	Informal Form Pronunciation/ Spelling	Examples
necessity *have to* *have got to*	*hafta* *gotta*	**(a)** I have to get some milk. **(b)** We('ve) got to get out of here!
future activity *be going to*	*gonna*	**(c)** I'm going to work a little longer.
advisability *ought to*	*oughta*	**(d)** You ought to tell your parents.
past habitual action *used to*	*useta*	**(e)** I used to ride a bicycle to work.

- Some phrasal modals are **more formal** than their one-word counterparts:
  - *be able to*
    - **(f)** I'm **not able to** speak to you now. (more formal)
    - **(g)** I **can't** speak to you now. (less formal)
  - *be to*
    - **(h)** John **is to** leave for France within the week. (more formal)
    - **(i)** John **will leave** for France within the week. (less formal)

Focus 6

Clarifying Meaning

MEANING

- You can use phrasal modals to clarify meaning in situations in which there is more than one possible interpretation of a one-word modal:

  (a) Charley **may not** bring a date.

    two meanings:

    possibility: It's possible that he won't bring a date.

    permission: He doesn't have permission to bring a date.

  (b) Charley **isn't allowed to** bring a date.

    one meaning: He doesn't have permission to bring a date.

- Some one-word and phrasal modals have special meanings and uses. It may be necessary to use one form instead of the other for a specific meaning or use.

- **Necessity:**
  - **have to** and **must** have different meanings in negative sentences.

    (c) You **don't have** to do it.
       (It's **not required.**)

    (d) You **must not** do it.
       (It's **forbidden.**)

  - *have got to* is an emphatic form of *have to*. It is not used in questions or negatives.

  - *be to* is very formal. It usually appears in official contexts.

    (e) You are to report to the medical office at once.

- **Advisability:**
  - *had better* is an emphatic form. It often implies a threat. You can use it in affirmative and negative statements, but not with questions.

    (f) You **had better do** your grammar homework, and you **had better not cheat**, or else Santa Claus won't bring you any presents!

  - *ought to* almost never appears in negative statements or questions.

- **Future Activity:**
  - *be about to* is used to describe events in the **immediate future**:

    (g) I'm **just about** to leave.
       (I'm going to leave right away.)

    (h) Let's hurry. The store's **about to** close.

    (i) I'm **about to** start a new job, so I need some new clothes.

    You will learn more about *be going to* in Unit 20.

Exercise 7

Work with a partner. Ask your partner questions about daily life and activities involving necessity, permission, obligation, ability, and future activities. Ask at least one yes/no and one *Wh*-question for each of these phrasal modals. Report your partner's answers in full sentences to the rest of the class.

> **EXAMPLE:** *Do you have to take the bus to get to school?*
> *No, I don't. I get a ride with a friend.*
> *What time do you have to leave home?*
> *About 15 minutes before class.*
> *My partner doesn't have to leave her house until just before*
> *class, because she gets a ride in a friend's car.*

1. have to
2. be allowed to
3. be supposed to
4. be able to
5. be going to

Exercise 8

What are the duties of citizenship? Decide whether people in society **should have to do or shouldn't have to do these** things. Write sentences that reflect your beliefs.

- go to work wherever the government sends them
- work without pay on community projects
- follow one particular religion
- send their children to school
- always obey their leaders
- be required to vote in elections
- report criminals to the police
- get permission to leave the country
- serve in the army
- pay taxes

For each category, add three more ideas of your own.

Exercise 9

What does it mean to "speak another language"? Decide whether a person **must** be able to do these things in a new language in order to say that he or she "speaks the language," or whether these are things that a person only **should** be able to do if he or she is a native speaker?

- read a newspaper
- understand native speakers perfectly when they are speaking to each other
- understand native speakers when they are speaking to foreigners
- speak correctly enough that people can understand what you mean
- have a perfect accent
- never make mistakes
- discuss abstract philosophy
- take care of day-to-day needs
- sound exactly like native speakers
- read and understand literature and poetry

Add three more skills for each category.
Based on your definition, do you consider yourself to be fluent in English? Why or why not?

Activities

Activity 1

In the Task, you listed situations that might make someone decide to live permanently in a new country. In Exercise 8, you identified some of the rights and duties of citizenship. Here are descriptions of three prospective immigrants who have applied for citizenship in a new country.

- In a small group, pretend that you are a committee who has to decide who should be granted priority for a residence visa.
- Examine each applicant's reasons for wanting to immigrate and the likelihood of his or her being able to fulfill the basic duties of citizenship in the new country. As a group, decide which applicant most deserves the residence visa and which least deserves it.
- Present your priorities and your reasons to the rest of the class.

Applicant A	Applicant B	Applicant C
• belongs to a religion that is discriminated against in the home country • refuses to serve in any army because of religious reasons • plans on maintaining the family's religion and language • will not allow children of the family to go to public schools in the new country • has few employable skills and may need to be supported by public welfare • will probably be imprisoned or executed in the home country because of religious beliefs	• wants to earn higher wages and send the money back to relatives in the home country • has skills that are needed badly in the new country • does not intend to vote or become involved in the politics of the new country • may decide to retire in the home country some day • doesn't intend to learn the language of the new country • wants children of the family to have a better economic condition than is available in the home country • believes in obeying the law, but will try to avoid national service	• doesn't want to spend 3 years in a remote area doing "national service." • was jailed for political activity in college • doesn't believe in paying taxes • has been threatened by the secret police • doesn't agree with the politics or government of the new country • is engaged to someone from the new country • wants to take advantage of the free educational system in the new country • is very intelligent • has skills that are badly needed in the new country

Activity 2

In **Exercise 9,** you defined what you consider to be a fluent speaker of English. Compare your definition with the one that has been developed by the Foreign Service Institute of the U.S. State Department. Their rating system gives people a numerical rating of 1 to 5.

- Here are some of the skills listed for each level. How would you rate your own abilities in English? Give yourself a rating and explain why you think it's accurate. If you speak other languages, rate yourself in these as well.

S-1: ELEMENTARY PROFICIENCY

- able to satisfy routine travel needs (hotels, directions, prices, etc.) and minimum courtesy requirements
- able to ask, answer, and understand questions and statements about very simple topics related to daily life
- makes frequent errors in grammar and vocabulary, but can be understood by a patient listener

S-2: LIMITED WORKING PROFICIENCY

- able to satisfy routine social demands and basic work requirements
- able to speak with confidence, but not easily, on such topics as current events, personal information, and daily job requirements
- can understand the general meaning of most conversations and speak clearly enough to be understood by all native speakers
- can use simple basic grammar accurately, but may require help to express more complex ideas

S-3: MINIMUM PROFESSIONAL PROFICIENCY

- able to satisfy all normal social and work requirements with fluency and accuracy as well as professional discussions in a special field
- can understand all conversations at normal speed
- vocabulary is broad enough that one never has to grope for words
- errors in grammar and vocabulary are infrequent and never interfere with understanding

S-4: FULL PROFESSIONAL PROFICIENCY

- can handle any conversation with a high degree of fluency and precision
- errors of grammar and pronunciation are extremely rare, but still listeners would not assume one to be a native speaker
- can do informal interpreting to and from the language

S-5: BILINGUAL PROFICIENCY

- complete fluency in the language equivalent to that of an educated native speaker

Activity 3

Here are three advertisements for positions available in clerical administration, computer programming, and sales. Examine each of these want ads to determine the basic requirements for each job, and what additional skills may be desirable.

- For each position, identify

> the things that an applicant must be able to do,
>
> the things he or she should be able to do (although they may not be absolutely required),
>
> some things that are neither required nor recommended, but are still characteristics that "the perfect candidate" might have,
>
> what an interested candidate has to do in order to apply for the position.

- Would any of these jobs interest you? Why or why not?

JOB OPPORTUNITIES

PROGRAM ASSISTANT
Provide clerical and admin support to five public program coord. involved in developing educational materials and providing training for hazardous waste workers. Qualifications: exper. operating Wordperfect 5.0 and HP Laserjet Series II printer. Skill in establishing and maintaining master computer and paper files of program information. Ability to create and carry out the details of long-term training schedules, including posting enrollments, instructor confirmation, curriculum changes, and training equipment acquisition. Interpersonal skills required to commun. with numerous instructors and staff on various university campuses. Organizational skills to estab. priorities. Related exper. working in a public service/ public program atmosphere pref'd.
Salary: $1799–2124/mo. with excel. benefits.

Apply or send detailed resume to: Personnel Office, Box 10-602-66(I) 2539 Channing Way, Berkeley, CA 94702 Closing date 11/30/93 EEO/AA

PROGRAMMER
Law Firm
Programmer/Analyst
As an industry leader, we have set new standards for "cutting edge" law firm information systems. Exciting opportunities exist in our SF office as we continue to develop, install, refine, and enhance automated solutions to law firm information processing. If you are a do-professional with 5+ years of programming experience, have a background in 4 lgs (preferably with COBOL or Powerhouse on a YAX), and have business software development exper., we'd like to hear from you. We seek individuals who strive for excellence in their work product, who prefer a challenging, fast-paced environment, and who are service-oriented. Excellent communication skills are a must!

Please send your resume and salary history to: Human Resources, PO Box 7880 San Francisco, CA 94120
Equal Opportunity Employer.

SALES
CAREER OPPORTUNITY
College Textbook Sales McGruder-Hall Western Region Office in SF has immediate openings for two Assoc. Sales Reps. These positions involve both office sales support & selling textbooks to professors on college campuses.
Qualifications include:
*4 yr. College Degree
*Exc. Communications Skills
*Strong Organization Skills w/ Ability to Prioritize Multiple Tasks
*Desire to Move into Outside Sales Position
*Strong Motivation to Succeed
*Willingness to Travel
We offer excellent salary & benefits package. Please send resume to: Sales Manager, McGruder-Hall Inc., 55 Francisco St. Ste.738 SF, CA 94133
No Phone Calls Please

Activity 4

Write your own want ads, advertising the qualifications and skills necessary for these occupations. First decide on necessary and desirable qualifications and tell interested people what they should do in order to apply.

English teacher
fire fighter
executive secretary/ administrative assistant
computer programmer
United Nations translator
police officer

Activity 5

Look in the want ads of your local newspaper and find two examples of jobs that you think would be interesting. Describe the position to the rest of the class and tell why you think you would be a good candidate for the job.

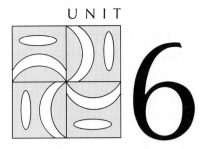

6

Infinitives

Task

John Tealhome is going to spend a year in France. He plans to study at the "Ecole des Langues et Langages" in Paris. He also hopes to enroll in some courses at Sorbonne University once his French is good enough to follow university lectures.

He's leaving in just two days, so he has a lot of things to do. He has also asked for some help from a couple of friends: Mary, his girlfriend (who is not very happy about his leaving for a year), and Charley, his roommate (who will stay on in their apartment).

Fortunately, he's a very organized person, so he makes lists to remind himself of everything he needs to get done, and crosses things off once he has accomplished them. He also reminds himself of the things he needs other people to do for him.

To Do
- buy Mary a present
- ~~say goodbye to Prof.~~
~~Montaigne~~
- get a letter of
introduction to Ecoles
des Langages
- ~~buy address book~~
- ~~buy suitcase~~
- ~~buy new jacket~~
- ~~buy small gifts for my~~
~~host family~~

- have farewell dinner with
Mom & Dad
- get traveler's checks
- reconfirm ticket and
get seat assignment

Check with Mary
- Does she really
understand why I'm
going?
- Is she still planning to
visit? When?

- move boxes to her
parents' garage
- ~~drive me to airport?~~
- have farewell dinner?
where?

Check with Charley
- remind about helping
move boxes to Mary's
garage?
- ~~check with landlord~~
~~about cleaning deposit~~

- clean the kitchen
- change name on the
bill for the electric
company
- ~~get address of his old~~
~~girlfriend (ballet~~
~~dancer) — don't tell~~
~~Mary!~~
- get money he owes me

- Examine this list with one or two other students in the class. How ready do you think John really is? What things does he still need to do? What things does he need Mary to do? Do you think she will agree to do them? What things does he want Charley to do? What things does he want Charley not to do? Why doesn't he want Charley to do them?

- Compare John's situation with your own experience or that of someone you know. Has he forgotten to do anything? If he doesn't have time for everything, what things should he be sure to do and what things could he decide not to do without creating problems?

- Present your ideas to the rest of the class.

Focus 1

FORM

Overview of Infinitives and Gerunds

FORM

- You can form infinitives and gerunds from verb phrases. They are used like noun phrases. Infinitives are of the form **to** + **verb**. Gerunds are of the form **-ing (verb + -ing)**.

Verb Phrase	Infinitive	Gerund
We **use infinitives and gerunds** like nouns.	We need **to use infinitives** in certain situations.	Other situations require **using gerunds.**

- You can use infinitives and gerunds in similar ways. They both function like nouns and you can use both forms like noun phrases in most situations. But there are also some very important differences between the two forms. This makes deciding which form to use—infinitive or gerund—somewhat difficult. Here are some common situations in which we need to use one form rather than the other.
  - as subjects in a sentence:
    - **(a) Knowing** how to use infinitives and gerunds can be tricky.
    - **(b) It** requires some experience **to know** which form is correct.
  - as objects of verbs:
    - **(c)** Some verbs **require using** gerunds as object forms, but with other verbs we **need to use** infinitive forms.
    - **(d)** Some verbs **allow using** both forms, but the situations in which we **are allowed to use** them may be different.
    - **(e)** Some verbs **require us to use** a "second subject," but other verbs **appear to use** only one.
  - as noun and adjective complements:
    - **(f)** Students often have a **hard time knowing** which **form to use.** But once you understand the principles, it's not **difficult to decide** on the correct form. You can learn to be **more confident using** gerunds and infinitives.
  - as objects of prepositions:
    - **(g)** This unit and the following one will focus **on using** infinitives and gerunds. By the end of the units, you should feel confident **about choosing** the correct form most of the time.

Exercise 1

Underline the infinitive and gerund forms in this passage. Tell how each one is used in the sentence.

EXAMPLE: Norman likes <u>to collect stamps</u>.
used as object of verb **likes**

(1)Norman likes to collect stamps. (2)He likes getting them from anywhere, but he is particularly interested in collecting stamps from Africa. (3)He has tried to get at least one stamp from every African country. (4)This hasn't always been easy to do. (5)He has tried writing to the post offices of various countries, but they haven't always responded to his request. (6)A friend suggested looking in commercial stamp catalogs for hard-to-find stamps, and Norman has had pretty good luck finding rare or unusual stamps there. (7)He has also begun corresponding with stamp collectors in other countries, and has asked them to send him stamps when they first come out. (8)They are usually happy to do it, and have urged him to do the same thing for them. (9)He enjoys learning about other countries, and finds that collecting stamps is a good way to do this.

Focus 2

FORM ● MEANING

Infinitive Forms and Their Meaning

FORM
MEANING

- Infinitives have no tense in themselves, but they have a basic general meaning. They refer to the idea or possibility of an action occurring. They have a future implication.

  (a) I want **to go** to Tahiti next year.

  (b) I am afraid **to open** that door. Something bad might happen if I do.

- You can add the same kind of additional information to infinitives that any verb phrase contains:

  - affirmative/negative:

Affirmative Infinitive *to* + **verb**	Negative Infinitive *not to* + **verb**
(c) John decided **to go** to Paris.	**(d)** John decided **not to go** to Paris.

(e) We want **to find** another restaurant because they have asked us **not to smoke** in this one.

- active/passive:

Active Infinitive *to* + verb	Passive Infinitive *to* + *be* + past participle
(f) I need **to wash** my car.	**(g)** My car needs **to be washed.**
(h) Brenda intends **to become** active in student government, and hopes **to be elected** to the student council.	

- time relationships:

Perfect Aspect: *to* + *have* + past participle	Progressive Aspect: *to* + *be* + verb + *-ing*
(i) I would prefer **to have left yesterday,** but John would prefer **to leave tomorrow.**	**(j)** We want **to be studying** when he gets here. (We'll study **before** he gets here.) **(k)** We want **to study** when he gets here. (We'll study **after** he gets here.)
Perfect infinitives indicate that the possible action occurred **before the main verb.**	Progressive infinitives indicate that the possible action is **in progress** at the time of the main verb.

- specific subject of the infinitive:

No Specific Subject: *to* + verb	Specific Subject: *for* + noun phrase + *to* + verb
(l) This question is easy **to answer.** (It's easy for everyone.)	**(m)** This question is easy **for us to understand.** (It's only easy for us; it's not easy for other people.)
The subject of an infinitive can be a noun or an object pronoun (*him, us,* and so on.)	

Exercise 2

Complete the sentences by expressing the idea in the infinitive as a verb phrase.

>   **EXAMPLE:** I hope **to be elected** to the student council.
>   I hope that I <u>will be elected to the student council</u>.

1. Morris claims **to have been born** in Russia.

   Morris claims that he_____.

2. We expected you **to have done** the assignment already.

   We expected that you___*had done*_____.

3. The teacher reminded the students not to forget to do their homework.

   The teacher said, "____*don't fo*_____."

4. We expected John **to be studying** when we got home.

   We expected that John would_____.

5. My sister is never happy **to be left alone** on a Saturday night.

   If my sister___*is left alone .*_____ , she is never happy.

Exercise 3

Interview a partner to get two or three answers to each of these questions.

>   **EXAMPLE:** What things do your teachers expect you **to do**?
>   *They expect me to speak up in class.*
>   What things do your teachers expect you **not to do**?
>   *They expect me not to copy my homework from other students.*

1. What things does your partner's family expect him or her **to do**?
   What things do they expect him or her **not to do**?

2. How does your partner like **to treat** people he or she has just met?
   How does your partner like **to be treated** by his or her teachers?

3. What things do your partner's teachers expect him or her **to do** at the beginning of class?
   What things do teachers expect your partner **to have done** before the beginning of class?

4. What does your partner plan **to do** when school ends?
   What does your partner plan **to be doing** when school ends?

Focus 3

Overview of Infinitive Verb Complements

FORM

- You can use infinitives as verb complements with three different kinds of verb patterns:
  - **Pattern 1:   verb + infinitive**

(a) Norman **decided to specialize** in African stamps when a friend **offered to give** him some stamps from Guinea.	The subject of the main verb also performs the action described by the infinitive.

  - **Pattern 2:   verb + noun phrase + infinitive**

(b) A friend **advised Norman to order** rare stamps from commercial companies, and **encouraged him to be** persistent.	The object of the main verb performs the action described by the infinitive. The subject of the main verb is different.

  - **Pattern 3:   verb (+ noun phrase) + infinitive**

(c) Norman **likes to send stamps** to other people, and also **likes other people to send stamps** to him.	If the subject of the main verb performs both actions, there is no object after the first verb. If there is a different performer of the second action, it is the object of the first verb and the subject of the infinitive.

Exercise 4

In these sentences, identify who performs the action described by the infinitive.

> **EXAMPLES:** We were expecting John to arrive before now.
> *John arrives.*
> We were asked to bring presents to the party.
> *We bring the presents.*

1. Malcolm claims to be speaking for the entire class.
2. This hotel requires people to turn in their room keys by 11:00.
3. Wendy requested Peter to bring her book to the party.
4. My sister promised to stay after the party.

5. Gladstone intends to lose 30 pounds by Christmas.
6. The child dared his friend to put a frog in the teacher's desk.
7. Norman wasn't allowed to stay up late when he was a child.
8. My parents encouraged all their children to start working part-time while they were still in high school.

Focus 4

FORM ● USE

Pattern 1: Verb + Infinitive

FORM
USE

- Some verbs describe situations in which the main subject also performs the action of the infinitive.
  (a) I **decided to go** shopping, but I **neglected to bring** my checkbook.
  (b) Peter **offered to help** Denise, but she **refused to accept.**
  (c) She **seemed to have** too much work, but she **was only pretending to be** busy.

Exercise 5

There are 17 different Pattern 1 verbs in the following passage. Identify them and list them in the blanks on the side of the passage:

Pattern 1 Verbs

_____agree_____ (1)The Acme Stamp Company agreed to send Norman some stamps, but

_____appear_____ when he got them they didn't appear to be in good condition. (2)The com-

_____ pany claimed to be reputable, but Norman still felt the stamps were bad.

_____ (3)He didn't care to pay good money for bad stamps and he felt that he

_____ deserved to get a refund. (4)So he decided to phone the company directly.

_____ (5)He demanded to speak to the manager. (6)The manager pretended to

_____ be concerned, but he hesitated to make any firm promises about refunds.

_____ (7)The company offered to exchange the stamps, but Norman refused to

_____ accept them. (8)All the stamps from that company seem to be of poor quality.

_____ (9)The company also tended to be very slow in filling orders. (10)Norman

_____ has learned to make sure a company is reputable before placing a large order

_____ with them. (11)He neglected to do this with the ACME Stamp Company.

_____ (12)Norman still hopes to get a refund. (13)He is waiting to see if the com-

_____ pany will do that before he files a formal complaint with the post office.

_____

_____

_____

Exercise 6

Practice using Pattern 1 verbs in sentences by completing these sentences with infinitives. Add information that expresses your real opinion. Compare your answers with those of other students in the class.

1. An honest person should never pretend . . . .
2. A good parent should never neglect . . . .
3. Most children in elementary school learn . . . .
4. Most poor people can't afford . . . .
5. The world situation today seems . . . .
6. Shy students sometimes hesitate . . . .
7. Selfish people rarely offer . . . .
8. A good friend should never refuse . . . .
9. Criminals deserve . . . .
10. Most children hope . . . .
11. In general, good students tend . . . .
12. Most American teenagers can't wait . . . .
13. Most good teachers seem . . . .
14. An honest person should never agree . . . .
15. Excellent athletes often appear . . . .

Exercise 7

Interview a partner and find out about five of the following topics. Report your information to the rest of the class in full sentences.

EXAMPLE: *My partner often neglects to do her homework.*

1. a responsibility he or she often neglects
2. a skill he or she learned in English class
3. a luxury he or she can't afford
4. a kind of assistance that she or he would never hesitate to accept
5. something he or she would refuse to do, no matter how much she or he were paid to do it

6. a reward she or he thinks he or she deserves
7. how he or she tends to react in a room full of strangers
8. a favorite make-believe fantasy he or she had as a child
9. how people in this class appeared on the first day of school
10. a famous person she or he would never care to meet

Focus 5

FORM

Pattern 2: Verb + Noun Phrase + Infinitive

FORM

- Some verbs describe situations in which the subject of the main verb causes or influences someone or something else to perform the second action. In such sentences, the object of the main verb functions as a "second subject" for the second action described by the infinitive.

  Other stamp collectors have **advised Norman to order** stamps from catalogs, but they **warned him not to spend** a lot of money unless he could **trust the stamp company to send** genuine stamps.

- Verbs that occur exclusively with this pattern are

advise	force	allow	tell
persuade	require	permit	remind
urge	forbid	invite	warn
encourage	command	trust	teach
convince	order	cause	hire

Exercise 8

Create sentences using the cues given:

EXAMPLES: (advise/study) *My parents advised me to study English.*
(force/cancel) *The heavy fog forced the airport to cancel all flights.*

1. remind/pay
2. warn/not forget
3. convince/help
4. hire/work
5. require/pay

6. forbid/marry
7. invite/join
8. teach/speak
9. allow/leave
10. order/send

11. urge/vote
12. trust/spend
13. tell/eat
14. encourage/ask
15. force/leave

Focus 6

FORM

Pattern 3: Verb (+ Noun Phrase) + Infinitive

FORM

- You can use many verbs either with or without a "second subject."
  (a) We **expect to leave** in an hour, and we **expect you to come** with us.
  (b) Norman **wants to get** stamps from every country, and he **wants us to help** him.
- A few verbs of this kind must use *for* to mark the second subject:
  (c) Mary's father **arranged for John to get** a cheap ticket. He never **intended for Mary to be** unhappy. But she will just have to **wait for John to return**.
- Verbs that follow this pattern are **arrange, hope, intend, consent, afford**.

Exercise 9

Interview other students in the class to find out information on one of the following topics. Report your answers in full sentences:

EXAMPLES: *My partner likes to do the dishes, but he prefers someone else to do the cooking.*
My partner needs to write a statement of purpose for her university application, but she needs a native English speaker to check her grammar.

1. things they **like to do** vs. things they **like someone else to do**
2. things they **expect to do** vs. things they **expect someone else to do**
3. things they have **asked to do** vs. things they have **asked someone else to do**
4. things they **need to do** vs. things they **need someone else to do**
5. things that they have **arranged to do** vs. things that they have **arranged for other people to do**

Exercise 10

Combine these sentence pairs. Replace the indicated word with an infinitive complement made from the first sentence.

> **EXAMPLE:** John will spend a year in France. Mary doesn't want **this**.
> *Mary doesn't want **John to spend** a year in France.*

1. John will write a long letter once a week. Mary has requested **this**.
2. John might postpone his trip until next year. Mary would prefer **this**.
3. She will try to visit him while he's there. She has decided **this**.
4. She was upset by the news of his plans. He didn't expect **this**.
5. John got a very cheap ticket. Mary's father arranged **this**.
6. John didn't apply for a passport. He neglected **this**.
7. John will report to the police when he arrives. French law requires **this**.
8. Mary will begin to study French herself. John has encouraged **this**.
9. Mary feels hurt that John is leaving. John never intended **this**.

Focus 7

FORM

Using Infinitive Complements with Passive Verbs

FORM

- You can use Pattern 2 and Pattern 3 verbs with second subjects (except the verbs that require *for*) in passive sentences. In such cases, the object of the main verb, or "second subject," becomes the subject of the sentence, and the main verb is in passive voice.
  - (a) **People warned Norman not to pay** a lot of money for stamps from unfamiliar companies.
  - (b) **Norman was warned not to pay** a lot of money.

Exercise 11

Make the "second subject" the main subject of a passive sentence:

> **EXAMPLE:** We expected John to arrive on the 10:00 flight.
> *John was expected to arrive on the 10:00 flight.*

1. Mary warned John not to fall in love with a French girl.
2. They asked John to study in a special accelerated program.
3. John's family encouraged him to apply for a scholarship.
4. The school chose him to receive a partial tuition discount.

5. Her family convinced Mary to give John permission to leave for a year.
6. People taught John to use French for all daily activities.
7. A French family invited John to have his meals with them.
8. Many people consider French cooking to be the best in Europe.

Exercise 12

Complete these sentences with infinitives. Use real information that expresses your true opinion. Compare your ideas with those of other students in the class.

1. Most people can be trusted....
2. Children should be allowed....
3. All teachers should be encouraged....
4. Noisy people should be told....

5. Teenagers should be warned....
6. Students should be expected....
7. Guests should be invited....
8. Rich people should be required....

Focus 8

FORM ● USE

Infinitives as Subjects of a Sentence

FORM
USE

- You can use infinitives as subjects in a sentence. We usually begin such sentences with *it* and put the infinitive at the end of the sentence.

Awkward	Better
(a) To **collect stamps** is fun.	**(b) It's** fun **to collect stamps.**
(c) To **have been introduced** to you is an honor.	**(d) It's** an honor **to have been introduced** to you.
(e) For John to study in France is a good idea.	**(f) It's** a good idea **for John to study** in France.

Exercise 13

Complete these sentences with ideas that express your true opinion. Compare your answers with other students in the class.

1. It's always a good idea....
2. It's enjoyable....
3. It's never wise....
4. It's every parent's dream....

5. It's never a teacher's responsibility....
6. It's sometimes difficult....
7. It's usually necessary....
8. It's seldom easy....

Activities

Activity 1

In the Task, you examined the things on John Tealhome's mind a couple of days before his departure for a year overseas. Have you ever left for a long trip? How prepared and well-organized were you two days before your departure?

- Make a list like John's that indicates the things you still needed to do for the trip you took, and some of the things that you needed other people to do for you. Compare your list and John's. Who was better organized?
- Write a paragraph describing your experience. Did you have a chance to do everything you needed or wanted to do? Was there anything you forgot to do? What advice would you give someone preparing for a similar trip?

Activity 2

Write about your favorite hobby or leisure time activity. What is it? Why do you like to do it? What skill does someone need to develop or what special equipment does a person need to buy if he or she wants to pursue this hobby?

Activity 3

Do parents treat boys and girls differently? Interview some classmates and find out what things children in their culture are taught to do when they are growing up.

	Boys are encouraged to . . .	Boys are encouraged not to . . .	Girls are encouraged to . . .	Girls are encouraged not to . . .
	Examples be brave defend their sisters	cry play with dolls	be neat and tidy play with dolls	play rough get dirty
Student 1				
Student 2				
Student 3				

- Compare the responses of the people you interviewed. Do some cultures make more gender distinctions in child-raising than others? What things are taught to all children regardless of their gender or culture?

Activity 4

Below is a list of some effective and ineffective strategies for learning to speak a foreign language. Think about your own language learning habits and decide whether the listed strategy is something that language learners should **try to do** or something that they should **try not to do**, in order to become better in English.

> try to use new vocabulary in writing and conversation
>
> stop to look up every unfamiliar word in the dictionary
>
> be very careful not to make any mistakes
>
> guess the meanings of unfamiliar words by using other clues in the sentence
>
> become discouraged if you don't understand 100 percent of everything you hear
>
> always think of your ideas in your own language first, and then translate them word-by-word into English
>
> listen for the general idea in conversations
>
> look for opportunities to speak English as often as possible
>
> go over your mistakes on homework and try to understand why you made them
>
> go over your mistakes on homework and write the correct answer
>
> find ways to punish yourself if you make a mistake
>
> don't speak unless you are sure the answer is correct

- Add at least three additional strategies to your list of things language learners should try to do, and three things to your list of things they should try not to do.
- Compare your list with several other students and present any interesting similarities and differences to the rest of the class.

Activity 5

A superstition is a folk belief about lucky or unlucky events. In many societies, people used to take these beliefs quite seriously, but nowadays, they follow these beliefs more out of custom than out of fear of bad luck. Even so, you can still see the present-day results of some old superstitions. For example, in the United States the number 13 is often considered to be an unlucky number. Some people try to stay at home on Friday the 13th (which is supposed to be a particularly unlucky day). Some people don't want to attend a party or sit at a table where there are 13 people. Many buildings, especially hotels, do not have a 13th floor. Other superstitions still affect basic manners in society. Because of an old superstition, it is considered polite to say "God bless you" when someone near you sneezes, even if that person is a complete stranger.

- Work with other students to develop a presentation for the rest of the class about some modern superstitions and their results. Identify some things that people try to do and some things they try not to. You may wish to compare the superstitions of several different cultures. Are there any superstitions that are universal? Why do you think superstitions come into being?
- Present your ideas to the rest of the class.

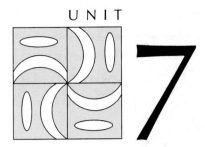

UNIT

7

Gerunds

Task

How do you like to spend your free time? Researchers have found that most people fit into one of two categories: **Do-ers and Be-ers.**

The first category (**do-ers**) is made up of those who like **doing** things during their leisure time. They have hobbies, projects, and interests that keep them busy. They structure their free time and measure a successful vacation by what they have done, seen, or accomplished.

The second category (**be-ers**) is made up of those who prefer **not doing things.** They are content to spend an afternoon relaxing in an easy chair, reading a magazine, or just doing nothing at all—sleeping, day-dreaming, whatever. They measure a successful vacation by how relaxed they feel by the end of it.

- Spend some time thinking about how you typically spend your free time. Identify some activities that you enjoy doing on your "day off." Next, identify some things that you like not doing during your free time. Finally, identify some things that you don't like or resent having to do during your leisure time. Use this table to help organize your thoughts. Some examples have been provided. Try to think of at least five or six other activities for each category. Which category has the most items?

Activities I enjoy doing in my free time (I do them, and I enjoy that.)	Activities I enjoy *not* doing in my free time (I don't do them, and I enjoy that.)	Activities I don't enjoy doing in my free time (I do them, but I don't enjoy that.)
reading the paper talking with friends	not getting up early not driving to work	doing chores, like cleaning and laundry taking work home from the office

- Next, describe your typical free-time activities and preferences to a partner. Your partner should decide whether you appear to be a do-er or a be-er. What category does your partner seem to be in?
- Present your findings about each other to the rest of the class.

Focus 1

Gerund Forms
and Their Meaning

FORM
MEANING

- You can form gerunds (like infinitives) from a verb phrase and use them like noun phrases in other sentences. Form them by adding **-ing** to the simple form of the verb. You can use them in many of the same ways that you use infinitives.

Verb Phrase	Gerund
(a) Norman **collects stamps**. He **pays a lot of money** for rare ones.	**(b)** Norman enjoys **collecting stamps**. He doesn't mind **paying a lot of money** for rare ones.

- Gerunds (like infinitives) have no tense by themselves. In general, they refer to an action that is already happening or completed. They imply that the action is in progress.

    (c) The librarian doesn't like **people talking**. Please stop.

    (d) I hate **listening** to boring lectures. I wish this class were over!

- You can add the same kind of additional information to gerunds that any verb phrase contains.

    - affirmative/negative:

Affirmative Gerund verb + **-ing**	Negative Gerund **not** + verb + **-ing**
(e) I enjoy **staying in bed** on Sunday mornings.	**(f)** I like **not getting up** early.
(g) Peter likes **having a responsible job**, but he hates **not having enough time** for his family.	

    - active/passive:

Active Gerund verb + **-ing**	Passive Gerund *being* + past participle
(h) Matt and Jeff enjoy **inviting friends** for dinner.	**(i)** Matt and Jeff enjoy **being invited** to their friends' homes for dinner.
(j) Denise likes **giving orders**, but she hates **being told** what to do.	

    - time relationships:

Simple Aspect verb + **-ing**	Perfect Aspect *having* + past participle
(k) John was nervous about **taking** tests.	**(l)** John was happy about **having gotten** a good grade on his exam.
Because the base meaning of gerunds usually indicates simple or progressive aspect, you do not often use perfect gerunds, and there is no progressive gerund.	

• specific subject of a gerund:

No Specific Subject verb + -ing	Specific Subject noun phrase + gerund
(m) My boss doesn't approve of **taking** time off. (She doesn't like anybody doing it.)	(n) My boss doesn't approve of **my taking taking time off**. She doesn't like **me leaving** early. (Perhaps she doesn't mind if other people do these things.)

You can use possessive noun phrases (possessive nouns and possessive pronouns), nouns and object pronouns (**my** taking time off, **me** leaving early) to mark the subject of a gerund. Possessives are more formal. They are more common in written English. Object forms are less formal. They are more common in spoken English.

Exercise 1

Complete the sentences by expressing the idea in the gerund as a verb phrase.

EXAMPLE: I enjoy **not doing** anything on Sunday mornings.
I don't do anything on Sunday, and I enjoy that.

1. We hate **being asked for** money all the time.

   When _____ , we hate it.

2. I really appreciate **your having taken** such good care of my dog while I was on vacation.

   I really appreciate that _____ .

3. They suspected him of **taking** the money.

   They suspected that ____ *had taken* ____ .

4. We didn't plan for **their having** problems with the homework.

   We didn't plan for the fact that _*they would / might have*_ .

5. I think John resents **not being invited** to the party.

   I think John resents the fact that _*he wasn't invited*_ .

93

Exercise 2

Interview a partner and find out two or three things for each of these topics.

EXAMPLE: Things your partner enjoys doing:

What things do you enjoy doing on Sunday mornings? I enjoy reading the paper.

Things your partner enjoys not doing:

What things do you enjoy not doing on Sunday mornings? I enjoy not getting up early.

1. Things your partner enjoys **doing** on the weekends.
   Things your partner enjoys **not doing** on the weekends.
2. Things your partner hates **doing**.
   Things your partner doesn't mind **other people doing.**
3. Things or services your partner likes **giving to other people**.
   Things or services your partner likes **other people giving to him or her.**
4. Things that being in a university typically requires **doing**.
   Things that being in a university typically requires **having done.**

Focus 2

FORM

Overview of Gerund Verb Complements

FORM

- You can use gerunds as verb complements with three different kinds of verb patterns:
  - **Pattern 1: verb + gerund**
    - **(a)** Charley **can't help falling** in love with a new woman every week.
    - **(b)** The doctor told me that I've got to **quit smoking.**
  - **Pattern 2: verb +** $\begin{Bmatrix} \text{gerund} \\ \text{noun phrase + infinitive} \end{Bmatrix}$
    - **(c)** Doctors **advise reducing** fats in one's diet.
    - **(d)** The doctor **advised me to reduce** fats in my diet.
  - **Pattern 3: verb (+ noun phrase) + gerund**
    - **(e)** I **don't mind sleeping late** when I get the chance, and I **don't mind other people doing it** either.

Exercise 3

In these sentences, identify who performs the action described by the gerund.

> **EXAMPLE:** Is there any way we can delay taking the test?
> *We take the test.*
>
> No politician will ever admit not having a solution to the budget problem.
> *Politicians don't have a solution to the budget problem.*

1. Jeff enjoys living in San Francisco.
2. I really appreciate your helping us get ready for the party.
3. Peter has considered looking for a new job.
4. Matt could never imagine leaving San Francisco.
5. Mary resents John's spending a year overseas.
6. Miss Manners will never excuse her having behaved so rudely.
7. We wanted to postpone leaving for the trip, but we didn't anticipate not being able to change our tickets.
8. We'll really miss your singing and dancing in the school talent show.

Focus 3

FORM

Pattern 1: Verb + Gerund

FORM

- A number of verbs take gerund complements.
  - **(a)** Charley **can't help falling** in love with a new woman every few weeks. Most women I know **avoid going out** with him.
  - **(b)** The doctor told Mary to **give up smoking**, but she **keeps on doing it**, even though she knows it's bad for her health.

Exercise 4

There are 14 verbs in this passage that follow Pattern 1. Identify them and underline them. The first two have been done for you.

(1) Nutritionists <u>recommend</u> reducing the amount of fat in one's diet. (2) They <u>suggest</u> eating foods that are high in fiber and avoiding foods that are high in fat. (3) Some people <u>deny</u> having a high-fat diet, and would never <u>consider</u> changing their eating habits. (4) Other people <u>admit</u> consuming more fat than they would really like to. (5) But nutritionists feel that everyone could benefit from these changes in their diet:

(6) Most people <u>can't help</u> consuming a certain amount of fat, no matter how careful they are. (7) But there are a few very simple basic changes in eating and cooking habits that will greatly decrease the amount of fat in a person's diet.

(8) They can <u>give up</u> using rich creamy sauces and use natural cooking juices to give their food flavor. (9) They should <u>avoid</u> consuming large amounts of red meat, and <u>quit</u> having such foods as bacon or sausage on a regular basis. (10) They can <u>practice</u> cooking their food in different ways. (11) Such changes <u>include</u> not frying foods in oil, and steaming or boiling whenever possible. (12) Initially these adjustment may be difficult, and people may <u>resist</u> following the recommendations. (13) But nutritionists feel that if people <u>keep on</u> following these techniques, it will get easier to <u>keep</u> doing it.

Exercise 5

Use the verbs that you found in Exercise 4 to talk about some of your own health habits. Describe some of your healthy habits. Include things that you regularly avoid doing and things that you do regularly and intend to keep on doing.

Focus 4

FORM

Pattern 2:
Verb + { Gerund / Noun Phrase + Infinitive }

FORM

- Some verbs take gerund complements if there is no second subject, and infinitives if there is a second subject.

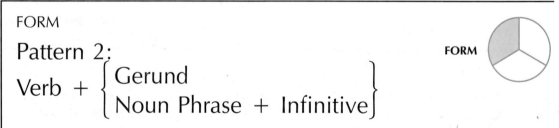

Gerund (No Second Subject)	Infinitive (Second Subject)
Doctors **advise reducing** fats in one's diet. They **urge giving up** fried foods. They **encourage steaming or boiling** food but **forbid frying** things in oil. Changing food habits **requires changing** old habits.	The doctor **advised me to reduce** my fat intake. He **urged me to give up** fried foods. He **encouraged me to steam or boil** my food but **forbid me to fry** things in oil. This has **required me to change** a lot of old habits.

Focus 5

Pattern 3: Verb (+ Noun Phrase) + Gerund

FORM

- Other verbs can appear with or without a second subject.

Without Second Subject:	With Second Subject:
(a) I **don't mind borrowing** money,	but I **dislike other people doing** it.
(b) I **dislike swimming** in cold water,	but I **don't mind other people doing** it.

- Common verbs that follow this pattern are

dislike	anticipate	appreciate	miss	resent
don't mind	consider	deny	tolerate	postpone
enjoy	delay	excuse	understand	imagine

Exercise 6

For five of the verbs listed above write two sentences, one with a second subject and one without. If you wish, you can write a single sentence that uses both patterns.

EXAMPLES: *Most people appreciate taking a nice hot bath.*

Most teachers don't appreciate their students copying each other's homework.

Exercise 7

Complete these sentences with true information. Use gerunds in your answers, and if the main verb can take a second subject, try to use a second subject in your answer:

1. I usually avoid....
2. When I was a child, I used to imagine....
3. My English teacher recommends....
4. I would like to quit....
5. I am considering....
6. Honest people shouldn't tolerate....
7. To be a good soccer player, it's necessary to practice....
8. A teacher's responsibility includes....
9. Becoming a really good speaker of a foreign language requires....
10. I appreciate guests....

Exercise 8

Combine these sentence pairs. Replace the indicated word with a gerund complement made from the first sentence.

EXAMPLE: John will spend a year in France. Mary resents **this**.

Mary resents John's spending a year in France.

1. John sings a funny song whenever he sees her. Mary will miss **this** a great deal.
2. He wants to become really fluent in French. Mary doesn't really understand **this**.
3. He applied to the program without consulting Mary. She resents **this**.
4. She will not have a chance to talk with him every day. She's not looking forward to **this**.
5. John is leaving in two weeks. He is quite excited about **this**.
6. John needs at least three weeks to get a passport. He didn't anticipate **this**.
7. This will make his departure even later than expected. John wanted to avoid **this**.

Focus 6

FORM

Gerunds in Other Positions in a Sentence

FORM

- You can use gerunds in other places in the sentence where nouns normally appear. They can be used as
  - **subjects:**

Gerund Subjects	Infinitive Subjects
(a) Collecting stamps is fun.	**(c) It's** fun **to collect** stamps.
(b) AWKWARD: **It's** fun **collecting stamps.**	**(d)** AWKWARD: **To collect stamps** is fun.

Gerund subjects commonly begin a sentence and are not usually used with *it* constructions.

 • You must use gerunds rather than infinitives as objects of prepositions and two-word verbs:
  - **(e)** I am happy **about meeting** you.
  - **(f)** This steak is too tough **for frying** in butter.
  - **(g)** He is exhausted **from staying up** all night.
  - **(h)** I'm **looking forward to going** on vacation.
  - **(i)** I won't **put up with your copying** homework.

Exercise 9

Complete these sentences with information that describes your true feelings about these topics. Compare your answers to those of other students in the class.

1. Studying English. . . .
2. Passing TOEFL. . . .
3. I'm nervous about. . . .
4. I'm never afraid of. . . .

5. My friends are concerned about. . . .
6. I would like to give up. . . .
7. Growing older. . . .
8. I get tired of. . . .

Focus 7

FORM

Choosing Infinitive versus Gerund Verb Complements Based on Form

FORM

- In many cases, students often have trouble deciding whether to use a gerund or an infinitive. You may use both form and meaning to help decide which is correct.

Form: Some verbs take **only** gerund complements; others take only infinitives. Verbs also fall into the specific patterns that we have studied. The verb itself determines whether you should use an infinitive or gerund complement.

Exercise 10

Review the basic patterns and common verbs in each pattern. Work with a partner and try to write as many additional verbs for each pattern as you can remember without looking back in your book. A couple have been done for you.

Verbs that Take Infinitive Complements			Verbs that Take Gerund Complements		
pattern 1	**pattern 2**	**pattern 3**	**pattern 1**	**pattern 2**	**pattern 3**
appear	advise	expect	can't help	encourage	appreciate
refuse	remind	arrange	keep on	urge	anticipate
seem	advise	————	————	————	dislike
————	————	————	————	————	————
————	————	————	————	————	————
————	————	————	————	————	————
————	————	————	————	————	————
————	————	————	————	————	————
————	————	————	————	————	————
————	————	————	————	————	————

Verbs that Take Infinitive Complements			Verbs that Take Gerund Complements		
_____	_____	_____	_____	_____	_____
_____	_____	_____	_____	_____	_____
_____	_____	_____	_____	_____	_____
_____	_____	_____	_____	_____	_____
_____	_____	_____	_____	_____	_____
_____	_____	_____	_____	_____	_____
_____	_____	_____	_____	_____	_____
_____	_____	_____	_____	_____	_____

Are there any verbs that can be used with both infinitives and gerunds? Which ones are they?

Focus 8

MEANING

Choosing Infinitive and Gerund Complements Based on Meaning

MEANING

- You can also use basic meaning to help decide which form to use. Infinitive complements usually indicate that the action is imagined or in the future. Gerund complements indicate that the action is happening at the same time as, or has taken place before the main verb. If there is no difference in meaning, we can use both forms:

    (a) I **hate telling** you this, but you have to take the test again.

    (b) I **hate to tell** you this, but you have to take the test again.

- If there is an important difference in meaning, you must choose one form instead of the other.

  - **forget:**

    (c) I **forgot to mail** the letter. (I didn't mail it.)

    (d) I **forgot mailing** the letter. (I mailed it, but I can't remember when.)

  - **try:**

    (e) We **tried closing** the windows, but it was still cold. (It was an experiment.)

    (f) We **tried to close** the window, but it was stuck. (We made an attempt.)

  - **remember:**

    (g) Did you **remember to mail** the letter? (You didn't forget, did you?)

    (h) I **don't remember mailing** it, but I'm sure I did, because it's not in my briefcase. (I can't recall.)

  - **stop:**

    (i) I have to **stop smoking**! Every time I climb a flight of stairs, I have to **stop to catch** my breath.

tried eating
tried book

• The same is true with noun complements and adjective complements. Choosing a gerund or infinitive depends on the implied meaning.

Infinitives	Gerunds
(a) My **plan to visit every bar in town** has become very expensive. (I made the plan before I started visiting.)	**(b)** I had a **problem visiting every bar**. I ran out of money. (I began visiting, and then the problem developed.)
(c) I'll be **happy to discuss** possible solutions. (The discussion hasn't started.)	**(d)** I am always **happy discussing** possible solutions. (I have discussed possible solutions before, and this has always made me happy.)
(e) I am too **nervous to study**. (I won't be able to study.)	**(f)** I get **nervous talking** to large groups of people. (When it happens, I get nervous.)
(g) He was very **anxious to speak** to the doctor. (He hadn't spoken to her yet.)	**(h)** He got more and more **anxious waiting** for the doctor. (The longer he waited, the more anxious he got.)

Exercise 11

Fill in the blank with the gerund or infinitive form of the word given. There may be more than one correct answer, so prepare to explain why you chose the answer that you did.

1. If you want to lose weight, you should try _____ (avoid) all sweets. That might be better than going on a diet. *either*

2. I know John was at the party, but I don't remember _____ (talk) to him. *ing*

3. On her way home, my mother stopped _____ *to* _____ (pick up) a few things at the store.

4. Suddenly all the dogs in the neighborhood began _____ *either* (bark) at the same time.

5. My sister has never been able to quit _____ *ing* (smoke).

6. Ruth couldn't watch TV because she forgot _____ *to* _____ (bring) her glasses with her.

7. Nowadays, children have stopped _____ *ing* _____ (play) traditional children's games and seem _____ *to* _____ (prefer) _____ *either* (play) video games instead.

8. I'll try _____ *ing* _____ (eat) any kind of food once.

Exercise 12

Underline the gerunds and infinitives in the numbered sentences. The first paragraph has been done for you as an example. Tell why you think the author chose to use one form rather than the other.

(1)Many Americans are having a hard time <u>doing nothing in their free time</u>. The amount of leisure time in the United States has decreased by nearly 30% in the last 20 years. Americans now have less leisure time than people in any other industrialized country in the world, (2)and this amount will probably continue <u>to decrease in the future</u>. Where is this time going to?

Employment practices in the U.S. are one cause. (3)The average American company requires employees to work 40 hours per week. (4)They are allowed to take 11 paid holidays, and have an average of 12 vacation days (about two weeks) per year. Compare that to the Germans. (5)They are required to work a 38-hour week, and get to enjoy a yearly total of 10 holidays and 30 days (six weeks) of paid vacation. (6)Even the hard-working Japanese (who spend an average of 42 hours a week working at the office) are encouraged to take 16 paid vacation days, and have an additional 20 days of holidays.

A second reason for this growing lack of free time comes from changing social patterns. (7)Today, in most American families, both the husband and the wife need to work full-time outside the home. (8)They are forced to postpone doing household chores until the weekend. (9)As a result, most Americans now need to spend at least one entire day of their weekend doing household chores, such as shopping for food, cleaning the house, doing the laundry, etc.

(10)But the American mania for keeping busy doesn't stop there. A third reason for decreased free time is how Americans spend what little free time they actually have. (11)More and more Americans are using their vacations to undertake large-scale projects that they wouldn't otherwise have a chance to do, such as painting their houses, repairing their automobiles, or even writing grammar books. There has also been a rapid growth in the popularity of "working vacations." (12)Travel agencies can now arrange for people to work on scientific research projects or to assist ecologists with collecting and cataloging plant and animal species in national parks. (13)Other popular "working vacations" include going on digs at archaeological sites or participating in community development projects in other countries. (14)Still other people arrange to enroll in travel-study courses in foreign languages, history, or geography. (15)For some Americans, their idea of a relaxing vacation is to take a 300-mile bicycle trip or to spend a week climbing mountains in South America.

Exercise 13

Fill in the blanks with the correct form of the verbs given. There may be more than one correct answer, so be prepared to explain why you chose the answer you did.

Before the invention of radio and television, people spent much of their leisure time

(1) _____ (pursue) activities that involved (2) _____ (do) or (3) _____ (make) something. They practiced (4) _____ (play) a musical instrument or studied (5) _____ (sing). Most people learned (6) _____ (keep busy) by

(7) _____ (try) (8) _____ (improve) their abilities in some way or by

(9) _____ (practice) a skill. People who couldn't afford (10) _____ (spend) much money on hobbies often started (11) _____ (collect) simple objects, such as matchbook covers or stamps, or even things like buttons or bottle caps. Of course, most people spent a lot of time (12) _____ (read), and (13) _____ (write) letters to friends. Children played games in which they pretended (14) _____ (be) pirates or Indians or people they remembered (15) _____ (read about) in books. Many women were extremely clever at (16) _____ (make) and (17) _____ (decorate) articles of clothing. Men often kept busy by (18) _____ (make) toys for children, or (19) _____ (carve) small sculptures out of wood.

Nowadays, people don't find it as easy (20) _____ (fill) their time with such productive activities. Television has encouraged many people (21) _____ (stop) (22) _____ (work on) their hobbies or amateur accomplishments. Children are spending more and more time (23) _____ (watch) TV or (24) _____ (play) video games. As a result, traditional children's games, which have been played for hundreds of years, are beginning (25) _____ (forget). Traditional skills such as embroidery, crocheting, and wood carving are failing (26) _____ (pass on) from parent to child. People seem (27) _____ (prefer) activities that allow them (28) _____ (be) passive observers rather than active participants. If these traditional forms of recreation keep (29) _____ (disappear) at the current rate, many of the things that people used to enjoy (30) _____ (do) will only be found on television documentaries about how people attempted (31) _____ (use) their leisure time in the days before television.

Activities

Activity 1

In the Task, you decided whether you are a **do-er** or a **be-er** in the way that you spend your free time.

- Form a group with other people who are in the same category as you. Together, come up with a list of the five or ten best ways to spend a rainy afternoon.
- Compare your list of activities with that of a group from the other category. What does this tell you about the differences between **do-ers** and **be-ers**?

Activity 2

Choose a partner that you know pretty well.

- Describe three things you can not imagine him or her ever doing. Then identify three things that you expect that your partner does on a routine basis.
- Explain your reasons for thinking why your partner would or wouldn't do the things you have described. What is it about your partner that makes you think he or she would ever behave that way? Your partner should then do the same thing with you.
- Were you or your partner surprised by any of the things you heard? For example, did your partner tell you that he couldn't imagine your doing something that you actually do quite frequently? Or perhaps your partner mentioned an expectation that you would never consider doing in a million years. Report any surprises to the rest of the class.

Activity 3

We all have bad habits that we would like to stop. We all have things that we know we should do that, for some reason, we always seem to neglect. New Year's Eve is a popular time to make resolutions about ways to improve our behavior.

- Make a list of "New Year's Resolutions":

    What are some things you would like to stop doing? (For example, watching so much TV, eating ice cream before bed, gossiping about people behind their backs)

    What are some things you would like to start doing? (For example, getting more exercise, reading for an hour every night, writing letters to friends)
- Compare your New Year's Resolutions to those of other people in the class. Are there any common categories or characteristics?

Activity 4

What are the reasons for choosing someone as a friend and what are the reasons to exclude someone from that category? Everyone has good and bad habits or personal characteristics. Some people find it easy to forgive certain faults, and decide that they like someone even if he or she isn't perfect. But other faults can result in deciding that you don't want that person as a friend. What actions or characteristics in other people do you feel can't be excused? What annoying habits do you tolerate?

- Write a brief paragraph on personal characteristics that you cannot stand but many other people do not seem to mind. (For example, I can not stand for people to be too serious about their work, and have no other interests in life.) Include characteristics that you do not mind, but that many other people can not stand. (For example, I do not mind people being late.)

Activity 5

Prepare a short talk for the rest of the class on one of these topics:

- your likes and dislikes: activities that you do not mind, can not stand, love, hate, resent, and enjoy;
- your future plans: activities that you anticipate, hope, intend to do and things that would make you postpone or delay them or consider not doing them at all.

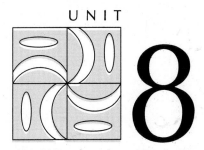
Conjunctions

Task

There is one thing we all know: Everybody is different in some way. Everybody likes and dislikes different things. Some people love to go to discos, but other people hate the smoke and the noise. Some people like a peaceful vacation with nothing to do but relax, while others prefer a vacation with lots of activities.

Make a list of the things you like and don't like in the following categories. Think of at least three items that you like and three items that you don't like for each category.

General Category	Things I Like	Things I Don't Like
styles of cooking		
fruits and vegetables		
sports		
music		
artists		
movie stars		
places to go on a date		
places to go for a vacation		
animals		
people		
feelings		

- Compare your list with a partner and identify
  things that you both like;
  things that neither of you likes;
  things that one of you likes, but not the other.
- Report your findings to the rest of the class.

Focus 1

Using Coordinating Conjunctions

- You can use the coordinating conjunctions *and, but, or,* and *nor* to join two or more parallel structures. These structures can be
  - **nouns:**
    (a) **Jeff** and **Matt** are roommates.
  - **verbs:**
    (b) They **live** and **work** in San Francisco.
  - **adjectives:**
    (c) They are **poor** but **hardworking** fellows.
    (d) They are neither **lazy** nor **rich.**
  - **adverbs:**
    (e) Every Saturday they clean their apartment **quickly** but **thoroughly.**
  - **prepositional phrases:**
    (f) They hurry **down the street** and **around the corner** to the store to do their shopping.
  - **infinitives:**
    (g) They're always in a hurry **to go bike riding,** or **to take** their dog to the park.
  - **gerunds:**
    (h) On Saturday nights, they like **dancing at discos** and **going to nightclubs** to meet friends.
  - **clauses:**
    (i) They enjoy living together **because they have many common interests** and **because it's cheaper than living alone.**

Exercise 1

Circle the coordinating conjunctions in this passage and underline the elements that each connects. The first paragraph has been done for you as an example. What elements are connected? Are there any conjunctions that don't connect similar constructions?

(1)Matt (and) Jeff first came to San Francisco in 1980, after they had graduated from college. (2)Both of them had grown up in small towns. (3)Jeff was from Wisconsin (and) Matt grew up in Kansas, but neither one enjoyed living in a small town. (4)There wasn't enough freedom (or) excitement for their tastes. (5)Each one decided to move to San Francisco because he had heard that it was a beautiful city (and) that it was filled with interesting people.

(6)When they first met, they were surprised and delighted to discover how many things they had in common, and how similar their interests were. (7)Jeff liked weightlifting and so did Matt. (8)Matt loved opera, and Jeff did too. (9)Jeff wasn't entirely comfortable with "big-city" life, nor was Matt, but neither one missed living in a small town at all. (10)They both liked dogs and wanted to have one for a pet, so they decided to look for an apartment and live together. (11)They both thought it would be cheaper and more fun to have a roommate.

(12)However, when they moved in together and took up house-keeping, they found that there were also a lot of differences between them. (13)Jeff was very tidy, but Matt wasn't. (14)Matt preferred to let the dishes pile up until there were "enough" to bother with, nor did he pick up his clothes or keep things neat. (15)Jeff, on the other hand, always wanted things to be washed immediately, even if there were only one or two dishes. (16)Matt liked staying out late every Friday night, but Jeff always wanted to get up early on Saturday mornings to clean the house, and to finish chores so they could spend the afternoon relaxing or playing with their new puppy in the park. (17)They soon realized that they would either have to start making compromises with each other or start looking for separate apartments, and neither Matt nor Jeff wanted to do that. (18)Fortunately, their similarities outweighed their differences, and they settled into a life of harmony and mutual interests.

Focus 2

Meaning of Coordinating Conjunctions

MEANING

- Conjunctions join two grammatical structures that have a logical relationship:
  - *And* has an additive meaning. Both structures share some characteristic.
    - **(a)** I like beans **and** carrots.
    - **(b)** Matt **and** Jeff enjoy swimming.
  - *But* has a contrastive meaning. It shows a difference between two similar elements. One of the elements has a characteristic but not both.
    - **(c)** I like beans **but** hate beets.
    - **(d)** Jeff enjoys swimming **but** not waterskiing.
    - **(e)** Matt is poor **but** very honest.
  - *(Neither)/Nor* has both an additive meaning and a negative meaning.

	Implied Meaning
(f) Neither Jeff **nor** Matt **wants** to live in a small town.	**Both** Jeff and Matt **don't want** to live in a small town.
(g) I like **neither** beets **nor** turnips.	I **don't** like **either** beets **or** turnips.
(h) Jeff doesn't want to leave San Francisco, **nor does** Matt.	Jeff doesn't want to leave San Francisco, **and** Matt **doesn't** either.

- *Or* has an additive meaning in negative sentences and a contrastive meaning in affirmative sentences.

	Implied Meaning
(i) I **don't like** beets **or** lima beans.	I dislike them **both**.
(j) I **need** to borrow a pencil **or** a pen.	I only need one, **not both**.

Exercise 2

Add the appropriate conjunction, **and, but, or, nor**, to these sentences.

1. Jeff likes opera _____ not rap music.

2. Matt is tall _____ good-looking.

3. Matt doesn't like getting up early _____ cleaning the house.

4. Jeff always wanted a German shepherd _____ a collie as a pet.

5. Jeff _____ Matt have been roommates since 1986.

6. Matt didn't enjoy small-town life, _____ did Jeff.

7. Matt likes to go dancing, _____ Jeff prefers quiet evenings at home.

8. Jeff usually takes the dog for a walk _____ goes bike-riding on Saturday

   afternoons.

9. Jeff does most of the cleaning, _____ Matt does most of the cooking.

10. Matt and Jeff love living in the city, _____ sometimes miss the small–town

    atmosphere of their hometowns.

Focus 3

MEANING

Expressing Additive and Contrastive Relationships

MEANING

- There are several ways to express these additive and contrastive relationships.

Meaning	Form	Examples	
		Matt and Jeff	**You and your partner**
ADDITIVE affirmative sentences	*and*	**(a)** Jeff likes carrots **and** peas	
both: X and Y do/are	*and* _____ , *too*	**(b)** Jeff likes spinach . . . **and** Matt **does, too.**	
	and so _____	**(c)** . . . **and so does** Matt.	
	both _____ *and*	**(d) Both** Jeff **and** Matt like spinach.	

Meaning	Form	Examples	
		Matt and Jeff	**You and your partner**
CONTRASTIVE not both: X does, but not Y. Y does, but not X. X doesn't but Y does. Y doesn't but Y does.	*but*	**(e)** Matt likes peas **but not** spinach.	
		(f) Jeff likes spinach, **but** Matt **doesn't**.	
		(g) Matt **doesn't like** spinach, **but** Jeff **does**.	
	(either) ——— *or*	**(h)** Jeff likes (**either**) spinach **or** carrots. I can't remember which.	
ADDITIVE negative sentences both: X and Y don't/aren't.	*not . . . or*	**(i)** Matt does**n't** like spinach **or** beets.	
	not . . . and ——— *not either*	**(j)** Matt doesn't like spinach, ... **and** Jeff **doesn't either.**	
	not . . . and neither ——— .	**(k)** . . . **and neither does** Jeff.	
	neither/nor	**(l) Neither** Matt **nor** Jeff like spinach.	
	not . . . nor	**(m)** Matt does**n't** like spinach, **nor** does Jeff.	

Exercise 3

Write sentences that describe the likes and dislikes that you discussed with your partner in the Task. Use the same patterns that are shown in the chart above in Focus 3 and write your sentences in the spaces provided in the chart.

Exercise 4

Match the sentences in Column A with the sentences in Column B that mean the same thing. Sentences may have more than one match.

EXAMPLE: Jeff doesn't care for rap music, nor does Matt.
The example sentence has the same meaning as Sentences A, C, and G.

Column A

1. Jeff and Matt like swimming, but not listening to rap music.
2. Jeff doesn't like rap music, and Matt doesn't either.
3. Jeff likes swimming and so does Matt.
4. Jeff likes washing dishes, but Matt doesn't.

Column B

a. Matt doesn't like rap music and neither does Jeff.
b. Matt likes swimming and Jeff does too.
c. Both Matt and Jeff dislike rap music.
d. Both Matt and Jeff like swimming.
e. Matt doesn't like washing dishes, but Jeff does.
f. Matt and Jeff don't like listening to rap music, but like swimming.
g. Neither Jeff nor Matt likes rap music.
h. Either Jeff or Matt likes washing dishes, but one of them doesn't.

Exercise 5

Change these sentences to similar sentences that mean the same thing, using the cue given.

EXAMPLE: Canada and the United States are in North America. (too)
Canada is in North America, and the United States is too.

1. Canada isn't in South America, and the United States isn't either. (neither)
2. Canada and the United States were once colonies of Great Britain. (and so)
3. Canada is part of the British Commonwealth; the United States isn't part of the British Commonwealth. (but)
4. Most Canadians and Americans speak English. (too)
5. The Winter Olympics will be held in Canada, or they will be held in the United States. (either)
6. Canada has a democratic government, and so does the United States. (both)
7. Neither Canada nor the United States have solved the problem of acid rain. (either)
8. Canada has a large French-speaking minority; the United States doesn't have a large French-speaking minority. (but)

Focus 4

USE

Emphasizing Additive and Contrastive Relationships

USE

- You can use these forms to emphasize additive relationships in affirmative sentences:
  - *and/also:*
    - **(a)** Jeff likes weight lifting, **and also** opera.
    - **(b)** Jeff likes weight lifting **and** opera **also**.
    - **(c)** Jeff washes the dishes **and also** cleans the living room.
  - *both/and:*
    - **(d)** Jeff likes **both** weight lifting **and** opera.
    - **(e)** **Both** Jeff **and** Matt like living in San Francisco.
    - **(f)** Jeff **and** Matt **both** like living in San Francisco.
  - *not only/but also* is even more emphatic:
    - **(g)** Jeff likes **not only** weight lifting **but also** opera.
    - **(h)** Jeff **not only** washes the dishes **but also** cleans the living room.
- Use these forms to emphasize additive relationships in negative sentences:
  - *not either/or:*
    - **(i)** I **don't** like **either** beets **or** okra.
  - *neither/nor:*
    - **(j)** **Neither** Jeff **nor** Matt **liked** living in a small town.
    - **(k)** I like **neither** beets **nor** okra.
  - *nor:*
    Nor without *neither* can only be used to join independent clauses.
    - **(l)** Jeff wasn't entirely comfortable with "big-city" life, **nor** was Matt.
    - **(m)** NOT: I like beets **nor** okra.
- Use this form to emphasize contrastive relationships in both affirmative and negative sentences:
  - *either:*
    - **(n)** Jeff **grew** up in **either** Kansas **or** Wisconsin. I can't remember which.
    - **(o)** On Saturday afternoon they **either** relax **or** take the dog to the park.

Exercise 6

Combine these sentences using *not only/but also, both/and, neither/nor* or *either/or.*

> **EXAMPLE:** Canada is in the Northern Hemisphere. The United
> States is in the Northern Hemisphere.
> *Both Canada and the United States are in the Northern*
> *Hemisphere.*

1. Winters in Northern Canada can be very cold. Winters in Northern Canada can be a lot longer than in the Southern United States.
2. Canada might host the Winter Olympics. America might host the Winter Olympics.
3. Canada harvests a lot of wheat. Canada produces a lot of lumber.
4. The United States has a larger population than Canada. The United States has a larger economic output than Canada.
5. Many Canadians speak English as their first language. Many Canadians speak French as their first language.
6. The United States doesn't use Spanish as an official language. Canada doesn't use Spanish as an official language.
7. Canada was originally settled as a British colony. The United States was originally settled as a British colony.
8. In another 50 years, the largest Spanish-speaking city in North America might be Mexico City. In another 50 years, the largest Spanish-speaking city in North America might be Los Angeles.

Exercise 7

Review the likes and dislikes you identified in the Task. Answer these questions with single sentences, using emphatic forms of conjunctions.

> **EXAMPLES:** Name two possible places that you would go on a date.
> *Both discos and movies theaters are good places to go on a date.*
> Name two kinds of food you don't like.
> *I like neither beets nor raw mushrooms.*

1. Name two sports that you play well.
2. Name two characteristics that people you like have.
3. Name two characteristics that people you don't like have.
4. Name two things you might do on your next vacation.
5. Name your favorite male and female movie star.
6. Name two good reasons to study English.

Focus 5

USE

Avoiding Redundancy

USE

- We usually use conjunctions to avoid redundancy (information that is repeated unnecessarily).

Redundant	Less Redundant
(a) Jeff likes weight lifting, and he likes opera.	**(b)** Jeff likes weight lifting and opera.
(c) Jeff likes weight lifting, and Matt likes weight lifting.	**(d)** Jeff likes weight lifting, and so does Matt. **(e)** . . . and Matt does too. **(f)** Jeff and Matt both like weight lifting. **(g)** Both Jeff and Matt like weight lifting.

- When using conjunctions, repeated information is usually omitted.

Redundant	Less Redundant
(a) Jeff enjoys cleaning, **but he doesn't like to clean** on Saturday mornings.	**(b)** Jeff enjoys cleaning **but not** on Saturday mornings.
(c) Jeff didn't like life in a small town, and Matt **didn't like it either.**	**(d)** Jeff didn't like life in a small town, **nor did** Matt. **(e) Neither** Jeff **nor** Matt liked living in a small town.

Exercise 8

Combine these pairs of sentences to make them less redundant. There is more than one way to combine most of the sentences.

> **EXAMPLE:** Jeff lives in San Francisco. Matt lives in San Francisco.
> *Jeff lives in San Francisco, and so does Matt.*
> *Both Jeff and Matt live in San Francisco.*

1. Jeff likes cleaning. Matt doesn't like cleaning.
2. Jeff might go home for a visit on his vacation. Jeff might travel to France on his vacation.
3. Matt doesn't plan to return to his hometown to live. Jeff doesn't plan to return to his hometown to live.

4. Jeff likes getting up early. Matt doesn't like getting up early.
5. Jeff always wanted to have a dog. Matt always wanted to have a dog.
6. Matt might take the dog to the park this afternoon. Jeff might take the dog to the park this afternoon.
7. Matt likes dancing at discos. Matt likes meeting friends at discos.
8. Matt comes from a small town in Kansas. Jeff comes from a small town in Wisconsin.

Focus 6

FORM

Parallel Construction

FORM

- In formal and written English, structures joined with conjunctions should have the same grammatical form.
  - **(a)** Jeff likes neither **playing** football nor **swimming.**
  - **(b)** NOT: Jeff likes neither **football** nor **swimming.**
  - **(c)** Matt **is** originally from Kansas but now **lives** in San Francisco.
  - **(d)** NOT: Matt **is** originally from Kansas but now **living** in San Francisco.
- In parallel structures you should omit repeated parallel elements such as prepositions, auxiliaries, articles, and so on, if the meaning is still clear.
  - **(e)** Matt and Jeff get phone calls **from** their parents **and from their friends** almost every week.
  - **(f)** Matt and Jeff get phone calls **from** their parents **and friends** almost every week.

Exercise 9

Omit the repeated elements in the joined structures in these sentences:

1. Jeff likes to get up early and to finish the cleaning on Saturdays.
2. By the time Matt finishes reading the Saturday paper, Jeff has washed the dishes and has vacuumed the living room.
3. Jeff cleans the kitchen and the living room every Saturday morning.
4. Jeff and Matt come from Kansas and from Wisconsin, respectively.
5. Matt vacuums the living room and dining room every Saturday morning.

Exercise 10

Add words to the blank spaces in this passage. Be sure to keep the added element parallel in structure to the other part.

My parents have been married for almost 50 years. (1) They are both kind and _____ .

(2) They are _____ but _____ . (3) My mother _____ ,

but my father _____ . (4) He is _____ , but she is _____ .

(5) My father not only _____ but also _____ . (6) My mother

neither _____ nor _____ . (7) They both _____ .

(8) They either _____ or _____ . (9) Neither my mother nor my

father _____ . (10) I not only _____ but also _____ .

Focus 7

MEANING

Joining Independent Clauses

MEANING

- You can join two or more independent clauses with the conjunctions *and, but, nor, or, for* and *so* to reflect the logical relationship between them.
  - *And* joins clauses with a similar idea or logical connection:
    (a) On Saturday mornings, Jeff usually washes the dishes, **and** Matt reads the paper.
  - *But* joins clauses that contrast in some way.
    (b) Jeff likes to go dancing, **but** Matt usually prefers to watch TV.
  - *Nor* joins two negative clauses.
    (c) Jeff doesn't intend to go back to Wisconsin, **nor does** Matt **want** to return to Kansas.
  - *Or* joins two alternative possibilities.
    (d) I might go to the beach, **or** I might stay home.
  - *Or* can also indicate a conditional relationship. (See Unit 15.)

Clauses Joined with *or*	Implied Conditional
(e) Turn down that music, **or** (else) we will have to ask you to leave.	If you don't turn down that music, we will have to ask you to leave.
(f) We had better clean the kitchen, **or** (else) Matt won't be happy.	If we don't clean the kitchen, Matt won't be happy.

- *For* joins an action and the reason for the action.
  - **(g)** Matt and Jeff decided to live together, **for** they enjoyed each other's company and wanted to save money.
- *So* joins a reason and a result:
  - **(h)** Matt and Jeff wanted to save money, **so** they decided to live together.
- When clauses are joined with negative conjunctions (*nor* or *not only/but also*), the clause with the negative conjunction at the beginning must take question word order:
  - **(i)** Jeff doesn't plan to leave San Francisco, **nor does Matt want** him to.
  - **(j)** **Not only do** the two **have** similar interests, **but they also have** similar personalities.
- See Unit 13 for more practice with joining independent clauses.

Exercise 11

For the two passages below, join the numbered pairs of sentences with *and, but, or, nor, for,* and *so.* Make any necessary changes to remove redundancy or to correct word order.

1. (1)My mother doesn't smoke. My father doesn't smoke. (2)My father gave up smoking years ago. My mother only quit last year. (3)My mother had wanted to quit for a long time. She knew it was bad for her health. (4)She wasn't able to smoke only one or two cigarettes. She had to give it up entirely. (5)My mother sometimes still wants a cigarette. My mother won't smoke a cigarette no matter how much she wants to. (6)My father is proud of her for quitting. My father gives my mother a lot of praise for quitting.

2. (1)Canada has a large French-speaking minority. The United States has a large Spanish-speaking minority. (2)Many people in Canada speak French. All government publications are printed in both languages. (3)Canada has two official languages. The United States discourages the use of languages other than English for official purposes. (4)In Canada, the French-speaking minority is concentrated primarily in the Province of Quebec. In the United States, Spanish-speaking concentrations are found in New York, Florida, New Mexico, and California.

Activities

Activity 1

Let's play a game called *Silly Sally*. In the Task, you identified things you like and dislike. Silly Sally also likes and dislikes various things. There is one single reason for all the things she likes or doesn't like.

- If you think you know the secret of the game, don't tell anyone else. Just give an example of something that Silly Sally likes and something that she doesn't like. Your teacher will tell you if you're correct. **Don't give away the secret!** Just help other students guess by giving them more examples of things she likes and doesn't like.

SILLY SALLY'S LIKES AND DISLIKES:

styles of cooking: Silly Sally loves cooking but hates to eat. She likes Greek but not Chinese cuisine. She won't touch anything from Brazil or Japan or Germany or Sweden, but she likes Moroccan cooking a great deal.

fruits and vegetables: She's wild about beets, carrots, and apples, but she can't stand potatoes, oranges, or especially cauliflower.

sports: She not only loves tennis and baseball but also skiing. However, she hates horseback riding and hockey. She doesn't mind jogging, but she hates to walk. She hates splashing in the water, but she doesn't mind swimming, as long as it's in a pool and not in the ocean.

music: She can't stand rap music, but she swoons for Beethoven.

artists: She likes Picasso and Klee, but she doesn't like Rembrandt or Michelangelo.

movie stars: She likes films with Pee-Wee Herman and Meryl Streep but not Marlon Brando or Elizabeth Taylor. She hates Sidney Poitier but loves Whoopie Goldberg, Morgan Freeman, and Harry Belafonte.

places to go on a date: She likes going to nice restaurants for dinner but not for lunch. She'll go to an art gallery but not a museum. She likes walking in the moonlight but not at night. She loves to kiss, but she hates to hug. She wants to get married, but she doesn't want to get engaged.

places to go for a vacation: She loves Greece but hates Italy. She likes inns, but she hates hotels. She wants to go to Hawaii but not to Tahiti. She'll go to the Philippines but not to Indonesia. She'll travel in the summer but not in the winter.

animals: She doesn't mind sheep, but she's allergic to goats. She hates cats and dogs but is fond not only of puppies, but also kittens.

people: She likes queens and princesses but neither kings nor princes. She loves Matt and Jeff, but she likes neither Peter and Denise nor John and Mary. She hates Charley but loves his fiancee.

feelings: She likes feelings but hates emotions. She likes sleeping and hates to wake up. She'll do a little napping in the afternoon but never at night.

Activity 2

Have you ever had a roommate? A roommate is someone you live with who is not a member of your family. How did you get along with him or her? Was there a good relationship between you? Why or why not?

- In a brief essay or oral presentation, describe the similarities and differences between you and your roommate, and whether you did or did not get along because of, or in spite of, those similarities and differences.

Activity 3

Do you think you are typical of people with your cultural background? Consider these two issues:

What things make you **different** from other people from your cultural background? Write a paragraph about typical characteristics of people from your culture and explain how you are different. Here is an example to get you started:

> I am not a typical American. Most Americans are very direct in giving criticism. However, I tend to be more indirect or diplomatic when I'm upset about something. Most Americans love football, but I don't. I think football is rather boring, and I prefer soccer. Most Americans don't know very much about other countries. I, on the other hand, have traveled a lot and lived overseas. . . .

In what ways are you **similar** to other people from your cultural background? Write a second paragraph about the typical characteristics of people with backgrounds similar to yours, and explain how you are similar, or how you share those characteristics.

- Show these two paragraphs to another student in the class. He or she should read your paragraphs and decide whether you are more typical of or more different from other people from your culture.
- Report your partner's decision, and whether you were surprised by it, to the rest of the class.

Activity 4

There are two sayings in English with contradictory messages:

- "Birds of a feather flock together" means that people like to be with others who are similar to them.
- "Opposites attract" refers to the two poles of a magnet, and implies that it is differences that attract people to each other.
- What is the secret to a happy relationship with someone—being similar or being different? From your own experience, describe two friends or a married couple that prove one or the other of these sayings. Describe their similarities and differences, and the effect those had on their relationship. You can make this description in written or oral form, depending on the instructions from your teacher.

Activity 5

Would you ever consider falling in love with someone from another culture? Would you ever consider marrying someone from a different culture? In a small group, discuss the advantages and disadvantages of a bicultural relationship. Report your discussion to the rest of the class, using some of these coordinating structures:

> Some of us felt . . . , but others felt . . . .
> Not only do bicultural relationships . . . , but they also . . . .
> Bicultural relationships can be . . . , and . . . .
> Such relationships are neither . . . nor . . . .
> They can also be . . . , but . . . .

- If you prefer, you can make a written report of your discussion. All members of the group should help write the report.

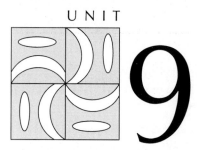

Intensifiers

Task

The word *workaholic* has an interesting history. The term describes people who like their jobs so much that they are "addicted" to them. Workaholics usually have no other important interests outside of their jobs. They often neglect other responsibilities (to their families, to their own physical health, etc.) in order to concentrate on their jobs and do them well.

The original word, *alcoholic*, is used to describe a person who is addicted to alcohol. In recent years, the suffix *-aholic* has been applied to other things. Although you will not find these words in a dictionary, you may hear them in conversations or on television, or read them in popular magazines. In addition to workaholics, people can sometimes be **sportaholics** (addicted to sports), **shopaholics** (addicted to shopping), **TVaholics** (addicted to watching television), or even **chocaholics** (addicted to chocolate).

Another word, *enthusiast*, also describes someone who likes something a great deal. However, there is an important difference in meaning between an enthusiast and an *-aholic*. An enthusiast balances that interest with other things in life. The interest is **very** important but not **too** important.

- Think about two people you know, one who is an **enthusiast about something** and one who is a **somethingaholic**. You could consider someone who loves his or her job, compared to someone who is a workaholic, or someone who likes chocolate, compared to someone who eats large amounts of it every day.

- Write a brief paragraph about each person, describing his or her character, what he or she does, and how (how fast, how hard, how often, how intensely) he or she does it.

- Work with a partner. Read each other's descriptions and decide on five characteristics that people have if they are **enthusiasts**, and five characteristics they have if they are **somethingaholics**. Present your ideas to the class.

Focus 1

Modifying Adjectives and Adverbs

- Intensifiers describe the **amount** or **degree** (how much) of a quality that is described by an adjective or adverb.

    (a) Denise is **extremely devoted** to her job. She's **quite a hard worker,** and even spends her weekends at the office.

    (b) Peter is **slightly bored** with his job. He works **steadily enough,** but **rather slowly,** and thinks that perhaps someday he may start looking for another line of work.

- Their position in the sentence varies:
    - All intensifiers come before the adjective or adverb, except *enough*, which comes after.

        (c) Denise works **extremely hard**.

        (d) Peter works **steadily enough**.

    - In noun phrases, intensifiers come between the determiner (*a, the, some*, etc.) and the adjective, except for *quite*, which comes before the determiner.

        (e) Denise is **a very dedicated worker**.

        (f) She is **quite a dedicated** worker.

121

Exercise 1

Circle the intensifiers in the following passage. Underline the words they modify. The first sentence has been done for you.

(1)Denise Driven is a (very) <u>dedicated</u> employee, but she's a (little) (too) serious. (2)Although she's extremely hardworking and quite efficient, she's also rather competitive and not very friendly. (3)She comes to work an hour earlier than everyone else, and is always the last one to leave. (4)At the end of the day, she's really too tired for other activities. (5)She has no hobbies and few friends. (6)She's actually a bit dull, since she's not really interested in anything but her job.

(7)Peter Principle is a rather easygoing fellow. (8)Although he works fairly hard and is reasonably serious about his work, his job is not the most important thing in his life, and he likes to have time to pursue other interests. (9)He lives a fairly normal life. (10)He likes spending time with his children, and he is quite active in his church. (11)He is also a rather accomplished musician. (12)He plays the clarinet in a jazz band with some of the other people from the office.

(13)Peter and Denise really don't get along. (14)She thinks he's a little lazy and "insufficiently motivated." (15)He thinks she's a rather humorless workaholic who is "not very nice." (16)It's somewhat difficult to decide who's right.

Focus 2

Formal and Informal Intensifiers

MEANING
USE

- Listed here are common intensifiers. You can use certain intensifiers in both formal and informal English, but others occur only in informal spoken English.

Meaning	More Formal Intensifiers	Less Formal (Conversational) Intensifiers
an excessive degree	**(a)** That's **too** expensive.	**(b)** She's **way too** serious.
a great degree	**(c)** Denise is **quite** busy. **(d)** She's **extremely** dedicated. **(e)** She works **very** hard.	**(f)** Denise is **really** busy. **(g)** She works **so** hard! **(h)** She's **awful(ly)** serious.
a moderate degree	**(i)** He's a **rather** accomplished musician. **(j)** It's **somewhat** difficult to decide who is right. **(k)** He's **fairly** hard-working. **(l)** He does his job **reasonably** well. **(m)** He works hard **enough.**	**(n)** Peter's **pretty** dedicated. **(o)** Denise is **kind of** depressed. **(p)** He's **sort of** easygoing.
a small degree	**(q)** He gets **slightly** annoyed. **(r)** She's **a bit** single-minded. **(s)** Work can sometimes be **a little** monotonous.	**(t)** He's **a tad** lazy and **a touch** stupid.
an insufficient degree	**(u)** He was **insufficiently** motivated. **(v)** He doesn't work hard **enough.**	**(w)** Peter doesn't get paid **near(ly) enough.**

Exercise 2

Create sentences using the intensifiers in Focus 2 that describe the skills and activities listed below. Example answers are provided, but you should think of other answers that are true for you:

1. a skill you are proud of: something you do well to a moderate degree:
   I'm a pretty good tennis player.

2. a favorite food: a kind of food you like to a great degree:
   I'm extremely fond of popcorn.

3. something that is not enjoyable for you but you don't hate: an activity you dislike to a small degree:
   Doing homework can be slightly boring.

4. an ability you want to develop: a skill you have in an insufficient degree:
   I don't speak English fluently enough.

5. a bad habit: something you do to an excessive degree:
   I eat too much ice cream.

6. a special talent: something you do well to a great degree:
   I'm a really good musician.

Exercise 3

Are the following sentences formal or informal? If they are written in informal/conversational style, change the intensifier to make the sentence more formal. If they are written in formal style, provide an intensifier that is more appropriate in less formal casual conversation. There are several possible answers, so prepare to explain why you chose the answer you did.

EXAMPLE: That sun is so hot! (informal)
That sun is very hot. (more formal)
I'm rather tired, so I won't be able to attend your party. (formal)
I'm pretty tired . . . . (more informal)

1. I'm kind of sick today.
2. I'm somewhat confused by all your questions.
3. She's really unfriendly.
4. He's quite annoyed about the broken window.
5. I'm sort of busy right now.
6. It's rather hot here, don't you think?
7. Peter works pretty hard.
8. Denise is pretty serious.
9. That man is awfully hard to understand.

124

Focus 3

Too versus Very

MEANING

- *Too* and *very* have an important difference in meaning. *Too* in affirmative sentences indicates something that is **excessive** (so much of something that it is not good).

A Great Degree	An Excessive Degree
(a) This car is **very** expensive, but maybe I'll buy it anyway.	**(b)** This car is **too** expensive. I can't afford it.
(c) Denise is **very** serious about her work. She's a good worker.	**(d)** Denise is **too** serious about her work. She's a workaholic.

- Only a few intensifiers can work with *too*:
  - **(e)** It's **way too** difficult!
  - **(f)** It's **really** too hot.
  - **(g)** It's **a little** too expensive.
  - **(h)** It's **a bit** too late.

Exercise 4

Decide whether *too* or *very* is the appropriate intensifier in these sentences.

1. We got there _____ late. The plane had already taken off.

2. I'm really _____ busy, but I think I can finish the report for you.

3. Denise works _____ hard for her own good. She's going to get sick if she's

   not careful.

4. Denise works _____ hard, because she's ambitious and wants to get ahead.

5. Don't bother to invite Jack to the party. He's _____ serious to have any fun!

6. The accident happened _____ quickly, but I'm _____ sure that the driver

   of the sports car didn't use his turn signal.

7. Children are growing up _____ quickly these days. They try to act like adults while they're still kids!

8. We arrived at the party _____ late, but there was still a little food left.

9. I really like Mary. I think she's _____ intelligent and has a great personality!

10. It's _____ hot. Let's forget about the tennis game.

Exercise 5

For the following sentences, decide on an appropriate rejoinder using an intensifier with *too:*

EXAMPLES: You just missed the plane.
   *We arrived **a bit too** late.*
   I can't reach the top shelf.
   *It's **a little too** high.*

1. I don't have quite that much money.
2. I wish she would smile more.
3. There's no way I can help you finish that report.
4. Only a couple of students passed the test.
5. This coffee needs more sugar.

Exercise 6

Pick five things from the list below that you don't like or think of other things that aren't on the list. State the reason why you feel that way, using *too* and an intensifier.

EXAMPLE: *I don't like workaholics. They're really too serious.*

babies	workaholics	studying grammar
dogs	diamond necklaces	being away from my family
cats	weather in the summer	rap music
spinach	sports cars	police officers
liberals	conservatives	

Focus 4

Using Intensifiers with *Not*

USE

- You can use only a few intensifiers in negative sentences. You can use them to "soften" a statement or make it more indirect or polite. Intensifiers with **not** imply that the opposite is true to a small or moderate degree.

Intensifiers that can be used with *not*	Implied Meaning
(a) Tom's new dog is **not too bright.**	It's **rather stupid.**
(b) Sometimes Peter does**n't** work **very hard.**	Sometimes he's **a bit lazy.**
(c) Please **don't** drive **so fast.**	Please drive **a little more slowly.**
(d) She's **not really interested** in sports.	She's **somewhat bored** by sports.
(e) I'm **not quite** ready.	I'm **almost** ready.

Exercise 7

Make these sentences less blunt or direct by changing the intensifiers to ones that use *not*. There may be more than one way to "soften" your comment.

EXAMPLES: This movie's pretty boring.
It's not too interesting.
He dances rather badly.
He doesn't dance too well.

1. She's quite unfriendly.
2. I almost understood what you said. Could you repeat it?
3. Mary's somewhat unhappy with you.
4. I hate Brussels sprouts.
5. Wait a minute! Be more polite!
6. Mark is a terrible cook.
7. Beth dislikes listening to other people's problems.
8. It's too crowded for me. Would you move over?

Focus 5

Using Intensifiers To Modify Verbs

MEANING
USE

- *Really* and *quite* are the only two intensifiers that are commonly used to modify verbs:
  - *really:* This word is common in spoken English. In negative sentences, the position of *really* can change the meaning of the sentence.

really + verb	Implied Meaning
(a) Denise **really loves** her work.	She loves it very much.
(b) Denise **really hates** inefficiency.	She hates it a great deal.
(c) Peter and Denise **really don't like** each other.	They hate each other.
(d) Peter and Denise **don't really like** each other.	They are not very friendly.

- *quite:*

  In American English, *quite* appears mostly in very formal written English. It is much more common in spoken British English. *Not quite* is more common in both formal and informal American English and means *almost:*

quite + verb	Implied Meaning
(e) I **quite understand** your position.	I understand it **completely.**
(f) I **quite agree** with you.	I agree with you **completely.**
(g) He **didn't quite get** there in time.	He **almost** got there in time.
(h) I **don't quite understand** what you're saying.	I **almost** understand you.

128

Exercise 8

Are these sentences correct or incorrect? If they are incorrect, identify the problem and correct the sentence.

1. The answer isn't a little complicated.
2. Learning a language so requires a lot of practice.
3. Henry's a quite intelligent fellow.
4. Rebecca isn't enough tall to reach the top shelf.
5. I'd like you to meet a friend of mine. He's too intelligent.
6. It's quite too hot to even think about going for a run.
7. Peter's not kind of busy.
8. Tom felt the lesson was insufficiently challenging.

Activities

Activity 1

Do you work in order to live, or live in order to work? Write a brief essay that describes how you feel about the importance of work in your life. Here are some questions you may wish to answer in your essay:

- Is work more or less important than other things in your life?
- What kind of a worker do you think you are?
- Could you ever become a workaholic? Why or why not?
- Who would you rather work with, Denise Driven or Peter Principle? Why?

Activity 2

What things are important for happiness? Working with a partner, make a list of ten things that are necessary for a happy life. Then rate those things in terms of how important they are to each of you individually. Which things do you think are really important? Which things are somewhat important? Only a little important?

- Compare your ratings with those of two other pairs of students. Working together, decide on the three things that you all agree are the most important and the three things that are the least important.
- Also decide on an answer to this question: If you could have only one of the things from your list, which would it be?
- Present your list and mention any interesting similarities and differences in opinion to the rest of the class.

Activity 3

Are you a perfectionist? Why or why not? Write a brief essay that describes how you approach your life and work.

Activity 4

Were you ever in a situation in which you were really frightened? Describe the events and your behavior.

Activity 5

What kinds of **"aholic"** people can you think of? You have read about workaholics, TVaholics, and chocaholics. Work with a partner and invent at least three other terms for people who carry their enthusiasm about something too far. Present your terms and definitions to the rest of the class.

Activity 6

There's a popular saying in America that it's not possible to be too rich, too good-looking, or too thin.

- Do you agree? Are there some qualities or characteristics that no one can have too much of? If so, what are they? Why do you feel that nobody can have too much of those qualities?
- Do you disagree? Is there a negative aspect to being extremely pretty, wealthy, or in excellent physical condition?
- Decide on your position and write an essay on whether or not it's possible to have too much of a good thing.

Adjective Modifiers

10

Task

If you want to buy something without spending much money, you should think about buying it **secondhand**. A secondhand store (also known as a thrift shop, or a junk shop) is a place where you can buy used possessions—things that people have sold or given away because they no longer need or want them. You can also find used possessions at **flea markets** (places such as parking lots where people gather every week to buy and sell secondhand goods), **swap meets** (where people exchange things instead of using money), or **garage sales** or **yard sales** (where people put out used items for sale in their driveways or on the sidewalk).

- Think of five things you own that you don't really need any longer. They could be old clothes, furniture, gifts you have received that you have never liked—anything you wouldn't mind getting rid of.
- Write a brief description for each item, following these examples:

  FOR SALE: ONE SLIGHTLY USED, ANTIQUE, BLUE MOROCCAN DISH
  FOR SALE: TWO UGLY LITTLE WOODEN STATUES FROM CHINA
  FOR SALE: A LARGE SQUARE TABLE AND TWO MATCHING CHAIRS
  FOR SALE: A REALLY BEAUTIFUL OLD ITALIAN GLASS BOWL
  FOR SALE: A COLLECTION OF RARE, USED ENGLISH TEXTBOOKS

- Show your list of items to other people in the class and find out what other people have for sale.
- Find three things they want to sell that you might be interested in buying, and tell the rest of the class what they are and why you want to buy them.

Focus 1

Order of Modifiers

- The term **modifier** refers to the different kinds of words we add to a noun to make a noun phrase. Modifiers can be
  - quantifiers:
    many books
  - determiners (articles, demonstratives, and possessives):
    many of **these** books
  - participles:
    many of these **interesting used** books
  - adjectives (with or without intensifiers):
    many of these interesting **really beautiful** books
  - other nouns:
    many of these interesting really beautiful **grammar** books
- Although it is rare to have more than three or four modifiers for a single noun phrase, there is a usual order for different categories of modifiers. Modifiers occur in the following order:

1 Quantifiers	2 Determiners	3 Intensifiers	4 Descriptive Adjectives (See Focus 2)	5 Reference Adjectives	6 Noun Modifiers	7 Head Noun
some many a few of, etc.	a/ an/ the these/ those my/ his John's, etc.	really slightly too absolute certain previous etc.	**evaluation** good, bad **appearance** big, round, chipped **age** old, new **color** red, green **origin** French, brass, etc.	medical retired well-known economic etc.	spring university three-day etc.	book building vacation theory etc.

Exercise 1

For each of the noun phrases indicated in boldface, list the modifiers according to their category. You will not use every kind of modifier in every noun phrase. Identify the head nouns.

EXAMPLE: one of those really expensive gold pocket watches

category	modifier
quantifiers	one of
determiners	those
intensifiers	really
descriptive adjectives	expensive, gold
other modifiers	– – – – – – – – –

HEAD NOUN	pocket watches

1. I bought **an ugly little statue** at the thrift store today.
2. Christine has collected **lots of rather cute miniature circus animals.**
3. **One of your more experienced English teachers** will know the answer.
4. I spoke to **a certain retired police officer.**
5. We need **some of that imported French goat cheese** for the picnic.
6. **Many very famous university professors** are not terribly talented when it comes to teaching.
7. George is **one of the most graceful amateur ballroom dancers** that I have ever seen.
8. He's planning on taking **a wonderfully relaxing three-week vacation.**

FORM

Order of Descriptive Adjectives

FORM

- Different categories of descriptive adjectives tend to occur in the following order:

Evaluation/ Opinion	Appearance	Age	Color	Origin
good *bad* *ugly* *interesting* *nice* *intelligent* etc.	**size/measure** *big* *small* *low* *high* *heavy* **shape** *round* *square* *triangular* **condition** *chipped* *broken* *rotten* etc.	*old* *young* *new* *antique* etc.	*red* *green* *blue* *mottled* *bright green* *dark blue* *deep purple* etc.	**geographical** *French* *Italian* *Japanese* **material** *wooden* *vegetable* *cotton* *brass* etc.

- Within a particular category, there is some possible variation. Adjectives of **appearance** tend to follow this order: **size, shape, condition.** Adjectives of **origin** tend to follow this order: **geographical, material.** But other orders are also possible:

  a big, round, shiny apple
  a big, shiny, round apple
  a shiny, big round apple
  a silk Japanese fan
  a Japanese silk fan

Exercise 2

(a) Identify the categories of descriptive adjectives in these noun phrases by listing them in the appropriate box in this grid. Not every category occurs in each noun phrase. The first two have been done for you as an example.

(b) Are there some noun phrases that do not follow the basic order listed in Focus 2? Why do you suppose the author changed the basic word order?

1. handsome, small, well-polished Italian leather shoes
2. a shiny big new red sports car
3. a fat little brown puppy
4. some beautiful old Thai silk pajamas
5. an antique round wooden tea tray
6. a black lacquer Japanese screen
7. an interesting young French physics professor
8. a funky, broken-down old Chevrolet

Category	Adjective 1	2	3	4
evaluation/ opinion	handsome			
appearance: size shape condition	- - - - - - - - small - - - - - - - - well-polished	- - - - - - - - big - - - - - - - - shiny		
age	- - - - - - - -	new		
color	- - - - - - - -	red		
origin: geographical material	Italian leather	- - - - - - - - - - - - - - - -		
NOUN	shoes	sports car		

Category	Adjective 5	6	7	8
evaluation/ opinion				
appearance: size shape condition				
age				
color				
origin: geographical material				
NOUN				

Exercise 3

Add the modifiers in the correct order to the following passages. The first one has been done for you as an example.

My friend Wolfgang is a shopaholic. Whenever he goes out of the house, he returns with

some (1) <u>strange, new</u> (new, strange) "bargain." He rarely buys any

(2) _____ (useful, really) items. Once he came home with

(3) _____ (bright, flannel, purple) blankets. "They match

my (4) _____ (pretty, French, new) curtains," he said.

But those curtains were still in their (5) _____ (plastic, original)

wrappings. He was so busy shopping that he hadn't had time to hang them up.

Fortunately, Wolfgang refuses to buy anything secondhand. I can imagine all the

(6) _____ (useless, incredibly ugly, antique) "art ob-

jects" he would bring home. He already has (7) _____

(brand-new, European, expensive, plenty of, bright-colored) shirts and sweaters. But that

doesn't stop him from buying more. He just piles them into his

(8) _____ (little, dark, bedroom, overcrowded) closet.

He has some (9) _____ (Italian, nice, handmade) shoes

that I have never even seen him wearing.

He's running out of space to put things. He has such a (10) _____

(new, nice) apartment with lots of storage space, but his closets look like some

(11) _____ (old, poor) shopkeeper's (12) _____

(frightening, terrible) nightmare!

136

Exercise 4

Are these sentences correct or incorrect? If they are incorrect, identify the problem and correct it.

1. I bought a green, old, pretty vase at the flea market.
2. He's a university, brand-new dormitory resident.
3. It's an antique, genuine, black, old-fashioned umbrella.
4. Would you like some of these delicious, little, chocolate bon-bons? ✓
5. Would you like to hear about my summertime, exciting, vacation plans?

Focus 3

MEANING

Compound Nouns

MEANING

- Compound nouns resemble modifier-noun combinations, but they function as single words. The same elements that make up modifier-noun combinations can be used to make compound nouns. Look at these differences:

Modifier + Noun	Compound Noun
adjective-noun: a hot day (a day that is hot), a rainy month (a month that is rainy)	a hot dog (a sausage), cold cream (a cosmetic), top hat (a kind of hat)
participle-noun: running water (water that is running)	a bathing suit (a suit for bathing), waiting room, swimming pool, drinking establishment
noun-noun: class clown (clown of the class), company president (president of the company), New York streets (streets of New York)	bus stop (a place where buses stop), house painter (a person who paints houses), dog catcher, beauty parlor, emergency room

- Compound nouns can also have adjective and noun modifiers:
    the Senate barber shop
    a hospital emergency room
    a sexy bathing suit

Exercise 5

Decide whether the highlighted structures are compound nouns or modified nouns.

1. Mary likes to put **cold cream** on her face before going to bed. C
2. I think **that green house** on the corner might be for sale. M N
3. Blanche is going to start taking **singing lessons** next week. C ?
4. They took the injured child to **the emergency room.** C
5. His office is on the **top floor** of that building. M N
6. He left **his calling card** on the table in the hall. C
7. Please call me at home only if there is **an emergency situation** that you can't deal with. M N
8. These strawberries will taste better with **cold cream** on them. M N
9. They call Jerry **the singing firefighter** of Miami Beach. M N
10. These tomatoes were raised in **a greenhouse.** How nice to have fresh vegetables in the middle of winter! C

Focus 4

FORM

Pronunciation of Compound Nouns versus Modified Nouns

FORM

- The pronunciation of noun phrases depends on the kind of modifiers in the noun phrase. When pronouncing noun phrases with compound nouns or most noun-modifiers, the stress falls on the noun modifier or the first element of the compound noun:

   (a) a well-known university **physics** professor

   (b) part of Miss Chantelle's new summer **swimwear** collection

   (c) a famous New York **drinking** establishment

- When pronouncing noun phrases modified by adjectives, the primary stress usually falls on the noun, instead of the modifiers:

   (d) a little old **lady**

   (e) a plump little German shepherd **puppy**

   (f) a few of those bright, new, red cotton **blouses**

   (g) a three-day **vacation**

- The primary stress falls on adjective and participle modifiers only when there is a contrast in meaning:

Contrastive Stress	Implied Meaning
(h) I want the **old** green chair.	Not the new one.
(i) He's a **high school** math teacher.	Not a university teacher.

Exercise 6

Underline the word that should receive the primary stress in the highlighted noun phrases in these sentences and read them aloud with appropriate stress.

EXAMPLE: Mary uses **<u>cold</u> cream** to keep her skin soft.

1. Johnny has started **a new paper route.**
2. Rachel is really proud of **her newly painted, professionally decorated living room.**
3. Jack's **the neighborhood expert** on how to get rid of squirrels.
4. He's probably over at **the university dormitory** visiting his brother.
5. The man had **no living relatives**, so his estate will probably go to the government.
6. We need **some paper decorations** for the birthday party.
7. I've got an appointment with **your antique dealer.**
8. The library was filled with **university students** studying for exams.
9. I refuse to work for that company. They don't even pay **a living wage.**
10. That's **a genuine antique French teacup.**

Exercise 7

Based on the indicated stress, decide on the implied meaning of the following sentences.

EXAMPLES: Please give me a glass of cold **water.**
I'd like some water.
Please give me a glass of **cold** water.
This water isn't cold enough.

1. I'm looking for a **French** grammar book.
2. I'm looking for a French **grammar** book.
3. He's the **short** dog catcher.
4. She's a telephone **operator.**
5. She's a **telephone** repairperson.
6. Charley only falls in love with **fat** ballerinas.
7. Charley only falls in love with fat **ballerinas.**
8. I think Dr. Jocelyn is a **retired** physics professor.
9. I think Dr. Jocelyn is a retired **physics** professor.

Activities

Activity 1

Go to a flea market, thrift shop, or garage sale. Write brief descriptions of things you find there that fit these categories.

something really cheap

something costing more than $25

something very surprising that people threw away or sold
   It could be valuable or rare, (like an antique) or very personal
   (like a book of photographs or a bundle of old letters)

something you might like to own

something funny

something ugly

Activity 2

What is the difference between an antique and junk? What are the qualities that make a used item valuable? Make two lists. For each junk item, write a description of a similar item you would consider an antique. Think of five examples of each. Here's an example:

junk   **antique**

a dirty old cup   a fine, unbroken, hand-painted porcelain teacup

- Compare your list to a partner's, and together develop a list of qualities that make junk worthless and antiques valuable.

Activity 3

Play **Adjective Tennis** with a partner. Here's how it's done: One person thinks of a modifier (quantifier, determiner, intensifier, descriptive adjective, or noun modifier) that can be added to the basic noun. The adjective has to make sense. (For example, if the noun is *radio,* the adjective *intelligent* is not an acceptable adjective.) The other person must place the modifier in its correct position. The person who can't think of a modifier or who puts the modifier in the wrong place loses. Here's an example:

Student 1: a ball . . . tennis

Student 2: a **tennis** ball . . . old

Student 1: an **old** tennis ball . . . rubber

Student 2: an old **rubber** tennis ball . . . dirty

Student 1. a **dirty** old rubber tennis ball . . . incredibly

Student 2: an **incredibly** dirty old rubber tennis ball . . . huge

Student 1: an incredibly dirty, **huge** old rubber tennis ball . . .

etc.

Keep going until one person puts an adjective in the wrong place or can't think of something new to add. You may want a third student to act as your referee.

Activity 4

Practice correct stress with a partner. Indicate which picture you are looking at by using stress. Your partner should indicate that he or she has understood by asking about the opposite picture. Here's an example:

Student 1: I'm looking at a **dirty** little dog.
Student 2: Not the **clean** one? I'm looking at a clean big **cat**.
Student 1: Not the **dog**? I'm looking at a dirty **little** cat.
Student 2: Not the **big** one?

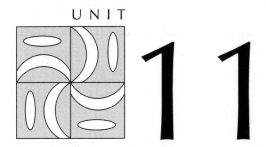

UNIT
11
Participle Modifiers

Task

Are certain kinds of behavior universal or do they vary from person to person or from culture to culture? How do you react in certain situations? What kinds of situations cause you to react in that way?

- First, name three physical or psychological reactions you have when you feel each of the emotions listed below, and three situations that cause you to feel that emotion. The first one has been done as an example.

HOW I REACT WHEN I FEEL BORED:	SITUATIONS THAT I OFTEN FIND BORING:
1. yawn, get sleepy, fidget	**1.** long meetings
2. think about other things	**2.** gossip about people I don't know
3. draw pictures in my notebook	**3.** talking about things that don't interest me

embarrassed	**embarrassing**
depressed	**depressing**
confused	**confusing**
excited	**exciting**
annoyed	**annoying**
worried	**worrying**
amused	**amusing**

- Compare your responses and the situations that cause those responses with those of other students in the class. Discuss these questions:

  Are there universal reactions to certain emotions?
  Which category showed more individual variation, the reactions or the situations?
  Do some cultures express emotions more readily than others?

- Present your ideas to the rest of the class.

142

Focus 1

FORM

Modifying Noun Phrases

FORM

- You can modify nouns with several structures that give us important additional information:

  - **adjectives:**
    The **large** man
  - **nouns:**
    The **delivery** man
  - **prepositional phrases:**
    The man **at the table**

  - **relative clauses:**
    The man **that you told me about**
  - **present and past participles:**
    The **interesting** man
    The **confused** man

- You can form present participles by adding **-ing** to the verb. You can form past participles by adding **-ed** to regular verbs or by using the third form (**-en** form) of irregular verbs.

Verb	Present Participle	Past Participle
study	studying	studied
forget	forgetting	forgotten

- For a review of irregular past participle forms, see Unit 30.

Exercise 1

Identify all the underlined modifiers (Are they adjectives, present or past participles, etc?) in the following passage and tell what noun they modify. The first sentence has been done as an example.

EXAMPLES: 1) unconscious—adjective, modifies "expressions"
2) body—noun modifier, modifies "language"
3) revealing—present participle, modifies "information"

(1)<u>Unconscious</u> facial expressions and (2)"<u>body</u>" language" often convey (3)<u>revealing</u> information to other people. Many people's (4)"<u>hidden</u>" emotions are actually quite obvious to anyone who knows how to read faces. Some reactions are so universal that there seems to be a (5)<u>physical</u> basis for them. All people react the same way to certain (6)<u>exciting</u> situations— whether that excitement is positive (exhilaration) or negative (fright or panic)—by breathing more rapidly. They also experience (7)<u>increased</u> (8)<u>heart</u> rates. (9)<u>Seriously depressed</u> individuals actually have more (10)<u>easily compromised</u> immune systems than people who are not suffering from depression. (11)<u>Facial</u> expressions of basic emotions, such as anger, surprise, and amusement, appear to be universal.

143

Other reactions are more varied. Many, but not all, individuals respond to an (12)<u>embarrassing</u> situation by "blushing," a phenomenon in which the face and neck turn bright red. Some people respond to boredom by growing sleepy or inattentive. Others show boredom by such signs as (13)<u>jiggling</u> feet or (14)<u>wiggling</u> fingers. For other people, these reactions may be (15)<u>unintended</u> indications of nervousness or anxiety. When someone experiences a (16)<u>confusing</u> situation, he or she may unconsciously try to hide that confusion by smiling, thus doing what is known as "the (17)<u>stupid</u> grin."

Certain kinds of (18)"<u>silent</u> language" give one particular message in one culture but a (19)<u>conflicting</u> message in another culture. For example, eye contact—looking directly into the eyes of the person you are speaking to—has a very different meaning from one culture to another. In American culture, if you do not look directly into someone's eyes, the listener will think that you are being dishonest. If someone is described as "shifty-eyed," it means that he or she cannot be trusted. But in many Asian cultures, avoiding eye contact is a sign of politeness and respect, and (20)<u>prolonged</u> eye contact (which indicates sincerity in American culture) means aggression or hostility. (21)<u>Mistaken</u> "body language" can result in even more misunderstanding than using the (22)<u>wrong</u> word or incorrect grammar.

Focus 2

MEANING

Active and Passive Meanings of Participles

MEANING

- English makes a distinction between agent and recipient.
  - The *agent* is the doer or performer of the action.
    (a) The boy was jumping.
       (The boy did the jumping.)
  - The *recipient* is the receiver of—or is affected by—the action.
    (b) The man was beaten.
       (Someone beat the man.)
       This is discussed in more detail in Unit 4.
- Participle modifiers maintain this agent or recipient relationship.
  - Present participles modify **agents**.
    The agents perform the actions suggested by the participle.
    (c) the **jumping boy**
       (The boy did the jumping.)
  - Past participles modify recipients.
    The recipients receive the action suggested by the participle.
    (d) the **beaten man**
       (Someone else beat the man.)

Exercise 2

Paraphrase these sentences by choosing the correct participle for the cues given.

      EXAMPLES: Most of my friends enjoy reading novels.

                  Most of my friends are _interested_ (interest) in reading novels.

                  Novels are _interesting_ (interest) to most of my friends.

1. The audience didn't understand the lecture.

   The audience was _____ (confuse).

   The lecture was _____ (confuse).

2. The students didn't do well on the exam.

   The exam results were _____ (disappoint).

   The students were _____ (disappoint).

3. Children who watch scary movies may not be able to sleep afterward.

   (frighten) _____ children may not be able to go to sleep.

   (frighten) _____ movies may keep children from sleeping.

4. That was quite a delicious snack.

   The snack was quite _____ (satisfy).

   We were quite _____ (satisfy).

5. Most students enjoy studying grammar.

   Most students are _____ (interest) in grammar.

   Grammar is _____ (interest) to most students.

Exercise 3

Use present or past participles to complete these definitions.

> **EXAMPLES:** Information that reveals thoughts can be described as <u>*revealing*</u> information.
> Emotions that people hide can be described as <u>*hidden*</u> emotions.

1. Situations that excite people can be described as _____ situations.

2. Heart rates that stress increases can be described as _____ heart rates.

3. A situation that embarrasses people can be described as an _____ situation.

4. Indications that people don't intend to show can be described as _____ indications.

5. News that depresses people seriously can be described as _____ news.

6. Individuals who some bad news depresses seriously can be described as _____ individuals.

7. A question that puzzles people can be described as a _____ question.

8. People that a question puzzles can be described as _____ people.

Focus 3

Adding Other Information to Participles

FORM MEANING

- You can add information to participles by combining **noun or adverb + hyphen** with a participle construction. Some common expressions and adverbs that end in *-ly* do not need a hyphen.

Noun + Hyphen	Adverb + Hyphen
(a) a **trend-setting** phenomenon (The phenomenon sets a trend.)	**(c)** a **fast-moving** train (The train moved fast.)
(b) a **male-dominated** society (The society is dominated by males.)	**(d)** some **home-grown** tomatoes (The tomatoes were grown at home.)

- Hyphenated present participles can indicate
  - the recipient of the action as well as the agent:
    (e) a **man-eating** tiger (a tiger that eats men)
    (f) an **all-consuming** interest (an interest that consumes all one's energy and time)
    (g) a **fire-breathing** dragon (a dragon that breathes fire)
    (h) a **show-stopping** finale (a finale that stopped the show)
- Hyphenated past participles can indicate
  - the agent as well as the recipient:
    (i) a **flea-bitten** dog (a dog that is bitten by fleas)
    (j) a **self-made** man (a man who made himself)
  - certain characteristics or physical attributes:
    (k) a **shifty-eyed** criminal (a criminal with shifty eyes)
    (l) a **sharp-tongued** woman (a woman with a sharp tongue)
- You can also add adverbial information to present and past participles:
    (m) a **much-visited** attraction (The attraction is visited a lot.)
    (n) a **fast-disappearing** custom
    (o) a **well-known** grammar book

Exercise 4

Restate these noun phrases as nouns plus relative clauses.

EXAMPLES: a much-loved story: *a story that is loved very much*
an all-consuming interest: *an interest that consumes all*
a fire-breathing dragon: *a dragon that breathes fire*

1. a death-defying stunt
2. a store-bought cake
3. a world-renowned expert
4. a mind-boggling fact
5. a handmade sweater

6. a weight-reducing machine
7. a face-saving maneuver
8. a well-trained employee
9. a love-starved kitten
10. a belt-tightening economic policy

Exercise 5

Write original sentences with these participles.

1. boring
2. self-satisfied
3. surprised
4. amazing
5. deeply depressed

6. exhilarating
7. worried
8. modern-thinking
9. disinterested
10. irritating

Exercise 6

Choose the correct participle form for these sentences from the cues given.

Problems in communication can arise when some of the voluntary and involuntary cues of the (1) _____ (nonspeak) part of a language are misinterpreted. There can sometimes be (2) _____ (confuse) misunderstandings between teachers and students in the classroom.

Teachers in American classrooms, for example, may often become (3) _____ (annoy) when students don't volunteer answers to general questions in class. Such behavior in American classrooms often means that the students are (4) _____ (bore), (5) _____ (disinterest), or (6) _____ (uninvolve) in the class activity. Similarly, teachers interpret eye contact from students as a sign that the lesson is (7) _____ (interest) and (8) _____ (involve) for them, and that they are (9) _____ (actively engage) in the learning process.

Students may sometimes become (10) _____ (confuse) about the best way to show they are paying attention. In an American classroom, asking questions is a good way to do this, but students from other cultures may be (11) _____ (embarrass) by having to admit that they are (12) _____ (confuse). Sometimes they are (13) _____ (worry) that asking questions may be interpreted as (14) _____ (teacher-challenge) behavior, or as a (15) _____ (slightly insult) suggestion that the teacher has not explained things clearly enough.

Talking about such interpretations and expectations is a good way to solve these misunderstandings. Teachers and students alike are often very (16) _____ (surprise) to find out about the (17) _____ (sometimes-mistake) assumptions that they have been operating under.

Focus 4

FORM

Participial Modifiers

FORM

- You can also use participial phrases as modifiers. You can learn about these structures in more detail in Unit 17 as reduced forms of relative clauses containing **be**.
    - **(a)** The man **who is speaking to John** told him some shocking information.
    - **(b)** The man **speaking to John** told him some shocking information.
    - **(c)** The woman **who was introduced at the party last week** is a world-renowned expert on infectious diseases.
    - **(d)** The woman **introduced at the party last week** is a world-renowned expert on infectious diseases.
- Such participial phrases can precede or follow the noun they modify. Participial phrases usually come
    - after the noun, if they identify the noun (tell which particular noun we are talking about):
        - **(e)** The man **speaking to John** (not the man dancing in the corner or the man standing by the punch bowl) told him some shocking information.
    - before the noun, if that noun has already been identified and the participial describes more about the noun:
        - **(f)** **Speaking to the man**, John found out some shocking information.
          (There is only one person named John.)

Exercise 7

Underline each of the participial phrases and paraphrase it as a relative clause. The first sentence has been done for you as an example.

> **EXAMPLE:** *that is frequently mentioned by researchers who are discussing cross-cultural differences*

(1) One aspect of "silent language" <u>frequently mentioned by researchers discussing cross-cultural differences</u> is the varying size of the "conversation bubble" in each culture. (2) This bubble is the amount of physical distance maintained between people engaged in different kinds of conversation.

(3) Americans carrying on polite social conversations tend to stand about an arm's length apart. (4) Closer distances are permitted only between people having a more intimate relationship. (5) Breaking that arm's length bubble is usually interpreted as overly aggressive (either socially or sexually).

(6) People in Latin America tend to have a smaller bubble, and as a result North Americans sometimes come across as cold or standoffish to people raised in Latin societies. (7) In general, Middle Eastern cultures tend to have the smallest bubble, while North Asian and Northern European cultures tend to have the largest.

149

Activities

Activity 1

What things should a teacher do to make a class more interesting? Think about the teachers you have really enjoyed working with and list three or four things they did to make their students more involved and committed to the class. Write a brief paragraph about a memorable class you had, using present participles to describe the teacher and past participles to describe the students.

Activity 2

Some cultures value people who express their emotions easily, while others value people who can keep their feelings to themselves. Some people have what is called *a poker face.* That means that their facial expressions rarely show what they are really thinking. This expression comes from the gambling game of poker, where it is very important not to let your opponents know whether or not you have a good hand of cards. The opposite of a poker face is someone who *wears his heart on his sleeve.* This means his or her emotions are near the surface and not hidden from other people.

- What are the advantages and disadvantages to each kind of behavior? Think of as many situations as you can where having a poker face can be advantageous—playing poker is an obvious example—and think of situations where it is a disadvantage— such as when trying to communicate in a language that you don't speak too well. Do the same for wearing your heart on your sleeve.

- Look over your answers. The number of responses should give you some clues about whether you tend to one style or the other. Now compare them with other people in the class. Do you see any parallels between the preferred styles of people from one particular cultural group compared to another? Discuss your thoughts with other students in the class.

Activity 3

What characteristics make somebody fascinating? What characteristics make someone boring? Think of at least five characteristics for each category. Compare your answers with those of three or four other people and compile a list of characteristics that everyone has mentioned. Present your list to the rest of the class.

Activity 4

Are facial expressions universal? Here is a chart used to teach a common "vocabulary" of facial expressions to deaf students.

- Examine these expressions in a small group made up of people from different cultures (if possible). Are there any feelings that are expressed in your culture by very different facial expressions than the ones shown? Are there any cultural generalizations you can make about nonverbal communication between one culture and another?

- Present your ideas to the rest of the class.

Activity 5

Here are some other expressions. The emotions they portray have been omitted.

- Decide on adjectives or participles that you feel describe these expressions. Be ready to explain why you have chosen the description that you did.

- Compare your answers with those of three or four other students in the class. What differences in interpretation did you discover? Do these differences give you any further insight into the role of facial expressions in other cultures?

- Report any significant differences or insights to the rest of the class.

151

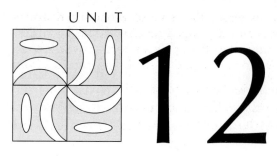

UNIT

12

Comparatives

Task

Rich countries and poor countries: The economics of development

Some experts feel that political conflicts in the next century will occur not because of cultural differences or differences between political systems, but rather because of important economic differences between rich countries and poor countries. Here are some statistics about two pairs of countries that were all once colonies of Great Britain.

People's Republic of Bangladesh	Islamic Republic of Pakistan
area 55,000 square miles **population**: 110 million **growth rate**: 2.7% **density per square mile**: 2,000 **languages**: **(national)** Bengali; **(official)** English **religion**: Islamic (83%),Hindu (16%) **literacy rate**: 25% **GNP**: $15 billion **per capita income**: $150 per year **politically independent since**:1947 from Britain/1974 from Pakistan	**area:** 310,000 square miles **population:** 108 million **growth rate:** 2.9% **density per square mile:** 346 **languages:** **(national)** Urdu, **(official)** English, **(regional)** Punjabi, Sindhi, Pashtu, Baluchi **religion:** Islamic (97%), all other (3%) **literacy rate:** 26% **GNP:** $36.5 billion **per capita income:** $360 per year **politically independent since:** 1947
United States of America	**Canada**
area: 3.5 million square miles **population:** 246 million **growth rate:** 0.7% **density per square mile:** 68 **languages:** English **religion:** Protestant (56%), Catholic (38%), Jewish (4%) **literacy rate:** 95% **GNP:** $4,490 billion **per capita income:** $16,000 per year **politically independent since:** 1776	**area:** 3.8 million square miles **population:** 26 million **growth rate:** 0.8% **density per square mile:** 6.8 **language:** English, French **religion:** Protestant (41%), Catholic (47%), Jewish (1%) **literacy rate:** 98% **GNP:** $347 billion **per capita income:** $13,700 per year **politically independent since:** 1867

- What information do these statistics give us about the issue of economic disparity between developing (Third World) countries and developed (industrialized) countries? Work with a partner or small group, using these statistics and your own knowledge and experience about various countries in the world to respond to the following questions:

  What are some things that developed countries have in common?

  What are some things that developing countries have in common?

  What are the differences between developed and developing countries? Are there similarities? What are they?

  What do these differences and similarities mean for world peace and global development?

  Which do you think is a more common source of conflict between nations: economic differences or cultural differences? Can you give examples to support your opinion?

- Present your ideas to the rest of the class.

Focus 1

FORM ● MEANING

Comparisons of Degree: Adjectives and Adverbs

- You can make comparisons in English, as in the international language of mathematics, in several different ways:
  - $X > Y$ (X is greater than Y.)

    (a) Pakistan is **larger than** Bangladesh.
  - $Y < X$ (Y is less than X.)

    (b) Bangladesh is **smaller than** Pakistan.
  - $X = Y$ (X is as great as Y.)

    (c) The population in Pakistan is growing **as quickly as** in Bangladesh.
  - $Y \neq X$ means the same thing as $Y < X$.

    (d) Bangladesh is **not as large as** Pakistan.

    (e) Bangladesh is **smaller than** Pakistan.
- You can use intensifiers with comparative adjectives and adverbs to indicate whether the difference between X and Y is small or large.

  (f) Pakistan is **considerably larger** than Bangladesh.

  (g) Bangladesh's growth rate is **slightly lower than** Pakistan's.

  (h) Pakistan's population is **not quite as large as** Bangladesh's.

153

- This chart summarizes the patterns that are used to compare adjectives and adverbs in English.

Comparisons of Degree (comparing adjectives and adverbs):

Meaning	Form Intensifier + Comparative	Examples Pakistan & Bangladesh	Exercise 1 Canada & USA
More $X > Y$	X is (intensifier) $\begin{Bmatrix} adjective + \text{-}er \\ more + adjective \\ more + adverb \end{Bmatrix}$ than Y	**(a)** Pakistan is **much larger than** Bangladesh **is**.	
		(b) The people of Pakistan are **slightly more** literate than the people of Bangladesh.	
large difference ↕ small difference	considerably substantially much somewhat slightly/a bit	**(c)** Bangladesh is growing **somewhat more** quickly **than** Pakistan.	
The Same $X = Y$	X is (intensifier) as $\begin{Bmatrix} adjective \\ adverb \end{Bmatrix}$ as Y exactly just	**(d)** Pakistan's post-colonial history is **just as recent as** Bangladesh.	
Less $X < Y$ small difference	X is (intensifier) as $\begin{Bmatrix} adjective \\ adverb \end{Bmatrix}$ as Y almost nearly	**(e)** Bangladesh's literacy rate is **nearly as high as** Pakistan's	
small difference ↑ ↓ large difference	X is not (intensifier) as $\begin{Bmatrix} adjective \\ adverb \end{Bmatrix}$ as Y quite nearly	**(f)** Pakistan is **not quite as** crowded as Bangladesh is.	
		(g) Bangladesh is not **nearly as large as** Pakistan.	
small difference ↑ ↓ large difference	X is (intensifier) less $\begin{Bmatrix} adjective \\ adverb \end{Bmatrix}$ than Y slightly/a bit somewhat much/many substantially considerably	**(h)** Bangladesh is growing **slightly less rapidly than** Pakistan.	
		(i) Bangladesh is **substantially less** prosperous than Pakistan.	

Exercise 1

Using the information in the Task, write statements of comparison about the United States and Canada that use the same forms as the examples in the chart on the previous page. Write your sentences in the space provided in the chart. You may need to use different intensifiers to express the information accurately.

Exercise 2

Underline the comparative structures in the following paragraph. For each structure you find, identify X and Y, identify the feature that is being compared, decide whether X or Y is greater and whether the difference is large or small. The first sentence has been done for you as an example.

EXAMPLES: X = population of Bangladesh; Y = population of Pakistan
$X > Y$ (small difference)
X = land area of Bangladesh; Y = land area of Pakistan
$X < Y$ (large difference)

(1)Although <u>the population of Bangladesh is slightly larger than that of Pakistan, its land area is considerably smaller.</u> (2)This means that the population density of Pakistan is not nearly as great as that of Bangladesh, and as a result, the general standard of living is substantially higher. (3) Although the population of Bangladesh is not growing quite as quickly as Pakistan's, its GNP is quite a bit lower, and as a result, it will be a very long time before the standard of living for Bangladeshis becomes as high as for Pakistanis. (4)While educational development is almost as high in Bangladesh as in Pakistan, economic development is substantially lower, and people in Bangladesh are generally less prosperous.

Exercise 3

Make comparative statements about Pakistan and Bangladesh using the cues given. Add an appropriate intensifier to indicate whether the difference is large or small. Refer to the information in the Task.

EXAMPLE: land area: Pakistan > Bangladesh (large)
The land area of Pakistan is considerably larger than the land area of Bangladesh.
people: Pakistan < Bangladesh (poor)
The people of Pakistan are not nearly as poor as the people of Bangladesh.
The people of Pakistan are much less poor than the people of Bangladesh.

1. GNP: Bangladesh < Pakistan (high)
2. GNP: Pakistan > Bangladesh (high)
3. Literacy rate: Pakistan > Bangladesh (high)
4. Literacy rate: Bangladesh < Pakistan (high)
5. Population: Bangladesh < Pakistan (quickly)

6. Population: Pakistan > Bangladesh (quickly)
7. Population: Bangladesh > Pakistan (large)
8. Population: Pakistan < Bangladesh (large)
9. Population: Bangladesh > Pakistan (dense)
10. Population: Pakistan < Bangladesh (dense)

Focus 2

FORM ● MEANING

Comparisons of Amount: Noun Phrases

FORM
MEANING

- You can compare noun phrases in English in the same way that you compare adjective and adverbs.
  - **X > Y** (X has more something than Y.)
    (a) Pakistan has **more land area than** Bangladesh.
    (b) Bangladesh has **somewhat more people than** Pakistan.
  - **Y < X** (Y has less something than X.)
    (c) Bangladesh has **substantially less land area than** Pakistan.
    (d) Pakistan has **somewhat fewer people than** Bangladesh.
  - **X = Y** (X has the same amount as Y.)
    (e) Pakistan has as many national and official languages as Bangladesh.
  - **Y ≠ X** means the same thing as Y < X
    (f) Bangladesh does **not** have **as many regional languages as** Pakistan.
    (g) Bangladesh has **fewer regional languages than** Pakistan.
- As in comparisons of degree, you can add intensifiers to comparative noun phrases to indicate whether the difference between X and Y is small or large.
  (h) Pakistan consists of a **considerably larger** land area than Bangladesh.
  (i) Bangladesh has a **slightly lower growth rate than** Pakistan.
  (j) Pakistan does **not** have **quite as many people as** Bangladesh.

- This chart summarizes the patterns that are used to compare amounts in English.

Comparisons of Amount (Comparing Noun Phrases)

Meaning	Form Intensifier + Comparative	Examples Pakistan & Bangladesh	Exercise 4 Canada & USA
More X > Y	*X verb (intensifier) more noun phrase than Y*	**(a)** Pakistan has **much more land area than** Bangladesh does.	
large difference ↑ ↓ small difference	considerably substantially much/many somewhat slightly/a bit	**(b)** Bangladesh has **slightly more people than** Pakistan.	
The Same X = Y	*X verb (intensifier) as much/many noun phrase as Y* exactly just	**(c)** Pakistan sends **just as many representatives** to the U.N. **as** Bangladesh does.	
		(d) One has **as much representation as** the other.	
Less X < Y	*X verb (intensifier) as much/many noun phrase as Y*	**(e)** Pakistan has **almost as many people** as Bangladesh.	
small difference	almost nearly		
	X adverb (intensifier) as much/many noun phrase as	**(f)** Pakistan does not have **quite as many people as** Bangladesh does.	
small difference ↑ large difference	quite nearly	**(g)** Bangladesh doesn't have **nearly as much land area as** Pakistan.	
	X verb (intensifier) fewer/less noun phrase than Y	**(h)** Pakistan has **slightly fewer people than** Bangladesh.	
small difference ↑ ↓ large difference	slightly somewhat much/many substantially considerably	**(i)** Bangladesh has **much less** land than Pakistan does.	

Exercise 4

Using the information in the Task, write statements of comparison about the United States and Canada that use the same forms as the examples in the chart on the previous page. Write your sentences in the space provided in the chart. You may need to use different intensifiers to accurately express the information.

Exercise 5

Underline the comparative structures in this paragraph. For each structure you find, identify X and Y, identify the feature that is being compared, tell whether X or Y is greater, and tell whether the difference is large or small. The first sentence has been done for you as an example.

> **EXAMPLE:** X — *Bangladesh has (a number of) people. Y — Pakistan does too.*
> $X > Y$ *(small or medium difference)*
> X — *Bangladesh has (an amount of) land area. Y — Pakistan does too.*
> $X < Y$ *(large difference)*

(1) Although <u>Bangladesh has somewhat more people than Pakistan, it has considerably less land area</u>. (2) This means that Pakistan does not have nearly as many people per square mile as Bangladesh does, and as a result, there is much less pressure on economic infrastructure, roads, water supply, and so on. (3) As a rule, people in Bangladesh have somewhat fewer opportunities for economic progress than people in Pakistan. (4) Bangladesh has just about as many literate people as Pakistan, but it has fewer people living above the poverty line, so there is somewhat less political and economic stability in Bangladesh than there is in Pakistan. (5) However, Pakistan has more regional ethnic groups than Bangladesh, and there are more incidents of ethnic unrest in Pakistan than there are in Bangladesh. (6) Thus, in the political arena overall, Bangladesh has fewer overt conflicts than Pakistan.

Exercise 6

Make comparative statements about Pakistan and Bangladesh using the cues given. Add an appropriate intensifier to indicate whether the difference is large or small. Refer to the information in the Task.

> **EXAMPLE:** Pakistan > Bangladesh (land area)
> *Pakistan has considerably more land area than Bangladesh.*
> Pakistan < Bangladesh (non-Muslim citizens)
> *There are fewer non-Muslim citizens in Pakistan than there are in Bangladesh.*
> *Pakistan doesn't have as many non-Muslim citizens as Bangladesh.*

1. Bangladesh < Pakistan: regional ethnic groups
2. Pakistan > Bangladesh: regional languages
3. Bangladesh > Pakistan: people
4. Pakistan < Bangladesh : literate people
5. Bangladesh > Pakistan: Hindu citizens
6. Pakistan < Bangladesh: Hindu citizens

158

Exercise 7

Use the statistics in the Task to write sentences that compare Pakistan and Bangladesh in terms of

1. population
2. growth rate
3. literacy
4. economic development
5. ethnic groups
6. level of prosperity

Compare your sentences with those of other students in the class. How many different patterns can be used to express the same comparative relationship?

Exercise 8

Use the statistics in the Task to write sentences that compare the United States and Canada in terms of

1. land area
2. population growth rate
3. percentage of Protestants
4. official languages of the two countries
5. literacy rate
6. population density
7. per capita income
8. GNP
9. overall population

Compare your answers with those of other students in the class. How many different patterns can be used to make the same comparisons?

Exercise 9

For each of the sentences you wrote in Exercises 7 and 8, change your basic comparison to the opposite country and change the information accordingly. There are several different ways to express such comparisons, so compare your answers to those of other people in the class.

EXAMPLE: Canada's land area is somewhat larger than that of the United States.
The United States has a slightly smaller land area than Canada.

Focus 3

FORM ● MEANING

Comparisons of Similarity and Difference—Noun Phrases

FORM
MEANING

- You can also make comparisons in terms of similarity and difference, rather than in terms of amount and degree. Once again there are parallels to the language of mathematics in these comparisons.
  - $X = Y$ (X is the same as Y.)
    - **(a)** Pakistan had **the same colonial administration as** Bangladesh.
    - **(b) Pakistan and Bangladesh** had **the same colonial administration.**
  - $X \approx Y$ (X is similar to Y.)
    - **(c)** American English is **almost the same as** Canadian English.
    - **(d) American English and Canadian English** are **almost the same.**
  - $X \neq Y$. (X and Y are different.) With comparisons of similarity and difference, this does **not** mean that $X < Y$, but only that X and Y are different.
    - **(e)** Pakistan doesn't have **the same ethnic minorities as** Bangladesh.
    - **(f) Pakistan and Bangladesh** don't have **the same ethnic minorities.**
      (This doesn't mean that Pakistan has **fewer** minorities, just **different** ones.)
- This chart summarizes the patterns that are used to compare amounts in English.

Comparing Noun Phrases:

Meaning	Form Intensifier + Comparative	Examples
Identical $X = Y$	*X verb (intensifier) the same noun phrase as Y(does)* *X & Y verb (intensifier) the same noun phrase* exactly precisely	**(a)** Pakistan uses **exactly the same** official language **as** Bangladesh. **(b)** Pakistan and Bangladesh use **the same official language.**
Similar $X \approx Y$	*X verb intensifier the same noun phrase as Y (does)* *X & Y verb (intensifier) the same noun phrase as Y (does)* great similarity | very much ↑ | basically ↓ | almost small similarity | somewhat	**(c)** Pakistan has **almost the same growth rate as** Bangladesh (does). **(d)** Pakistan and Bangladesh have **almost the same growth rate.**

160

Comparing Noun Phrases:

Meaning	Form Intensifier +Comparative	Examples
Different X ≠ Y	*X not verb (intensifier) the same noun phrase as Y (does)* *X & Y not verb (intensifier) the same noun phrase*	**(e)** People in Bangladesh don't speak at all **the same regional languages as** people in Pakistan do.
small difference ↕ large difference	quite nearly at all	**(f)** People in Pakistan and Bangladesh do not speak **at all the same national language.**
	X verb (intensifier) different noun phrase from/than Y *X & Y verb (intensifier) different noun phrase*	**(g)** People in Bangladesh have **a much different** culture **from** people in Pakistan. **(h)** People in Pakistan and Bangladesh have **very different cultures.**
small difference ↑ ↓ large difference	slightly/a bit somewhat substantially much/very considerably	

Exercise 10

Underline the statements of similarity and difference in the following passage. For each comparative structure you find, a) identify the things that are being compared, and b) decide whether the comparison describes things that are identical, similar, or different. What gives you this information? The first two sentences have been done for you as an example.

> **EXAMPLE:** 1) a) *kinds of English;* b) *similar*
> 2) a) *things like vocabulary and pronunciation;* b) *different*

(1)Although English is spoken in many countries, <u>English speakers don't all speak quite the same kind of English.</u> (2)<u>Things like vocabulary and pronunciation are often substantially different.</u> (3)The differences between some varieties of English are easy to identify. (4)No one would mistake Indian English for Australian English. (5)The pronunciation features of these two "Englishes" are quite different. (6)British English is substantially different from American English, not only in terms of accent but also spelling and vocabulary—especially slang.

(7)But the differences between some regional varieties are more subtle. (8)For example, many people think that Canadian and American varieties of English are exactly the same, but, in fact, there are some differences, and not all words are pronounced alike. (9)In America, the vowel sound in the word *out* is pronounced different from that in *boot*. (10)But in Canada many people pronounce *shout* basically like *shoot*. (11)To most people, Canadian English and American English seem very much alike. (12)But the careful listener will be able to find a number of examples of the ways Americans speak the language differently from their northern neighbors.

Exercise 11

Use the information that you learned in the Task and your own knowledge to make statements about similarities and differences between Canada and the United States. When compared with the United States, identify some things in Canada that are

a) identical.
b) similar.
c) somewhat different.
d) very different.

Write two sentences for each category. Compare your answers with those of other students in the class.

Exercise 12

Make expressions of similarity and difference about Pakistan and Bangladesh following the same categories as Exercise 11.

Exercise 13

Make expressions of similarity and difference about two other countries you are familiar with. Discuss the same categories that were compared in Exercise 8.

Focus 4

FORM ● MEANING

Comparisons of Similarity and Difference—Verb Phrases

FORM
MEANING

- In expressions of similarity and difference about verb phrases, different intensifiers express whether the two things are identical or similar, and how similar they are. This chart summarizes comparisons of similarity and differences concerning verb phrases.

Comparing Verb Phrases

Meaning	Form Intensifier + Comparative	Examples
Identical or Similar (degree of similarity is conveyed by intensifiers)	*X verb phrase (intensifier) the same as Y (does)* *X&Y verb phrase (intensifier) the same.* *X verb phrase (intensifier) like Y (does)* *X&Y verb phrase (intensifier) alike*	**(a)** Canadians pronounce most words **just the same as** Americans (do.)
Identical exactly just		**(b)** Canadians and Americans pronounce most words **very much the same.**
Similar more similar ↕ less similar almost very much quite much somewhat		**(c)** Canadian English sounds **almost** like American English (does).
		(d) American and Canadian English sound **very much** alike.
Different small difference ↕ large difference exactly quite much at all	*X not verb phrase (intensifier) like Y (does)* *X&Y not verb phrase (intensifier) alike*	**(e)** Some Canadian words aren't pronounced **exactly like** American words (are).
		(f) Australian and American pronunciation are **not much alike**.
small difference ↕ large difference quite a bit at all	*X not verb phrase (intensifier) the same as Y. (does)* *X&Y not verb phrase (intensifier) the same*	**(g)** Canadians do **not** pronounce *out* **quite the same as** Americans. (do)
		(h) Americans and Canadians **don't** pronounce *out* **at all the same**.
small difference ↕ large difference *a bit* *somewhat* *quite*	*X verb phrase (intensifier) differently from/than Y* *X&Y verb phrase (intensifier) differently.*	**(i)** Canadians pronounce english **a bit differently from** Americans.
		(j) Australians and Americans pronounce English **quite differently.**

Exercise 14

Use the information you read in Exercise 10 and your own experience to make statements of similarity and difference using these cues. Use intensifiers to indicate whether these differences are large or small.

EXAMPLES: Indians/ Australians/ pronounce English/ like
Indians don't pronounce English at all like Australians.
Canadians/ Americans/ pronounce English/ alike
Canadians and Americans don't pronounce English quite alike.

1. British/ American/ use slang expressions/ differently
2. No two countries/ speak a common language/ the same
3. Spanish in Spain/ in Latin America/ differently from
4. The word *color*/ in Britain/ in America/ is spelled/ not alike
5. Many Canadians pronounce *shout*/ *shoot*/ the same as
6. grammar/ in regional varieties of English/ alike

Exercise 15

Underline all the comparatives and statements of similarity and difference in the following passage. (Not all sentences contain such statements.) For each one you find, answer these questions:

a) What is being compared?
b) Do the statements indicate that the issues being compared are identical, very similar, somewhat similar, different, or very different?
c) What words or structures convey this information?

The first two have been done for you as examples.

EXAMPLE: 1. a) *groups of languages/ linguistic structure*
b) *somewhat similar*
c) *somewhat*
3. a) *groups of cultures/values, attitudes, and beliefs*
b) *very similar*
c) *more or less the same*

(1) We know that there are large "language families" — groups of <u>languages that have somewhat the same linguistic structure.</u> (2) Some anthropologists have suggested that there are also large "culture families," as well. (3) Culture families might be defined as groups of <u>cultures that have more or less the same basic values, attitudes, and beliefs.</u> (4) Anyone who has traveled extensively would agree that one "European" culture (which may also include areas outside of geographical Europe, such as Australia and North America) has many of the same basic characteristics as any other European culture. (5) Countries in Latin America are quite different from each other in terms of customs and social structures. (6) However, people from Colombia will probably think more like people from Venezuela than like people from Nepal. (7) And a Nepalese and an Indian will be more alike than a Nepalese and a Viennese.

(8) No culture has exactly the same set of values as another culture. (9) But there are a number of factors that make a particular culture more like one culture than another. (10) One important unifying factor is religion.

(11)People who have the same religion also tend to have the same general "world view" and moral values. (12)Their specific beliefs and practices may not be exactly alike. (13)Indeed, one group of followers may be quite different from another group; they may even have serious conflicts. (14)Nevertheless, they will still share certain important fundamental similarities, especially when compared to some other "culture family." (15)For example, Sunni Muslims and Shi'ite Muslims have some fundamentally different ideas, but both groups share the same five basic precepts of Islam, and view the world quite differently from Buddhists. (16) Roman Catholics worship somewhat differently from Protestants, but both groups observe Christmas and Easter in very much the same way.

(17)Another factor that determines "culture families" is historical development. (18)Cultures that have a shared historical background tend to have somewhat the same outlook on the world. (19)It is this factor that allows the different cultures in India, for example, to share the same political system.

(20)But it is also important to remember that the differences between cultures can sometimes be more important than the similarities. (21)Many developing countries were founded as political unions, not cultural ones. (22)No matter how much their economic and political interests may be alike, cultures that think quite differently from one another may choose to act quite differently as well. (23)Any student of geography knows that political boundaries change much more frequently and more rapidly than cultural boundaries.

Focus 5

USE

Informal Usage of Comparisons

USE

- There are differences between formal (written) and informal (spoken) English when making comparative statements.
  - **structure differences:**

Less Formal/Conversational Style	More Formal/Written Style
(a) The culture of Pakistan is **different than** Bangladesh.	**(b)** The culture of Pakistan is **different from that** of Bangladesh.
(c) Canadians pronounce certain words **differently than** Americans.	**(d)** Canadians pronounce certain words **differently from** Americans.
(e) Pakistan had **much the same** colonial experience **that** Bangladesh **did.**	**(f)** Pakistan had **much the same** colonial experience **as Bangladesh.**

- **intensifier differences:** (These differences are discussed in Unit 9.)

Less Formal	More Formal
(g) Canadian English is not **so** different from American English.	**(h)** Canadian English is not **very** different from American English.

Exercise 16

Change these informal comparisons to their more formal variations.

1. Sunni Muslims follow the same five basic precepts of Islam that Shi'ite Muslims do.
2. Catholic Christians regard the Pope differently than Protestant Christians.
3. Mahayana Buddhists don't put the same emphasis on being a monk that Theravada Buddhists do.
4. The social values of Germany are quite different than Italy.
5. Many people in Washington, D.C., have a different attitude toward the role of the federal government than many people in San Francisco.
6. The Civil War in the United States was caused in large part by the fact that people in the North felt differently on the subject of slavery than people in the South.
7. The Indians of Peru speak almost the same language that the Indians in Bolivia do.
8. The English spoken in New Zealand is slightly different than in Australia.

Focus 6

USE

Other Uses of Like and As

USE

- You can use *like* and *as* to make comparative statements about similarities and differences. You can also use them to make **similes**. A simile is an implied comparison that can answer questions such as "how." Similes are a common way to make language more descriptive. Similes can be formed

With Noun Phrases	With Clauses
(a) Tom dances **like a bear.** (b) He runs **as fast as the wind.** (c) Love is **like a beautiful poem.** (d) You solved that problem **like an expert.**	(e) He looked **like he had seen a ghost!** (f) Denise works **as if there is nothing else in the world worth doing.**

- In informal usage, you can use **like** to introduce clauses, but in formal usage we use **as if** or **as though** to introduce clauses.

Informal/Conversational	Formal/Written
(g) Charley looks **like** he didn't get much sleep last night. (i) Mary acted **like** she never wanted to see John again.	(h) Charley looks **as though** he didn't get much sleep last night. (j) Mary acted **as if** she never wanted to see John again.

Exercise 17

What is the function of *like* or *as* in these sentences? Does it indicate a true comparative statement, or does it express a simile or some other meaning?

    EXAMPLE: Many people feel that a policy of "political correctness" can be just as dangerous to free speech as a policy of political censorship. (***As*** *expresses a comparative statement.*)

                Peter thinks that Denise is as cold as ice. (***As*** *expresses a simile.*)

1. Pakistan, like India, received its independence in 1947.
2. African countries like Nigeria, Mali, and the Ivory Coast have several important different cultural and linguistic minorities.
3. Italy is predominantly Roman Catholic, as are Spain and Portugal.
4. Life in Rio de Janeiro can be as sweet as honey, if you're not poor.
5. Sometimes Denise acts like she is so important. I don't like it when she is like that.
6. The party was a success, just exactly like I told you it would be.
7. My school isn't like it was before so many people had to drop out in order to work.
8. This doesn't feel like silk. I think it's rayon.
9. I don't feel like there's much point in studying for the exam.
10. The people of East Pakistan felt like the government of West Pakistan was treating them like a colony.
11. Some British people think Americans all pronounce English like cowboys or gangsters do.
12. The crazy man acted like he was being pursued by devils.
13. Most governments spend money like there was no tomorrow.
14. The little girl looked like an angel in her new party dress.

Activities

Activity 1

The Task in Unit 17 describes the true story of two identical twins who were separated at birth. Refer to that Task and write statements of similarity and difference about the twins.

Activity 2

How can you tell if someone is from another country? What are some things people do differently when they come from another culture?

- Working with a partner from another culture, talk about how you know when someone is a foreigner. If you can, be sure to ask two or three Americans how they know when someone is from another country.
- Identify some **generic differences** in behavior, dress, and so on, that are true for all cultures. Some examples of generic differences are speaking with an accent, clothing styles, and so on.

Activity 3

What are the similarities between people of a particular group? Decide on a particular group of people. The group could be determined by nationality, culture, age, political beliefs, religion, or some other characteristic: Boy Scouts, people with blue eyes, teachers, tourists. The choices are unlimited!

- As you think about things that define a particular group of people, make sure you are able to avoid stereotypes in making your generalizations. **Generalizations** are statements of observation: Many people in culture X usually take a nap in the afternoon. **Stereotypes** are statements of judgment: People of culture X are lazy. A stereotype is an incorrect assumption that individual members of a group all share some observed generalized characteristic.
- Write a paragraph describing things that members of this group do or have in common.

Activity 4

Have you ever met someone who reminds you of someone else? What characteristics and actions of the two people were similar? In what ways were they different? In a brief essay or oral presentation, tell about two people who reminded you of each other.

13

Logical Connectors

Task

Bambang Soetomo asked his English teacher to point out grammatical problems in an essay he wrote for his cross-cultural communication class about culture shock. She indicated places where there were grammatical problems with his essay. With a partner, go over the essay and her comments.

My experience with culture shock.

Every person has experience with culture shock. However I am no exception. And I have experience with culture shock. Although I have lived in the United States for almost 1 year. I still often feel homesick and I miss my family. When I first came to the U.S., I was very comfortable and because everything was new everything was interesting for me. I enjoyed my independence from my parents. I enjoyed to experience new food and making new friends. Everything was strange, nevertheless I enjoyed the new experiences.

Soon I got used to many differences. Even though I was used to them. Still I wasn't comfortable. Little by little I grew tired of the differences. Because the things in America weren't new to me anymore. The differences weren't interesting they were boring. However I began to miss things in Indonesia. For example, food, my friends, the warm climate. I became depress and homesick. I stayed in my room, because I was tired of speaking English all the time. Even though I studied, however my grades weren't good.

So I visited my advisor. He told me about culture shock. I learned that every person has this kind of experience and it can't be avoid. I learned that this culture shock is temporary but universal. My advisor told me I must to keep busy and talk about my culture shock with my friends. This was a good advice, as a result, my culture shock became less and in spite I sometimes still miss my life in Indonesia. I don't feel depression the same as before.

- What kinds of grammatical problems is Bambang having? Identify at least three kinds of mistakes.
- Which mistakes might be examples of one-time "careless errors," and which ones reflect a reoccurring problem?

- What suggestions would you give to Bambang in order to improve his writing?
- Can you correct his essay?

After you and your partner have made your corrections, compare your version to one possible corrected version in Exercise 1.

Focus 1

FORM

Overview of Logical Connectors

FORM

- You can indicate the logical relationships between clauses in a sentence, sentences within a paragraph, or even between paragraphs within a longer text by using **logical connectors.** There are three kinds of logical connectors.
  - **Coordinators:** These connect two independent clauses. See Unit 8 for information about the independent clauses.
    - **(a)** Matt grew up in Kansas, **but** he now lives in San Francisco.
    - **(b)** Bambang **not only** misses his family, **but** he **also** wishes a few friends were in America with him.
  - **Sentence adverbials:** These do not give more information about the verb, but instead indicate a logical connection between the sentence and other sentences.
    - **(c)** Matt grew up in Kansas. **However,** he now lives in San Francisco.
    - **(d)** Bambang misses his family. **In addition,** he wishes that a few friends were in America with him.
  - **Subordinators:** These connect a dependent noun clause or a gerund phrase with the main clause. They are like other adverbial clauses that we studied in Unit 3.
    - **(e) Although** Matt grew up in Kansas, he now lives in San Francisco.
    - **(f) In addition to missing** his family, Bambang wishes that a few friends were in America with him.
- In formal written English, students often have trouble using connectors. Some logical connectors have specialized meanings. Some have grammatical restrictions on how you can use them. Incorrect use of connectors can result in unclear meaning, awkward writing, sentence fragments or run-on sentences. Such sentences are considered wrong in formal written English.

170

MEANING

Common Logical Connectors

MEANING

- There are many logical connectors with different meanings and emphases, but they fall into four general categories:

Meaning	Form		
	Coordinators	**Sentence Adverbials**	**Subordinators**
Additive			
addition	**(a)** Bambang misses his family, **and** they miss him.	**(b)** Bambang misses his family. He also misses his friends. **In addition,** he is suffering from culture shock.	**(c) In addition to missing** his family. Bambang misses his friends.
emphasis	**(d) Not only** does Bambang miss his family, but he is **also** experiencing culture shock.	**(e) Furthermore,** he's not doing well in school. **In fact,** he failed two midterms. He's **actually** quite depressed.	**(f) Besides being depressed,** he's having trouble in school, **not to mention** feeling lonely all the time.
Contrastive			
contrast	**(g)** Everyone experiences culture shock, **but** it eventually passes.	**(h)** Some people have severe culture shock. Others, **however,** just feel a mild depression. Bambang's culture shock is almost over. Yours, **on the other hand,** may be beginning. Mild culture shock is a universal experience. Deep depression, **in contrast,** is not.	**(i) While** some people have severe culture shock, others just feel a mild depression.
concession	**(j)** The advisor told him culture shock can't be avoided, **yet** it is fortunately temporary.	**(k)** Bambang feels homesick. **Even so,** he will stay until he finishes his studies. Bambang studies hard. **Nevertheless,** he isn't getting good grades.	**(l) Although** he feels homesick, Bambang will stay until he finishes his studies. He isn't getting good grades, **even though** he studies hard. **In spite of** experiencing culture shock, Bambang has decided not to go home.

Meaning	Form		
	Coordinators	**Sentence Adverbials**	**Subordinators**
Cause and Effect			
reason	**(m)** Bambang went to see his advisor, **for** he was worried about his grades.	**(n)** Bambang was worried about his grades. **Accordingly,** he went to see his advisor.	**(o)** He found it difficult to concentrate, **due to** being depressed. **Because/Since** Bambang was worried about his grades, he went to see his advisor.
result	**(p)** He was depressed, **so** he went to see his advisor.	**(q)** His advisor told him that culture shock is universal. He **consequently** felt much better about his depression. **As a result,** he decided not to go home early. He **therefore** cancelled his plane reservation.	**(r) As a result** of feeling depressed, he decided to talk with his advisor. He made an appointment, **so that** he could find out about leaving school early. **In order** to find out more about culture shock, he decided to read some articles about it.
conditional	**(s)** The advisor told Bambang to keep busy, **or else** he would become more depressed.	**(t)** Bambang didn't want to go home early. **Then** he would feel that he had failed. **Under such circumstances** he might even feel worse than he had in America.	**(u)** His advisor told him to get a lot of exercise, **providing/if** he could do that without neglecting his studies
Sequence			
	(v) He made an appointment, **and** he went directly to see his advisor.	**(w) First**, one must recognize culture shock. **Then** one must deal with it. **Eventually** everyone gets over it	**(x)** Bambang felt much better **after** he talked with his advisor. **When** he found out about culture shock, he was glad he hadn't decided to have **before** talking with his advisor.

Exercise 1

Identify the form and the general meaning of the highlighted logical connectors. Not every logical connector in this essay appears in the chart. For those that do not, decide which category they belong in and add them to the chart. The first sentence has been done for you as an example.

> **EXAMPLE:** **and**—*form: coordinator,* **meaning:** *additive*
> **since**—*form: subordinator,* **meaning:** *reason*

My Experience with Culture Shock

(1)Every person who has lived in a new culture has had some experience with culture shock, **and** I am no exception, **since** I, too, have had an experience with culture shock. (2)**Although** I have lived in the United States for almost one year, I sometimes still feel homesick, and still miss my family. (3)**When** I first came to the U.S., I was very excited. (4)**Because** everything was new, everything was interesting. (5)I enjoyed my independence from my parents; I **also** enjoyed experiencing new situations and making new friends. (6)**Although** everything was a little strange, I **nevertheless** enjoyed these new experiences.

(7)**Eventually** I got used to many of the differences, **but even though** I was used to them, I still wasn't comfortable. (8)**In fact,** little by little I grew tired of the differences. (9)**Because** the things in America weren't new to me anymore, the differences weren't interesting. (10)**Indeed,** they had **actually** become boring. (11)**As a result,** I began to miss things about Indonesia, such as food, friends, and the warm tropical climate more and more. (12)I **soon** became depressed and homesick. (13)I stayed in my room, **because** I was tired of speaking English all the time. (14)**Even though** I studied hard, my grades weren't good. I wanted to go home.

(15)**Because of** these feelings, I decided to see my advisor **so that** I could get some advice about returning home without finishing my studies. (16)He told me two important things about culture shock. (17)**First,** I learned that any person in a new culture has a similar kind of experience, **and** that culture shock can't be avoided. (18) **Furthermore,** I learned that culture shock is not only universal, but also temporary. (19)**As a result of** his advice, I realized that I should be patient, and that I shouldn't go home just yet. (20)My advisor **also** suggested that I try to keep busy and talk about my culture shock with my friends.

(21)I followed this good advice, **and, as a result,** my culture shock has become less troublesome. (22)**In spite of the fact that** I sometimes still miss my life in Indonesia, I don't feel as depressed as I did. (23)**Moreover,** I no longer want to return home before I finish my studies. I know that I can adjust to this new life.

Exercise 2

Choose an appropriate logical connector from the options provided. Make sure your choice reflects the correct, logical relationship and the grammatical constraints. There may be more than one correct choice, so prepare to explain why you chose your answer.

Both Canada and the United States have large minorities that speak languages other than English. Canada has a large French-speaking minority. (1)The United States, **(on the other hand, furthermore, consequently, yet)** has a large Spanish-speaking minority. (2)**(But, However, So)** the way the two countries deal with this fact are rather different.

Canada has adopted a policy of bilingualism, and has two official languages. All students study both languages in school. (3)**(Moreover, Nevertheless, Therefore)** all official government activities are conducted in both languages.

However, in the United States, there is a movement to make English the only official language. (4)**(So, So that, As a result)**, some people may be officially discouraged from using languages other than English at work. In some parts of the country, there are very few facilities available to people who can't speak English, (5)**(and, but, yet, so)** (6)**(under such circumstances, on the other hand, in addition to)** Spanish-speaking people may be required to provide their own translators in such places as hospitals or government offices. (7)**(In Spite of, Even though, Consequently)** all students in the public schools are taught English, (8)**(but, and, for, no connector)** English-speaking students are not usually required to study Spanish.

These differences in bilingualism may spring from geographical considerations. In Canada, the French-speaking minority constitutes a majority in certain parts of the country, primarily in the Province of Quebec. In the United States, (9)**(however, on the other hand, in spite of this, therefore)** Spanish-speaking concentrations are spread around the country. Large concentrations of Spanish-speaking people are found in New York, Florida, New Mexico, and California. (10)**(As a result, Under such circumstances, In addition, Besides)** there are significant concentrations in many other large cities. (11)**(Although, However, In spite of)** they do not constitute a majority in any single region.

Exercise 3

Complete these sentences using information provided in Exercises 1 and 2.

1. In addition to missing his family, Bambang. . . .
2. In spite of sometimes still missing his family,. . . .
3. Before he talked to his advisor about culture shock,. . . .
4. Bambang now understands that his depression was the result of culture shock. Because of this. . . .
5. Bambang sometimes does poorly on tests, even though. . . .
6. Bambang sometimes does poorly on tests, in spite of. . . .
7. Canada has an official policy of bilingualism. The United states, however,. . . .
8. Canada has an official policy of bilingualism. Consequently,. . . .
9. As a result of Canada's official policy of bilingualism,. . . .
10. Canada's French-speaking minority is concentrated in a particular part of the country. Consequently. . . .
11. Canada's French-speaking minority is concentrated in a particular part of the country. Nevertheless. . . .
12. Since all government business is conducted in both languages,. . . .

Focus 3

FORM ● USE

Problems with Using Coordinating Conjunctions

FORM
USE

- **Form:** When you use coordinating conjunctions to connect independent clauses, they must be preceded by a comma. Without a comma, such sentences are called **run-on** or **run-together sentences.** They are considered incorrect in formal written English.

  (a) Bambang Soetomo studies **hard, but** he sometimes has trouble understanding assignments.

  (b) NOT: Bambang Soetomo studies **hard but** he sometimes has trouble understanding assignments.

- **Use:** In formal written English, using coordinating conjunctions a great deal or using them to connect independent sentences is often awkward and shows poor style. Most formal writing uses other kinds of logical connectors—sentence adverbials and subordinating conjunctions—more frequently.

  (c) AWKWARD: I began to miss my family, **and** I was getting more and more depressed, **so** I decided to talk with my advisor.

  (d) BETTER: **In addition to** missing my family, I was getting more and more depressed. **As a result,** I decided to talk with my advisor.

Focus 4

Problems with Using Sentence Adverbials

FORM
MEANING

- **Form:** You can use sentence adverbials with sentences or with independent clauses connected by a semicolon. Using them with commas to connect clauses produces run-on sentences.

    (a) I was getting more and more depressed. **As a result,** I decided to talk with my advisor.

    (b) NOT: I was getting more and more depressed, **as a result,** I decided to to talk with my advisor.

- **Use:** Most sentence adverbials normally occur at the beginning of a sentence, but they can also appear in the middle or at the end. There is a slight difference. Placing the sentence adverbial in the middle makes the logical connection more emphatic. Placing the sentence adverbial at the end makes it less emphatic.

	Implied Meaning
(c) Jeff grew up in Wisconsin. **However,** Matt comes from Kansas.	basic contrast.
(d) Matt, **however,** comes from Kansas.	This contrast focuses on Matt (not Peter or Louis).
(e) Matt comes from Kansas, **however.**	This indicates the information about Matt is an afterthought or digression

- Some sentence adverbials do not occur in the middle of a sentence or at the end.

    (f) **Besides**, Matt likes having a roommate.

    (g) NOT: Matt **besides** likes having a roommate.

    (h) NOT: Matt likes having a roommate **besides.**

    (i) Alice had a lot of money in her bank account. **Thus,** she was able to pay cash for her new car.

    (j) She was **thus** able to pay cash for her new car.

    (k) NOT: She was able to pay cash for her new car **thus.**

176

Exercise 4

Correct these run-on sentences from Bambang's essay. You can correct the punctuation or try using a sentence adverbial of similar meaning. Compare your solution to other students' solutions.

1. I still often feel homesick and I miss my family.
2. Everything was strange nevertheless I enjoyed the new experiences.
3. The differences weren't interesting they were boring.
4. I learned that every person has this kind of experience and it can't be avoided.
5. This was good advice, as a result, my culture shock became less but in spite of this I still miss my life in Indonesia.

Exercise 5

These sentences have problems with sentence adverbials. Identify the problems and correct them.

1. Every person has experience with culture shock. However, I am no exception.
2. Even though I studied however my grades weren't good.
3. In Canada all official government activities are conducted in both French and English. Under such circumstances, students also study both languages in school. Nevertheless, in the United States, there is no official bilingual policy in government operations. Besides, some local governments have policies that prohibit the use of any language other than English for official business.

Focus 5

FORM

Problems Using Subordinating Conjunctions

FORM

- **Form:** Subordinating conjunctions can introduce dependent clauses, gerunds, or noun phrases. You cannot use them with sentences. This produces a **sentence fragment**, which is considered ungrammatical in formal written English.

Sentence Fragment	Correct Subordination
(a) Because things were no longer new to Bambang. **He** began to miss his friends and family back home.	**(b) Because** things were no longer new to Bambang, **he** began to miss his friends and family back home.
(c) Even though Bambang Soetomo studies hard. **Sometimes he** has trouble understanding assignments.	**(d) Even though** Bambang Soetomo studies hard, **sometimes he** trouble understanding assignments.

- There are some subordinating conjunctions that you cannot use with dependent clauses. You must use them with gerunds or noun phrases instead.

    (e) **Besides missing his family,** Bambang also missed his friends.

    (f) NOT: **Besides Bambang missed his family,** he also missed his friends.

    (g) Bambang sometimes doesn't do well on tests, **in spite of studying** carefully.

    (h) Bambang sometimes doesn't do well on tests, **in spite of the fact that he studies** carefully.

    (i) NOT: Bambang sometimes doesn't do well on tests, **in spite of he studies** carefully.

Exercise 6

Here are some problems with subordinating conjunctions that appeared in Bambang's essay. Identify the problems and correct them.

1. Although I have lived in the United States for almost one year. I often feel homesick and miss my family.
2. Even though I was used to them. Still I wasn't comfortable.
3. However I began to miss things in Indonesia. For example, food, my friends, the warm climate.
4. In addition to he told me about culture shock, my advisor suggested that I should be patient.

Activities

Activity 1

Give your teacher a piece of your writing. This may be something that you have written for another class, or it may be something you have written for another unit in this book. Ask your teacher to indicate places where there are grammatical problems. Follow the same procedure that you used in the Task to analyze your problems and correct your mistakes.

Activity 2

Describe your own experience with culture shock. Write a brief essay. Be sure to connect your ideas with logical connectors. Be sure to avoid run-on sentences and sentence fragments.

Activity 3

What are some common logical connectors in your native language? How does "good style" affect their use? This unit taught us that although it is grammatically possible to join sentences with coordinating conjunctions, it is not always "good writing." Think about the words you use to join ideas in your native language. Identify two instances where "good writing" may be different in your first language than it is in English. Present your ideas to the rest of the class.

Activity 4

What do you think are the different implications of choosing one logical connector instead of another?

- With a partner or in a small group, discuss the following three groups of sentences. What differences in meaning do they imply? What kind of situation would each one be appropriate for?

   Indian food is spicy, and I love it.
   Indian food is spicy, but I love it.
   Indian food is spicy, so I love it.

   Although Indian food is spicy, I love it.
   Although I love Indian food, it's spicy.

   Not only is Indian food spicy, but I also love it.
   Because Indian food is spicy, I love it.

- Most grammar teachers would say that these sentences below are incorrect because they are illogical. Why? With a partner or in a small group, discuss these three sentences. How does the incorrect use of a logical connector make the meaning strange or unclear?

   I love Indian food, and it is spicy.
   I love Indian food, so it is spicy.
   Because I love Indian food, it is spicy.

Activity 5

In this unit, you compared writing with incorrect logical connectors (Task) to writing that uses them correctly (Exercise 1). Compare what you produced in Exercise 2 with the following passage, which contains no logical connectors.

> Canada has a large French-speaking minority. The United States has a large Spanish-speaking minority. Many people in Canada speak French. All government publications are printed in both languages. Canada has two official languages. The United States discourages the use of languages other than English for official purposes. In Canada, the French-speaking minority is concentrated primarily in the Province of Quebec. In the United States, Spanish-speaking concentrations are found in New York, Florida, New Mexico, and California.

- With a partner, or in a small group, examine the writing in this passage and in Exercise 2. Find at least three examples where you think the use of logical connectors has made the author's point clearer.
- Examine Exercises 1 and 2. Which kind of logical connector (subordinating conjunction, coordinating conjunction, or sentence adverbial) appears most frequently? Which appears least frequently?

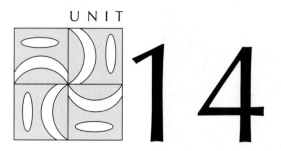

14

Degree Complements:
Too/Enough ... To and *So/Such ... That*

Task

When humans try to change the balance of nature, they often get unexpected, unwanted results. When a new species of plant or animal is transported to a different environment, it sometimes takes over and wipes out other species that had been there before.

For example, the African water hyacinth was originally brought to Florida as an ornamental flower, because other kinds of European water lilies didn't grow well in the warm Florida waters, but people still wanted a beautiful flower to grow in fish ponds. The water hyacinth grew so well in Florida that it soon became a major problem for navigation.

The same thing happens with animal species. When men brought rabbits to Australia, the new animal had few natural enemies, because the wild dogs that might have eaten them had all been killed to protect the herds of sheep. The rabbit population exploded. Soon, rabbits began to destroy crops and even natural vegetation. In both cases there weren't enough natural enemies to control the growth of the imported species.

Here is some information about what happened when a plant species and an animal species were introduced to new environments. In a small group, share information about other examples of unforeseen ecological change that you are familiar with. Choose one of the examples and write a paragraph about the events of the past and how the situation is today.

CASE 1: **Species Imported**	**African Water Hyacinth**
new environment	**the Southern United States**
reason for importation	people wanted an ornamental flower for their fish ponds
initial result	rapid growth
unforeseen problem	no hippopotamus to eat the plant
long-term result	water hyacinths clogged streams and rivers; got tangled in propellers of boats; slowed stream flow; caused flooding
attempted remedy	spraying with weed killer
current situation	most rivers and canals must be cleared by expensive machines on a continual basis

CASE 2: Species Imported	European Rabbits
new environment	Australia
reason for importation	to raise for food
initial result	rabbits escaped, became wild, and multiplied very quickly
unforeseen problem	most of the wild dogs that used to live there had already been killed to protect the sheep and didn't eat the rabbits
long-term result	rabbits began to destroy agriculture
attempted remedy	poison; traps; built hundreds of miles of fences to keep rabbits away from crops
current situation	rabbits still a serious problem in many parts of the country

CASE 3: Species Imported	
new environment	
reason for importation	
initial result	
unforeseen problem	
long-term result	
attempted remedy	
current situation	

Focus 1

Statements of Degree and Result versus Degree Complements

MEANING

- Degree complements are similar to statements of cause and effect. They answer the question *how much* by describing the **result** of a particular situation.

Statement of Degree	Result	Degree Complement
(a) Denise is **very** dedicated to her work.	She doesn't think much about leisure activities.	Denise is **too dedicated** to her work **to think** about leisure activities
(b) Peter has **a number** of outside interests.	He keeps from getting too serious about what happens in the office.	Peter has **enough outside interests to keep** from getting too serious about what happens in the office.
(c) Today rabbits in Australia are an **extremely serious** problem.	They have caused food production to decline.	Today rabbits in Australia are **such a serious problem that** food production has declined.
(d) Rabbits have **few** natural enemies.	They have multiplied very quickly.	Rabbits have **so few** natural enemies **that** they have multiplied very quickly.

- There are two ways to state degree complements:
  - *Too* and *enough* express degree; the **infinitive** expresses result:
    - **(e)** Water hyacinths grew **too quickly to be controlled**.
    - **(f)** Authorities didn't respond **quickly enough to eliminate** the problem.
  - *so* and *such* express degree; a clause with *that* expresses result:
    - **(g)** Water hyacinths grew **so quickly that they couldn't be controlled**.
    - **(h)** Authorities made **such a slow response that they couldn't eliminate** the problem.

182

Exercise 1

Identify the degree complements in these two paragraphs. For each structure, describe the implied statement of degree and the implied statement of result.

EXAMPLE: 1. Denise is too serious to be able to appreciate Peter's laid-back point of view.

   Statement of degree: *Denise is extremely serious.*

   Result: *She isn't able to appreciate Peter's laid-back point of view.*

2. We are burning so much coal and oil that we won't have much left in 100 years.

   Degree: *We are burning a lot of coal and oil.*

   Result: *We won't have much left in 100 years.*

1. Remember Denise Driven and Peter Principle from Unit 9? They're still not getting along. (1)Denise is so rushed at work these days that she doesn't have any free time. (2)She has too little energy at the end of the workday to pursue any hobbies. (3)She's feeling a little lonely, but she's too busy to have made any close friends. (4)Peter has suggested that she take some time off, but she always says that there's too much going on at work for her to take a vacation right now. (5)Nothing moves fast enough for her. (6)Even her secretary types too slowly to keep up with all the letters she writes. (7)Peter, on the other hand, still works hard enough to avoid being fired. (8)But, unlike Denise, he isn't so dedicated to his job that he is willing to sacrifice everything else in order to get ahead. (9)He loves his family enough to make their needs his most important priority. (10)He's just not competitive enough about his job for Denise to consider him a threat to her authority.

2. (1)In the second half of the twentieth century, there has been such a rapid growth in population that many countries have started to develop lands that only a few years ago were uninhabited, dense, tropical rain forest. (2)The need for lumber for export and land for agriculture has become so great that literally hundreds of square miles of tropical rain forest are now disappearing every day. (3)Scientists fear that unless this deforestation stops, the world's rain forests will be completely gone in just another 30 years. (4)And once the rain forests have been cut down, there is too little fertility in the soil of most tropical areas for the jungle to grow back again. (5)The problem has gotten serious enough for the United Nations to become involved.

   (6)There are two primary reasons why the destruction of the rain forests poses a global threat. (7)First, rain forests contain so many plants with possible medical uses that scientists are worried that many valuable species will be destroyed before we can find out how useful they are. (8)But there is a second, more important reason why the destruction of the rain forests is too important to be ignored. (9)There is a clear relationship between rain forests and the climate and weather patterns of the entire world. (10)Rain forests are disappearing so quickly that scientists are afraid that this may already be causing changes in the atmosphere and weather. (11)There are signs that it may already be too late for us to stop this process of global warming and climatic change.

Focus 2

Degree Complements with *Too* and *Enough*

FORM
MEANING

- You can use *enough* and *too* to make degree complements about adjectives, adverbs, and nouns. *Too* and *enough* express degree; an infinitive expresses the result.

TOO:

too + **adjective:**

(a) Some teenagers are **too immature** to make really wise decisions.

too + **adverb:**

(b) They grow **too quickly** for clothes to fit for very long.

too much/too little + **non-count noun**

(c) They have **too little patience** to wait for complete freedom.

(d) They have **too much pride** to ask for advice from their elders.

too many/too few + **count noun**

(e) They have **too many controls** to be able to feel truly independent.

(f) They have **too few chances** to exercise responsibility.

verb + *too much/too little*

(g) Teenagers think they know **too much** to listen to their parents, and **too little** to be responsible for their actions.

ENOUGH:

adjective + *enough*

(h) Most teenagers are **responsible enough** to do a good job.

adverb + *enough*

(i) They work **hard enough** to get the same wages as adults.

verb + *enough*

(j) They have **learned enough** to make wise decisions.

enough + **noun**

(k) They don't make **enough money** to live without their parents support.

- An infinitive, with or without a second subject, always expresses the result portion of degree complements with *too* and *enough*. (See Unit 7 for more practice with these structures.):

Statement of Degree and Statement of Result	Degree Complement
Same Subject: **(l) Denise** is extremely serious about her career. **She** isn't able to appreciate Peter's laid-back point of view.	**(m) Denise** is too serious about her career **to be able** to appreciate Peter's laid-back point of view.
Different subjects: **(n) Peter** is not very competitive about his job. **Denise** doesn't consider him a threat to her authority.	**(o) Peter** isn't competitive enough about his job **for Denise** to consider him a threat to her authority.

- The underlying meaning of the infinitive depends on which degree word we have chosen. Degree complements with *too* and *not enough* have an implied negative meaning in the result clause.

   Degree complements with *enough* do not have this negative implication. If the statement of result with *enough* contains a negative meaning, you must add *not* to the infinitive:

Degree Complement	Implied Meaning
(p) Mr. Green is **too old** to **worry** about losing his hair.	He **doesn't worry** about losing his hair.
(q) Mr. Green is **not young enough** to **wear** the latest fashions.	He **doesn't wear** the latest fashions.
(r) He is **wise enough** to **avoid** taking sides in the argument.	He **avoids** the situation.

Exercise 2

Choose the correct implied meaning for these degree complements:

1. Teenagers are too young to buy alcoholic beverages.
   - (a) They can buy alcoholic beverages.
   - (b) They cannot buy alcoholic beverages.
2. Peter does not work hard enough to be promoted.
   - (a) He will be promoted.
   - (b) He will not be promoted.
3. Mr. Green is wise enough to avoid taking sides in the argument.
   - (a) He avoids taking sides in the argument.
   - (b) He never avoids taking sides in the argument.

4. Teenagers think they are smart enough not to make mistakes.
   (a) They think they might make mistakes.
   (b) They think they will not make mistakes.

Exercise 3

When do teenagers become old enough to take on the privileges and responsibilities of adulthood? Read the sentences below and decide whether you agree with the statements or not. Use one of these degree statements and an infinitive to make statements that reflect your opinion on things that 15-year-olds are old enough or too young to do.

> **15-year-olds are old enough . . . .**
> **15-year-olds are too young . . . .**

> **EXAMPLES:** *15-year-olds are old enough to drive.*
>
> *15-year-olds are too young for their parents to let them live in their own apartments.*

1. They should be able to drive.
2. Their parents should give them some financial responsibility.
3. They can fall in love.
4. Schools should let them choose what classes they want to take.
5. Teachers should talk to them as adults.
6. They shouldn't be able to buy alcohol or cigarettes.
7. Their parents shouldn't let them live in their own apartments.
8. The law shouldn't treat them as adults.
9. They shouldn't be police officers or soldiers.
10. Society shouldn't give them total freedom.

Exercise 4

Restate these pairs of sentences with statements of degree using *too* and *enough*:

> **EXAMPLES:** Denise is very serious about her career. She doesn't understand why Peter is so relaxed.
>
> *Denise is too serious about her career to understand why Peter is so relaxed.*
>
> Peter isn't terribly serious about his job. He doesn't want to spend every weekend at the office.
>
> *Peter isn't serious enough about his job to want to spend every weekend at the office.*

1. Denise has lots of responsibilities. She can't take a vacation right now.
2. The pace of work is extremely hectic. Denise can't do her best work.
3. Denise's secretary types very slowly. Denise can't catch up on her correspondence.
4. Mr. Green hasn't assigned Denise much additional clerical support. Denise can't meet the contract deadline.
5. Denise is very proud. She doesn't want to ask her boss for more help.
6. Denise has often behaved rudely to Peter. He won't offer to help her with the contract.

7. There is always a little free time. Peter spends it on his friends, his music, and his family.
8. Peter plays the clarinet quite well. He could be a professional musician.
9. He doesn't like Denise. He won't help her meet her contract deadline.
10. Work is not that important. Peter doesn't make it the focus of his life.

Exercise 5

Working with a partner, ask and answer the following "stupid" questions. Answer the question with *yes* or *no* and give a reason for your answer, using *too*.

> **EXAMPLE:** Can you swim to Hawaii?
> *No. It's too far to swim.*

1. Do you have any great grandchildren?
2. Can you walk 150 miles in a single day?
3. Is $50 a fair price for a cup of coffee?
4. Can dogs read?
5. Do banana trees grow wild in Russia?
6. Can one person lift a grand piano?
7. Can you learn to speak English fluently in a week?
8. Can a 100-year-old woman still have babies?
9. Do you remember what you did on your first birthday?
10. Can you eat 50 hamburgers in a single meal?

Think of five other stupid questions. Report your questions and your partner's answers to the rest of the class.

Exercise 6

Working with a partner, ask and answer these questions. Give your real opinions. Use *enough* in your answer. Report your partner's answers to the class.

> **EXAMPLE:** Why don't some people pass the TOEFL?
> *Because they don't know enough English to get a high score.*

1. How much money do you need for a happy life?
2. How well do you speak English?
3. When should children move out of their parents' home?
4. When should people get married?
5. How quickly or slowly should a person drive on the freeway?
6. What's an ideal age to retire?
7. What kind of a person should be President?
8. What is an important characteristic for a basketball player?
9. Why can't monkeys learn languages?

Focus 3

Degree Complements with *So* and *Such*

FORM
MEANING

- You can make statements of degree and result using *so* and *such*. Phrases with *so* or *such* express the degree. The result is expressed with a **that clause.**

SO:
so + adjective:

> **(a)** The water hyacinth has become **so dense** that boats can no longer navigate on southern waterways.

so + adverb:

> **(b)** It has spread **so quickly** that authorities have not been able to keep it under control.

so + many/few + (count noun)

> **(c)** Australia now has **so many rabbits** that they have had to build a fence across the country.
>
> **(d)** The rabbits had **so few natural enemies** that they multiplied rapidly.

so + much/little + (noncount noun)

> **(e)** The rabbits caused **so much destruction** that agriculture was seriously affected.
>
> **(f)** They ate **so much** that wild plants didn't provide a sufficient food supply.
>
> **(g)** They have had **so little success** with natural remedies that the government is considering using poisons to control the problem.

SUCH:
such + (a/an) + (adjective) + noun

> **(h)** The water hyacinth has become **such a serious problem** that there is no easy solution.
>
> **(i)** Waterways contain **such large amounts** of the weed that boats can no longer navigate.
>
> **(j)** Canals have suffered from **such destruction** from the weed that there isn't much chance of being able to repair them.

In spoken English and less formal written English, you can omit *that* in constructions using *so* and *such*.

(k) I'm so happy **that** I could fly.	**(l)** I'm so happy, I could fly.
(m) Denise is such a serious person **that** she probably doesn't know the meaning of the word *fun*.	**(n)** Denise is such a serious person, she probably doesn't know the meaning of the word *fun*.

Exercise 7

Restate these pairs of sentences as single sentences using *so* and **such**.

> **EXAMPLE:** There are many plants in the rain forest with possible medical uses. Scientists fear we may lose valuable medical resources if they are destroyed.
>
> *There are so many plants in the rain forest with possible medical uses that scientists fear we may lose valuable medical resources if they are destroyed.*

1. The world's forests are being destroyed at an alarming rate. We can't ignore the problem any longer.
2. The world population is growing quickly. We can't continue our old habits.
3. We have few alternative materials. We haven't stopped using trees for fuel.
4. There has been a rapid growth in population. There are no other places for people to live except the rain forests.
5. Some countries have few other natural resources. They are forced to exploit the rain forests for economic development.
6. The problems appear insurmountable. Some countries haven't even begun to address the problems.
7. The United Nations considers deforestation a problem. It is trying to establish conservation programs throughout the developing world.
8. The loss of the rain forests is a major global threat. The future of mankind may be at stake.

Exercise 8

Restate the ideas in these sentences by using *so* or **such**. Remember to take the negative implications of **too** and **not enough** into account as you write your result clause.

> **EXAMPLE:** The problem is too serious to be ignored any longer.
>
> *The problem is so serious that we can't ignore it any longer.*
>
> *This is such a serious problem that we can't ignore it any longer.*

1. Plant species are being wiped out too quickly for us to find out if they have important medical uses.
2. We don't know enough about the relationship between rain forests and weather patterns to take a chance.
3. Too little is known about the various medical uses of plants in the rain forests to risk destroying them.
4. Too many people are hoping to become rich from cutting down the rain forests for us to expect much change in the situation.
5. Some people fear that others are too greedy to consider the long-term effects on the planet.

Exercise 9

Identify the degree complements in this passage by underlining the result clauses where *that* has been omitted. The first paragraph has been done for you as an example.

(1)In American English, we use the term *tall tale* to describe stories that are so exaggerated <u>they become funny.</u> (2)No one really believes that they're true. (3)That's part of the fun. (4)The point of a tall tale is to tell such incredible lies <u>everyone ends up laughing.</u> (5)American folklore is filled with examples of tall tales.

(6)One famous tall tale is the story of the winter when the weather was so cold everything froze. (7)Each day things got a little colder. (8)First the usual things froze: water, plants, pipes, machinery. (9)Then it got worse. (10)It was such a cold winter, dogs and cats froze when they went outside, and birds fell out of the sky, frozen solid. (11)Then it got even worse. (12)It got so cold, people's words froze whenever they tried to talk. (13)You couldn't hear a single sound. (14)Of course, people like to talk, no matter how cold it is. (15)So people kept talking, and their words kept freezing just as soon as they came out of their mouths.

(16)Then suddenly the cold weather came to an end. (17)One day it was so cold, nobody could carry on a conversation because the words just froze right up, and the next day it was warm enough to wear shorts. (18)The change in weather was so great and so sudden, everything became unfrozen all at the exact same minute. (19)All those frozen words thawed out at once, and the resulting noise was so loud everyone became deaf.

Exercise 10

Give true answers to these questions using *so/such*:

EXAMPLE: What kind of a student are you?
> *I'm such a good student that I always do my homework before class.*

1. What kind of a student are you?
2. How quickly or slowly do you walk or drive?
3. Have you ever wanted something a great deal? How badly did you want it?
4. Did you ever eat a huge amount of food? What happened?
5. How high are the Himalayan Mountains?
6. Do you remember what you did on your first birthday?
7. How tall was the tallest person you've ever seen.
8. How hard is the TOEFL?
9. What happened in the most boring class you've ever been to?
10. How wonderful is your grammar teacher?

Activities

Activity 1

In the United States, children become adults in some ways at the age of 18. They are old enough to leave home, to do many things without permission from their parents, and to vote. But they are still not old enough to buy alcoholic beverages, and in some states, they still need their parents' permission to get married. At the age of 21, they are granted full "legal adulthood." But in the United States, teenagers are "growing up" so quickly that some sociologists have suggested that the age of adulthood should now be lowered to age 15.

- Poll your classmates to find out their opinions about when someone should or should not become an adult. Interview five people and find out what things they think people are old enough to do at the age of 15, and what things they feel people are still too young to do. Determine their opinions about the issues listed below and their reasons for these opinions. In addition, ask each person to think of two other examples of things that people are old enough to do at age 15, and two things they're still too young to do. For the things that they feel people are still too young to do, find out what age they feel is old enough for those things.

Activities	Old Enough/ Too Young?	Why?
marry and raise a family		
decide on a future career		
go on dates without a chaperone		
live independently outside the home		
serve in the army		
get a part-time job		
take care of young children		
vote in national elections		
fall in love		
drive a car		
make wise decisions about life		
pay taxes		
get a full-time job		
write poetry		
be a professional athlete		
have control their own money		

additional examples:

(1) _____

(2) _____

- Once you have gathered your information, summarize your findings for the class. Be sure to report any especially interesting reasons or additional issues that were mentioned by the people you interviewed. Can you make any generalizations or detect any interesting cultural patterns about how people feel about this subject?

Activity 2

In the Task, you read about two environmental problems from the past. Can you think of a similar problem or situation that might have a negative effect in the future? Some scientists believe that population growth, acid rain, ozone depletion, pollution, and increasing nuclear and industrial waste are all problems that need solutions very soon, before they get out of control.

- Working with a partner or in a group, identify some current ecological or environmental problems that are becoming serious. Present your list to the rest of the class. Each person should report on a specific problem.
- Describe the current situation, and the possible results if nothing is done about the problem.
- Discuss what you think needs to be done. What are the available solutions? What might prevent those solutions from happening?

Activity 3

In Exercise 9, you read a passage about **tall tales** and looked at an example of one.

- Work with some other people to invent a tall tale of your own to tell to the rest of the class. The more unbelievable the story, the funnier it will be.
- The class should decide which group told the tallest tale.

Activity 4

Do things like this ever happen to you?

- The driver of a bus I was riding on got so mad and shouted so loudly that his false teeth actually flew out of his mouth.
- My brother was so excited to get to Hawaii that he left his sweater and overcoat on the plane. He was pretty cold when he returned to Chicago.
- I was once in such a hurry to get to work that I left the house wearing one black shoe and one brown shoe.

Embarrassing experiences are universal. Most people have had an experience in which they have lost their temper, made a foolish mistake, or said or done something without realizing it. Have you ever "lost control"? Have you ever been so angry, frightened, happy, sad, or nervous that you did something without realizing it?

- Describe your experiences, or those of someone you know. You may wish to use one of the following situations, or think of some of your own:

  > I was once so happy that . . . .
  > My sister was so hungry that . . . .
  > When I was a child, I was once so frightened that . . . .
  > A student I know once got so nervous in class that . . . .
  > I once experienced such frustration that . . . .
  > I was once so angry that . . . .
  > A friend once got so drunk that . . . .
  > My friend Charley was so in love with his new girlfriend that . . . .

- Share some embarrassing moments with other people in the class. Listen to their stories.

Activity 5

Do you have all the money or all the free time you wish you had? Are there some things you are not able to do because you do not have enough resources or too many responsibilities, or because you are too busy?

- Make a list of these activities and what keeps you from doing them.

  EXAMPLES: I don't have enough time to read novels.

  I'm too poor to take a vacation this summer.

- Show your list to a partner. For each problem you have mentioned, your partner should make at least two suggestions on how to change or solve this difficulty. If you do not feel the suggestion will work, explain.
- Help your partner by suggesting solutions to his or her problems.

Activity 6

When are children old enough to move away from home? Different cultures have different opinions about when (and if) this should happen. In the United States, many young people begin to think about independent living as soon as they graduate from high school and begin a job or university studies. Although adult children may return to live at home for brief periods in their lives, such as immediately after college or during a divorce, it is rather unusual to see people in their mid-twenties still living with Mom and Dad.

- What are the opinions about this issue in other cultures? Interview people from three or four different countries. What is the average age at which people move away from home? What do other people think if someone leaves home at a much younger or much older age than the average? Are there different standards for men and women?
- Make a report on what you have discovered. It can be a written report or an oral presentation to the rest of the class.

Activity 7

When children become adults, they gain many rights and privileges. But they also lose some things as well. Many people sometimes wish that they could return to the days of their childhood.

- What are some of the disadvantages of becoming an adult? What things are you too old to do anymore? Write a paragraph about some of the things adults have to give up.

Factual, Inferential, and Predictive Conditionals

Task

In science classes, most people study some of the basic laws of mathematics, physics, and chemistry. Test your general knowledge of some of the principles of cause and effect. Tell what happens when certain general situations occur. Then test your ability to apply these principles to specific situations by telling what you think will happen as a result of a particular sequence of events. If you do not know the answers to the general questions (What happens when...), try to find someone in the class who does. Or, you can try to figure out the general rule based on what you know about the specific application. Work with other people and compare your answers to other groups in the class.

PRINCIPLES
What happens when...

- an acid is mixed with a base?

- light passes through a prism?
- a liquid reaches its boiling point?
- a solid reaches its melting point?

- two objects of different mass fall from the same distance?

- a moving object is acted upon by a force?

- a wave source is moving toward or away from the observer?
- objects in a system undergo rapid circular motion?

SITUATIONS
What will probably happen if...

- you mix vinegar and baking soda in a glass?
- you put on a pair of really cheap sunglasses?
- you leave a teakettle on a hot stove?
- you don't eat your ice-cream cone quickly enough?
- you drop a cannonball and a pea at the same time?
- you drop a pea and a feather at the same time?
- you try to aim a stream of water on a windy day?
- a car blows its horn as it passes by you at a high speed?
- you spin a plate full of marbles?

Focus 1

Identifying Conditional Statements

MEANING

- Conditional statements express one kind of cause-and-effect relationship: the relationship between a condition and a result. A conditional statement expresses a situation that is necessary for a given result to occur. There are a number of ways to express conditional relationships:

   (a) Both overeating and lack of exercise **can result** in obesity.

   (b) **Whenever** the temperature of water drops below 32°F, ice forms.

   (c) You should do well on the test, **providing** you have read the book.

   (d) **If** you have gone over the lectures, the test should be easy.

Exercise 1

Identify the sentences in these two passages that express conditional relationships. For each sentence, identify the condition and the result. The first paragraph has been done for you as an example.

1. (1)Chang and Eng were famous Siamese Twins in the nineteenth century. (The term *Siamese Twin*—identical twins, whose bodies are not completely separated—came from these two men.) (2)They were born in Siam (as Thailand was called in those days) and became famous in America as part of the Barnum and Bailey Circus. (3)In those days, if someone had a physical deformity (**condition**), they usually ended up working in a circus (**result**). (4)Extensive publicity in newspapers made people curious to see "Prodigies of Nature," and such shows were part of every circus. (5) Whenever the circus came to town, (**condition**)   people would stand in long lines and pay large amounts of money for the opportunity to see Chang and Eng (**result**).

   (6)The twins had bodies that were joined together at the hip, and they shared a single set of digestive organs. (7)Although they were twins, they had distinctly different personalities, and they didn't always get along. (8)Chang was friendly and outgoing and loved parties, but Eng was rather shy and withdrawn. (9)If Chang drank whiskey, Eng got drunk. (10)Whenever Eng felt hungry, Chang (who spoke better English) had to ask for food. (11)If they got into an argument about something, they would sometimes spend days not speaking to each other. (12)Each man got married (to a different woman), and each was the father of several normal children. (13)They died within a couple of hours of each other.

2. (1)Scientists fear that global warming will have a profound effect on the economy and standard of living of the world's people. (2)If the climate continues to grow warmer, the polar ice caps will begin to melt and the level of the world's oceans will rise. (3)Weather patterns will be affected, and areas of the planet that now get a lot of rain will get considerably less. (4)The climate may stabilize, providing the world can control its output of CO_2. (5)CO_2 is produced by burning fossil fuels, such as coal and oil. (6)If the world community can slow the wide-scale destruction of the world's rainforests, this might also slow down the process a little bit. (7)There are already indications that we may be too late. (8)Many regions of the world are experiencing their worst droughts in recorded history. (9)If these droughts continue for another year, there will not be enough water to support the present populations in those areas, and it will be necessary to ration water, or perhaps to sell it like gasoline, a liter at a time.

Focus 2

FORM

Conditional Sentences

FORM

- Conditional sentences (*if*/*then*) are the most common way to express cause-and-effect relationships and statements of condition and result.
- The adverbial clause (the *if*-clause) expresses the condition. The main clause expresses the result (the *then*-clause). Note that the word *then* is usually optional. See Focus 8 for a situation in which it is not.

Condition	Result
Adverbial Clause (IF)	**The Main Clause (THEN)**
(a) If I drive to work,	it usually takes about 45 minutes.
(b) If Chang and Eng got into an argument,	they would sometimes spend days not speaking to each other.
(c) If the climate continues to grow warmer,	the polar ice caps will begin to melt.

- The adverbial clause can precede or follow the main clause, but usually the condition precedes the result. When the adverbial clause precedes the main clause, it must be followed by a comma:

(d) If I take the bus to work, it takes about an hour and a half, but **providing I drive**, I can get there in 45 minutes.	**(e)** It takes about an hour and a half to get to work **if I take the bus**, but I can get there in 45 minutes **providing I drive.**
(f) Whenever a glass of water is exposed to air, some evaporation occurs.	**(g)** Some evaporation occurs **whenever a glass of water is exposed to air**

- Both condition and result clauses can be either affirmative or negative:
  - **(h)** If you **don't cover** a glass, the water eventually evaporates.
  - **(i)** If I take the bus to work, I **don't get** there as quickly.

Exercise 2

Express the conditions and results listed here as conditional sentences about a typical daily routine.

> **EXAMPLE:** **Condition**
>
> It is a regular workday.
>
> **Result**
>
> I always follow the same routine.
>
> *If it's a regular workday, I always follow the same routine.*

Condition	Result
There is milk.	I have cold cereal for breakfast.
I have forgotten to buy milk.	I usually have toast.
I have an early meeting.	I leave at 6:00.
It's a normal day.	I leave at 7:00.
I drive to work.	It usually takes about 45 minutes.
I take the bus.	It usually takes an hour and a half.
There is a traffic jam on the freeway.	It can take an hour or even an hour and a half.
Traffic continues to get worse.	I don't know what I'll do.
Current trends continue.	It will soon take four hours a day to get to and from work.

Focus 3

MEANING

Overview of Factual, Inferential, and Predictive Conditionals

MEANING

- This unit discusses three kinds of conditionals: **factual**, **inferential**, and **predictive**. Other conditionals are discussed in Unit 22 (Hypothetical Statements).
- Factual conditionals express a general cause-and-effect relationship. These can be about
  - timeless truths or generic relationships:
    - **(a)** If a glass of water is exposed to air, it eventually evaporates.
    - **(b)** When a baby duck hatches from an egg, it generally follows the first living thing it sees, because it thinks that thing is its mother.
  - habitual or recurrent situations:
    - **(c)** If I take the bus to work, it takes about an hour and a half, but if I drive, I can get there in 45 minutes.
    - **(d)** If there is an accident on the freeway, it takes a lot longer to get to work.

- Inferential conditionals express an inference about a specific situation. This inference can refer to
  - present time:

    (e) If your skin is covered with itchy red spots, you probably **have** chicken pox.

    (f) If Denise was at the meeting, she already **knows** about the new policy.
  - past time:

    (g) If the window is broken, the children **must have done** it.

    (h) If Peter was at the meeting, you can be sure that Denise **was** there too.
- Predictive conditionals express a prediction about a specific future situation.
  - future time:

    (i) If I need help, I**'ll be sure to ask** for it.

    (j) If the climate continues to grow warmer, the polar ice caps **will begin to melt** and the level of the world's oceans will rise.

Exercise 3

Decide whether these conditional statements are factual, inferential, or predictive.

1. If an acid is mixed with a base, a chemical reaction occurs.
2. If you were there, you must have seen the reaction.
3. If you leave that teakettle on the stove, all the water will eventually boil away.
4. If a liquid reaches its boiling point, it turns into a gas.
5. If you don't get a gas, you've done the experiment incorrectly.
6. If we mix this vinegar and baking soda in a container, there will be a chemical reaction that will produce CO_2, which in turn will put out the flame on this candle next to it.
7. If a solid reaches its melting point, it becomes liquid.
8. If you don't eat your ice-cream cone quickly enough, you'll have to drink it instead!
9. If objects in a system undergo rapid circular motion, they demonstrate the principle of centrifugal force.
10. If you spin that plate of marbles, they will all roll off the plate.

Focus 4

Factual Conditionals

- Factual conditionals generally (but not always) use the same tense in both the **if-clause** clause and the **then-clause** clause.
  - generic relationships and timeless truths:

Present Condition	Present Result
(a)If a glass of water **is exposed** to air,	it eventually **evaporates**. it **will eventually evaporate**.
(b)When a baby duck **hatches** from an egg,	it generally **follows** the first thing it sees.

  - habitual and recurrent situations:

Past Condition	Past Result
(c)If Change **drank** whiskey	Eng **got** drunk.
Present condition	**Present result**
(d)If I **drive** to work	it usually **takes** 45 minues

- In factual conditionals, you can substitute *when* or *whenever* for *if* with no change of meaning.
  - **(e) When** vinegar is added to baking soda, CO_2 is produced.
  - **(f) Whenever** I take the bus to school, it takes about an hour and a half, but **if** I drive I can get there in 45 minutes.

Exercise 4

Work with a partner and explain the meaning of each of these proverbs by restating the idea in a conditional sentence. Compare your paraphrases to those of other people in the class.

EXAMPLE: A man is known by the company he keeps.

If/Whenever you associate with people who behave in a certain way, other people will think you behave like that too.

A fool and his money are soon parted.

If you spend money foolishly, you lose it in a hurry.

1. Spare the rod and spoil the child.
2. People who live in glass houses shouldn't throw stones.

3. A stitch in time saves nine.
4. Don't cry over spilled milk.
5. Marry in haste, repent at leisure.
6. All work and no play makes Jack a dull boy.

Focus 5

FORM

Inferential Conditionals

FORM

- With inferential conditionals, there is no strict parallelism of tense. This is because we use the conditional to make a present or past inference. The result clause often contains an inferential modal such as *must*.

Condition	Inferred Result
Past Time:	**Past/Present Time:**
If Denise **was** at the meeting,	she probably **kept** a careful record of what happened. (**past**) she **knows** about the new policy. (**present**)
Present Time:	**Past/Present Time:**
If the window **is** broken,	the children **must have done** it. (**past**) we **need to be** careful of the glass on the floor. (**present**)

Exercise 5

Work with a partner. Ask each other questions about your childhoods: When you were a child, what happened in the following situations? Answer with an *if*-clause and a main clause with an adverb of frequency (*usually*, *sometimes*, etc.) Report each other's answers to the rest of the class.

EXAMPLE: be sick:

When you were a child, what happened if you were sick?

If I was sick, my mother usually gave me ginger ale.

1. get bad grades in school
2. tell a lie
3. hit your brother or sister
4. get good grades in school

5. help with chores
6. fall down and hurt yourself
7. disobey your parents
8. not want to go to bed

Focus 6

Predictive Conditionals

FORM

- Predictive conditionals normally have a simple present tense in the if-clause, and some explicit indication of future time (i.e. a future modal) in the result clause.

Condition	Predicted Result
(a) If John **arrives** tomorrow,	we **will have** a big party in his honor.
(b) If he **comes** on time,	we **might be able to get** to the show as well.

Exercise 6

Discuss the differences between classrooms in America and classrooms in other countries. Make statements that describe what happens in the two countries in the following situations:

> **EXAMPLE:** *In the United States, if a student comes late to class, the teacher will probably be annoyed.*
>
> *In Indonesia if a student comes late to class, the teacher probably won't be upset.*

- In the United States, what happens if:
- In Country_____ , what happens if:

A Teacher:	A Student:
sits on a desk	comes late to class
wears bluejeans to school	doesn't understand the lesson
says "I don't know."	asks a question
makes a lot of jokes in class	makes jokes in class
hits a student	doesn't do the homework
makes a mistake	copies another student's answers
doesn't give the students homework	makes a mistake

Exercise 7

Decide whether these sentences are predictive or inferential conditionals.

> **EXAMPLE:** If my brother runs out of money, he'll probably ask me for a loan.
>   *predictive*

1. If Bambang was at the lecture yesterday, he'll be able to help you with tomorrow's assignment.
2. If the TV is missing, someone must have broken into the apartment.
3. If Frans was born in Switzerland, he is still eligible to have a Swiss passport.
4. We'll definitely go to the concert if John is able to get tickets.
5. If Steve finishes the project by the end of next month, he might take a short trip to Mexico.
6. If the semester ends next week, we'll have a lot of unfinished assignments.
7. Peter knows what to do, if he was paying attention at the meeting.
8. If John is having a good time in Paris, he'll probably stay for a long time.

Focus 7

FORM

Modals in Future Predictions

FORM

- You can indicate the likelihood of a specific inference or prediction by choosing an appropriate modal form.

	Implied Meaning
(a) If you wash the dishes, I **will** give you **$5.**	The result will definitely happen if the condition is fulfilled.
(b) If you wash the dishes, I **may** give you **$5.**	The result may or may not happen, if the condition happens.
(c) If you have answered correctly, you **might** be a prizewinner.	It's quite possible that the result won't happen.

Exercise 8

What conditions are necessary for these situations to happen? Here are some results. Supply actual conditions that reflect the likelihood of the result:

EXAMPLE: I might not pass the TOEFL... .
> *I might not pass the TOEFL if I don't study hard.*
> *I might not pass the TOEFL if I go out to discos every night.*

1. You will pass the TOEFL... .
2. We might stop global warming... .
3. My teacher will be surprised... .
4. There won't be world peace... .
5. Traffic may continue to get worse... .
6. We could have to look for a new apartment... .
7. We may not have enough energy resources in the future... .
8. I might not be able to continue my studies... .
9. I will give my grammar teacher $500... .
10. The use of computers will become more widespread... .

Exercise 9

Here are some likely conditions. Supply a true result using the modal specified:

EXAMPLE: If I study really hard (won't)
> *If I study really hard I won't get bad grades.*

1. If I study really hard (might)
2. If the world climate continues to change (could)
3. If traffic continues to get worse (may)
4. If I get the opportunity to speak with my family back home (will)
5. If I don't pass the TOEFL (won't)
6. If I don't pass the TOEFL (will)
7. If my teacher gives me an A in this class (won't)
8. If I haven't done my homework (will)

Exercise 10

Work with a partner. Find out what he or she does or will do if he or she

1. is called to serve in the army
2. gets the flu
3. needs money for school
4. wins the lottery
5. falls in love with an American
6. gets lost in a strange city
7. sees someone committing a crime
8. starts getting homesick

Report your partner's answers to the rest of the class.

Focus 8

Implied Conditional Relationships

- You can also indicate conditional relationships between independent sentences. A condition can have multiple results that we express in more than one sentence.

  (a) If too many rats are crowded into a small area, they begin to show signs of aggression. They exhibit abnormal activity in feeding patterns and social behavior.

- In conversations, two different speakers can express a single conditional relationship. In such cases, you usually mark the result clause with *then*.

  (b) "I'm finally going to give you the money I owe you."
  "Oh really? **Then** I'll buy that book I've been wanting to read."

- You can also mark such results with clause substitutes *if so* and *if not*.

	Implied Meaning
(c) I hope John pays me the money he owes me. **If so**, I'll be able to buy that book Professor Montaigne told us about. **If not**, I might try to get it from the library.	If he pays me . . . If he doesn't pay me . . .
(d) Mary says she'll probably be at the party. **If not**, we won't need to worry about having enough soda.	If Mary isn't at the party . . .

Exercise 11

These sentences are implied conditions. Make a statement of appropriate result with *then*. Compare your answers to those of other students in the class.

EXAMPLE: Donald will probably be able to come to your party.
   Then we had better buy another case of beer.

1. The teacher says we're going to have a test tomorrow.
2. I'm worried about gaining weight.
3. This room is too warm.
4. I need some new clothes.
5. I don't have anything to do this Saturday night.
6. I'm worried about the high cost of hospital care.
7. I wasn't in class yesterday, so I didn't hear the lecture.

Exercise 12

These statements may or may not be true. Make two appropriate statements of result, one with *if so* and one with *if not*:

EXAMPLE: There may be a surprise quiz in grammar class next week.
If so, I'll be ready for it.
If not, I will have done a lot of studying for nothing!

1. Industrial pollution may be causing changes in the world climate.
2. Wearing a seatbelt could increase your chances of surviving a serious automobile accident.
3. There may be a link between breathing other people's cigarette smoke and developing lung problems.
4. A high TOEFL score may be a somewhat unreliable indicator of future academic success.
5. There appears to be a possible connection between certain kinds of fat in the diet and the development of cancer of the colon.

Focus 9

MEANING

Conditionals with *Whether or Not*

MEANING

- *Whether or not* indicates that a particular result will happen if the condition does or doesn't happen. *Or not* can precede or follow the adverbial clause.

	Implied Meaning
(a) We'll go on a picnic if it doesn't rain.	If it rains, we won't go.
(b) We'll go on a picnic **whether** it rains **or not**. **(c)** We'll go on a picnic **whether or not** it rains.	We will go **regardless** of the weather.

Exercise 13

Indicate if the results below **depend** upon the conditions given. If the results do **not depend** on the conditions, join the clauses with *whether or not*. If the results do depend on the given conditions, join the sentences with *if*.

EXAMPLES: **result:** The plane will leave on time.

condition: We are on board.

not dependent: *The plane will leave on time* **whether or not** *we are on board.*

result: The plane will leave on time

condition: There aren't too many other planes waiting to take off.

dependent: *The plane will leave on time* **if** *there aren't too many other planes waiting to take off.*

Result	Condition
1. Boiling water will eventually evaporate.	It is boiled rapidly.
2. People must pay taxes in the United States.	They are American citizens.
3. Students in American classrooms are expected to do homework.	They are absent from class the day before.
4. Marbles will roll to the outside edges of a plate.	The plate is rotated rapidly.
5. Two objects will fall at the same rate of speed.	They have the same weight.
6. Two objects will fall at the same rate of speed.	They have the same mass.
7. Most universities will admit foreign students.	They get a high score on the TOEFL.
8. Automobile accidents may occur.	The driver is wearing a seat belt.
9. Injuries may be less serious.	
10. The rate of global warming will decrease.	Worldwide emissions of CO_2 are decreased.

Focus 10

Conditionals with *Unless*

FORM

- You can also state conditional relationships with *unless*. *Unless* identifies a particular condition that must **not** happen in order for a result to occur.

	Implied Meaning
(a) We'll eat outside tomorrow **unless** it's raining.	We will eat outside tomorrow **if** it **isn't** raining.
(b) Denise refuses to come to the party **unless** Peter **is not** going to be there.	Denise refuses to come to the party **if** Peter **is** going to be there.
(c) Bambang won't begin university study this next semester **unless** he **passes** the TOEFL.	Bambang won't begin university study this next semester **if** he **doesn't pass** the TOEFL.
(d) John plans to stay in Paris for a whole year **unless** he **doesn't have** enough money.	John plans to stay is Paris for a whole year **if** he **has** enough money.

- Conditionals with *unless* most commonly follow the main clause. Conditionals with *if* most commonly precede the main clause.
  - **(e) If** I have enough money, I'll definitely go with you to Palm Springs.
  - **(f)** I'll definitely go with you to Palm Springs **unless** I don't have enough money.

Exercise 14

Identify conditions that could keep these results from happening, using *unless*.

> **EXAMPLE:** I will enter the university next semester
> *I will enter the university next semester unless I don't pass the TOEFL test.*
> *I will enter the university unless I decide to go home.*

1. You won't pass the TOEFL.... .
2. Global warming will continue to worsen.... .
3. There won't be world peace.... .
4. Traffic should continue to get worse.... .
5. Peter could have to look for a new job.... .
6. We may not have enough energy resources in the future.... .
7. I might not be able to continue my studies.... .
8. The incidence of AIDS will become more widespread.... .

Activities

Activity 1

What are the important differences between educational values in the United States and in other countries?

- Review the statements you made in Exercise 6. You were asked to compare the results of certain situations in an American classroom with those in a classroom in some other country.

Situation	Result in USA	Result in Another Country
A Teacher		
sits on a desk		
wears bluejeans to school		
says "I don't know."		
makes a lot of jokes in class		
hits a student		
makes a mistake		
doesn't give the students homework		
A Student		
comes late to class		
doesn't understand the lesson		
answers a question		
makes jokes in class		
doesn't do the homework		
copies another student's answers		
makes a mistake		

- In a small group, compare your responses. Then discuss the differences between what is expected of teachers and students in the United States compared to other countries that your group is familiar with.
- Decide on the 3–5 most important differences between the United States educational system and the systems of other countries you are familiar with.
- Present your differences and the reasons why you feel they are important to the rest of the class in either a written or oral report.

Activity 2

Choose some important ongoing current event or situation. It could be a news item (war between two countries, a new economic policy, etc.) or it could be an ongoing social or environmental trend (the increase in traffic and pollution, the change in world climate, etc.).

- Write a brief essay or make a presentation to the rest of the class explaining at least two possible scenarios for how the situation might be resolved. Be sure to mention what factors will be necessary for those scenarios to happen.

Activity 3

Should drugs be legalized? What do you think will happen if the government legalizes drugs? What do you think will happen if the government maintains the *status quo* (the situation as it is now)?

- Form a small group with three other students in the class to discuss one another's opinions on these issues:
- Three things that might happen if the government legalizes the use of drugs:

Your Opinion	Student A	Student B	Student C
1.			
2.			
3.			

- Three things that might happen if the government maintains the current policies:

Your Opinion	Student A	Student B	Student C
1.			
2.			
3.			

• Should drugs be legal? Why or why not?

Your Opinion	Student A	Student B	Student C
1.			
2.			
3.			

• Based on the information you have obtained by interviewing other students in your group, your group should decide these two questions:
What are the strongest reasons in favor of legalization?
What are the strongest reasons against legalization?
• Choose at least two reasons in each category and present them to the rest of the class.

Activity 4

Write a paragraph that discusses the conditions that result in variations in some part of your daily routine, such as how you travel to and from school or how you spend your evenings. See Exercise 2 for an example of the kinds of variations you may want to discuss.

Activity 5

Here are some well-known principles of economics. Write an explanation of these "laws." If you do not know about these relationships, find someone in the class who can explain them to you.

The relationship between supply and demand
The relationship between interest rates and levels of investment
The relationship between management style and worker productivity

UNIT

16

Adverbials of Purpose and Reason

Task

Nearly a billion people in the world are currently studying English. This means that we could probably identify nearly a billion different individual reasons to study English. What do you think some of those might be? What are your personal reasons and purposes for studying English?

- Identify three things that convinced you to study English.

  Sample reasons: It was required in my school.
  I've always liked American films.
  I knew that English has become the international language of business and technology.

- Identify three things that a good knowledge of English should enable you to do.

  Sample purposes: I want to study at an American university.
  I want to be able to understand English-language films without reading subtitles.
  I want to work in an import-export business.

- Next, poll three other students in the class to find out their answers to these questions.
- Form a small group with three other students whom you did not interview. Your group should have had interviewed at least ten other students total. Based on the samples you have, identify the five most common reasons for studying English and the five most common purposes. Rank these reasons and purposes in order from most frequent to least frequent.
- Write a brief essay or make an oral presentation to the class that reports your ranking of the most popular reasons and purposes for studying English.

Focus 1

Identifying Statements of Reason and Purpose

MEANING

- The question *Why?* asks about cause-and-effect relationships. We can answer such questions with two kinds of adverbial statements: reasons and purposes.

  (a) Why did you visit your grandmother? (**action**)

  (b) Because she was lonely. (**reason**)

  (c) In order to cheer her up. (**purpose**)

- **Statements of reason** refer to causes—situations that happen before an action. Adverbials identify the cause of an action, and the main clause (the action itself) identifies the effect.

Action—Main Clause	Cause—Adverbial of Reason
(d) John is studying in France	**(e)** because he loves French culture. Because of the school's reputation for fine teaching.
	(f) since the school has an exchange program with his university.
	(g) for he loves French culture.

- **Statements of purpose** refer to effects—situations that happen as the result of an action. Adverbials identify the result of an action, and the main clause (the action itself) identifies the cause.

Action—Main Clause	Effect—Adverbial of Purpose
(h) John is studying in France	**(i)** so (that) he can get a job with an international company.
	(j) (in order) to improve his chances for a job in Paris.
	(k) for fun.

212

Exercise 1

The following are answers to the question, Why is John leaving home and spending a year in France? Decide whether the answers are statements of purpose (result) or reason (cause).

> **EXAMPLES:** He is fascinated by French literature. (*reason*)
>
> He wants to spend an extended period of time in Europe. (*purpose*)

1. He has always wanted the experience of living in another culture ever since he was a child.
2. He knows that French is still widely spoken throughout West Africa, and he has made plans to travel there someday.
3. Being fluent in French will make him more employable in companies with overseas operations.
4. He got to know a French foreign exchange student very well when he was in high school.
5. He wants to visit the exchange student at her home.
6. He has always been interested in French cooking techniques.
7. His uncle told him that Paris was the most beautiful city in the world.

Exercise 2

Underline the adverbials of reason and purpose in this passage. Mark statements of purpose with *P* and statements of reason with *R*. The first paragraph has been done for you as an example.

(1) People may have many different motivations for doing things. (2) For example, people
(R)
may follow exercise routines <u>because they enjoy being physically active</u>, or they may do it
(P)
<u>to control their weight</u>, or have a more muscular physique or improve their cardiovascular

fitness.

(3) Behavioral scientists have identified two broad categories of motivation: **extrinsic motivation** and **intrinsic motivation.** (4) When somebody does something for a particular purpose, this is extrinsic motivation. (5) When somebody does something because they enjoy the activity itself, this is intrinsic motivation.

(6)For many people, one kind of motivation is more effective than the other. (7)People usually do things because they enjoy the experience, but they will also do unenjoyable things to obtain a particular benefit. (8)However, if the benefit is too hard to achieve, they will usually stop doing the unenjoyable activity after a time. (9)For example, people who have successfully lost weight have done so because they were able to develop new eating habits and to enjoy those new habits. (10)People who have dieted only to improve their physical appearance often regain the weight they have lost as soon as they stop dieting, because they no longer have the extrinsic motivation to eat less and they have not developed the intrinsic motivation to eat more sensibly.

Focus 2

FORM

Expressing Purpose and Reason

FORM

- These structures indicate **reason:**
  - *because of* with a noun phrase:
    (a) The picnic was canceled **because of** the bad weather.
  - an adverbial clause with *because, since,* or *for*:
    (b) The picnic was canceled **because** it was raining.
    (c) The picnic was canceled **since** the weather was so bad.
    (d) I didn't call, **for** I knew you wouldn't be there.
       (*For* is no longer commonly used in modern American English.)
- These structures indicate **purpose:**
- *for* with a noun phrase
  (e) She stood on the chair **for a better view.**
- an infinitive phrase (with or without *in order*):
  (f) She stood on the chair **to get** a better view.
  (g) She stood on the chair **in order to see** better.
- a clause with *so* or *so that*:
  (h) She stood on the chair **so she could see** better.
  (i) She stood on the chair **so that she could get** a better view.

Exercise 3

Think of a plausible reason (because) and a plausible purpose (in order to) for each of these questions. Compare your answers to those of other students in the class.

1. Why do people smoke?
2. Why do people decide to move to other countries?
3. Why are people interested in the private lives of famous people?
4. Why should people be careful about what they eat?
5. Why is it important to be an active participant in a language class?
6. Why are some people attracted to political careers?
7. Why is the TOEFL required of foreign students for admission to most American colleges and universities?
8. Why do most people get married?

Exercise 4

Underline the infinitives in this paragraph. Circle the ones that express purpose. (**Hint:** You can paraphrase infinitives of purpose with *in order to*.) The first two sentences have been done for you as an example.

(1)John was anxious to find a French family who he could live with. (2)He wanted to stay with a family (to improve his conversational ability.) (3)He was about to give up looking when he saw a notice on the bulletin board at school. (4)He called right away to make sure that the family was still looking for someone. (5)He was delighted to hear that they were, and he made an appointment to meet them that very afternoon. (6)The family appeared to be friendly, so John decided to move in the following week. (7)He started eating meals with the family right away to get an opportunity to practice what he was learning in his classes, and to start getting to know them as quickly as possible.

Focus 3

USE

Position of Adverbials of Reason and Purpose

USE

- Adverbials of reason and purpose (like most other adverbial clauses) can appear before or after the main clause.

main clause	adverbial clause
(a) I decided to study English	because my parents recommended it.

adverbial clause	main clause
(b) Because my parents recommended it,	I decided to study English.

- If the adverbial clause appears before the main clause, it may be because the writer wishes
  - to emphasize the reason or purpose instead of the action:
    - **(c)** Just because you're all being so nice to me, I won't assign any homework.
    - **(d)** In order to make sure things are sterile, all laboratory equipment must first be boiled.
  - to establish a context, which may apply to several sentences.
    - **(e) In order to apply to a university**, it is **first** necessary to do some research on the kind of institution you would like to attend. **Then**, you need to choose at least three possible schools and request application forms from each of them.
- There are some exceptions to this general rule:
  - Clauses of reason with *for* cannot appear before the main clause. *For* is actually a conjunction, like *and, but,* and *or,* rather than a true adverbial. The clause it introduces must come after the main clause.
    - **(f)** I visited my grandmother, for I knew she had been sick.
    - **(g)** NOT: For I knew she had been sick, I visited my grandmother.
  - Adverbials of purpose with *for* + **noun** can precede the main clause.
    - **(h) For practice**, John would regularly read French newspapers without a dictionary.
    - **(i) For excellent soup**, it's necessary to cook all the ingredients very slowly.
  - Clauses of purpose with *so* and *so that* do not usually precede the main clause.
    - **(j)** John went to France so that he could be immersed in a French-speaking environment.
    - **(k)** AWKWARD: So that he could be immersed in a French-speaking environment, John went to France.

Exercise 5

In the following sentences, decide why the author chose to put the adverbials before the main clause.

1. For want of a nail, a shoe was lost.
   For want of a shoe, a horse was lost.
   For want of a horse, a rider was lost.
   For want of a rider, a message was lost.
   For want of a message, a battle was lost.
   For want of a battle, a kingdom was lost.
   A kingdom was lost for want of a nail.

2. In order to improve vocabulary, it is necessary to read extensively, to try to guess the meanings of words from context, and to use a bilingual dictionary as little as possible.

3. Of course Hawaii is a good place for a vacation, but for a great vacation, I prefer Disneyland.

4. Since it's already so late, why don't we just forget about the meeting?

5. Because of technical difficulties, the program scheduled for this time will not be shown.

6. Because the test results had been rather disappointing, the teacher decided to spend the rest of the semester reviewing previously taught material.

Activities

Activity 1

Which form of motivation is more prevalent in your day-to-day activities: extrinsic motivation or intrinsic motivation?

> Extrinsic motivation is **purpose.** You do something in order to achieve something else, such as studying business in order to get a high-paying job in the future.

> Intrinsic motivation is **cause.** You do something because you like the activity itself, such as studying business because you love being a student and enjoy economic theory.

- Classify your basic motivations for these activities:

studying English	cooking	watching TV
reading newspapers	cleaning the house	sports activity/exercise
doing homework	meeting Americans	driving a car
keeping up with friends	going to church	shopping

- Using these and other activities and examples, write a brief essay about which form of motivation is more prevalent in your life.

Activity 2

Name three things you do because of intrinsic motivation. Interview three other students in the class and record their answers also. Here is a grid to help you record and organize the results of your data-gathering:

Your Activities	Classmate 1	Classmate 2	Classmate 3
1)_____	1)_____	1)_____	1)_____
_____	_____	_____	_____
_____	_____	_____	_____
2)_____	2)_____	2)_____	2)_____
_____	_____	_____	_____
_____	_____	_____	_____
3)_____	3)_____	3)_____	3)_____
_____	_____	_____	_____
_____	_____	_____	_____

- Compare your results to those of two or three other students in the class (whom you did not interview). This should give you a group of at least ten sets of answers to look at.
- As a group, decide on answers to these questions and present your ideas to the rest of the class.

> **What are the three most common characteristics shared by things that people do because of intrinsic motivation?** For example, do intrinsically motivated activities result in self-improvement? Are they inherently pleasurable for the person who does them? Do people feel deprived if they do not have an opportunity to pursue these activities?
>
> **Can you identify other characteristics that are not true for all but are true for most?** For example, can some, but not all, of these activities be classified as hobbies?
>
> **Are there identifiable categories of activity?** For example, are all athletic activities inherently intrinsically motivated? What about activities that can be classified as hobbies?

Activity 3

Is there an objective standard for right and wrong behavior, or does the morality of an action depend on your reason for doing it? Are bad actions ever justifiable because of pure motives?

- In a small group, discuss the following situations. For each situation decide whether there are ever any justifiable reasons or purposes for the following actions:

  leaving your family forever

  getting married to someone against your family's wishes

  not reporting a criminal to the police

  falling in love with someone other than your spouse

  taking something that doesn't belong to you

- Based on your discussion, decide whether a person's motivation or merely the actions themselves should determine the morality of his or her deeds.
- Present your opinions and your reasons to the rest of the class.

Activity 4

There is a famous American children's song that almost every American child learns this song at a very early age.

"I Know an Old Lady Who Swallowed a Fly."

Verse 1:
I know an old lady who swallowed a fly.
I don't know why she swallowed the fly.
Perhaps she'll die.

Verse 2:
I know an old lady who swallowed a spider
It wriggled and jiggled and tickled inside her.
She swallowed the spider to catch the fly
I don't know why she swallowed the fly.
Perhaps she'll die.

Verse 3:
I know an old lady who swallowed a bird.
How absurd! She swallowed a bird!
She swallowed the bird to catch the spider.
She swallowed the spider to catch the fly,
I don't know why she swallowed the fly,
Perhaps she'll die.

(Each verse adds another animal.)

Verse 4:
I know an old lady who swallowed a cat
Fancy that! She swallowed a cat.

She swallowed the cat to catch the bird,
She swallowed the bird to catch the spider
. . . (etc.)

Verse 5:
I know an old lady who swallowed a dog.
What a hog! She swallowed a dog.
She swallowed the dog to catch the cat.
She swallowed the cat to catch the bird . . .
(etc.)

Verse 6:
I know an old lady who swallowed a goat.
She opened her throat and swallowed the goat.
She swallowed the goat to catch the dog . . .
(etc.)

Verse 7:
I know an old lady who swallowed a cow.
I don't know how she swallowed the cow.
She swallowed the cow to catch the goat
. . . (etc.)

Last Verse: (This one's very short.)
I know an old lady who swallowed a horse.
She's dead, of course!

- How would this song be different if it had been about reasons instead of purposes? Would the grammatical structures need to be changed? What about the order? Would the song still begin with "I know an old lady who swallowed a fly" and end with "She's dead, of course"? Discuss your ideas with other students in the class. Can you rewrite the song so that it's about reasons instead of purposes?

- Many other cultures have similar kinds of songs. If you know another song like this, translate it into English, if you can, and teach it to the rest of the class.

17 Relative Clauses

Task

In 1943, two identical male twins were born in Ohio. Their mother wasn't married, so she gave the children up for adoption. They were separated the day after they were born, and grew up in different parts of the country, unaware of each other's existence. Neither one knew he had a twin brother until one twin moved to the same state where the other twin was living. Then friends began telling each of them that they had seen a man who looked just like him. The two men each began doing research and discovered their backgrounds and the fact that they were twins. They finally met each other in 1989.

Many researchers are interested in this case because they want to see if the two men have any similarities in spite of the fact that they have been raised in completely different environments. The researchers have found that there were, of course, many differences between the two men, but there are also some very intriguing similarities: They each had a blond wife and three children. They each had a yellow house. They both had dogs, and shared similar interests and hobbies. They both had jobs that called for a lot of travel.

Here is some information about one twin:

He has a modern ranch-style home.

His house is painted bright yellow.

He is married to a woman named Betty.

His wife has blond hair.

He has three children—all boys.

His eyes are each a different color.

He didn't tell his children that he had been adopted.

He sells plumbing supplies and his job involves a lot of travel.

He has a German shepherd named Prince.

His hobbies are stamp collecting and watching sports on TV.

His favorite beer is Miller.

He likes to play football.

Here is some information about the other twin:

He has an old-fashioned bungalow-style home.

His house is painted bright yellow.

He is married to a woman named Bernice.

His wife has blond hair.

He has three children—all girls.

His eyes are each a different color.

His children knew that he had been adopted.

He sells advertising space in magazines, and his job involves a lot of travel.

He has a poodle named King.

His hobbies are stamp collecting and watching sports on TV.

His favorite beer is Budweiser.

He likes to play basketball.

- Identify which characteristics both twins have and which are different. Use the information that describes the differences to answer the following questions with complete sentences. Start each answer with "The twin who . . . ." Here is an example:

  Which twin is married to Bernice?

  The twin who has an old-fashioned bungalow is married to Bernice.

  Which twin has children that are all girls?

  The twin who _____

  Which twin owns a dog named Prince?

  The twin who _____

  Which twin told his children that he had been adopted?

  The twin who _____

  Which twin drinks Miller?

  The twin who _____

  Which twin prefers basketball?

  The twin who _____

  Which twin lives in a ranch-style home?

  The twin who _____

- Check the accuracy of your answers by comparing them with those of another student. Which information did each you use to identify the appropriate twin?
- Taking both the differences and similarities between the two men into account, discuss the following question with your partner and decide whether you think the answer is *yes* or *no*.

  Is there a relationship between genetic makeup and personality traits?

- Present your opinion and at least two pieces of information that support your opinion to the rest of the class.

Focus 1

Combining Sentences

USE

- There are a number of structures that you can use to combine sentences in English:
  - **coordinating conjunctions** (see Unit 8):
    - **(a)** Jeff likes weight lifting. Matt likes weight lifting.
    - **(b)** **Both** Jeff **and** Matt like weight lifting.
    - **(c)** Jeff likes weight lifting, **and so does** Matt.
  - **subordinating clauses and phrases** (see Unit 13):
    - **(d)** Bambang Soetomo has decided to study in the United States. He wants an advanced degree in mechanical engineering.
    - **(e)** **In order to** get an advanced degree in mechanical engineering, Bambang Soetomo has decided to study in the United States.
    - **(f)** **Although** he is a little homesick, he still thinks his decision was a good one.
  - **relative clauses (embedding one sentence into another):**
    - **(g)** I visited an old friend last week after school. The friend lives in my apartment building.
    - **(h)** I visited an old friend **who lives in my apartment building** last week after school.
- Complex academic, technical, and literary prose generally tends to use embedding and subordination more often than coordinating conjunctions.

Exercise 1

Restate these combined sentences as two independent sentences. There may be more than one way to state the ideas, so compare your answers with those of other students in the class.

> **EXAMPLES:** Both Biff and Gladstone are trying to improve their appearance.
>
> *Biff is trying to improve his appearance. Gladstone is trying to improve his appearance also.*
>
> Although John is a little homesick, he still plans to stay in France for at least a year.
>
> *John is a little homesick. He still plans to stay in France for at least a year.*
>
> I wrote to an old friend who went to school with me last night after dinner.
>
> *I wrote to an old friend last night after dinner. She went to school with me.*

1. Jeff likes to get up early most days, but prefers to sleep late on weekends.
2. Denise has so much work to do to that she can't even consider taking a vacation.
3. Because they feel war is so destructive, many people are opposed to military solutions for international problems.
4. I once met a man who looked just like a friend of mine.
5. Bob is looking for a part-time job because he needs some extra money.
6. On Saturday mornings, I either clean the house or go shopping.
7. I know an old lady who swallowed a fly.
8. Although I have many friends, I still enjoy getting to know new people.

Focus 2

MEANING
Using Relative Clauses

MEANING

- You can combine sentences by modifying any noun with a relative clause. You can use relative clauses
  - in affirmative and negative statements:
    (a) I have a friend **who likes opera.**
    (b) I don't know anyone **that can give you that information.**
  - in questions:
    (c) Do you know any doctors **that don't charge too much for an office visit?**
    (d) Where can I find a plant **that doesn't need much water?**
  - to modify nouns that are either subjects or objects in the main sentence:
    (e) Charley told me about a beautiful woman:
    - subject
      (f) The woman that Charley told me about is very beautiful.
    - object
      (g) Last night I met **the woman that Charley told me about.**
    - indirect object
      (h) I sent **the woman that Charley told me about** a long letter.
    - object of a preposition
      (i) I'm crazy about **the woman that Charley told me about.**
  - to modify an indefinite noun—give more information about it:
    (j) I read **a book that was written by your economics professor.**
    (k) I finally met **a person who likes classical Japanese music as much as I do.**
  - to identify a definite noun—make the noun specific:
    (l) I want to visit **the hotel that I read about in the newspaper.**
    (m) Please pass me **the notebook that has my name on it.**

Exercise 2

Underline each relative clause in this passage and circle the word it modifies. The first two have been done for you as an example.

(1)My friend Charley has fallen madly in love. (2)He says that he has finally met (the woman) that he has been looking for all his life. (3)He has always been attracted to (women) that are intelligent and independent, and who have a good sense of humor and a love of adventure. (4)The woman that he has fallen in love with has all those things and more, according to Charley. (5)Even though physical appearance isn't the most important characteristic that Charley is looking for, he is quite happy his new friend is attractive and athletic. (6)She not only runs and skis, but also goes skin-diving, and has several other interests that Charley also shares.

(7)Charley was never completely happy with the women that he used to go out with. (8)There was always something that he wasn't satisfied with. (9)I used to tell him that he was too fussy. (10)The "perfect woman" that he was looking for didn't exist. (11)No real person can equal the picture that someone has in his or her imagination. (12)But I'm glad he has found someone that he thinks is perfect. I've never seen him happier.

Focus 3

FORM

Forming Relative Clauses with Relative Pronouns

FORM

- The term for a noun that is modified by a relative clause is **head noun**. To form a relative clause, change the noun that repeats the head noun to a relative pronoun and move it to the front of the relative clause.

            head noun   **repeated element**
(a) I read **a book.** Charley really likes **it.**

                relative pronoun
(b) I read a book **that** Charley really likes.

- The relative pronouns are *who/whom, that,* and *which.* Use *who* and *whom* with humans. Use *which* with nonhumans. Use *that* for either.

(c) I met the *man who* you told me about.

(d) I read the *book which* Kevin had recommended.

(e) I met the *man that* you told me about.

(f) I read the *book that* Kevin had recommended.

224

Exercise 3

Replace the relative pronoun *that* with *who*, *whom*, or *which* in the following sentences.

(1)I finally met the woman that Charley has fallen in love with. (2)She seems to be the kind of person that likes being active and adventurous. (3)She has a responsible position in a company that produces computer programs. (4)That's a field Charley is also interested in. (5)She likes hobbies that involve athletics and being outdoors. (6)She seems to like all of Charley's friends that she has met so far, including me. (7)Maybe one of these days, I'll meet a woman that's like Charley's new girlfriend. (8)In the meantime, Charley had better hope that she doesn't meet a man that's like me! I just might try to ask her out myself!

Focus 4

FORM

Relative Pronouns in the Relative Clause

FORM

- You can use relative pronouns to replace any noun or pronoun within the relative clause.

Underlying Sentence	Relative Clause
Subjects: (a) **The book** was published last year.	(b) I read the book **that** was published last year.
Objects: (c) Your professor wrote **the book.**	(d) I read the book **that** your professor wrote.
Indirect Objects: (e) Charley gave **the person** flowers.	(f) I met the person **that** Charley gave flowers to.
Objects of Prepositions: (g) Charley told me **about the person.**	(h) I met the person **that** Charley told me about.

- Remember that the replaced noun or pronoun of the underlying sentence does not appear in the relative clause.

(i) I read the book **that** was published last year.

(j) NOT: I read the book that **it** was published last year.

(k) I read the book **that** your professor wrote.

(l) NOT: I read the book that your professor wrote **it.**

(m) I met the person **that** Charley gave flowers to.

(n) NOT: I met the person that Charley gave **her** flowers.

(o) I met the person **that** Charley told me about.

(p) NOT: I met the person that Charley told me about **her.**

Exercise 4

In the following passage, circle the head noun of each relative pronoun *that, who, whom,* or *which*. Show the position of the replaced noun in the relative clause by drawing an arrow from the head noun to the place where the replaced noun has been removed.

EXAMPLE: I read (a book) that was published last year.

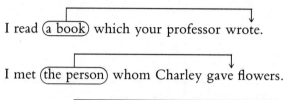

I read (a book) which your professor wrote.

I met (the person) whom Charley gave flowers.

I met (the person) who Charley told me about.

(1)I read an article the other day that interested me a great deal. (2)It reported on a survey that some sociologists conducted recently. (3)They examined the attitudes that American women have about men, and they identified some of the things that women consider to be important characteristics in a good husband or boyfriend. (4)The study determined that women seem to prefer men who can express their feelings. (5)Most women prefer husbands who they can talk to easily, and who they can share their problems with. (6)There were also several other things that women consider important in a partner. (7)A man's character or personality is more important to many women than the type of job that he has, or the amount of money that he makes. (8)Not surprisingly, most women want a husband that will take on an equal share of housekeeping and child-raising duties. (9)But the bottom line is this: Women want husbands who they can trust and depend on. (10)Unfortunately, more than 70 percent of the women who answered the questionnaires said they had husbands who did not meet these basic requirements in some way.

Focus 5

Deleting Relative Pronouns

FORM

- You can delete relative pronouns if they function as objects in the relative clause.
  - direct objects:
    - **(a)** I read the book **that** your professor wrote.
    - **(b)** I read the book your professor wrote.
  - indirect objects:
    - **(c)** The lady **that** Charley sent flowers is on the phone.
    - **(d)** The lady Charley sent flowers is on the phone.
  - objects of prepositions:
    - **(e)** I read the book **that** Charley was so excited about.
    - **(f)** I read the book Charley was so excited about.
- You can delete relative pronouns if they are in relative clauses with *be* as a main verb or auxiliary. In such cases, both the relative pronoun and *be* are deleted:
  - passive forms:
    - **(g)** I want a book **that was written** by an expert.
    - **(h)** I want a book **written** by an expert.
  - progressive forms:
    - **(i)** I think I know that woman **who is carrying** the blue suitcase.
    - **(j)** I think I know that woman **carrying** the blue suitcase.
  - prepositions:
    - **(k)** I tried to get an autograph from the baseball player **who is beside** the fence.
    - **(l)** I tried to get an autograph from the baseball player **beside** the fence.
  - adjective phrases:
    - **(m)** Anyone **who is** foolish enough to use drugs should be free to do so.
    - **(n)** Anyone **foolish enough** to use drugs should be free to do so.
- You cannot delete relative pronouns if they are subjects of a relative clause without **be.**
    - **(o)** Have you read the book **that** made Darryl Brock famous?
    - **(p)** NOT: Have you read the book made Darryl Brock famous?

Exercise 5

Delete the relative pronouns where possible and make the other necessary changes. (You cannot delete all the relative pronouns in this passage.) Prepare to explain your choices. The first paragraph has been done for you as an example.

(1)The kind of people ~~that~~ I like are usually people who have a good sense of humor. I like people who take other people's feelings into account, and people ~~who are~~ actively involved in making the world a better place.

(2)I like people who don't take themselves too seriously. (3)I find people who are lacking a sense of humor often tend to be pessimistic about many things. (4)A person who can't laugh at himself may not be able to distinguish between the things that are really important in life and the things in life that only seem important at the moment.

(5)I dislike people who strive to be important and powerful without also trying to be kind, fair, and helpful. (6)I dislike people who intentionally try to hurt other people's feelings. (7)People who are too concerned with their own power and position often try to take power from other people by making them appear or feel bad.

(8)I like people who think about important issues, such as the purpose of life and death or how to increase cooperation between different countries and people. (9)I prefer them to people who are only worried about the color that they want to paint their living room, or the kind of clothes that they would like to wear to a party that a friend is having next weekend.

(10)But I guess most of all I like people who are like me, and who also like me in return.

Exercise 6

Underline all the relative clauses in this passage. Make sure that you also include the ones that have deleted relative pronouns. The first two relative clauses have been done for you as an example.

(1)When World War I was finally over, it was called "The war to end all wars." (2)It was the most destructive war <u>the world had fought up to that time</u>. (3)Enormous numbers of young men <u>sent to battle from both sides</u> were killed or permanently crippled. (4)The war introduced weapons and techniques the world had never before seen. (5)The use of the airplane enabled armies on both sides to drop bombs with an effectiveness and precision that had been previously impossible. (6)Heavy casualties were also caused by the wide–scale use of a poison gas, called mustard gas, which permanently damaged the lungs of soldiers caught without gas masks. (7)There were more than 8.5 million casualties. (8)Most of these were people killed in action. (9)But many also died from intestinal diseases caused by the unsanitary conditions on the battlefield, or by infections that developed in lungs damaged by mustard gas.

(10)The peace established by "the war to end all wars" lasted less than a generation. (11)The most destructive war the world had ever known, like most wars, only provided a very temporary solution to the political and economic problems facing European governments at that time. (12)Just 20 years after the signing of the economically damaging treaty the winners had forced the losers to accept, Europe was again at war.

Focus 6

Differences Between Formal and Informal Usage

USE

- In formal English, use *who* as the relative pronoun for subjects in relative clauses. Use *whom* for objects in relative clauses.

  (informal) **(a)** This is the person Charley met at the party.

  ↑ **(b)** This is the person **that** Charley met at the party.

  ↓ **(c)** This is the person **who** Charley met at the party.

  (formal) **(d)** This is the person **whom** Charley met at the party.

- In formal written English, it is considered bad style to separate the preposition and its object. As a result, the preposition precedes the relative pronoun.

  (informal) **(e)** That's the situation I was so worried about.

  ↑ **(f)** That's the situation **that** I was so worried about.

  ↓ **(g)** That's the situation **which** I was so worried about.

  (formal) **(h)** That's the situation **about which** I was so worried.

  - In such cases, you must use *whom* or *which*, instead of *that* or *who*.

    (i) That's the situation **about which** I was so worried.

    (j) NOT: That's the situation **about that** I was so worried.

    (k) That's the woman **about whom** Charley told us.

    (l) NOT: That's the woman **about who** Charley told us.

Exercise 7

Make these sentences more appropriate for formal written English by putting the preposition at the beginning of the relative clause:

EXAMPLE: Pollution is a problem people are just becoming concerned about.

Pollution is a problem about which people are just becoming concerned.

1. Charley has fallen in love with the woman his cousin introduced him to.
2. I no longer have a friend I can go to the movies with, now that Charley is spending all his free time with his new girlfriend.
3. World War I did not really provide a solution to the problems it was fought for in the first place.
4. Turkey was one of the countries Germany was allied with during World War I.
5. This is the article I told you about.
6. Women prefer husbands they can discuss their troubles and concerns with.
7. Some of the issues my friends are concerned about are environmental destruction, political activism, and developing alternative energy sources.

Exercise 8

Change the second sentence in each of these pairs into a relative clause and insert it into the first sentence. Delete the relative pronoun wherever possible.

> **EXAMPLE:** Charley introduced the woman to his parents. He had been dating her for several weeks.
>
> *Charley introduced the woman he had been dating for several weeks to his parents.*

1. Last month Charley fell in love with a young woman. He had been introduced to her by some mutual friends.
2. She had a number of positive characteristics. Charley found them quite attractive.
3. She was careful to leave time for other activities and interests. These helped keep her healthy, and reflected her commitment to the needs of her friends and family.
4. She had a wonderful sense of humor. This made their times together relaxing and enjoyable.
5. From the first time they met, Charley felt there was a "special understanding" between them. He was unable to explain it.

Focus 7

MEANING

Whose in Relative Clauses

 MEANING

- When a relative clause contains a possessive form, you can use *whose* + **noun** in the same way that you use relative pronouns. You can use *whose* with
  - the subject of the relative clause:
    - **(a)** I met **a man. His house** was destroyed in the earthquake.
    - **(b)** I met a man **whose house** was destroyed in the earthquake.
  - the object of a relative clause:
    - **(c)** I got a letter from **a man.** We visited **his house** last week.
    - **(d)** I got a letter from the man **whose house** we visited last week.
  - the object of a preposition in a relative clause:
    - **(e)** I spoke to a man. We got an invitation **to his party.**
    - **(f)** I spoke to the man **whose party** we got an invitation to.
- You can never delete **whose** from a relative clause. It must always be used with a noun.
  - **(g)** I got a letter from the man **whose house** we visited last week.
  - **(h)** NOT: I got a letter from a man **house** we visited last week.
  - **(i)** NOT: I got a letter from a man **whose** we visited last week.

Exercise 9

Write the two underlying sentences that have been combined.

> **EXAMPLE:** I spoke to the man whose party we got an invitation to.
> *I spoke to a man. We got an invitation to his party.*

1. Bernice is married to the twin whose dog is named King.
2. The twin whose children are all girls told them about his background.
3. The children whose father didn't tell them that he had been adopted are all boys.
4. Betty is married to the twin whose dog is named Prince.
5. The modern ranch-style home belongs to the twin whose favorite sport is football.
6. Bernice is the wife of the twin whose friends first reported that they had seen his "double."
7. Twins whose upbringings are different still tend to have many characteristics in common.
8. People whose physical characteristics are identical also tend to have similar personalities and interests.

Exercise 10

Combine these sentences using *whose*.

> **EXAMPLE:** I got a letter from a man. We visited his house last week.
> *I got a letter from the man whose house we visited last week.*

1. Florence met a man. His twin brother is a well-known geneticist.
2. Jeff and Matt are roommates. Matt's nickname is "Akbar."
3. People may have similar personalities. Their genetic makeups are similar.
4. Joan took a class from a teacher. She knew his wife in college.
5. Mary Rae would like to go to the lecture by the mountain climber. She read about his latest climb in *Adventure Magazine*.
6. My friend has a dog. Its eyes are different colors.
7. I keep getting phone calls for some stranger. His last name is apparently the same as mine.
8. Charley finally succeeded in meeting the artist. He had been admiring her work for years.

Focus 8

USE

Using *Whose* vs. *Of Which* in Relative Clauses

USE

- *Of which* can indicate possessive meaning in relative clauses instead of *whose*. Choosing the appropriate form depends on the head noun and the level of formality. You generally use *of which* to refer to
  - nonliving, physical objects:
    - **(a)** At the back of the restaurant was **a shabby wooden table.** The top **of the table** was incredibly dirty.
    - **(b)** At the back of the restaurant was a shabby wooden table, **the top of which** was incredibly dirty.
  - abstract concepts, characteristics, ideas:
    - **(c)** I read a novel, **the ending of which** was so shocking that I couldn't sleep after I finished it.
    - **(d)** Crete was a civilization, **the beginnings of which** are now lost in the mists of time.
- In formal writing and speech, *whose* usually refers to living (usually human) things. In informal writing, you can use *whose* for concepts, ideas, and so on, or even physical objects:
  - **(e)** This is the man **whose** book we were talking about.
  - **(f)** I read a novel **whose** ending was so shocking that I couldn't sleep after I read it.
  - **(g)** Crete was a civilization **whose** beginnings are now lost in the mists of time.
  - **(h)** That's the car **whose** owner lives next door.
- Because using *of which* seems very formal and using *whose* may seem illogical, writers try to avoid both *of which* and *whose* constructions when discussing abstract antecedents or physical objects. They more commonly express the same idea with different relative clauses or without relative clauses.
  - **(i)** The ending of the novel **(that)** I just read was so shocking that I couldn't sleep after I read it.
  - **(j)** **The beginnings of Cretan civilization** are now lost in the mists of time.
  - **(k)** That car **belongs to** my next-door neighbor.

Exercise 11

Combine these sentences using *whose* and *of which*. Decide how formal each choice is, and whether the informal version is logical or not. Then try to restate the ideas in a way that avoids the problem, by avoiding *whose* and *of which*.

EXAMPLE: Scientists have discovered a new disease. Its causes are still unknown.

Scientists have discovered a new disease the causes of which are still unknown. (very formal)

Scientists have discovered a new disease whose causes are still unknown. (informal—and a little illogical, since a disease is not a person)

The causes of the new disease that scientists have discovered are still unknown. (possible restatement)

Although scientists have discovered a new disease, they still don't know its causes. (possible restatement)

1. My brother bought a used car. Its tires need to be replaced immediately.
2. We'll be going to an opera. The synopsis of the opera can be found in the program.
3. I saw a mysterious-looking symbol. Its meaning was as mysterious as its design.
4. Darryl has finished his latest book. Its cover had his picture on it.

Focus 9

MEANING ● USE

Using *Where* and *When* in Relative Clauses

MEANING
USE

- There are two relative adverbs *where* and *when*, which behave very much like *whose*.

Form/ Use	Sentences with Relative Adverbs	Implied Meaning
where Reference to *there* or prepositions meaning *in/on/at* that place.	**(a)** We arrived at a hotel **where** we were told we had no reservation.	We arrived at a hotel. We were told that we had no reservation **there**. We arrived at a hotel **at which** we were told that we had no room.
when Reference to *then* or to prepositions meaning *in/on/at* that time.	**(b)** Please come to my house at another time **when** I will be able to see you. **(c)** I can't remember a time in my childhood **when** I was completely happy.	Please come to my house at another time. I will be able to see you **then**. I can't remember a time in my childhood **during which** I was completely happy.

- You cannot delete *when* and *where*. Most writers prefer them over *at which* or *during which* for all but extremely formal contexts.

Exercise 12

Combine these pairs of sentences, using *when* or *where*.

> **EXAMPLE:** In yesterday's newspaper, I read about a demonstration.
> All the protesters blew whistles and stopped traffic at the demonstration.
> *In yesterday's newspaper, I read about a demonstration where all the protesters blew whistles and stopped traffic.*

1. My father can remember the old days. There were no televisions or computers in those days.
2. I'm going to start reading again. I stopped reading at the bottom of the page last night.
3. Jeff grew up in a small town in Kansas. Everybody there knew everybody else.
4. Most people think New Orleans is a great place. Everyone can live as they please there.
5. Do you remember that Halloween party at Alice's house? That evening everyone ran outside in their costumes and surprised the neighbors.

Exercise 13

Combine these numbered pairs of sentences in this paragraph, using *when* or *where*.

(1) The Sixties were a time of rapid social change. Many people explored alternative life-styles at that time. (2) The change was greatest in urban areas. There were a lot of young people studying at universities and colleges in those areas. (3) San Francisco was one center of the hippie movement. Many people gathered there during the famous "Summer of Love" in 1968. (4) The Haight-Ashbury was the center of activity. People from all parts of the city came to Haight-Ashbury to listen to rock and roll concerts. (5) People today look back upon the Sixties as an important time. Old values were brought into question, and people experimented with new answers at that time.

Exercise 14

Combine these numbered pairs of sentences in this paragraph, using *when* or *where*.

(1) We stayed at a hotel in Mexico. They had trained monkeys in the lobby of the hotel. (2) We arrived at the hotel during a festival. All the hotels in town were full during the festival. (3) Someone had put our reservation in the wrong file. No one else could find it in that place. (4) They put us in a very small room. There were no windows there. (5) Our vacation became much more pleasant on the next day. We were moved to a larger room on the next day.

Exercise 15

Combine these numbered pairs of sentences in this paragraph using *whose*, *where*, and *when* or *relative pronouns.*

(1)Charley wants to make some changes in his life. These changes involve both his life-style and his social activities. (2)Charley wants to find a new place to live. There is enough room for a dog. (3)He plans to move next year. The lease on his old apartment expires then. (4)He's looking at a new apartment. There is a balcony in the apartment, so he can grow some flowers. (5)Charley also wants to get married to someone. Her political beliefs are similar to his own. (6)He hasn't found anyone yet. No one seems to share his interest in politics and sports. (7)He often goes to coffee shops. People of similar interests go there on weekends. (8)He's thinking of putting a personals ad in a paper. A lot of people advertise in that paper in order to meet others with similar interests and backgrounds.

Activities

Activity 1

In Exercise 4, you read about some of the things that American women consider important in a husband. Divide into groups of men and groups of women. In your group, discuss the characteristics of **"the ideal spouse."**

- Prepare a list of 10–15 statements like these:

    "The ideal husband is someone who takes an equal responsibility for raising the children."

    "The ideal wife is a person who is able to maintain a good sense of humor."

    What ideals do you all agree on? Are there ideals that are controversial?

- Present your statements to the other groups. Compare the ideals presented by women's groups and the ideals presented by men's groups.

- Discuss these questions as a whole class or in groups of mixed sex: What are the important similarities and differences between the statements of the two kinds of groups? Are there some ideals that all men share, no matter what culture they come from? Are there some ideals that all women share, no matter what culture they come from? Are there some ideals that everyone shares, regardless of gender?

Activity 2

What kind of people do you like most? What personal characteristics do you appreciate and respect in other people? What personal characteristics do you find distasteful?

- Write a brief essay describing personal characteristics in people that you like and dislike. You may wish to look at the essay in Exercise 5 for some ideas about the kinds of characteristics other students have identified, and for an example of the kind of essay you should write.

Activity 3

The word *daffy* means "silly." A *daffynition* is a made-up definition for a word that doesn't really exist. In fact, the word *daffynition* is, itself, a made-up word. Try to invent daffynitions for these made-up words.

Here's an example: **Murphler:** A murphler is someone who makes a lot of noise when he eats.

Daffynitions:

Who or what is a **murphler**?

What do **parahawks** do?

What does **chemicophysiologicalistic** mean?

What do **flurps** and **mompsquats** have in common?

What are **quatchels**?

Define **hypervoraciosity**.

- Share your daffynitions with the rest of the class. The class should decide who has the most believable daffynition, and who has the most amusing daffynition for each term. Make up some of your own imaginary words and provide daffynitions for them as well.

Activity 4

A *pacifist* is someone who doesn't believe in fighting wars, under any circumstances. Are you a pacifist, or do you believe that there can be such a thing as a "justifiable" war? Is there a difference between a *war* and a *revolution*? Give some examples of armed conflicts that you feel were or were not justifiable. Under what circumstances is it acceptable to take up arms against your own government, other countries, or other groups of people within your own country?

Organize a debate between the doves (a slang term for pacifists) and the hawks (people who believe that wars are justifiable). You may wish to discuss the issues in terms of wars in general, or a specific conflict that you are familiar with (such as the Second World War, the Vietnam War, or the War in the Persian Gulf).

Activity 5

All languages have words that describe concepts or ideas that are not found in other languages. For example, in English the words *alone* and *lonely* have quite different meanings. One can be alone without being lonely, and lonely without being alone. But in many languages, these concepts are expressed by a single word.

- Choose a word from another language that you are familiar with that expresses a concept that doesn't exist in English, or that suggests a very different implication than its English counterpart.

- Present your word to the rest of the class, give a definition of it, and explain why you think that there is not a word for that concept in English.

Activity 6

In American English, we often make a "dramatic introduction" in certain formal situations. A dramatic introduction lists a person's characteristics and accomplishments and ends with the individual's name. Here's an example of a "dramatic introduction":

> Ladies and Gentlemen, it is my great pleasure to introduce an individual whose honesty and sincerity are well-known, whose commitment to education is serious and wide-reaching, whose work in the field of linguistics has helped many students understand English better, whose wit and kindness make working together a pleasure. Ladies and Gentleman, I give you our English teacher, Rebecca Buckley.

- Make a dramatic introduction for one of your classmates, or a real person whose life and accomplishments you are familiar with.

Activity 7

Describe the qualities and characteristics of the ideal location for

a vacation
meeting new people
spending a rainy afternoon
retiring
raising a family

- Think of at least three statements for each category. (An ideal place for a vacation is a place where there is lots of sunshine.)
- Compare your descriptions to those of several other people.

Activity 8

Nicknames are often given to people to describe some physical characteristic or aspect of their personality. For example, someone with red hair is often called "Red." Someone with curly hair (or sometimes someone who is bald) is called "Curly." Someone whose nickname is "Sunny" is probably a cheerful, outgoing person.

- Here is a list of some other common American nicknames. Working with a partner, decide what characteristics would be likely for someone whose nickname is

Blondie	Cowboy	Muffin
Bubbles	Doc	Sport
Butch	Gramps	Tiger
Buster	Honey	Tubby

- Report your ideas to the rest of the class by using this kind of sentence: We think that someone whose nickname is_____ is probably a person who. . . .
- What else can you say about these nicknames? Are they used for children or adults? Could you apply them to both men and women? Do you think people would use these nicknames with people to their faces or behind their backs?
- Discuss how nicknames are used in other countries. Do you have a nickname? Why do people call you that name?

18

Special Problems in Using Present Time:
Temporary versus Permanent, Actions versus States

Task

Mary Rae is on a vacation in Florida, but she's not relaxing on the beach. She is participating in a program called Outward Bound. This program involves a lot of strenuous physical activity. People go to Outward Bound in order to challenge themselves and test their limits for physical and mental endurance. They come from ordinary jobs and spend two weeks in a wilderness environment hiking long distances, rowing many miles, and sleeping under the stars in primitive camps. The program is physically exhausting, but most people find it deeply satisfying as well. Many people say that Outward Bound has taught them things about themselves that they never knew. Most people are surprised to learn that they are much braver, stronger, and more capable than they originally thought.

   Here is some information about Mary Rae and her life in New York, where she lives. There is also information about the things she is doing as part of her Outward Bound Program.

Mary Rae in New York	Mary Rae at Outward Bound
• Occupation: advertising account executive: visits clients, supervises a 25-person office • lives in a studio apartment • often eats take-out Chinese food • worries a lot about her career • doesn't get much exercise • doesn't spend much time outdoors • often has trouble falling asleep • doesn't feel particularly challenged by her daily routine • is somewhat bored with life • is not learning anything new • doesn't make new friends easily	• Occupation: program participant: rows, hikes, climbs trees, builds fires, catches fish, picks wild fruit, cooks • sleeps in a tent, lives in a canoe • cooks all her own food, catches fish, and picks wild fruit • doesn't think about her career at all • hikes or rows 12–14 hours each day • doesn't spend any time indoors • falls asleep almost instantly • feels considerably challenged by each day's activities • is excited about growing stronger and more capable • is learning something new every day • is making new friends easily

- What differences are there between the life she usually lives and the life she is living at Outward Bound? Write a paragraph comparing Mary Rae's normal life with her life at Outward Bound. Each sentence should contrast some aspect of her life in New York with her life in Florida. Here are some examples to get you started.

  Mary Rae normally spends her day as an account executive in a busy advertising firm, but here at Outward Bound she is spending 12 to 14 hours a day in vigorous physical activity. In New York, she supervises 25 employees, but here in Florida she is only supervising herself. . . .

- Once you have written your paragraph, compare it to that of another member of the class. Did you use the same verb tenses to describe the activities, states, and situations in New York and Florida?

- Based on Mary Rae's experience, would you ever consider going to an Outward Bound Program? Why or why not?

Focus 1

USE

Using the Present Time Frame in Generic Statements

USE

- We use the Present Time Frame most often to talk about general truths and relationships that are either true now or always true. Generic statements, conditional statements, and frequency adverbs are often used to indicate this generic meaning. This use of the Present Time Frame is extremely common in scientific and technical writing.

  (a) Supply **affects** demand in several ways. **If** supply exceeds demand, the cost of the commodity **generally decreases**.

  (b) **When** cost increases, demand often **drops**. Decreased demand **eventually results** in decreased supply.

Exercise 1

Here are reports of two scientific experiments. Change them into the Present Time Frame so that they serve as statements of general scientific principles, rather than as accounts of specific experiments.

EXAMPLE: *When baking soda is added to vinegar, a chemical reaction occurs....*

EXPERIMENT 1:

(1)When baking soda was added to vinegar, a chemical reaction occurred.(2) The baking soda bubbled, and CO_2 was produced by the combination of elements. (3)When a candle was put next to the container while the chemical reaction was taking place, the flame on the candle went out.

EXPERIMENT 2:

(4)We wanted to determine whether weight affected the rate of acceleration of objects falling through space. (5)Two objects of similar size and shape, but substantially different weights— a cannonball and a volleyball—were dropped from the same height. (6)We found that both objects hit the ground at the same time. (7)This indicated that the acceleration due to gravity was constant.

Exercise 2

This is a case study illustrating the economic principle of supply and demand. A case study is an account of a specific situation. Rewrite this case study so that it becomes a general statement of basic economic principles and applies to more than this particular situation. You will need to change some of the specific references as well as the verb forms. Change *Kansas* to *rural areas,* change *wheat* to *commodities,* change *farmers* to *producers*.

(1)In Kansas, before the development of good interregional transportation, the price of wheat was determined by the relationship between its supply and the demand for it. (2)Supply was determined by how much wheat was available. (3)Demand was determined by how many people needed to buy it. (4)When the demand for wheat rose, the price also rose. (5)Farmers responded to the price increase by producing more wheat, since they could get a more profitable return on their investment of time and effort because of the higher prices. (6)With more wheat available, the competition to sell wheat also increased, and the prices of the wheat began to drop. (7)Fluctuations in wheat prices were extreme and continuous.

(8)But with the development of better interregional transportation, a more constant supply became available, since extra wheat could be brought in from other places. (9)Similarly, a more constant demand existed, since wheat could be sent to other areas of the country where harvests had not been as good.

Focus 2

Choosing Present Progressive or Simple Present Tense

USE

- When you use the Present Time Frame to talk about specific actions instead of general relationships or recurring events, it is necessary to make a basic distinction between things that are **true now** as opposed to things that are **always true.** Present progressive verb forms describe specific ongoing actions, and simple present verb forms describe things that are always true.

Recurring Activity, Habit, or Skill	Ongoing Activity Happening Now
(a) My friend **speaks** Spanish.	**(b)** He **is speaking** Spanish. He must be talking with Carlos.
(c) Bob **plays** the piano.	**(d)** Bob **is playing** the "Minuet in G" by Beethoven. It's so pretty!
(e) The children **sleep** in the upstairs bedroom	**(f)** Don't make too much noise. The children **are sleeping.**

Permanent Situation Extended Duration	Temporary Situation Limited Duration
(g) I **live** in Texas.	**(h)** I'm living with my uncle for the summer.
(i) Baking soda **works** well as a cleansing agent.	**(j)** The refrigerator **is working** well. I just had it repaired.

Exercise 3

Decide whether the verbs in these sentences refer to habits, skills, and recurring situations or to ongoing events. Choose the correct verb tense (**simple present** or **present progressive**) to indicate the difference in use. More than one answer may be correct, so be ready to explain why you chose the form you did.

1. Don't turn on the TV. I _____ (talk) to you!

2. My brother _____ (speak) a little Spanish. Let's ask him to help us with

   this letter from Mexico.

3. Janet _____ (study) for a biology midterm, so I don't think she can come

   to the party.

4. I _____ (leave) for work about 7:30 every morning.

5. Peter _____ (make) a big mess in the kitchen. You'd better go help him.

6. Gladstone _____ (do) his best, but he still can't run as fast as the others.

7. I _____ (try) to understand you, but you will have to speak more slowly.

8. Scientists _____ (discover) that many forms of mental illness are caused by chemical imbalances in the brain.

9. The traffic situation _____ (get) worse every year.

10. Learning a language _____ (get) easier when you practice outside of class.

Exercise 4

Decide whether these sentences talk about a permanent or temporary situation. Choose the correct verb tense (**simple present** or **present progressive**) to indicate the difference in meaning.

Bob (1) _____ (not take) a vacation this summer, because he (2) _____ (not think) that he (3) _____ (have) enough money. He (4) _____ (teach) high school chemistry, so he (5) _____ (get) three months of vacation, but teachers (6) _____ _____ (not make) much money. So he (7) _____ (look for) a temporary job, since he can't afford to go anywhere. He (8) _____ (try) to find work as a computer programmer. But most companies only (9) _____ (hire) workers on a permanent basis. Bob (10) _____ (find) that it is difficult to locate short-term employment. He (11) _____ (get) depressed about the prospects of three months of nothing to do and nowhere to go. No matter how hard he (12) _____ (search), he (13) _____ (begin) to realize that he may have to take a vacation, whether he (14) _____ (want) one or not.

Exercise 5

Describe your daily routine. What activities do you do on a regular basis? Describe your typical day, starting from the time you wake up and ending with going to sleep at night. Write at least eight sentences about things you do on a regular basis.

Now describe three things that you are currently doing differently from normal, and why you have changed your routine. For example, "I'm living in a dormitory, because I have moved to a new city to go to school."

Focus 3

MEANING

Stative Verbs

MEANING

- Stative verbs describe conditions or states. They do not usually take progressive form.
  (a) I **know** that you are unhappy right now.
  (b) NOT: **I am knowing** that you are unhappy right now.
- They fall into several general categories:

Sensory Perception	Mental Perception	Emotional Perception	Logical Relationship	
Appearance	**Knowledge and Belief**	**Feeling and Attitude**	**Cause and Effect**	**Measurement**
see	agree/	love	result in	weigh
hear	disagree with	like	require	cost
feel	believe	hate	depend on	measure
appear	doubt	dislike	mean	equal
look	feel (believe)	appreciate		
seem	imagine	prefer	**Possession**	**Entailment**
smell	intend	want		
sound	know	need	belong to	contain
taste	recognize	mind	possess	consist of
resemble	realize		have	include
look like	remember		own	entail
	suppose		owe	
	think (believe)			
	understand			
	consider			

Exercise 6

Work with a partner and ask him or her *Wh*-questions for the cues given. Your partner should give true answers, and then ask the same questions of you:

> **EXAMPLE:** which parent/resemble most
> *Which parent do you resemble most?*
> *I resemble my mother more than my father.*

1. what kind of fruit/taste best
2. what way/think/most effective to learn a foreign language
3. how/a sick person/appear
4. what/your notebook/contain
5. what/a handshake/mean
6. what activity/your parents appreciate/your doing
7. what/getting a BA degree/require
8. how many _____/you/own
9. who /that _____/belong to
10. what/not understand/American culture

Exercise 7

Report your partner's answers from Exercise 6 to the rest of the class.

> **EXAMPLE:** *Yoshiko resembles her mother more than her father.*

Focus 4

Verbs with Both Stative and Action Meanings

MEANING

- You can also use some stative verbs to describe actions. When you use them as action verbs, they usually appear in present progressive to distinguish their meaning from their stative uses. Here are some common examples:

Verb	Stative Meaning	Action Meaning
have	**(a)** I **have** three brothers. **(possess)**	**(b)** We**'re having** a great time. **(experiencing)** **(c)** Mary**'s having** a party next week. **(giving)**
mind	**(d)** I **don't mind** smoke. **(object to)**	**(e)** He**'s minding** the children now. **(taking care of)**
see	**(f)** I **see** your point. **(understand)**	**(g)** John **is seeing** a specialist about his back. **(consulting)**
think	**(h)** I **think** you're right. **(opinion)**	**(i)** Be quiet! I**'m thinking.** **(mental activity)**
consider	**(j)** I **consider** money to be the root of all evil. **(opinion)**	**(k)** I**'m considering** going to Hawaii for vacation. **(mental activity)**
depends on	**(l)** Athletic ability **depends on** strength and practice. **(requires)**	**(m)** I**'m depending on** John to help me move next week. **(relying upon)**
be	**(n)** Jack **is** a teacher. **(identity)**	**(o)** Those children **are being** very noisy. **(behaving)**
feel	**(p)** I **feel** that you're the best choice. **(believe)**	**(q)** I**'m feeling** a little sick today. **(experiencing)**

- Other stative verbs can indicate the **act** of perception or measurement, or the perceptions or measurements themselves.

Verb	Perception/ Measurement	Act of Perception/ Measurement
smell	**(r)** The flowers **smell** wonderful.	**(s)** The dog **is smelling** the clothes of the missing boy.
taste	**(t)** That cake **tastes** delicious.	**(u)** Our host **is tasting** the soup to make sure it's not too salty.
weigh	**(v)** Joe **weighs** almost 100 kilos.	**(w)** The butcher **is weighing** that piece of meat.

Exercise 8

Decide whether these verbs express an action meaning or a stative meaning and indicate that meaning by writing the verb in **simple present** or **present progressive** tense in the blanks. In some cases, both answers may be correct, so prepare to explain why you chose the answer you did.

1. This cloth _____ (feel) really nice.

2. I _____ (consider) applying to go to Outward Bound.

3. Why did you ask that question? You _____ (be) really rude!

4. I _____ (believe) that Mary Rae _____ (have) a good experience at the Outward Bound program.

5. I don't like this beer. It _____ (taste) bitter to me.

6. I like people who _____ (mind) their own business and don't try to tell others what to do.

7. Bambang _____ (doubt) that he will be able to pass the TOEFL next week.

8. It _____ (look) as if we will get some rain later this week.

9. John _____ (feel) a little guilty about leaving Mary for so long. But I'm sure he'll get over it.

10. Learning a new language _____ (require) a lot of hard work.

11. These days the government _____ (require) people to take drug tests in order to get a government job.

12. Those children _____ (be) so naughty. I wish someone would make them stop teasing that poor kitten!

Focus 5

Other uses of the Present Time Frame

USE

- You can also use the Present Time Frame to
  - report actions as they are being performed. This use of the Present Time Frame is extremely common on radio and television shows that broadcast sporting events or "how-to" programs, such as cooking classes:
    - **(a)** Here's how we **make** cookies. First we **mix** a cup of flour and two eggs together in a bowl. Next, we **mix** in some sugar. A cup and a half **is** probably enough, but if we **want** sweeter cookies, we **add** at least 3 cups of sugar.
    - **(b)** Canseco **throws** the ball. Mays **hits** it. He **makes** a run to second base. He's **tagged** by Brown.
  - tell stories orally in more informal situations. This use of the Present Time Frame is most common with joke telling and stand-up comedians:

    One day I'm walking down the street. I see this guy talking on a pay phone. I know he's mad about something because I can hear him screaming all the way down the block. So, anyway, when I get up next to the pay phone, he stops shouting and asks me if I have an extra quarter. I tell him, "Sorry, man," and all of a sudden....

Exercise 9

Tell this story aloud, as if you were Mary Rae describing her own experience. Recount it using the Present Time Frame to make it more vivid and less formal. The first two sentences have been done as an example.

> **EXAMPLE:** *There I am, standing in dirty swamp water as deep as my waist, but I'm having a wonderful time! The canoe we're rowing has gotten stuck on a log, so somebody has to get into the water and try to lift one end of it.*

There I was, standing in dirty swamp water as deep as my waist, but I was having a wonderful time! The canoe we were rowing had gotten stuck on a log, so somebody had to get into the water and try to lift one end of it. I looked into the water. It looked really dark and dirty. I knew there were a lot of poisonous snakes in this area. I knew there were also alligators. All of a sudden, I realized that I wasn't afraid of any of these things. I had complete confidence in my ability to free the canoe and to avoid getting eaten or bitten. Without another thought, I jumped into the water and started to pull at the canoe. At that moment, I knew that there was nothing that I was afraid to do, and nothing that I couldn't do if I put my mind to it. Outward Bound was one of the most important experiences of my life!

Activities

Activity 1

Give a demonstration on how to do something for the rest of the class. (This could be how to prepare a favorite food, how to perform some physical activity, or how to make some simple object.) Give verbal instructions at the same time that you demonstrate the activity.

Activity 2

Describe how your life has temporarily changed from its more normal routines. What things are you doing that you do not normally do? What things are you not doing now that you normally do? If you have moved to a new country recently, you may wish to compare your life in the new country with the old country. Otherwise, you can talk about any period when you have experienced a departure from your normal routines.

- Use the Present Time Frame to describe the differences. Think of at least five temporary changes in your activities. You may wish to use the statements you wrote in the Task as examples of the kind of statements you should make about yourself.

Activity 3

"How much does that cost?" "How much money do you earn?" "How much do you weigh?" "How old are you?" Most Americans consider these to be rude questions. They would not ask these questions of someone unless that person was a very good friend. In other cultures, people do not consider these to be rude questions, but they might hesitate to ask other kinds of questions, such as "How many daughters do you have?" "What do you do—what kind of job do you have?" or even "What kind of house do you live in?"

- Form a group and talk about what are considered to be rude questions in other cultures that you are familiar with. Present your findings to the rest of the class.

Activity 4

Describe some of the things that are happening in the picture that illustrates the Task at the beginning of this chapter.

Activity 5

We all learn our basic cultural values when we are very young. By the time we are adults, these lessons are so much a part of us that they are almost unconscious. A first step in learning about different cultures is learning to identify some of the deep basic cultural values.

- Write down at least five things your parents told you that were general truths when you were growing up. Make sure that the things you write are not orders or requests (My parents told me to clean my room), but rather, statements about things that are always true. (Good manners are important.)
- Compare your list to the lists of several other students. Are any of the statements the same on all your lists? Are there any interesting similarities or differences based on differences of cultures? What does this tell you about the values your parents tried to teach you?
- Report your ideas to the rest of the class.

Task

North American Institute of International Studies
Application for Admissions

APPLYING FOR:

__ SPRING __ SUMMER __ FALL __ WINTER 19____

DEGREE OBJECTIVE:

Undergraduate _____ Graduate _____
Major _____ Minor _____

PERSONAL DATA:

Name _____
Address _____
Telephone _____
Birthdate _____ Sex _____ Ethnic Background _____

EDUCATIONAL BACKGROUND:

List all secondary and postsecondary schools attended, including language programs.

Name and location of school   dates of attendance   degree granted   GPA
_____
_____
_____
_____

PERSONAL ESSAY/WRITING SAMPLE:

All applicants must provide a writing sample. On another sheet of paper, write at least 200 words on the following topic. It must be handwritten, and written *only* by the applicant.

What are some characteristics that make you different from other people you know? How have your experiences in life shaped you as a person? What are some achievements that you have accomplished that you feel particularly proud of?

SIGNATURE _____ DATE _____

All application must be accompanied by official transcripts in English, proof of finances, and a nonrefundable $40 application fee.

When American students apply to colleges and universities, they often have to write a personal essay about their individual character and achievements. Such essays often require students to identify ways in which they are different from other people who might also be applying for admission. The question asked on this application is typical. You may want to follow this suggested process in developing your answer:

- Identify a characteristic about yourself that might be of interest to the university admissions committee. It should be something that is related to your proposed field of study. For example, an applicant in international business may want to talk about his or her familiarity with and adaptability to other cultures; an applicant in fine arts may want to stress creativity, an applicant in science or technology may want to emphasize mathematical abilities.

- Next, identify at least one formative experience that helped you develop that characteristic.

- Finally, describe at least one achievement that this characteristic has enabled you to do. Here is an example:

   characteristic: I am adaptable.
   formative experience(s): I have lived in four foreign countries.
   resulting achievement(s):
   I have learned three foreign languages.
   I have lived comfortably in primitive conditions.
   I have seen things and experienced things that none of my friends has ever done.
   I have learned firsthand what life was probably like in earlier centuries.

- After you develop your list, compare it to that of another student in the class. You should work together to help each other explain and clarify your ideas.

- Once you have followed this process to organize your ideas, write your essay. Make sure you mention all the topics that were included in the question on the application form. Make sure your answer (1) identifies the characteristic, (2) identifies the experiences that have made you that way, and (3) mentions one or two things that you have been able to achieve as a result of that characteristic.

- If you wish, use Exercise 1 as an example of the kind of essay you should write.

Focus 1

USE

Choosing Past Time Frame or Present Time Frame

USE

- When you describe past events in English, it is necessary to make a basic choice: whether to use the Past Time Frame or the Present Time Frame. In Unit 1, you learned that the moment of focus in the Present Time Frame is always NOW (the moment of speaking or writing). You also learned to use perfect aspect to describe sentences that are related to each other. Using the Past Time Frame instead of the Present Time Frame indicates that there is **no relationship** between the past event and NOW. This unit explores common situations where there is usually a relationship to NOW.
- You can use Past Time Frame to describe events that were fully completed in the past or occurred at a specified time in the past, but you must use the present perfect tense if those events continue to influence the present moment of focus in some way. Compare these sentences to see how a situation can determine whether to choose Past Time Frame or Present Time Frame:

Past Time	Present Time
(a) I **went** to Disneyworld three times while I was living in Florida. Now that I live in Ohio, it's too far away to visit.	**(b)** I **have gone** to Disneyworld three times, so I'm not really anxious to go again so soon after my last visit.
(c) I **worked** as a limousine driver during college. I **had** many opportunities to meet famous people.	**(d)** As a limousine driver, I **have had** many opportunities to meet famous people. It's one of the things I like about my job.
(e) I started that book, but I **didn't finish** it. It was too boring.	**(f)** I **haven't finished** that book yet. I've been reading it for several hours, and I hope to finish it soon.

Exercise 1

1) Underline all the verbs in the following passage. Mark verb phrases that refer to general truths or recurrent actions in Present Time Frame with (*a*). Mark verb phrases that refer to past events that have a relation to the present with (*b*). Mark verb phrases that simply refer to past events with (*c*). The first paragraph has been done for you as an example.

2) Why do you think the author changed from the Present Time Frame to the Past Time Frame in the second paragraph of her essay?

(1)One of the characteristics that <u>makes</u>^(a) me different from many people I know <u>is</u>^(a) my adaptability. (2)I <u>am</u>^(a) flexible and comfortable in new or unusual situations. (3)I think this <u>is</u>^(a) because <u>I have had</u>^(b) a lot of experience living in foreign countries. (4)This <u>has given</u>^(a) me a lot of opportunities to face unfamiliar situations and to learn about unfamiliar customs and beliefs.

(5)My first experience in a foreign country was more than 20 years ago in Afghanistan. (6)I taught English in a small town in a rural area. (7)Life in my town was very simple. (8)Because there was no electricity and rather little contact with the outside world, my life was a lot like living in an earlier century. (9)I have lived in more modern situations since that first experience, but everywhere I have lived it has been interesting and educational.

(10)As a result of my experiences in other countries, I have always been able to be comfortable with a simple life-style. (11)I have learned that relationships between people are very much the same, whether they have modern, busy lives, or old-fashioned, more peaceful lives. (12)I have learned to understand different ways of doing things and different ways of looking at the world. (13)Most of all, I have learned that *new* does not necessarily mean *better*. (14)This has made me adaptable, and this adaptability has helped me understand other people better.

Focus 2

USE

Relation to the Present: Still True versus No Longer True

USE

- One common way that past events relate to NOW is if they are still true. You can use present perfect to indicate that the situation being described is **still true.** You can use Past Time to talk about events that are **no longer true.**

Present Perfect Tense: (true now)	Past Tense: (not true now)
I **have worked** in a factory for three years. I **have been learning** how to operate complex machinery. I **have learned** how to operate three different kinds of machines so far. I still work at the factory.	I **worked** in an automobile factory for three years. I **was working** on the assembly line, but then they **promoted** me to foreman. I no longer work at the factory.

Exercise 2

Decide whether you should use the **past tense** or the **present perfect tense** for the verbs indicated in parentheses. More than one answer may be correct, so prepare to explain why you chose the form you did.

Bambang Soetomo (1) _____ (come) to the United States last January to get a degree in mechanical engineering. Since he (2) _____ (be) in the United States, he (3) _____ (have) many new experiences. At home in Jakarta, servants (4) _____ (cook) all his food. But here in the United States, Bambang (5) _____ (have) to prepare food for himself. In Indonesia, a lot of his university classes (6) _____ (require) the ability to memorize large amounts of information. But here, Bambang (7) _____ (find) that memorization is not considered to be a very important skill in many of his classes. Of course, he (8) _____ (be) ready for obvious differences in things like food and social customs, but he (9) _____ (not quite/adjust) to the subtle differences. He (10) _____ (learn) that knowing about differences and dealing with them are two different things. In fact, he (11) _____ (be) rather homesick. In Jakarta, he (12) _____ (have) a large group of friends, but here in the States, he (13) _____ (meet) only a few other Indonesian students, and none of them are in the same department he is. When he (14) _____ (be) planning his trip to America, he (15) _____ (plan) to go home for a vacation after his sophomore year, but he (16) _____ (change) his mind since he (17) _____ (get) here. He (18) _____ (speak) with his father about the possibility of coming home during his first summer vacation. His father (19) _____ (not decide) whether that's a good idea or not.

Focus 3

Chronological Relationships: Until Now

USE

- Another way past events relate to the present moment is through a chronological (time) relationship. You can use present perfect to describe events or situations that began in the past and continue until the present. Common ideas that typically occur in this time frame are
  - the number of times something has happened:
    - **(a)** Matt and Jeff **have seen** The Wizard of Oz over **a dozen times.**
    - **(b)** I've ridden a roller coaster **once,** but I'll never do it again!
  - very recent events with *just:*
    - **(c)** The doctor **has just left** the office. Maybe you can catch him if you hurry to the parking lot.
    - **(d)** We've **just been talking about** your suggestions. Won't you join us?
  - sentences with *ever, never, since*:
    - **(e)** I've **known** Stephanie **since** we **were** in high school.
    - **(f)** I've **never eaten** snake meat. **Have you ever tried** it?

Exercise 3

Work with a partner. Take turns asking each other these questions. You can use the suggested topics or make up questions of your own.

1. Have you ever . . . (ridden a horse, been in love, seen a flying saucer . . .)?
2. How many times have you . . . (eaten Chinese food, taken the TOEFL, driven a motorcycle . . .)?
3. Name three things you have never done but would like to do.
4. Name three things you have done that you don't particularly want to do again.

You should ask at least ten questions. Once you have collected the information, make a brief oral report about your partner to the rest of the class. The class should decide who has asked the most interesting or unusual questions.

Exercise 4

Do these sentences refer to situations that include the present moment or situations that are fully completed in the past? Indicate which by choosing the **past tense** or the **present perfect tense** for the verbs. More than one answer may be correct, so prepare to explain why you have chosen your answer.

My friend Bob is a very happy man. He just (1) _____ (find out) that he (2) _____ (win) a free trip to Hawaii. He (3) _____ (buy) raffle tickets for years, but he never (4) _____ (win) anything until six months ago, when he (5) _____ (win) an electric toaster. Since then, apparently, his luck (6) _____ (change). He (7) _____ (get) more than a dozen prizes from various contests. Most of the prizes (8) _____ (be) small, until last month, when he (9) _____ (win) a videocassette recorder and a color TV. I wonder if he (10) _____ (think about) sharing his good fortune with his dear, kind friends.

Focus 4

Logical Relationships to the Present

USE

- Past events can also have a logical relationship to the present moment. The past event, although completed in the past, still continues to affect the present situation in some way. The logical connection can be a present result.
- This present result can be stated explicitly:

Past Action	Present Result
(a) I have already seen that movie,	so I suggest we go see a different one.
(b) He has been wasting so much money	that I don't think we should give him anymore.
(c) I have always felt that beggars were lazy,	so I won't give this fellow any money.

- This result can be implied:

Past Action	Implied Present Result
(d) You **have spilled** ink all over my new tablecloth!	There's a mess.
(e) John **has obviously forgotten** about our meeting.	He is not at the meeting.

- The logical connection can also be the **speaker's or writer's attitude.** The event in some way is connected to the present in the speaker's mind. For example, reporters often introduce news stories with the present perfect tense to emphasize the connection with the present moment. Or a writer may mention a past event that has a connection to a point she or he is about to make.

Not Connected to the Present	Connected to the Present in the Speaker's Mind
(f) Did you find the article you were looking for?(a simple question)	**(g) Have you found** the article you were looking for? Because if not, I think I might know where you can find it.
(h) The White House **released** new figures **yesterday** concerning the balance of trade. (a simple fact)	**(i)** The White House **has released** new figures on the balance of trade in the last quarter. These figures **show** that imports continue to outstrip exports by more than 20 percent. (a news report)
(j) The historian Toynbee **once observed** that history repeats itself. (a simple fact)	**(k)** The historian Toynbee **has observed** that history repeats itself, and I believe that he is correct. (The writer is making a point.)

Exercise 5

Choose the sentence that reflects the most logical continuation of the ideas expressed in the first sentence. Both sentences are grammatically possible.

1. I **have told** you that I don't like the color green.
   (a) My brother didn't like that color either.
   (b) So why did you buy me a sweater in that color?
2. Jeff **met** Matt at a party.
   (a) They soon became the best of friends.
   (b) They share an apartment in San Francisco.
3. Bambang Soetomo **arrived** in America about eight months ago.
   (a) He has been adjusting to American life ever since.
   (b) He is living by himself in an apartment.
4. **I have been trying** to get in touch with my math professor since last week.
   (a) I didn't do well on the last exam.
   (b) Whenever I go there, she doesn't seem to be in her office.
5. Many historians **have noted** the parallels between the decline of Rome and the decline of the great nineteenth century colonial powers, such as Britain and France.
   (a) However, they have neglected to extend the parallel to the United States.
   (b) The purpose of this paper is to explore those parallels in relation to the United States, and its role in world economic development.
6. I **don't think** that Denise likes Peter very much.
   (a) Have you ever noticed the way she avoids looking at him when she speaks?
   (b) Did she say anything about her feelings to you at the meeting last week?

Exercise 6

Why do you think the speaker chose to use the present perfect tense instead of the simple past tense in these sentences? Is the relationship to the present a chronological one, a logical one, or a combination of both?

1. Scientists have discovered a number of interesting similarities between the atmosphere of Earth and that of Titan, one of the moons of Jupiter. They have found significant concentrations of water vapor, and other chemicals common to Earth. They hope to send another space probe to the planet within the coming decade.
2. If I have told you once, I've told you a hundred times: I hate broccoli!
3. Guess what? We've been invited to Liz's wedding. What should we get her for a gift?
4. Sociologists have often argued that easily available welfare payments to poor families do not significantly affect long-term poverty, but recent statistics show that this may not be true.
5. Shakespeare's reputation as a psychologist has grown in recent years. His plays have always reflected an uncanny understanding of human motivations.
6. Has Jill found a summer job? I was talking with my aunt, and she said her office might need a temporary computer programmer.

Focus 5

Present Perfect Progressive Tense

USE

- You can use the present perfect progressive tense to give additional information about events that have a relation to the present. Use the present perfect progressive instead of the present perfect to describe something that is
  - temporary rather than permanent:
    - **(a)** He **has been living** with his parents, but he hopes to move out now that he has found a job.
    - **(b)** He **has lived** with his parents since he dropped out of college.
  - a repeated rather than a single occurrence:
    - **(c)** I **have been thinking** about the problem, but I don't have a solution. Do you have any ideas?
    - **(d)** I **have thought** about the problem, and I have a solution.
  - continuous rather than repeated or recurring:
    - **(e)** It **has been snowing constantly** for the last three hours. I hope it stops soon!
    - **(f)** It **has snowed several times** since we got here, but there's still not enough snow for skiing.
  - uncompleted rather than completed:
    - **(g)** I **have been writing** my term paper. I still have to type it, proofread it, and staple it together.
    - **(h)** I **have written** my term paper. Let's go have a beer!
- Remember that stative verbs do not normally take progressive aspect even when they refer to states continuing until the present:
    - **(i)** Living in foreign countries **has required** a lot of flexibility.
    - **(j)** NOT: Living in foreign countries **has been requiring** a lot of flexibility.

Exercise 7

Choose the correct form, **present perfect** or **present perfect progressive,** to talk about these events. More than one answer may be correct.

1. I _____ (read) about the development of early forms of photography, and I _____ (learn) some very interesting facts about it. I would like to continue my research next semester.

2. That baby _____ (cry) constantly since we got here. I wish its parent would do something to make it be quiet.

3. Bob's brother _____ (resent) his winning that free trip to Hawaii ever since he heard the news.

4. I _____ (try) to explain that for the last 15 minutes. Aren't you listening?

5. I _____ (try) to explain that every way I know how. I give up!

6. I _____ (work) on this problem all afternoon. I think it's time for a break.

7. Rebecca _____ (expect) the police to call about the accident. That's why she wants to stay home this afternoon.

8. Bob _____ (tell) the office that he doesn't want to take a summer job until after returns from Hawaii.

9. The newspaper _____ (try) to contact Bob about some contest. They _____ (called) at least five or six times.

10. Bob _____ (dream) about visiting Hawaii ever since he read an article about volcanoes. He _____ (become) a real expert on them.

Exercise 8

Decide whether these passages should use the **simple present**, **present progressive**, **present perfect**, **present perfect progressive**, or **past tenses**. More than one answer may be correct, so prepare to explain why you made the choice you did.

PARAGRAPH 1

Bambang Soetomo (1) _____ (speak) English quite fluently. I wonder where he

(2) _____ (learn) it. He (3) _____ (study) mechanical engineering. He (4)

_____ (plan) to go to graduate school once he (5) _____ (get) his BS de-

gree. Bambang (6) _____ (live) by himself for the last few months. But he (7)

_____ (think) about getting a roommate. He (8) _____ (miss) his friends

back home a great deal, and this (9) _____ (affect) his studies. He (10) _____

(consider) asking his father for permission to come home during the summer, but he (11)

_____ (not do) so yet.

PARAGRAPH 2

Many historians (1) _____ (draw) a parallel between the decline of the Roman

Empire and more recent empires, such as Spain, Britain, and even the United States. Some

historians (2) _____ (argue) that such comparisons (3) _____ (be) not valid

because there (4) _____ (be) many variables that (5) _____ (affect) political or

economic development. For example, one of the biggest problems that the Roman Empire

(6) _____ (encountered) (7) _____ (be) transporting food to urban areas with

large populations. Technological advances (8) _____ (make) that particular problem

insignificant for today's modern "empires." Other historians (9) _____ (consider)

the parallel between ancient Rome and later empires invalid because they (10) _____

(feel) that today's empires (11) _____ (not consist) of political alliances, but rather

economic ones. The development of a global economy (12) _____ (change) the

way political powers (13) _____ (deal) with each other and with the people that

they (14) _____ (govern).

Activities

Activity 1

They say that everyone is an expert at something. Identify a special skill or ability that you have that enables you to do something better than most other people. Talk about the experiences you have had using that skill, and what you have learned from those experiences that would convince someone to give you a chance to use that expertise. Make a report to the rest of the class.

Activity 2

Bring in the front page of a daily newspaper and examine the articles with a partner or in a group. Find examples of sentences written in present time and past time. What tense are headlines generally written in? What tense are the introductory paragraphs generally written in? What tense is the body of the article generally written in? Can you find a pattern? Why do you think the author chose one time frame rather than another? Discuss your ideas with your partner or group, and present them to the rest of the class.

Activity 3

Experts in cross-cultural communication have found that most Americans tend to believe that most changes in life are usually good. This is not necessarily true in other cultures. Find out what important changes your classmates have made in their lives. Interview three other classmates. Ask them the following questions:

Have you changed any habits or routines recently?
Describe the changes.
Why have you made the changes?
How have the changes affected you?

Record your information on this chart:

Name	Description of Change	Reason for Change	Result of Change
Example	quit smoking	health concerns, price of cigarettes	stronger lungs, better energy, more money, more nervous, weight gain
1.			
2.			
3.			

- Based on the changes your group has experienced, decide whether you agree that changes in life are generally for the better. Present your group's ideas and reasons to the rest of the class.

Activity 4

American culture tends to value individualism, and, as a result, most Americans are taught from a very early age to look for ways that they are different from other people. Most Americans can easily identify a large number of personal experiences and characteristics that they feel make them different from other people.

- Interview three or four other people and ask them these questions:

  What experiences have you had that most other people have not?

  What things make you different from most other people?

Record your information on this chart:

Student's Name and Nationality	Different Individual Experiences	Different Individual Characteristics
1.		
2.		
3.		
4.		

- Of the people you interviewed, who was able to think of the greatest number of individual differences?

Activity 5

You may wish to compare the responses of Americans and other students in your class to the questions you asked in Activity 4. Were the Americans able to think of more differences than your classmates? Were they able to think of these differences more readily? Were there other cultural groups that could answer these questions more or less readily? What do the similarities and differences tell you about cultural differences? Discuss these questions in a small group and summarize your ideas for the rest of the class.

20

Special Problems with Future Time:
Using Present Tenses; Using *Will* versus *Going To*; Adverbial Clauses in Future Time

Task

Are you an optimist or a pessimist? Optimists generally look on the bright side of things. Pessimists tend to expect negative things to happen. What are your expectations about the future?

- Here are some current trends and issues. Share your knowledge about these issues with a small group of other students. Consider some of the issues and decide how they are likely to develop in the future.

    Positive trends: technological improvements, new medical treatments, longer life expectancy, better food crops, political changes, better communication, more rapid transportation, equal status for women, more education

    Negative trends: environmental problems (pollution, acid rain, global warming), population increase, new diseases, increased traffic, Third World debt, breakdown of traditional families, declining resources

- Based on your discussion and your own ideas, consider the following question:

    Do you think that life 100 years from now will be better or worse than it is today? Why or why not?

- Write a brief paragraph expressing your opinions and your reasons for them. Begin your paragraph by stating whether you are optimistic or pessimistic about the future of the world.

Focus 1

Recognizing Future Time

FORM

- Some linguists say that English doesn't really have future tense, because
  - you can often use the simple present and the present progressive tenses to talk about events in the future:
    (a) John **leaves** for Europe in three weeks.
    (b) We' **re having** a test next Tuesday.
    (c) When I **am** 50 years old, I will have a big party.
  - you can use modal forms for both the Future Time Frame and the Present Time Frame:
    (d) **Will** you open the window **now**?
    (e) There's someone at the door. It **should** be Peter.
    (f) Denise isn't here **now**. She **must be** at the office.

It is important to recognize when these forms refer to future events and when they refer to events happening now.

Exercise 1

Do the verbs in the passages refer to future time or do they have some other function (e.g., present time, request, or recommendation)? Underline the verb phrases. Mark future time verb phrases with *(a)*. Mark present time verb phrases with *(b)*. Mark other meanings with *(c)* and describe the meaning. The first passage has been done for you as an example.

1. *(b)*
   (1)School always <u>begins</u> in September in the United States. (2)This coming year school
   (a)   *(a)*
   <u>begins</u> on September 12. (3)Janet's <u>going to start</u> her third year of high school. (4)She's
   (a)   *(a)*
   <u>taking</u> chemistry, history, English, and advanced algebra. (5)She <u>might take</u> a theater
             (c—ability)
   class, if she <u>can fit</u> it into her schedule.

2. (1)We're having a class picnic in just a couple of weeks. (2)As you know, school ends on

   June 15, and the picnic will be on the next day, so we're already making plans. (3)Most

   people are being really cooperative. (4)For example, Martha makes great potato salad,

   so she's bringing some to the picnic. (5)There should be enough for everyone to have some. (6)But George is being difficult. (7)He says he will come, but he won't bring anything. (8)Will you explain something to me? (9)Will you tell me why George is so stubborn? (10)He really should be more cooperative. (11)Everyone else is bringing something. (12)Why won't he?

3. (1)The next century should be an extremely important time in the development of the human race, (2)but the time for government action should be **now!** (3)If certain things don't begin to happen, the next century could be a very unpleasant period in the history of the world. (4)The population is increasing at an alarming rate. (5)In spite of this fact, the current government will not put additional funding into birth control research or family planning programs, either at home or overseas. (6)Supplies of fossil fuels (coal, oil, gas) are decreasing rapidly, but the government will not adequately support programs to develop alternative energy sources, such as solar power or wind-generated electricity. (7)The new century starts in less than a decade, (8)but it is the actions that are or are not being taken today that will determine whether the human condition will be better or worse than it is now.

Focus 2

USE

Present Tenses in Future Time Frame

USE

- You can use the simple present and present progressive tenses to describe future activities that are already scheduled or planned to take place in the future.
    - **(d)** Christmas **happens** on a Sunday next year.
    - **(e)** John's **leaving** for France in a week.
    - **(f)** Next year **is** Leap Year.
- You must mark future events that are not already scheduled with *will, be going to* or a modal of prediction. (*may, could, might,* etc.)
    - **(d)** We **will** go shopping if they have a big spring sale.
    - **(e)** I **am going to** travel to the Amazon someday.
    - **(f)** There **might** be a surprise quiz on Friday.

Exercise 2

Make at least five questions about things that will happen in this class at a future time that have already been scheduled. Ask your questions to another person in the class.

EXAMPLE: *What time do classes start next Tuesday?*
When are we having our next grammar test?

Focus 3

USE

Will versus *Be Going To*

USE

- *Will* and *be going to* both talk about future actions, but they have different uses.
- You can use *be going to*
  - to introduce a topic:
    - **(a)** **I'm going to paint** my apartment. First, **I'll** go to the store to get some paint. **I'll** also get brushes and rollers. I **might** paint the walls green, but I haven't decided yet.
      Subsequent sentences often use *will* or other modal forms.
  - to indicate a strong intention:
    - **(b)** I'm **going to go** to the party, whether you're there or not.
      Will can be used in such cases, but it is stressed in speech.
    - **(c)** I **will** go to the party, whether you're there or not.
  - to indicate definite situations in the immediate future:
    - **(d)** We shouldn't go hiking this afternoon. It's **going to rain** any minute!
- You can use *will*
  - for future actions that do not stress intention:
    - **(e)** John **will** study in France next year.
    - **(f)** I had better do it now, because **I'll be** busy next week.
  - for offers and requests in future time:
    - **(g)** I need some milk from the store. Oh, **I'll** get it for you.
    - **(h)** I've been invited to a party next weekend. **Will** you go with me?
  - to indicate refusal of an invitation or request:
    - **(i)** I asked him to help us, but he **will not do** it. (He has refused our request.)
    - **(j)** Denise **won't go** with us, no matter how much we ask her. (Denise has refused our invitation.)
  - to express general truths:
    - **(k)** Plants **will die** if they don't get enough water.
    - **(l)** Boys **will be** boys.
    - **(m)** A criminal **will always return** to the scene of the crime.

- When there is a possibility of interpreting a future action as a request, you should use **be going to** instead of **will** future actions.
  - **(n) Are you going to** buy a new car? (I know you were thinking about it. What have you decided to do?)
  - **(o)** AWKWARD: **Will** you buy a new car? (This sounds strange in English. It sounds like a request.)
- When the context makes clear that we are talking about a future action, not a request, either form can be used:
  - **(p)** Are you going to Mary's party?
  - **(q)** I don't know. **Will** John be there?
  - **(r)** I don't know. **Is** John **going to be** there?

Exercise 3

Decide which form, *will* or *be going to*, should be used in the following sentences. In some cases, both answers may be correct.

1. Charley (1) _____ (not go) to Rebecca's party. Gladys (2) _____ (be) there, and she and Charley don't get along anymore. She (3) _____ (probably drink) too much, and then she (4) _____ (want) to tell everyone about how they used to be engaged to be married.

2. I've got an extra ticket to the opera. (1) _____ (you go) with me? It (2) _____ (be) a great performance. Pavarotti (3) _____ (sing) the part of Falstaff. I'm sure he (4) _____ (be) wonderful.

3. I don't know what to do for my vacation. Maybe I (1) _____ (go) to Mexico. I know the plane ticket (2) _____ (be) expensive. Perhaps I (3) _____ (take) the bus to save some money. Your brother's taken the bus before, hasn't he? (4) _____ (you ask) him how the trip was?

4. Janet (1) _____ (finish) her assignment tonight, even if she has to stay up until dawn. It (2) _____ (not be) easy. She has to finish reading *War and Peace*, and then write a 10-page paper. She (3) _____ (probably be) up all night. Maybe her roommate (4) _____ (make) some coffee for her and do the dishes, so that Janet (5) _____ (not have) to worry about anything else.

5. Different plants need different amounts of water. Too much water (1) _____ (kill) certain kinds of plants. Other kinds require daily watering, and they (2) _____ (die) if they don't get it. Setting out a garden (3) _____ (require) some advanced planning to make sure that plants with similar water requirements (4) _____ (be) planted in the same areas.

Focus 4

MEANING

Other Modals in Future Time Frame

MEANING

- You can use most one-word modals (**will, may, might, should,** and **could**) to make predictions about the **probability** of something happening in the future.

Form	Meaning	Use
will	**certain** 100% probability	**(a)** We **will** arrive in an hour.
should	**probable** 65%–80% probability	**(b)** Aunt Emily **should** like this movie.
may/may not	**quite possible** 35%–65% probability	**(c)** I **may** be a little late to the meeting.
might/might not *could*	**somewhat possible** 5%–35% probability	**(d)** Peter **might** not know the answer. **(e)** It **could** rain before we get there.
will not	**certain** 0% probability	**(f)** I **won't** be at the concert next week.

- ***Shall*** is not usually used in American English to talk about future actions or events. Using ***shall*** to talk about future actions sounds quite formal to the American listener. In American English, we use ***shall***
  - to make offers:
    (g) Shall I peel you a grape?
    Should and ***may*** are often used in this context.
  - to suggest activities that both speaker and listener will participate in:
    (h) Shall we dance?
    (i) Shall we begin with the first exercise?
    Let's is a slightly more informal variant of this use.
- See Unit 21 for more information about and practice with predictions about future events.

Exercise 4

What are some likely developments in the areas listed below and what are your reasons for thinking so? Use a modal to indicate how likely your answer actually is.

EXAMPLE: What will life be like 100 years from now?

Life should be more complex 100 years from now, because of so many technological developments.

1. Will life be better or worse than it is today?
2. Will there be enough coal and oil?
3. Will there be a decrease in air pollution?
4. Will the overall climate grow warmer?
5. Will the rate of population growth be greater?
6. Will there be increased use of automobiles?
7. Will there be political stability?
8. Will there still be large differences between developing and developed countries?
9. Will there be cures for cancer, AIDS, and other diseases?
10. What will the "problems" be that people face in the twenty-first century?
11. Will there still be wars between countries?

Make up three questions of your own.

Focus 5

FORM

Future Time Frame Adverbial Clauses

FORM

- In the Future Time Frame, adverbial clauses always use present tenses.
  - **(a)** I'll do it tomorrow, **when I finish school**.
  - **(b)** NOT: I'll do it tomorrow, **when I will finish school.**
  - **(c)** I'm going to watch TV **as soon as I have finished my homework.**
  - **(d)** NOT: I'm going to watch TV as soon as **I will have finished my homework**.
  - **(e)** John is planning to have a party **while his parents are visiting relatives in Canada.**
  - **(f)** NOT: John's planning to have a party while his parents **will be visiting relatives in Canada.**

Exercise 5

Join the second sentence in each of these pairs to the first sentence using the suggested linking word. Make sure to change nouns to pronouns where necessary.

> **EXAMPLE:** I'll go to the movies. I will finish my homework. (after)
> *I'll go to the movies after I finish my homework.*

1. All my friends will be very relieved. The semester will end in a couple of weeks. (when)
2. I'm going to go to the movies every day. I will have finished all the household chores that have been postponed all semester. (once)
3. It will be almost three weeks after the last day of class. Janet will finally get her research paper completed. (by the time)
4. I'm going to read that book about magic. I'll have some time after the exams. (when)
5. Peter's going to spend every afternoon at the beach. The weather will be sunny. (while)
6. Matt and Jeff will be really tired. They are going to arrive in Phoenix by bicycle. (by the time)
7. Kevin and Libby are leaving for Europe. They'll finish their last exam. (as soon as)
8. Doug and Kathy are going to get married. They will be on vacation in Mexico. (while)
9. Even our teacher's going to take some time off. She will have finished grading the final papers and correcting the exams. (when)
10. The vacation will be over. We will realize that sad news. (before)

Focus 6

USE

Sequence of Tenses in Future Time Frame

USE

- Time relations between verbs in the Future Time Frame are expressed in the same way as verbs in the Present Time Frame or the Past Time Frame. You can indicate these relationships using
  - adverbial information:
    John will travel around Europe **before** he returns home.
  - aspect markers:
    John **will have visited** several other countries by the time he leaves for home.

Exercise 6

Read the following passage and underline each verb phrase. For each verb phrase, identify the time relationship between the verb and the moment of focus (100 years from today, the end of the twenty-first century). Does the verb happen **(a)at, (b)before, (c)during, or (d)before and during** the moment of focus? Mark it accordingly. The first two sentences have been done for you as an example.

(1)A hundred years from now <u>will be</u> *(a)* a wonderful time to be alive. (2)By the end of the twenty-first century, several basic changes <u>will have occurred</u> *(b)* in human society. (3)Most of the diseases that are common today will have been wiped out. (4)Scientists will have found cures for AIDS, Alzheimer's Disease, heart diseases, and cancer. (5)People will be living longer and healthier lives than they currently are. (6)People in developing countries will have been eating more nutritiously for several generations; (7)so, as a result, human beings will, on the whole, be larger, stronger, and more intelligent than they are today. (8)Scientists will have been researching ways to produce cheap, clean, nonpolluting energy. (9)So it is likely that by the end of the next century, there will be no smog, no acid rain, and no fears about global warming and the greenhouse effect. (10)Political changes will have removed the threat of nuclear war. (11)People will have been thinking in global terms for so long that it will no longer be necessary to have passports.

Activities

Activity 1

What day and time is it at this moment? Imagine what you will be doing **at this exact moment** 10 years from now, 20 years from now, and 50 years from now. Describe these activities to a partner or write a brief essay.

Activity 2

Who has the most interesting plans for the next vacation?

• Describe your plans to two or three other people. Listen to their plans. Once everyone has described his or her vacation, answer these questions as a group:

> Whose plans sound like the most fun? Why?
> The easiest to arrange? Why?
> The best opportunity to practice English?
> Decide on one more original category of your own.

• Report your decision and reasons to the rest of the class.

Activity 3

Choose one of these three questions and write a paragraph or make an oral presentation expressing your ideas.

- What major **political and economic changes** are going to take place in your lifetime? Describe them and explain why you think they are going to happen.
- What major **social changes** are going to take place in your lifetime? Describe them and explain why you think they are going to happen.
- What major **scientific advances** are going to take place in your lifetime? Describe them and explain why you think they are going to happen.

Organize a debate between optimists and pessimists. Using the Task at the beginning of this lesson, decide whether you are an optimist or a pessimist. Form groups of four or more. Be sure to have an equal number of optimists and pessimists in each group. As a group, choose one of the following areas of world affairs and discuss the current trends that are suggested here. Add one or two significant additional trends of your own. Optimists will then decide on reasons why they think the current trends will result in a better situation 100 years from now. Pessimists will decide on reasons why they think the current trends will result in a worse situation 100 years from now. Present both sets of predictions to the rest of the class.

Area of World Affairs	Some Current Trends
political developments	<ul><li>wars between nations and within nations</li><li>political changes in specific countries</li></ul>
economic developments	<ul><li>Third World debt</li><li>the balance of trade</li><li>the collapse of Communist economies</li><li>the growth in numbers of poor people in industrial societies</li></ul>
environmental developments	<ul><li>global warming</li><li>the depletion of rain forests</li><li>the development of new energy sources</li></ul>
religious developments	<ul><li>the growth of Islamic and Christian fundamentalism</li><li>the spread of Eastern religions (Hinduism and Buddhism) to Europe and North America</li></ul>
artistic and literary developments	<ul><li>the spread of English as a world language</li><li>the impact of radio and TV on communication</li><li>the increasing importance of visual media (film, TV, photography) over print media (literature, newspapers)</li></ul>
scientific and technological development	<ul><li>genetic engineering</li><li>new medical treatments</li><li>the growth of computers</li></ul>

21

Modals of Prediction and Inference

Task

Have you ever wanted to be a detective? Let's see how good you are at solving some puzzles. The following are three mysterious events. Discuss the possible causes with other students. Which causes are likely and which causes are not so likely? When nobody can think of any other possible explanations, turn to the Activities, read the additional clues, and try to solve the mysteries.

Mystery #1

A man lives on the 40th floor of a very tall building. Every day he rides the elevator down to the ground floor. When he comes home, he rides the elevator to the 20th floor, but he has to walk the rest of the way.
Why?

Mystery #2

In a room, a dead woman hangs by a rope, more than three feet above the floor. There are no windows, and the door has been locked from the inside. The room is empty: no furniture, no ladder. The only thing in the room is a single piece of paper.
What happened to the woman?

Mystery #3

A police officer receives an emergency phone call. There has been a terrible automobile accident, and a boy and his father have been badly injured and are both in critical condition. The officer has been called in to fill out the report and figure out what happened. The police officer arrives, takes one look at the boy and his father, and says, "You'll have to find someone else to deal with this. I'm too upset. This boy is my son!"
How can the boy have two fathers?

Do not look at the additional clues until you have thought of at least five possible explanations for each mystery.

Focus 1

Modals of Prediction

MEANING

- Modals of prediction refer to the Future Time Frame. You can use them to indicate how likely or possible it is that some future event will occur.

Form	Meaning	Examples
will	certain	**(a)** We **will** arrive in one hour.
should	probable quite likely	**(b)** We **should** be able to get a good price for Andy's car.
may	quite possible possible	**(c)** I **may** be late tonight.
might **could**	somewhat possible	**(d)** You'd better take an umbrella. It **could/might** rain tonight.
may not **might not**	possibly not	**(e)** We **may/might not** get there in time.
shouldn't	probably impossible not likely	**(f)** This **shouldn't** hurt.
won't	impossible	**(g)** That **won't** happen.

Exercise 1

Make sentences from these cues using modals.

> **EXAMPLE:** certain: Andy/drive to New York for a vacation.
>
> *Andy will drive to New York for a vacation.*

1. probable: Andy/decide what to do about his car next week.
2. impossible: the car/work well enough for his trip to New York.
3. possible: Andy/get it repaired, if it can be done cheaply.
4. probably impossible: he/have trouble selling it.
5. quite likely: he/be able to get a good price.
6. possible: Andy's friend Paul/want to buy it.
7. possibly not: Andy/sell the car to Paul.
8. possibly not: the car/be in very good condition.
9. possible: Paul/expect a refund if he has troubles with the car.
10. certain: Andy/need the money to buy a plane ticket if he doesn't drive.

275

Exercise 2

Here are some activities. How likely is it that you will be doing these things next Saturday night at 8:00 P.M.?

doing English homework	taking a bath
watching TV	speaking another language
thinking about personal problems	sleeping
going to church	writing letters to the family
reading a magazine	having a good time with friends

Work with a partner. Ask questions with **will.** Answer questions with the appropriate modal of prediction. Prepared to report two or three of your partner's answers to the rest of the class.

EXAMPLES: *At 8:00 P.M. next Saturday, do you think you will be doing English homework?*
I won't be doing homework on a Saturday night. I might be at a disco.

Exercise 3

Write 12 true sentences about your plans for your next vacation, using modals of prediction:

two things that you will definitely do
two things that you will probably do
two things that you will possibly do
two things that you possibly won't do
two things that you probably won't do
two things that you definitely won't do

Exercise 4

Write 12 sentences about how you think life will be at the end of the next century, using modals of prediction:

two things that will definitely be true
two things that will probably be true
two things that will possibly be true
two things that possibly won't be true
two things that probably won't be true
two things that definitely won't be true

Focus 2

Modals of Inference

MEANING

- Modals of inference refer to the Present Time Frame. You can use them to describe logical conclusions about a current event or situation based on knowledge or evidence. Because they are statements of conclusion, you do not use these forms to ask questions.

Form	Meaning	Example
must	There is no other possible conclusion.	**(a)** That **must** be John. I've been expecting him.
should	This is a reasonable conclusion, but it is possible that there is another conclusion.	**(b)** John **should** be here somewhere. He said he was coming.
may/might/could	This is one of several possibilities.	**(c)** She **may** be unhappy. **(d)** They **might** have some problems. **(e)** John **could** be here.
may not/might not	This is one of several possibilities.	**(f)** She **may/might not** be here. I haven't seen her yet.
shouldn't	This is not a reasonable conclusion, but it could be possible.	**(g)** That **shouldn't** be Mary's brother. She told me he wasn't planning to be here.
must not	This is not a possible conclusion.	**(h)** I've looked everywhere for Mary. She **must not** be here.
can't/couldn't	This is impossible.	**(i)** That **can't** be John. I know he's still out of town. **(j)** He **couldn't** be in two places at the same time.

Exercise 5

Fill in the blanks with an appropriate modal of inference. There may be more than one correct answer, so prepare to explain why you chose the form you did.

1. There's someone at the door. That _____ be my brother. I've been expecting him. But it _____ be the mailman, or it _____ even be a salesman.

2. Someone is ringing the doorbell. It _____ be my brother; he has a key. It _____ be the mailman; he doesn't usually ring the bell. It _____ be a friend; all my friends think I'm still in New York. It _____ be a salesman. Let's not answer it!.

3. I hope I can go to the movies with you tonight, but I _____ have enough money. I _____ have enough, because I cashed a check yesterday. But I won't be 100 percent sure until I buy groceries and see how much money I have left. I really hope I can go. Everyone who has seen it says it's really good. It _____ be very funny.

4. Martha looks pretty unhappy. She and George _____ be having another one of their fights. I don't know what the problem is this time. It _____ be because George is always working on his car. It _____ be because Martha wants them to spend every weekend at her mother's house. It _____ be about money, though. That's the fight they had last week. They _____ have a very happy marriage.

5. Where have I put my wallet? It _____ be somewhere! It _____ just disappear by itself. It _____ be on my desk, since that's where I usually put it. But it _____ be in my briefcase too. I sometimes forget to take it out when I get home.

6. Naomi _____ need money. She's always eager to pay when we go out for a night on the town. She never seems to have a job. It _____ be nice to have enough money without having to work.

278

7. Frank _____ have no trouble finding a job when he moves to California. It

_____ take a while, but I know he'll find a good position. He seems unhappy

in New York. He _____ like living there very much.

Focus 3

MEANING ● USE

Other Modal Meanings
for *Will, Can,* and *Should*

- In the Present Time Frame it's easy to confuse the meaning of certain modals. **Can, will,** and **should** have other common meanings in the Present Time Frame that are easy to confuse with prediction and inference.
- You can also use **will** and **can** to make statements about the certainty or possibility of general truths in the Present Time Frame in addition to their use for predictions about the Future Time Frame.

General Possibility/Certainty	Specific Prediction
(a) My brother **can** be really grouchy when he first wakes up.	**(b)** He **might** be more cooperative after he has had breakfast.
(c) A criminal **will** always return to the scene of a crime.	**(d)** We **might** identify some suspects by watching to see who comes by.
(e) San Francisco **can** be cold and foggy in the summer.	**(f)** We **will** need our jackets if we go there.

- *Should* has two common uses in the Present Time Frame. You can use it to state a reasonable expectation or you can use it in hypothetical situations to imply that the opposite of what has been stated is actually true.

Reasonable Expectation	Negative Implication
(g) There's someone at the door. Oh, that **should** be my brother. He said he would drop by. **(h)** Is that Mary? Mary **shouldn't** be here. She had a date tonight.	**(i)** I **should** be happy that you're here. (I'm not happy.) **(j)** John **should** be here right now. (He's not here.) **(k)** I **shouldn't** be angry with you. (I'm angry.)

Exercise 6

Do these statements refer to a general truth, a specific prediction, or a statement of ability?

1. Babies will cry if they don't get fed.
2. Learning English can be quite rewarding.
3. Mrs. Smith can forget things if she's not careful.
4. I will be visiting your class.
5. People won't become fluent in a foreign language unless they practice.
6. Dogs won't eat vegetables.
7. Mary won't be very happy to hear the news about John's new "friend."
8. Mr. Merlin can do magic tricks.
9. Denise can be very difficult if she's in a bad mood.
10. Increased demand will always result in higher prices.

Exercise 7

Do these sentences express reasonable expectation or negative implication?

1. John should be pretty happy tonight. He just won $1,000.
2. You shouldn't have any problems with the car. The mechanic has checked it over.
3. Mary shouldn't be so disappointed about the test. Nobody else is.
4. I know the doctor should see you now, but he's still with another patient.
5. I know Bob should be here any minute, because I just saw his car pulling into the driveway.
6. You should be getting straight *A*'s in all your classes. What's the problem?

Focus 4

FORM

Phrasal Modals with Prediction and Inference

FORM

• You can use certain phrasal modals in statements of prediction or inference:

One-Word Modal	Phrasal Modal	Examples
will	be going to	(a) We're **going to** start the program a little late. It **will** begin at 8:20.
should	ought to	(b) Once the traffic starts moving, it **shouldn't** take too long. We **ought to** get there in about an hour.
must	have to/have got to	(c) That check **has to** be here someplace!

- You cannot use **ought to, have to**, and **have got to** to make negative inferences:

    (d) The test **shouldn't** be too hard.

    (e) AWKWARD: The test **ought not to** be too hard.

    (f) He **must not** care about his grade.

    (g) NOT: He **doesn't have to** care about his grade.

Exercise 8

Change the one-word modals in these sentences to phrasal modals if possible. (Not all the modals can be changed.)

    EXAMPLE: I think it will snow a lot this weekend.

        I think it's going to snow a lot this weekend.

        You shouldn't find the exam difficult.

        (Change to a phrasal modal is not possible because the statement is a negative inference.)

1. Traffic will get worse every year until we do something about the problem.
2. The traffic problem should begin to improve within ten years if we start making plans to solve it now.
3. It shouldn't be very difficult to find a parking place today, because it's Sunday.
4. Traffic is getting heavy; rush hour must be starting.
5. Jack must not have much money, because he drives a 15-year-old car.
6. The problem won't be solved by building more highways.
7. That will just increase the number of cars on the roads.
8. Traffic should flow more smoothly after they build the new tunnel.
9. This city must not have a very efficient public transportation system, because people seem to drive everywhere.
10. Commuters must be getting really tired of driving to work in such awful traffic.

FORM • MEANING

Modals of Prediction and Inference in Past Time Frame

FORM
MEANING

- You can make predictions and inferences about things that happened in the Past Time Frame by using **perfect modals:**

Modal + *Have* + **Past Participle**
Alice **might   have   seen**   that movie.

Modal	Present/Future Time	Past Time
must	**(a)** That **must be** John. I've been expecting him.	**(b)** That **must have been** John. I wasn't expecting anyone else.
should	**(c)** Peter **should be** here somewhere. He said he was coming.	**(d)** Let's ask Peter about the meeting. He **should have been** there.
may/might/could	Why is Martha crying? **(e)** She **may be** unhappy. **(f)** She **might be having** problems. **(g)** George **could be** the reason.	Why was Martha crying? **(h)** She **may have been** unhappy. **(i)** She **might have been having** problems. **(j)** George **could have been** the reason.
may not/might not	**(k)** She **may/might not be** here. I haven't seen her yet.	**(l)** She **may/might not have been** here. I didn't see her.
shouldn't	**(m)** That **shouldn't be** Mary's brother. She told me he wasn't in town.	**(n)** That **shouldn't have been** the reason.
must not	**(o)** I've looked everywhere for Mary. She **must not be** here.	**(p)** They didn't know what happened at the meeting. They **must not have been** there.
can't/couldn't	**(q)** That **can't/couldn't be** John. I know he's still out of town.	**(r)** I **can't have lost** it! **(s)** You **couldn't have forgotten** my name.

- In statements of prediction and inference, perfect modals indicate only Past Time Frame. For other modal uses, perfect modals indicate important changes in meaning. They are used for hypothetical statements, which are discussed in Unit 22.

   (t) Too bad you failed the test. You **should have** studied harder.

   (u) You **could have** helped me. Why didn't you?

Exercise 9

Change this passage to the Past Time Frame.

> **EXAMPLE:** Denise might not have enough time to finish the project today. That must be the reason why she isn't at the boss's birthday party.
>
> *Denise might not have had enough time to finish the project yesterday. That must have been the reason why she wasn't at the boss's birthday party.*

(1)Frank might be in California. (2)He should have no trouble finding a job. (3)It might take a while, but he has excellent qualifications and lots of experience. (4)He must be really unhappy in New York to want to move all the way across the country. (5)He must not like living in such a big city very much.

Exercise 10

Write the appropriate perfect modal form in the blank. There may be more than one correct answer.

1. Someone called me up in the middle of the night. They hung up before I could answer the phone. It _____ (be) my brother; he doesn't have a telephone. It _____ (be) someone I know, but why would they call in the middle of the night? It _____ (be) a wrong number.

2. Where were you last night? I thought you were going to join us at the movies. You _____ (have) enough money to go with us, because the tickets weren't that expensive. It's too bad you didn't come. I _____ (be) able to lend you the money. And probably Peter _____ (pay) for your ticket. He's so generous. The movie was really funny. You _____ (be) disappointed.

3. Janet looked really unhappy. She _____ (failed) another exam. I know she's already failed one midterm, and she had two more last week. It _____ (be) her chemistry test. I know she was really nervous about it. It _____ (be) her calculus exam. She's really good at mathematics, and I know she studied a lot for it.

4. Bob looked everywhere for the missing documents. They _____ (disappear) by themselves. He thought they _____ (be) on the desk, where he usually put things he was working on, or they _____ be in his briefcase too. But when he looked, they weren't in either place. Then he remembered working on them at the office. He _____ (leave) them there.

5. Who killed Judge Clarence? It _____ (be) his wife. She was in Switzerland learning how to ski. It _____ (be) his accountant. Apparently there was some trouble with money. But nobody thought his accountant would do such a thing. There were a few clues. His wallet was missing. His brother's fingerprints were found on the candlestick that was used to kill the judge. The murderer _____ (be) his brother. But Detective Nancy Mann was not convinced. It all seemed too simple. The brother was rich and didn't need the money. The murderer _____ (be) someone else, someone who was actually trying to get the brother in trouble with the law.

Exercise 11

Use modals of prediction and inference to give possible reasons for these situations.

EXAMPLE: The window was open. The TV was gone.
A thief must have broken into the apartment.
The students are quiet. They're listening carefully.
They might be taking a test.
The teacher could be telling them about their final examination.

1. Mary is crying. She's looking at a picture.
2. John's waiting at the airport. He's looking at his watch.
3. Rebecca was smiling. Her parents were congratulating her.
4. The men were digging holes. They were looking at an old map.
5. A woman was shouting happily. She had just received an envelope in the mail.
6. Bill studies every night. He sends applications to universities.
7. That man wears old clothes. He doesn't have enough to eat.
8. The firemen ran to the firetruck. They drove quickly to the house.

Activities

Task—Additional Clues:

- **Do not look at these** until you have thought of at least five possible explanations for each mystery.
  Mystery #1: The man is very, very short.
  Mystery #2: There's a big puddle of water in the room, and the paper is a delivery bill from an ice company.
  Mystery #3: The police officer is a woman.

Activity 1

Watch a television program (comedy or drama–not a news show or program with a narrator) for a few minutes without turning on the sound. You should be able to see, but not to hear, what's going on. Describe at least ten interactions between characters. Describe exactly what happened, your interpretation of what happened, and your reasons for thinking so.

Description of what happened	Interpretation of the action	Reason for your interpretation
Who did what?	What was the character's reason or purpose?	Why do you think so?

- Then write a paragraph that describes what you saw and what you think was happening. Be sure to distinguish between things that might have been going on versus things that must have been going on. Be sure to give reasons for all of your interpretations.
- Your teacher may want you all to watch the same program so that you can compare your interpretations with those of other students in the class.

Activity 2

Do you have friends or family living in another country? What time is it at this moment in that country? (How many hours' difference is there between that country and where you are now?) Taking the time difference into account, talk or write about what you think they are doing at this very moment.

Activity 3

These are pictures of six household items that are no longer used today. The size of each object has been indicated. Can you tell what function these objects had by looking at their form?

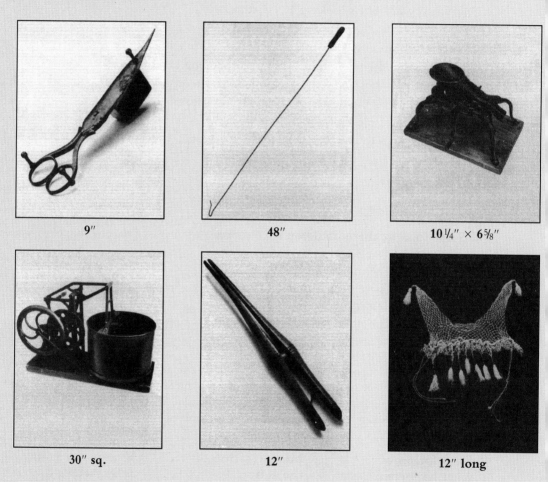

| 9″ | 48″ | 10¼″ × 6⅝″ |
| 30″ sq. | 12″ | 12″ long |

- Work with a partner and discuss what you think each object might have been used for. Explain what its function might have been, and your reasons for thinking so.
- Compare your ideas to those of other students in the class. After you have presented your ideas to the class, your teacher will tell you what the actual use of each of the objects was.

Activity 4

Do you know how to predict someone's future by looking at his or her palm? Here is a diagram of some of the important lines of the palm. If the line is deep and strong, the person should have favorable developments in those areas. If the line is weak or broken, this indicates that the person may have trouble in that area. Using this reference guide, choose a partner, examine his or her palm, and make predictions about his or her future.

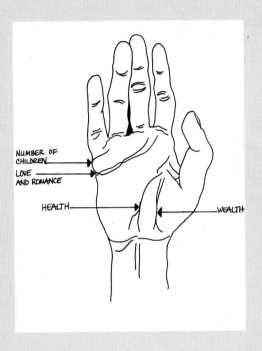

22

Hypothetical Statements

Task

What things about your life would you change if you had the chance? Nadine Stair, from Louisville, Kentucky, wrote the following essay at the age of 85.

IF I HAD MY LIFE TO LIVE OVER

I'd dare to make more mistakes next time. I'd relax. I would limber up. I would be sillier than I have been this trip. I would take fewer things seriously. I would take more chances. I would take more trips. I would climb more mountains and swim more rivers. I would eat more ice cream and less beans. I would perhaps have more actual troubles, but I'd have fewer imaginary ones.

You see, I'm one of those people who live sensibly and sanely hour after hour, day after day. Oh, I've had my moments, and if I had it to do over again, I'd try to have nothing else. Just moments, one after another, instead of living so many years ahead of each day. I've been one of those persons who never goes anywhere without a thermometer, a hot water bottle, a raincoat, and a parachute. If I had to do it again, I would travel lighter than I have.

If I had my life to live over, I would start barefoot earlier in the spring and stay that way later in the fall. I would go to more dances. I would ride more merry-go-rounds. I would pick more daisies.

- First, discuss this essay with a partner. What is Nadine Stair's philosophy of life? Do you agree or disagree with her attitude about what things are important? Do you think that she is speaking literally about swimming rivers, climbing mountains, and carrying a parachute, or do you think these are metaphorical examples of her attitude toward life? What does she mean by "moments"? You and your partner should summarize this essay in one or two sentences. Compare your ideas with those of the rest of the class.

- Next, decide how you would live your life differently if you could. Make a list of things that you are dissatisfied with, or things that you wish you could change. Once you have made your list, write how you would do it differently. Here are some examples:

DISSATISFACTIONS

- I don't have enough money.
- I have to spend too much time studying.

- I don't like living in a place with cold winters.

- Some people don't like me.

HOW MY "IDEAL" LIFE WOULD BE DIFFERENT

- I would have lots of money.
- I wouldn't have to spend a lot of time studying.

- I would live in a place that was warm all the time. (Or: I wouldn't live in a place that has cold winters.)

- Everyone would like me.

- Finally, use your list of the things you would or would not do to write a brief essay like Nadine Stair's. Write a paragraph on how you would live your life differently than you are currently doing, and what things you would change if you could.

Focus 1

MEANING

Hypothetical Meaning

MEANING

English makes a grammatical distinction between real situations, or **actual situations**, and **hypothetical situations.** Hypothetical situations are very common in both spoken and written English. You can use them

- to talk about things that are not true or are impossible.
- to imply that the opposite situation is actually true.
- to be more polite.

It is important to recognize hypothetical statements and to understand the implied meaning of these kinds of statements.

Hypothetical Statement	Implied Meaning
(a) If I had a million dollars, I would buy a nice house.	I don't have a million dollars, so I probably won't be able to buy a nice house.
(b) If we were in Hawaii right now, we wouldn't have to be studying grammar. We could be lying on the beach.	We're not in Hawaii; we're in English class. We can't lie on the beach because we're studying grammar.
(c) You should be happy with your life. Many people would love to have half the opportunities that you do. If I were you, I wouldn't feel so sorry for myself, and I would count my blessings!	You aren't happy with your life. Many people don't have even half the opportunities that you have. I am not you, but I think you feel sorry for yourself, and you don't count your blessings.
(d) I wish we weren't in school. If we weren't in school, we could be almost anywhere. We could be at the beach or at the movies. We could be relaxing or having fun. We wouldn't have to be studying English. Wouldn't that be interesting?	It's too bad we're in school. If you're in school, you can't be anyplace else. You can't be at the beach or at the movies. You can't be relaxing or having fun. You have to be studying English. Isn't that boring?

289

Exercise 1

Here are some other examples of hypothetical statements. Choose the sentence that correctly reflects their implied meaning:

1. If you had done your homework, you would have gotten an *A*.
   (a) You didn't get an *A* because you didn't do your homework.
   (b) You did your homework, and so you got an *A*.
2. You could have brought a friend to the party.
   (a) You had permission, but you came alone.
   (b) You were able to bring a friend.
3. You could have been more careful with your homework.
   (a) You had the ability to do good work.
   (b) You were careless with your homework.
4. You should have seen the doctor before you got so sick.
   (a) You followed my advice.
   (b) You did not follow my advice.
5. You might at least have cleaned the house before my mother got here!
   (a) It was still dirty when she arrived.
   (b) It is possible that you did it.
6. I would have been here early, but the traffic was terrible!
   (a) I arrived early.
   (b) I arrived late.
7. I wish you had come to the lake last weekend.
   (a) You did not come.
   (b) You were there.
8. Let's pretend that we had a new president.
   (a) We do not have a new president.
   (b) We have a new president.

Exercise 2

For these hypothetical statements in Nadine Stair's essay, write a nonhypothetical sentence describing the condition that was actually the case. The first few have been done for you:

Hypothetical Statement	Implied Meaning
1. I'd dare to make more mistakes next time.	1. I was afraid of making mistakes.
2. I would be sillier than I have been this trip.	2. I wasn't silly enough.
3. I would take fewer things seriously.	3. I took too many things seriously.
4. I would take more trips.	4.
5. I would eat more ice cream and less beans.	5.
6. I would perhaps have more actual troubles, but fewer imaginary ones.	6.
7. I would travel lighter than I have.	7.
8. I would start barefoot earlier in the spring.	8.
9. I would go to more dances.	9.
10. I would ride more merry-go-rounds.	10.
11. I would pick more daisies.	11.

Exercise 3

There are three nonhypothetical statements in Nadie Stair's essay. What are the sentences that describe her actual life and character, rather than the life she wishes that she had?

Exercise 4

Are these sentences hypothetical statements or predictions about actual events? If they are hypothetical statements, restate the implied meaning.

EXAMPLES: Those two are always together, so if she attended the meeting, he did too.

prediction about a real event

If the weather hadn't been so cold yesterday, the picnic would have been a lot more fun.

hypothetical statement. The weather was cold yesterday, so the picnic wasn't much fun.

1. I would come to your party if I didn't have to work.
2. If John went to Hawaii on vacation, he must have spent a lot of money.
3. If Bill could afford to retire, I'm sure he would have done so by now.
4. I wouldn't tease that dog if I were you.
5. Suppose you had your own private jet. Where would you go for the weekend?
6. If Bill left when he had planned, he should be here any minute.
7. If my brother needed money, he always asked to borrow it from me.
8. Suppose I cook a big casserole for the party. Do you think there would be enough food?

Focus 2

Hypothetical Conditionals

We often phrase hypothetical statements in terms of conditions and results. Compare these nonhypothetical conditionals (see Unit 15) with their hypothetical counterparts. Notice the important differences in implied meaning.

Factual, Predictive, or Inferential Conditionals	Implied Meaning
(a) If I **have** the time, I always **clean** the kitchen before I go to work.	I always do this whenever I have time.
(b) If I **don't have to work, I will come** to your party.	I don't know if I can come, because there's a chance that I may have to work.
(c) If Mary **was** at the lecture yesterday, I'm sure she **took** very complete notes.	Maybe she was there and took notes.

Hypothetical Conditional	Implied Meaning
(d) If I **had** the time, I **would clean** the kitchen before leaving for work.	I don't do it, because I don't have time.
(e) If I **didn't have to work, I would** come to your party.	I can't come, because I have to work.
(f) If Mary **had been** at the lecture, I'm sure she **would have taken** very complete notes.	She wasn't there, so she didn't take notes.

Exercise 5

Match these statements with their correct implied meaning.

Statement	Implied Meaning
1. (a) If John has the money, he always stops for a cup of espresso on his way to class. **(b)** If John had the money, he would always stop for a cup of espresso on his way to class.	**(a)** He doesn't usually do this, because he usually doesn't have the money. **(b)** He always does this whenever he has the money.
2. (a) If I had to work, I wouldn't be helping you with your homework. **(b)** If I have to work, I won't be able to help you with your homework.	**(a)** I may have to work. **(b)** I don't have to work.
3. (a) If Bambang took the TOEFL yesterday, I'm sure he did very well. **(b)** If Bambang had taken the TOEFL, I'm sure he would have done very well.	**(a)** Bambang didn't take the TOEFL. **(b)** Maybe Bambang took the TOEFL.

Focus 3

FORM

Hypothetical Statements in Present and Future Time Frames

FORM

You can use past tense forms to indicate that all these statements of condition and result are hypothetical and, therefore, not possible.

Past Tense Verb Forms Refer To	*Would/Could/Might* + **Verb Refer To**
Present Conditions	**Present/Future Results**
(a) If I **had** time, **(b)** If I **didn't have to work**, **(c)** If I **were** rich, **(d)** If I **could speak** English,	I **would clean** the kitchen before leaving for work. I **would come** to your party. I **would give** you a million dollars. I **wouldn't need** to read this unit.
Future Conditions	**Present Results**
(e) If we **didn't have to go** to school tomorrow,	we **could stay up** all night tonight.
(f) If John **weren't going to spend** next year in France,	Mary **might not be** so annoyed with him now.
	Future Results
(g) If I **graduated** next semester, **(h)** If I **were to graduate** one semester earlier,	it **would be** easier to find a job. it **would be** easier to get a teaching job right away.

These structures are an indication of hypothetical statements:

- *If*-clauses use *were* for singular subjects, rather than *was*, in most written and formal spoken English.
    - **(i)** If my mother **were** here, she would want us all to wash our hands.
    - **(j)** If Mary **were** coming to the party, she could bring the potato salad.
- Future hypothetical conditions are stated with past tense forms or *were to*. *Were to* is more common in formal English, and indicates that the possibility is very unlikely.
    - **(k)** If you **passed** TOEFL **next month**, you could probably begin academic studies next semester.
    - **(l)** I don't think you'll pass the TOEFL next month, but if you **were to do so**, we could have a party to celebrate.

Exercise 6

Change these statements of condition and result into hypothetical conditionals.

> **EXAMPLE:** (Condition) I'm not the teacher of this class.
> (Result) We have too much homework.
> *Hypothetical: If I were the teacher of this class, we wouldn't have so much homework.*

1. I don't have a million dollars. I can't afford to buy you a new car.
2. I don't yet speak English perfectly. I still have to study grammar.
3. Doctors have to spend so many years in medical school. Medical care is quite expensive.
4. My mother doesn't know how I am living now. She's not worried about me.
5. I am not President of my country. I don't have much influence on world events.
6. I have many good friends. My life is busy and rewarding.
7. The TOEFL is a difficult examination. Many people can't pass it on the first try.
8. There are too many irregular verbs in English. It isn't an easy language to learn.
9. There aren't enough places in universities in other countries. Many students come to the United States for university study.
10. The weather reporter has forecast heavy rains for the entire day tomorrow. We won't have the picnic.

Exercise 7

Here are some hypothetical conditions. Add hypothetical results that are true for you:

> **EXAMPLE:** If I could be anywhere in the world at this moment, . . .
> *I would be home in bed.*

1. If I were going to attend any American university tomorrow, ...
2. If I were President of the United States, ...
3. If my mother knew how I was living now, ...

4. If I were the teacher of this class, ...
5. If I didn't have to worry about the TOEFL, ...
6. If I were to go home next week, ...
7. If I had all the money I needed, ...
8. If I were the same age as my parents, ...

Exercise 8

Here are some hypothetical results. Add hypothetical conditions that are true for you.

EXAMPLE: I would take a vacation . . .

if I didn't have to pass the TOEFL.

1. I wouldn't need to work . . . .
2. I would bring my family here for a visit . . . .
3. We wouldn't come to school . . . .
4. We wouldn't need umbrellas . . . .
5. I wouldn't be studying English . . . .
6. I wouldn't have to take the TOEFL . . . .
7. The world would be a much better place . . . .
8. I would give my grammar teacher $1,000 . . . .

Exercise 9

Compare your answers to Exercise 7 and 8 with those of another student. Report some of his or her responses to the rest of the class:

EXAMPLE: *May says that if she were the teacher of this class, she would give me an A.*

Focus 4

Hypothetical Statements in Past Time Frame

FORM

You can use past perfect forms and past modals with *have* + **past participle** to indicate hypothetical situations in the Past Time Frame.

Past Perfect Verb Forms Refer to	***Would Have/Could Have/Might Have/ Should Have* + verb** Refer to
Past Hypothetical Conditions	**Past Hypothetical Results**
(a) If Mary **had been** at the lecture,	I'm sure she **would have taken** very complete notes. She **wouldn't have minded** sharing them. She **would have let** you borrow them.
	***Would/Could/Might* + verb** Refer to
	Present or Future Results
(b) If William the Conqueror **hadn't invaded** England in 1066, **(c)** If I **had been born** in the last century, **(d)** If we **hadn't saved** enough money last year,	the English language **would probably have** a lot fewer words of French origin. I surely **wouldn't be** alive today. we **wouldn't be able to take** a vacation next summer.

Focus 5

Inverted or Question Word Order for Hypothetical Conditionals

USE

In formal written English, you can indicate hypothetical conditions in clauses with a *were* or *had* auxiliary by omitting the *if* and using question word order. This is not very common in spoken English.

Inverted Form	**Regular Form**
(a) Had I known that you were coming so late, I wouldn't have waited.	**(b) If I had known** that you were coming so late, I wouldn't have waited.
(c) Were I in charge of this business, I would make some big changes.	**(d) If I were** in charge of this business I would make some big changes.

Exercise 10

Change these nonhypothetical statements of condition and result to hypothetical conditionals.

EXAMPLE: I wasn't alive 100 years ago. I have been able to fly all over the world.

If I had been alive 100 years ago, I wouldn't have been able to fly all over the world.

1. My parents didn't speak English when I was a baby. I have to learn it in school.
2. English became a language of international business after World War II. Most developing countries require students to study it in high school.
3. Modern English developed from several different languages: French, German, Latin, Dutch, and even Norwegian. As a result, the grammar and spelling rules are very irregular.
4. England was invaded by France in 1066. Many French words replaced the traditional Anglo-Saxon ones.

Exercise 11

Here are some past conditions.
Add past-time hypothetical results that are true for you.

EXAMPLE: If I had been born 100 years ago...

I wouldn't have had a chance to travel.

1. If my parents had spoken English when I was a baby....
2. If America hadn't won World War II....
3. If the grammar of English hadn't developed from so many different languages ;...
4. If advanced computer technology hadn't been developed in the United States....
5. If I had never studied English....

Add present or future time results to these sentences:

EXAMPLES: If I had been born 100 years ago...

I probably wouldn't be alive today.

my great grandchildren might be entering the university in the next few years.

6. If I had been born in this country....
7. If the Japanese had won World War II....
8. If my parents hadn't wanted me to learn English....
9. If computers hadn't become so inexpensive and widely available....
10. If I had already gotten a score of 650 on the TOEFL....

297

Exercise 12

The following are hypothetical results. Add appropriate past-time conditions.

> **EXAMPLE:** I wouldn't have had a chance to travel . . .
>
> *if I had been born 100 years ago.*

1. I wouldn't have asked you to join us . . . .
2. I would not be studying English now . . . .
3. English grammar would be much more regular . . . .
4. Fax machines wouldn't be so popular in Asian countries . . . .
5. America wouldn't be spending so much money on military expenditures . . . .
6. Transoceanic telephone calls wouldn't be possible . . . .
7. There wouldn't have been such sweeping political changes in Eastern European countries . . . .
8. Modern antibiotics might not have been discovered . . . .
9. Life today would be much more difficult . . . .
10. I wouldn't have to answer this question . . . .

Exercise 13

Compare your answers in Exercises 11 and 12 with those of another student. Report some of his or her responses to the rest of the class:

> **EXAMPLE:** *May says that if she had been born 100 years ago, she wouldn't have been able to study medicine.*

Exercise 14

From the sentences you made in Exercises 7, 8, 11, and 12, write new sentences in non-hypothetical language.

> **EXAMPLES:** If I had a million dollars, I would give you a new car.
>
> *I don't have enough money to give you a car.*
>
> I would take a vacation, if I didn't have to finish this project.
>
> *I have to finish this project, so I can't take a vacation.*
>
> *I can't take a vacation because I have to finish this project.*
>
> I wouldn't have asked you to join us, if I had known you were going to be so rude.
>
> *I asked you to come because I thought you would be more polite.*
>
> If I had been born 100 years ago, I wouldn't have had a chance to travel widely.
>
> *A hundred years ago people like me didn't have a chance to travel widely.*

Exercise 15

These passages contain hypothetical statements.

- Underline the hypothetical statements.
- Rewrite the sentences using nonhypothetical language. Be sure that your restatements reflect the actual time and preserve the actual meaning. The first paragraph of the first passage has been done for you as an example.

> **EXAMPLE:** (2) *Governments spend too much on arms, so not enough money is available for economic development, education, and health care.*

1. (1)Some students of international relations feel that individual governments shouldn't be spending so much money on military expenditures. (2)If governments stopped spending so much on arms, more money would be available for economic development, education, and health care.

   (3)Everyone agrees that some kind military force is necessary to maintain global stability, but these experts feel that it could be some sort of multinational peacekeeping force, administered by the United Nations. (4)If countries formed joint regional defense programs, one or two "superpowers" would be less likely to see themselves as responsible for maintaining global stability.

   (5)Pacifists point out that if the size of military forces were reduced — or even eliminated — then that money would be available for nonmilitary purposes. (6)This would enable governments to give more support to social programs. (7)Better social programs would improve social conditions. (8)Improved social conditions worldwide would reduce the need for wars even more.

2. (1)Many important developments in science have happened by accident. (2)Discoveries have often been made because someone was in the right place at the right time, or because someone made a mistake and got an unexpected result. (3)For example, if Sir Isaac Newton hadn't decided to take a nap under an apple tree, he wouldn't have been hit on the head by a falling apple. (4)It was this event that inspired him to formulate the Law of Gravity. (5)If Sir Alexander Fleming hadn't left his sandwich sitting on a laboratory windowsill and forgotten about it, he would not have discovered the mold that contains penicillin. (6)That's how he first found out about the antibiotic properties of certain fungi. (7)Had Christopher Columbus correctly calculated the actual size of the earth, he would never have tried to reach Asia by sailing west. (8)If that hadn't happened, the European discovery of the New World might have occurred in 1592, instead of 1492.

3. (1)The commercial development of the fax machine (which enables a person to send a photocopy of a document via telephone) has literally exploded in a phenomenally short period of time. (2)But its use wouldn't have grown as rapidly as it has, had certain Asian writing systems been able to adapt well to other forms of transmission. (3)If the writing systems of Chinese and Japanese were not so complex, people would be able to use other means (such as telegraph or digital computer display) to communicate information over long distances.

(4)Western languages use only 20 to 30 symbols to communicate ideas, so each individual letter can be easily translated into a specific series of electronic impulses. (5)Electronic digital transmission of western languages has been possible ever since the invention of the telegraph, nearly 150 years ago. (6)If Western languages used a writing system like that of Chinese, such digital transmission would probably never have been developed. (7)Chinese requires 3,000 to 5,000 different individual characters to communicate ordinary day-to-day events and ideas. (8)This makes digital transmission impractical. (9)If there weren't so many individual characters, or if the writing system had a clear correlation between a single symbol and a single sound, the fax would surely not have become so widely used in such a short period of time.

(10)In the last five years, fax machines have virtually replaced other communications systems, especially in Asia. (11)It is simply easier to write a character and transmit the image than it is to try to invent some system that "translates" a visually complex symbol into a series of electrical impulses. (12)Had this not been the case, the widespread use of fax machines would probably not have happened so quickly.

Focus 6

Mixing Hypothetical and Actual Statements

USE

- You can sometimes mix actual conditions and hypothetical results in a single statement.

Actual Condition	Hypothetical Result
(a) I had to work last night.	**(b) Otherwise** I would have come to your party.
(c) Peter brought a doctor's excuse to explain his absence.	**(d) Otherwise** Denise would have accused him of being irresponsible.
(e) It's going to rain tomorrow.	**(f) Otherwise** we could have the luncheon outside.

Hypothetical Result	Actual Condition
(g) I would have come to your party last night,	**but** I had to work.
(h) Denise would have accused Peter of being irresponsible,	**but** he brought a doctor's excuse to explain his absence.
(i) We could have the luncheon outside,	**but** it's going to rain.

Exercise 16

The following are some actual conditions. State a hypothetical result by using *otherwise* or *but*.

EXAMPLE: I'm not rich.

I'm not rich. Otherwise I would loan you the money you asked for.
I would loan you the money you asked for, but I'm not rich.

1. I don't have a million dollars.
2. I don't yet speak English perfectly.
3. Doctors have to spend many years in medical school.
4. My mother doesn't know how I am living now.
5. My father is not the leader of my country.
6. I have many good friends.
7. The TOEFL is a difficult examination.
8. English isn't an easy language to learn.
9. Many students come to the United States for university study.
10. The weather forecaster has predicted heavy rain for tomorrow afternoon.

Focus 7

USE

Using Hypothetical Statements

USE

You can use present and future hypothetical constructions
- to indicate theoretical rather than actual possibilities:

Actual Possibility	Implied Meaning
(a) If we **get** some free time, we **can go** to the movies.	There is a strong possibility that we **may get** free time.
Theoretical Possibility	
(b) If we **got** some free time this weekend, we **could go** to the movies.	The possibility of free time is not great, but we are discussing it anyway.
(c) If I **had** free time, I **would go** to the movies.	There is no possibility of free time, but this is what would happen if there were.

- to be more polite:

Very Direct/Less Polite	Less Direct/More Polite
(d) The room **will** be much more comfortable if we **open** a window.	**(e)** The room **would** be much more comfortable if we **opened** a window.
(f) If you **have** time, **can** you help me with my homework tonight?	**(g)** If you **had** the time, **could** you help me with my homework tonight?
(h) I **won't** help you with your homework because I **have** to work tonight	**(i)** I **would** help you with your homework if I **didn't have to** work tonight.

You can discuss certain "sensitive" topics more easily and diplomatically by using hypothetical constructions. Using hypothetical indicates that you are not implying that the sensitive topic is actually true or could actually happen.

Nonhypothetical	Implied Meaning
(j) If someone **gives** you a lot of money, **will** you help them cheat on an important examination?	I think you might be the kind of person who will do something dishonest for money.
Hypothetical	
(k) If someone **gave** you a lot of money **would** you help them cheat on an important examination?	This is not a real situation, just an example. I don't think that you would do something dishonest for money.

The most common use of hypothetical statements in the Past Time Frame is to talk about things that did not actually happen.

Hypothetical	Implied Meaning
(l) Had you done your homework, you would have gotten an *A*.	You didn't get an *A* because you didn't do your homework.
(m) You could have brought a friend.	You had permission, but you came alone.
(n) You could have been more careful with your homework.	You had the ability, but you didn't do it.
(o) You should have seen the doctor.	You didn't do it.
(p) You might have cleaned the house before my mother got here.	It was still dirty when she arrived.
(q) I would have been here early, but the traffic was terrible!	I arrived late.

Exercise 17

Would you ever consider doing these things? Decide whether these statements represent actual or theoretical possibilities for you, and make a hypothetical or nonhypothetical sentence that reflects that.

> **EXAMPLE:** marry an American
>
> *If I marry an American, I will probably become a citizen.*
> *(actual possibility—something that might actually be possible for you)*
> *If I married an American, my parents would be very disappointed.*
> *(theoretical possibility—something that you don't think will ever be possible for you)*

1. go home for the next vacation
2. pass the TOEFL the next time you take it
3. become President of your country
4. have eight children
5. buy a new car within the next three months
6. join the army
7. get sick later today
8. look for a new place to live
9. have free time before class tomorrow

Exercise 18

Make these statements and requests more polite by using hypothetical conditionals.

> **EXAMPLE:** Don't smoke here.
>
> *I wouldn't smoke here if I were you.*

1. Can I close the door?
2. Do you mind turning down the radio a little bit?
3. Eat some more of this pie, because it will make the cook happy.
4. I won't come to your party.
5. I'm too busy to take the time to help you.

Exercise 19

Do these sentences indicate statements of past possibility or hypothetical events that did not happen?

> **EXAMPLES:** I didn't see him, but he could have been there.
> *past possibility*
> If John had been at the concert, he would have been able to explain how the composer was able to get those effects.
> *hypothetical event*

1. My brother could have loaned me the money, but he's too cheap.
2. Assuming that the plane was on time, it should have landed a little while ago.
3. I don't know what the problem is. They should have been here by now.
4. You should have asked for a receipt when you bought those clothes.
5. John might have worked a little harder on this report. It's pretty sloppy.
6. The thief might have gotten in through the window. It appears to be unlocked.

Focus 8

Other Common Verbs Used with Hypothetical Statements

USE

- Use hypothetical constructions with **wish**. There is an important difference in meaning between the verbs **wish** and **hope**:
  - **Wish** describes situations that are not true:

	Implied Meaning
(a) I **wish** you **had come** to the lake last weekend.	You didn't come.
(b) I **wish** you **liked** Chinese food.	You don't like it.
(c) I **wish** you **would come** to my party.	You refuse to come.

- **Hope** expresses actual possibilities. The outcome can be in the past, present, or future:

	Implied Meaning
(d) I **hope** you **had** a nice time at the lake last weekend.	I don't know whether or not you did.
(e) I **hope** you **like** the new apartment.	I don't know if you will like it or not.
(f) I **hope** you'll **come** to my party next week.	I don't know if you'll be able to come or not.

- You should use hypothetical constructions with verbs that indicate imagination or hypothetical supposition:
  - **(g)** **Let's imagine** that we **had** a new President.
  - **(h)** **Pretend** that you **could** fly. Do you think you **would** still own a car?
  - **(i)** **Suppose** we **went** to Europe next summer. How much do you think it **would** cost? (We are only talking about it now. We're not making an actual plan.)
- In formal English, you can use hypothetical constructions with **as if** (See Unit 12):
  - **(j)** John looks **as if** he **were** thinking about something else.
  - **(k)** He drank **as if** there **were** no tomorrow.
  - **(l)** You act **as if** there **were** no reason to be embarrassed.

Exercise 20

Refer to the Task. Write five sentences that identify the things Nadine Stair wishes she had done differently.

> **EXAMPLES:** *Nadine Stair wishes that she had been more relaxed.*
> *She wishes she had dared to make more mistakes.*

Activities

Activity 1

They say that everyone has 20/20 hindsight vision. Things that may have been unclear when they were happening seem very clear when we look back on the experience.

- Think about some things that you would have done differently if you had known then the things that you know now.
- Make a list of
  - things you wish you had done that you didn't do.
  - things you wish you hadn't done that you did do.
- Write an essay about your hindsight or make a presentation to the rest of the class.

Activity 2

If you could have three wishes, what would they be and why would you wish them?

- Write down your three wishes.
- Compare your answers to those of someone else in class. What do someone else's wishes tell you about his or her life? What do your wishes tell someone else about you?
- Make one statement about **why** you think your partner made the wishes that he or she did. Tell that statement to your partner but not to the rest of the class.

Activity 3

Suppose that you had just been made Supreme Commander of the Entire World. What actions would you take to

    end world hunger
    develop renewable energy sources
    control population growth
    protect the environment
    abolish war
    ensure political stability
    maintain economic growth

- Choose one of these areas and devise a plan for things you would do if you had the power and resources to accomplish them.
- Report your hypothetical plan to the rest of the class.

Activity 4

What would you do for ten million dollars? Would you tell a lie? Would you betray a friend? Would you give a child up for adoption? Would you become a citizen of another country? Would you leave your family? What would you refuse to do, even if you were offered ten million dollars?

- Identify some things you would and would not do for ten million dollars and compare them to those of other people in class.

Activity 5

A *dilemma* is a problem for which there are a limited number of possible solutions that are all unsatisfactory for one reason or another.

- What would you do if you were faced with the following dilemmas:

    Your parents do not approve of the person you want to marry.

    Your friend and you both work at the same company. You feel very loyal to the company, but you find out that your friend has stolen some of the company's money.

    You have fallen in love with the husband or wife of your best friend.

    Your best friend needs to borrow some money "for a serious emergency," but he or she will not say what that emergency is. You had been planning to spend that money to buy a birthday present for your boyfriend or girlfriend. Your friend needs the money right away, and the birthday celebration is also today. You cannot get any other money, only what you have now.

- Discuss your solutions with others in a small group.
- Devise a list of general strategies or suggestions about what people can do if they are faced with any kind of dilemma.
- Present your list of strategies to the rest of the class.

Sensory Verbs

23

Task

Seeing is the sense that we rely on most. But when we are deprived of sight, our other senses become sharper. Test your other senses through the following exercise:

- Go to a place you know well. It could be this classroom, a favorite room in your house, or someplace outdoors. Close your eyes and keep them closed for three minutes. Listen for the sounds that you can hear, both inside and outside. Are there any smells that you notice? Are they pleasant or unpleasant? What can you feel? Is it hot or cold? Can you feel a draft?
- Make a list of things you have noticed about this place that you never noticed when your eyes were open.

    I heard . . . .

    I smelled . . . .

    I felt . . . .

- Compare your list with several other people's lists. As a group, decide what other kinds of things escape your attention when you can rely on eyesight for information about the world around you.
- Present your ideas to the rest of the class.

Focus 1

Describing Two Actions

MEANING

- Sensory verbs (also known as verbs of observation) are similar to Pattern 2 verbs that take infinitive and gerund complements. You can use them to report the observed action of a "second subject." The second subject can be a noun or an object pronoun.

Sensory Verb	Second Subject	Observed Action
(a) I **saw**	the dog	jump into the water.
(b) Mary **heard**	us	laughing.

Exercise 1

Identify the sensory verbs in the following sentences. Restate the observed action as a separate sentence.

EXAMPLE: Mary saw the dog come into the room and steal the cheese.
> *sensory verb: saw; observed action: The dog came into the room and stole the cheese.*

1. If you listen carefully, you can hear the birds singing in that tree.
2. Marlon likes to feel the wind blow through his hair when he rides his motorcycle.
3. Peter heard his voice get louder as he argued with Denise.
4. I saw the thief pick up the man's briefcase and begin to run away.
5. The doctor listened to the old woman complain about her arthritis.
6. When Deborah heard the baby crying, she hurried into the nursery.
7. We watched squirrels gathering nuts for the winter.
8. I smell something burning, so we had better check the stove.

Exercise 2

Answer these questions by using sensory verbs with a second subject.

EXAMPLE: What can you see at a disco?
> *You can see people dancing.*

1. What can you hear at a concert?
2. What can you see at a skating rink?
3. What can you smell at a bakery?
4. What can you hear at the beach?
5. What can you see at a shopping mall?
6. What will you hear at a playground?
7. What can you hear in an English class?
8. What can you see at a gym?

Focus 2

Actions in Progress versus Completed Actions

FORM
MEANING

- Unlike *verb + gerund* or *verb + infinitive* combinations, sensory verbs use either a **present participle (verb + *ing*)** or the **simple form** of a verb to express the second action:
  - **(a)** The teacher heard us **laughing**.
  - **(b)** NOT: The teacher heard **our laughing**.
  - **(c)** The teacher heard us **laugh**.
  - **(d)** NOT: The teacher heard us **to laugh**.
- Depending on the form that is used, there is a difference in meaning and use. Using **-*ing* form** indicates that the action was **in progress or unfinished** at the time of observation. Using the **simple form** indicates that the **complete action** was observed in its entirety.

Action in Progress/Unfinished	Complete Action
(e) Bob heard the thieves **breaking** into the house, so he called the police.	**(f)** Bob **saw** the thieves **load** the TV into the car and **drive** away.

- In many cases, there is little difference in meaning, but in some cases the situation requires one form instead of the other.

Same Meaning	Different Meaning
(g) I watched the boys **playing** baseball in the park next door.	**(i)** I saw Mary **leaving** school, **so I ran to catch her.**
(h) I watched the boys **play** baseball in the park next door.	**(j)** I saw Mary **leave** school, so **I'm sure she's not coming to the teachers' meeting.**

Exercise 3

Decide on which form of the verb to use, based on the context, and underline it. In some sentences, both forms may be possible, so prepare to explain your choice.

EXAMPLE: I saw smoke (come/<u>coming</u>) from the storeroom, so I called the fire department.

1. I heard the phone (ring/ringing), but I decided not to answer it.
2. The principal watched the students (take/taking) the test so that she could be sure there was no cheating.
3. Matt felt himself (get/getting) angry as he and his roommate argued about who should do the dishes.
4. On my way to the store, I saw Morris (ride/riding) his new bike.
5. As Mary listened to the radio (play/playing) her favorite song, she began to cry and hurried out of the room.
6. I heard the workers (leave/leaving) earlier today. I'm sure they haven't returned yet.
7. We could all smell something (burn/burning). Apparently somebody had tossed a lighted cigarette into the wastepaper basket.

Exercise 4

Restate the numbered sentences in these paragraphs as sensory verb complements:

EXAMPLE: Here is what Tom saw: (1)Three boys were swimming in the river. (2)They were splashing and playing. (3)One of them shouted that it was time to go. (4)They picked up their towels and left.

(1)Tom saw three boys swimming in the river. (2)He watched them splashing and playing. (3)He heard one of them shout that it was time to go. (4)He watched them pick up their towels and leave.

1. Here is what Doris observed: (1)A man came into the bank. (2)He got in line. When he reached the teller's window, he handed her a piece of paper and a brown paper bag. (3)The teller was putting money in the bag, when a loud alarm began to ring. (4)Guards rushed in, but the man had escaped through the side entrance.
2. When Mrs. McMartin looked out the window, this is what she saw: (1)There were a few children playing on the swings. (2)Others were climbing on the monkeybars. (3)One little boy was running very fast around and around the playground. (4)Suddenly he fell down. (5)He screamed in pain. (6)All the other children looked around to see where the noise was coming from. (7)One child ran toward Mrs. McMartin's office.
3. Here is what I saw, heard, and felt during the hurricane. (1)The wind grew louder. (2)The windows and doors shook. (3)The trees swayed in the garden outside. I thought the house was moving. (4)A tree crashed against the house. (5)There was a sound of breaking glass upstairs. I went upstairs. (6)Rain was pouring through the broken window. (7)A strong wind blew into the room. (8)The wind howled louder and louder.

Focus 3

Present Participle versus Simple Form

MEANING

- You can use present participles (**verb + –ing**) instead of simple verbs
  - to indicate repeated action instead of a single occurrence:

Repeated Action	Single Action
(a) I saw the woman **slapping** her child	**(b)** I saw the woman **slap** her child.
(c) The police watched the demonstrators **overturning trucks** and setting **them** on fire.	**(d)** The police watched the demonstrators **overturn a truck** and set **it** on fire.

- with verbs of position, if the "second subject" is an inanimate object that cannot move by itself:
  - **(e)** I saw the bicycle **lying** by the side of the road.
  - **(f)** NOT: I saw the bicycle **lie** by the side of the road.
- with verbs of interception (**find, catch, discover,** etc.), when the second action is interrupted or not completed:
  - **(g)** We **caught** the thief **taking** money out of the cash register.
  - **(h)** NOT: We caught the thief **take** money out of the cash register.
  - **(i)** We **found** the watchman **sleeping** at his desk.
  - **(j)** NOT: We found the watchman **sleep** at his desk.

311

Exercise 5

Choose the correct form of the verb given. In some cases, both answers may be correct, so prepare to explain why you chose your answer:

1. Brian heard the phone (ring/ringing), but by the time he reached it the person at the other end had hung up.
2. As the hurricane grew stronger, they heard many branches of the big oak tree (snap/snapping) and (fall/falling) to the ground.
3. John was relieved when he saw his lost wallet (sit/sitting) next to his checkbook on the shelf.
4. Mary watched the snow (fall/falling) gently through the trees.
5. Deborah heard Evan (cry/crying), so she went in to see what was wrong.
6. We heard the sound of laughter (drift/drifting) across the lake from the house where the party was.
7. When we arrived, we found the dog (wait/waiting) at the door for us.
8. I smell something (burn/burning). Did you remember to take the cookies out of the oven?

Activities

Activity 1

Describe this picture. Begin each sentence with "I see...."

312

Activity 2

In the Task, you had an opportunity to experience the world as a blind person does. How are blind people able to move around independently? In what ways do they compensate for lack of sight? How do they get information about where they are and where they are going? Consider people who cannot hear. How are they able to communicate with each other and the rest of the world?

- Discuss ways that people with sensory handicaps can compensate for those handicaps. Use your experience in the Task and any other experiences you have had with people who are blind or deaf.
- Present your ideas in a written or oral report.

Activity 3

Here are some general statements about human nature.

> People are generally in too much of a hurry.
> Children are spontaneous.
> Teenagers like to associate together in groups.
> Older people are generally slower than younger people.

Do you think such generalizations are true or not? This is an opportunity for you to test the validity of such generalizations through systematic observation.

- Choose a generalization that you want to test. It could be one of the statements listed above or some other generalization. You may want to test some generalization that involves cultural differences, such as "Americans are very outgoing" or "Asians are studious."
- Go to a place where you can watch lots of people. A shopping mall, a cafeteria, or a busy corner are all good places. Watch how people behave. Look for examples of behavior that reflect the generalization you are testing. Find as many examples as you can that either support or contradict the generalization and write a paragraph describing what you have observed.
  Here's an example:

  "They say that most people are generally friendly, and I have found that this seems to be true. At the mall yesterday, I saw many people smiling at each other. I saw two people meet by chance. They must have been old friends, because I saw them hug each other. I heard many people laughing and joking. I heard many of the salespeople say "Have a nice day" to customers. I saw one family arguing with each other, but strangers tended to be polite.

Activity 4

Have you ever been in a really strong storm, or a flood, or an earthquake, or some other large-scale natural disaster? Write a paragraph describing your experience and what you saw, heard, and felt.

UNIT

24

Causative Verbs

Task

How do you think children should be raised? What things should good parents do to give their children a good upbringing? What is the best way to teach children responsibility? What is the best way to reward and punish? Answers to questions like these can vary from culture to culture.

- Think about the way your parents raised you. Did you ever hear your parents say:
  "We're doing this for your own good."
  "Everyone needs to do something for the family."
  "You can do this because we know you enjoy it."
- Thinking about these situations will help you identify strategies your parents used to try to give you a good upbringing. Consider these questions:

  What things did your parents make you do that you did not want to do?
  What things did they have you do on a regular basis that you did not mind doing but probably would not have done on your own?
  What things did they let you do as a reward for good behavior?
- Try to think of at least three answers for each question. For each thing you remember, decide whether or not it was an effective strategy, and whether you will use (or are using) this strategy as you raise you own children.
- Ask these questions of other students in the class to find out about their own experiences and opinions. Collect information from at least three other people. Here is a checklist to help you organize your information:

Discipline/ Punishment A	Responsi- bilities B	Rewards/ Motivations C	Effective? yes/no/why	Will You Use It? yes/no/why
Example: (1) no TV for a week (2) spanking (3) no allowance	(1) cut the grass (2) sweep the sidewalk (3) take care of younger sister	(1) allowance $5 per week (2) stay up late on weekends (3) ice cream and candy	A1 Yes A2 Yes A3 Yes C1 Yes C2 Yes C3 Yes	A1 Yes A2 No A3 No C1 Yes C2 Yes C3 No
Student A: _____ _____ _____ _____ _____ _____ _____ _____ _____	_____ _____ _____ _____ _____ _____ _____ _____ _____	_____ _____ _____ _____ _____ _____ _____ _____ _____	_____ _____ _____ _____ _____ _____ _____ _____ _____	_____ _____ _____ _____ _____ _____ _____ _____ _____

Discipline/ Punishment A	Responsi- bilities B	Rewards/ Motivations C	Effective? yes/no/why	Will You Use It? yes/no/why
Student B:				
_____	_____	_____	_____	_____
_____	_____	_____	_____	_____
_____	_____	_____	_____	_____
_____	_____	_____	_____	_____
_____	_____	_____	_____	_____
_____	_____	_____	_____	_____
_____	_____	_____	_____	_____
_____	_____	_____	_____	_____

Discipline/ Punishment A	Responsi- bilities B	Rewards/ Motivations C	Effective? yes/no/why	Will You Use It? yes/no/why
Student C:				
_____	_____	_____	_____	_____
_____	_____	_____	_____	_____
_____	_____	_____	_____	_____
_____	_____	_____	_____	_____
_____	_____	_____	_____	_____
_____	_____	_____	_____	_____
_____	_____	_____	_____	_____
_____	_____	_____	_____	_____
_____	_____	_____	_____	_____

- Based on your findings, make ten recommendations for parents.
  Start five of them with **"Parents should . . . ."**
  Start five recommendations with **"Parents shouldn't . . . ."**
- Compare your recommendations to those of the people you interviewed. Decide on a list of recommendations that you all agree on and present the list to the rest of the class.
- Compile a list of recommendations that the entire class agrees upon.

Focus 1

Causative Verbs and Pattern 2 Verbs with Causative Meaning

FORM
MEANING

- Sentences with causative verbs (*make, let, have, help*) are similar to sentences with pattern 2 verbs (verb + noun phrase + infinitive). You can use them in situations in which the subject of the main verb causes the object of the main verb, the second subject, to perform a second action. But causative verbs are slightly different: The **simple form of the verb**, rather than the infinitive, expresses the second action. This group is limited to a few verbs, but they are used very frequently.

Verb + Noun Phrase + Infinitive	Causative Verb
(a) Parents should **require** their children **to brush** their teeth before bedtime. **(c)** They shouldn't **allow** them **to misbehave in school.**	**(b)** Parents should **make** their children **brush** their teeth before bedtime. **(d)** They shouldn't **let** them **misbehave** in school.

- Causative meanings indicate how much **force** or **persuasion** is necessary to cause the person to do the action.
  - *Make*

	Implied meaning
(e) Parents should **make** naughty children **stand** in the corner instead of spanking them.	Parents should **force** naughty children to stand in the corner **against their will**.
Pattern 2 verbs with a similar meaning are *require, force, order, demand,* and *compel*.	

  - *Get*

	Implied Meaning
(f) Parents should **get** their children **to read** instead of watching TV.	Parents should **persuade rather than force** their children to read instead of watching TV.
This verb does not follow the usual pattern. It requires an infinitive rather than a simple verb. Other Pattern 2 verbs with a similar meaning are *persuade, convince, inspire, motivate,* and *encourage*.	

  - *Have*

	Implied Meaning
(g) Parents should **have** the doctor **examine their children at least once** a year.	Parents should **routinely employ or hire** a doctor to examine their children.
Pattern 2 verbs with a similar meaning are *hire, employ,* and *engage*.	

• **Let**

	Implied Meaning
(h) Good parents **let** their children **play** outside on sunny days.	Parents want their children to play outside and should **allow** them to do so.
Pattern 2 verbs with a similar meaning are *allow* and *permit*	

• **Help**

	Implied Meaning
(i) Good parents **help** their children **learn good manners.** **(j)** Good parents **help** their children **to learn good manners.**	Parents should **assist and participate with** their children in learning good manners.
You can use this verb with either simple verb complement or with an infinitive. A Pattern 2 verb with a similar meaning: *assist*	

Exercise 1

a) Underline the causative verbs and the verb + infinitive constructions with a causative meaning in this passage. Mark the various elements with the letters given: *(a)* the causer, *(b)* the causative verb, *(c)* the doer, and *(d)* the action. Is the action marked by an infinitive or a simple verb? One sentence has been done for you as an example.

(1)Kilroy hated his life in the army from the very first day. (2)When he arrived at Fort Dix for

                               (a)   *(b)* *(c)*   *(d)*

basic training, <u>a drill instructor</u> <u>had</u> <u>him</u> <u>join all the other new recruits</u> on the parade ground.

(3)The officers made them stand in the hot sun for several hours, while clerks filled out forms.

(4)They would not allow the new recruits to joke or talk to each other, or even to move their

heads. (5)Then they had Army barbers cut their hair so short that Kilroy felt like he was bald.

(6)An officer ordered Kilroy to report to a long building called Barracks B, along with about

20 other men. (7)The sergeant at Barracks B had each man choose a bunk. (8)He let them put

their personal possessions in lockers next to each bunk. (9)Kilroy helped the man in the next

bunk make his bed, and that man helped Kilroy to do the same thing. (10)The sergeant then required the recruits to sweep the floors and clean the bathrooms. (11)Kilroy had wanted to join the army to learn how to be a soldier, but now he was beginning to worry that the army would only teach him how to be a janitor.

Exercise 2

Decide whether you think the policies suggested below are good ideas or not. Make statements with *should* or *shouldn't*, depending on whether you agree or disagree with the policy. Then supply a reason with *because* to explain why you feel the way you do. The first one has been done for you as an example.

EXAMPLE: *Parents should let their kids play actively every day, because vigorous physical exercise is important for growing bodies.*

Causer	Causative Verb	Doer of Action	Action
EXAMPLE: parents	let	kids	play actively
1. parents	make	children	go to bed at 6:00
2. teachers	help	students	learn things by themselves
3. police	allow	people	break laws
4. ministers	get	rowdy teenagers	come to church
5. people	have	a dentist	examine their teeth regularly
6. dog owners	let	pets	run around freely
7. the law	require	everybody	pay taxes
8. a government	require	all citizens	take drug tests
9. a good manager	allow	employees	do whatever they like
10. a good manager	motivate	employees	do their best

319

Exercise 3

Match the verbs listed in Group A with the verbs in Group B that have the same or similar meaning.

GROUP A	GROUP B
let	convince
help	hire
have	require
get	employ
make	permit
	assist
	encourage

Exercise 4

What should a teacher do in order to help students learn to speak English? Make sentences stating your opinion, using each of the causative verbs given in Exercise 3. Be careful to use the correct form (infinitive or simple verb).

> **EXAMPLE:** *Teachers should **have** students do homework every night.*
> *Teachers should **help** students guess the meaning of unfamiliar vocabulary.*

Exercise 5

What are the basic responsibilities of a government and the people it governs? For each statement of causer/doer/action listed, choose an appropriate causative that expresses your opinion. Write two complete sentences expressing that opinion: one with a causative verb and one with verb+infinitive complement.

> **EXAMPLE: causer:** government **doer:** citizens **action:** vote in regular elections
> *Governments should let their citizens vote in regular elections.*
> *Governments should allow their citizens to vote in regular elections.*

Causer	Doer	Action
government	citizens	• pay taxes • read any books and magazines they wish • be of service to the nation • meet national goals • defend the country
citizens	government	• be responsive to their wishes • work without corruption • establish national goals • maintain law and order • provide for basic defense

Focus 2

Passive Causative Verbs

- The causatives **make** and **help** and all Pattern 2 verbs with causative meaning can be made passive.

Active Causative Verbs	Passive Causative Verbs
(a) Parents should **make** their children **brush** their teeth before bedtime.	**(b)** Children should **be made to brush** their teeth before bedtime.
(c) Parents should **allow** children to have their own bank accounts.	**(d)** Children should **be allowed** to have their own bank accounts.
(e) Parents should **require** children to go to bed at a certain time.	**(f)** Children should **be required** to go to bed at a certain time.
(g) Parents should **help** their children learn good table manners.	**(h)** Children should **be helped to learn** good table manners.

- The passive is especially common when the causer of the action is understood or not stated, or is a law or an institution:

  (i) All children are required to go to school.

  (j) Minors aren't allowed to drink alcoholic beverages.

- When the verbs **make** and **help** are passive, their complements must be stated as infinitives, not simple verbs.

  (k) Students should **be made to study**.

  (l) NOT: Students should be **made study**.

  (m) Children should **be helped to understand** good manners.

  (n) NOT: Children should be **helped understand** good manners.

- The other common causatives, **get, have,** and **let** do not appear as passive verbs in causative sentences.

  NOT: Children should **be gotten** to read.

  NOT: Teachers should **be had** to teach.

  NOT: Children shouldn't **be let** to stay up too late.

Exercise 6

Decide whether the causative verbs in these sentences can be made passive without losing information or being ungrammatical. If so, write the passive version of the sentence.

EXAMPLES: The law requires parents to send their children to school.
Parents are required to send their children to school.

The doctor got the patient to take the bitter tasting medicine.
No change possible.

1. Tradition doesn't allow people to smoke in church.
2. Lack of time forced Kilroy to return to the barracks before the movie was over.
3. The law requires everyone who works to pay some income taxes.
4. People shouldn't let their dogs run free around the neighborhood
5. We had the janitor clean up the mess.
6. When I was a child, my mother didn't allow me to play in the street.

Focus 3

FORM ● USE

Passive Action Verbs

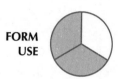

FORM
USE

- You can also use the passive voice with verbs that express the second action when the agent is understood or not important. There are some differences in form depending on which causative you use.
- For Pattern 2 verbs with causative meaning use a passive infinitive.

Active Action Verb	Passive Action Verb
(a) Parents should **require** their **children to finish homework** before TV time.	(b) Parents should require **homework to be finished** before TV time.
(c) Parents should **encourage** children **to do homework** carefully.	(d) Parents should encourage **homework to be done** carefully.

- With the causative *let*, omit *to* from the infinitive.

(e) Parents shouldn't **let** their children **be** neglected.	(f) NOT: Parents shouldn't **let** their children **to be** neglected.

- With the causative verbs *have* or *get*, you only need the past participle.

Active Action Verb	Passive Action Verb
(g) I had the barber cut my hair.	(h) I had my hair **cut**. (i) NOT: I had my hair **to be cut**.
(j) I got the judge to reduce my fine.	(k) I got my fine **reduced**. (l) NOT: I got my fine **to be reduced**.

- You can also use **had** and **get** to indicate simple passive meaning. (See Unit 4) Therefore, in some cases the meaning can be ambiguous:

Causative Meaning (Subject is the Agent)	Simple Passive Meaning (Subject is the Recipient)
(m) Mary had her car washed.	(n) Mary had her car stolen. (Someone stole Mary's car.)
(o) Mary got the thief arrested.	(p) Mary got herself arrested. (Mary was arrested)

Exercise 7

(a) Restate all the passive causatives in this paragraph as active constructions. Use *officers* as a probable agent. Sentence 1 has been done for you as an example.

Example: *Once again officers required the recruits to stand in the hot sun...*

(b) Sentence 4 is an example of passive meaning, not causative meaning. Can you restate this sentence so that the causative meaning is not ambiguous?

Kilroy's second day in the army was not much better than his first. (1) Once again the recruits were required to stand in the hot sun for several hours while clerks filled out even more forms. (2) They still weren't allowed to talk to each other, and they weren't allowed to sit down. (3) Next they were ordered to go to the medical building. (4) There they had their teeth examined and got their blood pressure measured. (5) Next was a test of physical endurance, where they were forced to run three miles in the hot sun. (6) Recruits who didn't run fast enough were required to run an extra mile as punishment. (7) By the time Kilroy was allowed to return to his bunk at the barracks, he was so tired he could barely walk. (8) As he lay on his bunk, he was sorry that he had been persuaded to join the army. (9) That night the men were allowed to write letters to their families, but Kilroy was too tired to do anything but sleep.

Exercise 8

Are these sentences correct or incorrect? For incorrect sentences, identify the mistake and fix it.

1. The students were got to do their homework.
2. The sergeant made the recruits to march for several hours.
3. A tailor was had to shorten my trousers.
4. Parents shouldn't let their children to watch too much television.
5. I had the waiter to bring the food to the table.
6. They encouraged all their children be independent.
7. Parents should make their children to brush their teeth.
8. Companies should be required to provide their employees with health insurance.
9. The babysitter made the children to fall a sleep by singing quietly.
10. Kilroy had his hair to be cut.

Activities

Activity 1

What routine jobs do you hate? Pretend that you do not have to worry about money. What things would you have other people do for you?

- Decide on 5 to 10 personal tasks that you would have someone else do, if money were no object. (For example: If money were no object, I would have somebody else do my grammar homework.)
- Compare your list to those of other students in class. What chores does everyone hate doing?
- Based on the other lists you have seen, what are the three most unpopular chores that people have to do on a regular basis?

Activity 2

In the Task, you examined the way people raise children. You identified things that parents should and should not do. Based on your discussion and your own experiences, state your opinion on this question:

Do good parents **make** their children do things or **get** their children to do things?

- Write a brief essay that explains your opinion, and why you feel the way you do. Support your opinion with examples from your own or other people's lives.

Activity 3

Based on the interviews that you conducted in the Task, did you find any interesting cultural or family patterns in the child-rearing practices of your classmates?

- Write a brief essay explaining any differences you found between the way children are raised in your own culture or family and some of the other culture or family patterns you learned about in the process of doing the Task.

Activity 4

There is a saying in English, "You can catch more flies with honey than you can with vinegar." What do you think are the best ways to get someone to do something? Support your ideas by describing a situation in which someone convinced you to do something you did not initially want to do. How did that person convince you? Were you glad you did it, or not?

Activity 5

If you were the leader of the country, what things would you change?

What laws would you establish for people to follow?
What would you require people to do?
What privileges would you allow people?
What things would you not allow them to do?
How would you get people to support you?

- Think of at least three answers to each of these questions, and present the information to the rest of the class in an oral presentation, explaining why they should let you be their leader.
- Take a vote to see who was the most convincing candidate.

25 Articles in Discourse

Task

Proverbs are well-known sayings that express general truths. They come into existence because many people in similar situations have seen similar results. Proverbs represent general lessons that many people have learned from actual individual experiences.

- Here are a number of proverbs. Choose one that you agree with, and think of an example from your own life (or that of someone that you know) that proves the truth of the proverb. Write a paragraph about that experience. The first proverb has been done for you as an example. Tell your own story to illustrate that proverb or another from the list.

A dog is man's best friend.	The leopard cannot change his spots.
Time is money.	Actions speak louder than words.
A fool and his money are soon parted.	Beauty is only skin-deep.
Experience is the best teacher.	Every cloud has a silver lining.
An idle mind is the devil's play-ground.	Time heals all wounds.
	Money is the root of all evil.
Absence makes the heart grow fonder.	A man is known by the company he keeps.

A dog is man's best friend. I once had a dog named Poppy. She was a very faithful friend. Every afternoon when I came home, the dog would greet me with kisses and a wagging tail. I liked the wagging tail, but I didn't enjoy the kisses very much. Even so, she was always glad to see me, and I was happy to see her too. There was a time in my life when I was feeling very lonely. I didn't think I had any friends. Every day I came home to an empty house with an empty heart. But Poppy was always at the door waiting for me. She seemed to know whenever I was sad or lonely, and at those times she would be extra friendly. One time she even gave me a gift: an old bone. Somehow she knew that I was especially sad. She must have thought the bone would cheer me up. Those bad times passed eventually, but they would have been a lot more difficult without my faithful companion, Poppy. She proved to me that a dog really is a wonderful friend.

Focus 1

Determiners in English

FORM

- Most noun phrases in English require a determiner. Determiners can be
  - **demonstratives:**
    (a) We need **this** pen. **That** pen is out of ink.
  - **possessives:**
    (b) **Peter's** information surprised us more than **his** appearance.
  - **quantifiers:**
    (c) Denise has **few** friends. She doesn't make **much** effort.
  - **articles:**
    (d) Denise has **a** new position. She has **some** work to do. She feels **the** work is quite important.
- There is only one determiner in each noun phrase.
  (e) NOT: Here is **a this** pen.
  (f) NOT: **That my** pen is green.

Exercise 1

Underline and identify the determiners in the sample paragraph of the Task. Are they demonstratives, possessives, quantifiers, or articles? Are the nouns count or non-count, singular or plural?

Focus 2

FORM

Definite and Indefinite Articles

FORM

- There are three indefinite articles:
  - *a/an:* used with singular-count nouns: *a* precedes nouns (or their modifiers) that begin with a consonant sound; *an* precedes nouns (or their modifiers) that begin with a vowel sound.

a book	a shiny apple	an uncomfortable situation
a church	an apple	
a hotel	an honest man	an hour
a university	an easy lesson	

- *some:* used with plural count nouns and non-count nouns to indicate a quantity or amount:
  - **(a)** I need some pencils.
  - **(b)** Some teachers will be arriving soon.
  - **(c)** I have some ideas about the party.
  - **(d)** Would you like some rice?
  - **(e)** Some water got on my notebook.
  - **(f)** I'm looking for some information.
- **No article (∅):** used with plural count nouns and non-count nouns in generic statements that do **not** refer to a quantity or amount. (See Focus 6 for other rules regarding **some** vs. ∅)
  - **(g)** Everyone needs **friends.**
  - **(h)** Teachers want **students** to succeed.
  - **(i)** **Ideas** can come from anywhere.
  - **(j)** **Rice** is eaten all over Asia.
  - **(k)** **Water** is necessary for life.
  - **(l)** I'm looking for **information** about public transportation.
- There is one definite article: **the.** You can use it with all nouns, count and non-count, singular and plural.

Focus 3

USE

Generic versus Particular Statements

USE

- Using articles depends on whether we are making a **generic** statement or a **particular** statement. In order to know which article you can use, you must first decide whether a sentence is particular or generic.
  - **Generic statements** talk about **concepts and ideas** and refer to **general classes or categories.** Such statements are true for the class or category and therefore they are also true for all members of that class.
  - **Particular statements** talk about **real situations** and refer to **actual members or items of a class or category.** Such statements are true only for the member, not necessarily the category itself.

- Compare these pairs of sentences:

Generic Statements	Particular Statements
(a) The lion is found throughout Africa. (a category of animal)	**(b)** I saw **the lion** at the circus. (a particular animal—not all lions are in the circus.)
(c) Bicycles are an excellent means of transportation. (a category)	**(d)** They went shopping for **bicycles** yesterday. (particular things they wanted to buy—they didn't buy all the bicycles in the world.)
(e) An angry customer is a frightening sight. (a category of person)	**(f)** We saw **an angry customer** complaining about the high price of tickets. (a particular person—not all customers are angry.)
(g) Some people never fall in love. (a category of people)	**(h) Some people** are joining us for dinner. (particular people, not a class of people)
(i) Information is increasingly communicated by electronic rather than printed media. (a category of things that things that are communicated electronically)	**(j)** Please give me **some information** on medical treatments for heart disease. (particular written or spoken facts)

- The rules for article use depend on whether the noun phrase occurs in a generic statement or a particular statement.
  - In generic statements, you can use both definite and indefinite articles in many of the same kinds of sentences.
    - **(k) The** lion is a mighty creature.
    - **(l) A** lion is a mighty creature.
    - **(m)** ∅ **Lions** are mighty creatures.
    - **(n)** Any large zoo will surely have **some lions** as part of its collection.
  - In particular statements, the use of articles depends on whether a noun is specific or nonspecific.

Exercise 2

Decide whether the highlighted noun phrases in these sentences are generic (refer to classes or categories) or particular (members of a class).

> **EXAMPLE:** An idle mind is **the devil's playground.**
> *generic*
>
> There is **a playground** next to the school down the street.
> *particular*

1. I wish we had **some mangoes** for the fruit salad, but they're so expensive!
2. **Mangoes** are a fruit found in most tropical places.
3. I saw **a doctor** about my cough.
4. **A doctor** is someone who has received training in medical science.
5. **Computers** have completely changed the way we live.
6. Don't go to that store for **computers.** They're cheaper at Smith Electronics.
7. **Many people** don't like spicy food.
8. There weren't **many people** at Jane's party.
9. If you really want to know how John is feeling, don't ask **the doctor**, ask **the nurses.** They will have better information.
10. Jane cooked a big pot of chili, but **many people** didn't eat it.
11. **Computers** are cheaper now than they were ten years ago.
12. There is a shortage of **nurses** in American hospitals today.
13. **Computers** for the new lab are being donated by **a company** in San Jose.
14. There aren't **many people** who actually like paying taxes.
15. Millions of people in this country can't afford to go to **the doctor** when they are sick.
16. **A company** needs to make sure that it is earning a profit.

Exercise 3

Write one generic sentence and one particular sentence for each of the cues listed here.

1. bicycles
2. a new car
3. the English language
4. transportation
5. tea
6. salespeople
7. books
8. hard work
9. Chinese food
10. trouble

Focus 4

MEANING

Specific versus Nonspecific Nouns

MEANING

- In particular statements, article use is determined by whether a noun is specific or nonspecific.
  - Specific nouns require definite articles. Specific nouns refer to an identified object. Both the speaker and the listener know specifically which object is being referred to. Both writer and reader can form a mental image of that particular object.

Definite Article	Implied Meaning
(a) Please give me **the** red pen.	There is only one red pen.
(b) Please pass **the** tea.	There is a teapot right here.

  - Nonspecific nouns require indefinite articles. A noun is nonspecific when either the speaker or the listener does not know specifically which object is being referred to.

Indefinite Article	Implied Meaning
(c) Please give me **a** red pen.	There are several pens. More than one of them are red. Any red pen is OK.
(d) Let's go to **a** restaurant and have **some** tea.	We don't know which restaurant it will be, or what kind of tea we will have.

- Use indefinite articles when
  - the speaker has a specific mental image of the noun, but the listener does not:

Indefinite Articles	Implied Meaning
(e) a/an: I bought **a new car.**	You haven't seen it yet.
(f) some: I had **some rice** for dinner last night.	I can remember it, but since you weren't there, you can't.
(g) Ø: There are **students** in my class who always do their homework.	I know which ones they are, but you don't.

  - the speaker does not have a specific mental image, but the listener does:

	Implied Meaning
(h) I hear you bought **a new car.** What kind is it?	You know, but I don't.
(i) You have **some mail** for me, don't you?	I don't know whether you do or not.
(j) Mary tells you **secrets** that she never tells me.	You know which secrets, but I don't.

331

• neither the speaker nor the listener has a specific mental image:

	Implied Meaning
(k) I hope we have **a wonderful time** on our vacation.	We don't know exactly what's going to happen.
(l) Let's get **some spaghetti** when we go out tonight.	We haven't decided on a restaurant.
(m) We should bring **food** to the picnic.	We haven't decided what kind.

Exercise 4

In the highlighted noun phrases, why was the particular article used? Indicate whether the noun was *(a)* specific for both speaker and listener, *(b)* specific for speaker but not listener, *(c)* specific for listener but not speaker, *(d)* nonspecific for both speaker and listener.

EXAMPLE: Do you want to go to **a movie** tonight? *(d)*

1. The Simpsons just bought **a beautiful new house.** You really ought to see it. I'm sure you'll think it's wonderful.
2. I want you to meet **a friend** of mine. You both have the same interests.
3. Did you have **a good time** at **the party?**
4. Let's have **some friends** over for dinner on Saturday.
5. I heard Charley has **a new girlfriend.** What's she like?

Exercise 5

Choose the correct implication for each of these sentences. (*I* refers to the speaker or writer. *You* refers to the listener or reader.)

1. The student from Japan is here to see you.
   a) There are several students from Japan who had appointments.
   b) There is only one student from Japan who had an appointment.
2. Let's go to a restaurant.
   a) We have already decided which restaurant to go to.
   b) Let's choose a restaurant.
3. Did a teacher say anything about a test?
   a) I am asking about one class.
   b) I am asking about all my classes.
4. Some friends are coming to dinner.
   a) You know who is coming to dinner.
   b) You don't know who is coming to dinner.

5. Let's invite the neighbors to dinner.
   a) You know which neighbors will be invited to dinner.
   b) You don't know which neighbors will be invited to dinner.
6. You should see a doctor about that cough.
   a) I have a specific doctor in mind.
   b) Any doctor should be able to help you.

Exercise 6

Decide whether these sentences require definite or indefinite articles. Add the appropriate article *(a/an, the, some,* or ∅) in the blank spaces. There may be more than one correct answer. Prepare to state your reason for choosing a particular article.

1. I didn't bring _____ roses that you asked for. I completely forgot them.

2. Sally wanted to buy _____ new dress, so she's gone out to find one.

3. _____ teacher was here to see you. I think it was your English teacher.

4. Did you give _____ musicians a nice tip? They certainly played beautiful music

   for your party.

5. Would you like _____ cold ice tea?

6. How did you enjoy _____ Chinese food last night?

7. I have _____ problems that I don't want to talk about.

8. John sent Mary _____ card for her birthday, but she says she never received it.

9. _____ bank where Doris works was robbed by _____ masked man with

   _____ gun.

10. When _____ police arrived, it was too late. _____ robber had disap-

    peared.

Focus 5

Using Articles in Discourse

USE

- Most nouns are marked with an indefinite article the first time they are mentioned because they are nonspecific: It is the first time the listener or reader has encountered the reference. In subsequent sentences, that same noun is specific: Both speaker/writer and listener/reader now know exactly which noun is being refered to, so you should use a definite article.

  (a) There once was **a** little old man who lived in **a** shack by **a** river. **The** shack was rather shabby, and so was **the** man.

  (b) I once had **a** big black dog and **a** little white dog. **The** black dog kept itself very clean, but **the** white dog loved to roll in mud.

- Nouns become specific
  - by direct reference. The noun is repeated:

    (c) I had **a dog** named Poppy. Every afternoon when I came home, **the dog** would greet me with **kisses** and **a wagging tail**. I liked **the wagging tail**, but I didn't enjoy **the kisses** very much.

  - by indirect reference. The noun itself is not repeated, but the reference is still clear from the context:

    (d) If you have **a dog** as **a pet**, you can always look forward to going home because of **the kisses** and **the wagging tail** that are there to greet you when you arrive.

    (e) I read **an interesting book. The author** suggests that all life came from visitors from another planet. **The first chapter** recounts stories of visitors from outer space that are found in many different cultures.

Exercise 7

Write articles *(a, an, Ø, some, the)* in the blank spaces. More than one answer may be correct, so prepare to explain why you chose the answer you did.

1. I have _____ foolish friend who is really careless with _____ money.

He has _____ good-paying job, but he doesn't even have _____ bank account. He says he doesn't need one because he spends his salary right away. He gets

_____ paycheck once _____ week. _____ money is always gone before _____ week is over. I can't tell you what he spends it on. And you know what? Neither can he!

2. I saw _____ "interesting" play last night. _____ actors were excellent, and _____ set was beautiful. However, _____ play itself was unfortunately not very well written.

3. Would you like _____ cake? _____ icing is _____ special recipe from _____ friend of my mother's. I made _____ cake and _____ icing myself.

4. Little Billy doesn't like _____ school. He says _____ teachers are boring. He doesn't like doing _____ homework. He much prefers to watch _____ cartoons on TV. As _____ result, his teachers aren't very happy with _____ way he performs in class. If he doesn't take _____ responsibility for doing _____ assignments, he may have to repeat _____ same grade next year.

Focus 6

USE

Repeating the Indefinite Article   USE

- There are certain situations in which you do not follow the usual rule of replacing an indefinite article with a definite article after the first time it is mentioned:
  - sentences with **there is/there are**.
    - **(a)** There once was **a** little old man who lived in **a** shack by *a river*. **The** shack was rather shabby, and so was **the** man. Although *there was a river* right next to **the** shack, **the** old man had to walk quite far to get clean drinking water.
  - sentences that identify someone or something as a member of a class or category:

	Implied Meaning
(b) I once had **a** dog. Her name was Poppy. She was **a** good dog.	She was a member of the category "good dogs."
(c) You know John. He's **a** teacher.	He's a member of the category "teachers."

- Do not use **some** for plural nouns that identify things as part of a group.

(d) John is **a** teacher. John and Fred are teachers. **(f)** Paris is **a** city in Europe. Paris, Rome, and Munich are cities in Europe.	**(e)** NOT: John and Fred are **some** teachers. **(g)** NOT: Paris, Rome, and Munich are **some** cities in Europe.

Exercise 8

Add the correct articles to the blank spaces in these sentences.

(1)I once had _____ experience that proved to me that _____ idle mind is _____ Devil's playground. Miss Kersell was my eighth grade science and math teacher. (2)She was _____ very strict teacher, and wouldn't allow any misbehaving in class. (3)To my friend Billy, this presented _____ tantalizing challenge. He found math and science very easy, so he was frequently bored in class. (4)As _____ result, he would try to play _____ tricks on her without getting caught. (5)It was _____ challenge that he could never resist, especially when he didn't have anything else to do. (6)One day we were taking _____ arithmetic quiz. (7)It was _____ easy quiz, but I have never been good at arithmetic, so it was taking me _____ long time. (8)But Billy had finished _____ quiz in just _____ few minutes. (9)I heard _____ strange noise coming from the back of the room. (10)It was _____ noise like no other I had ever heard. (11)Someone in _____ front of the class began to giggle. (12)Then there were _____ giggles in the back. (13)Soon there was _____ laughter everywhere. (14)Miss Kersell was furious, and looked everywhere to find out where _____ noise was coming from. (15)Billy had found _____ way to make _____ strange noise by rubbing his foot against _____ leg of his chair.

Focus 7

Unique Nouns

USE

- **Unique nouns** are specific for both the speaker and the listener without prior mention. This means that the **first** time they are mentioned, they are marked with a definite determiner. You do not need to introduce them in a nonspecific context.

  (a) I hear someone knocking at **the** door.

- A noun can be unique
  - because of a particular situation or setting:

Unique Nouns	Implied Meaning
(b) We were all having dinner. We were sitting around **the table**, and I asked my brother to pass **the butter**.	There was only one table and one dish of butter.
(c) "How did you do on **the exam** yesterday?" "Terrible! **The questions** were really difficult!"	There are two students in the same class. They both know which test is being referred to.
(d) This is going to be a wonderful vacation. I hope you remembered to ask **the neighbors** to pick up **the mail**.	We always ask the same neighbors each time we go away, and the mail is routinely delivered every day.

  - because it is a universal reference:
    (e) **The sky** is so beautiful tonight. **The moon** is bright, and **the stars** look like diamonds. (There is only one sky and one moon.)
    (f) My dog used to love to roll in **the mud**.
    (g) Let's go to **the beach. The ocean air** is supposed to be good for you.
  - because of immediate identification by a relative clause or prepositional phrase:
    (h) **The street where John lives** is lined with trees.
    (i) First we went to a hotel where **the man at the desk** told us we had no reservations.
    (j) **The book the teacher told us about** is available at **the bookstore across the street**.
  - because it is identified by rank in a sequence:
    (k) **The first time I ever went bowling**, I got **the highest score of anybody in the group**.

337

Exercise 9

Why do you think the highlighted nouns in the following sentences are unique? Decide if they are unique because of

   (a) prior reference (identify the reference);
   (b) a specific context or situation (identify the context or situation);
   (c) a universal context or situation;
   (d) being identified by a modifier (identify the modifier).

1. An idle mind is **the devil's** playground.
2. I saw a great movie last night. **The camera work** was fantastic.
3. **The newspaper** said it was going to rain tonight.
4. **The tallest mountain** in **the world** is on **the border** between Nepal and China.
5. **The place** we went last year is great for a vacation.
6. Let's go to **the club** for dinner tonight.
7. **The teacher** said we have to finish **the assignment** before Friday.
8. **The town** where I grew up was quite small.
9. **The noise** Billy made was like no other noise I had ever heard before.
10. What did **the doctor** say about **the medicine** you've been taking?

Exercise 10

Write the appropriate article *(a, an, the,* or ∅*)* in the blanks. There may be more than one correct choice, so prepare to explain why you have chosen the particular article.

(1)Peter Principle believes that every cloud has _____ silver lining. (2)He is _____ very optimistic person. (3)He thinks that _____ problem is really _____ opportunity in disguise. (4)As _____ result, he is always happy and reasonably content with _____ things that _____ life has given him. (5) _____ people like being around him, because he's _____ cheerful, positive person.

(6)Denise Driven is just _____ opposite. (7)She always looks on _____ dark side of _____ things. (8)If she encounters _____ problem, she sometimes blames it on _____ fact that she is _____ woman in _____ man's world. (9)She believes that _____ world isn't _____ fair place, and she, in particular, has always had _____ bad luck. (10)Although she's not _____ optimistic person, she doesn't spend much time feeling sorry for herself. (11)She rarely has time to listen to anyone's troubles or tell you about _____ troubles she is facing. (12)But whenever _____ friend does something nice for her, she always suspects that the person actually has _____ hidden motive. (13)She believes that every silver lining has _____ cloud.

Exercise 11

Write the appropriate article in the blanks. There may be more than one correct choice, so prepare to explain why you have chosen the particular article.

(1)The tall person in this picture is one of _____ most beautiful people I know, _____ woman by _____ name of Big Sue. (2)She proves _____ truth of _____ saying, "Beauty is only skin deep." (3)Perhaps people who don't know her well would say that she is not _____ beautiful person. (4)I guess that compared to _____ movie star or _____ fashion model, she isn't that attractive. (5)But anyone who knows her well thinks that she has _____ beautiful and courageous spirit. (6)Her beauty is in her personality. (7)She has _____ deep, booming laugh that makes other people laugh with her. (8)She's not self-conscious about her size.

(9)She makes _____ jokes about it. (10)She was _____ person who invented _____ name "Big Sue." (11)She says there are plenty of Sues in _____ world, but only one Big Sue. (12)If she gains _____ few pounds, she doesn't worry. (13)She just says, "There's more of me to love." (14)She is _____ incredible dancer, and moves around _____ dance floor with _____ grace and style. (15)She is _____ wonderful comedian. (16)She can tell _____ stories in _____ way that has _____ people falling down with laughter. (17)She has _____ friends all over _____ world. (18)She has turned down _____ dozens of proposals for marriage. (19)People can't help falling in love with her, once they get to know her well. (20)But she's not in _____ hurry to find _____ husband. She says, "I'll wait till I'm old and skinny. Right now I'm having too much fun."

Exercise 12

Write the appropriate article in the blanks. There may be more than one correct choice, so prepare to explain why you have chosen a particular article.

(1)When I first went to _____ university, I learned the truth of the proverb, "Absence makes _____ heart grow fonder." (2)It was _____ first time I had lived away from home. (3)I was surprised to discover how homesick I got, even after just _____ few days. (4)When I lived with my family, my brother and I used to fight about everything. (5)He wanted to watch one TV program and I wanted to watch another. (6)We fought about whose turn it was to do certain chores, like feeding _____ dog, sweeping _____ garage, cutting _____ grass, and taking out _____ garbage. (7)We argued about whose turn it was to use _____ car on Saturday night. (8)(I was allowed to use it one week, and then he was allowed to use it _____ other.) (9)But when I moved away, I realized that there were _____ lot of things about my brother that I missed. (10)I began to forget about all _____ tricks he used to play on me. (11)I started to remember only _____ happy times we had spent together. (12)By _____ time _____ year ended and I went back to spend _____ summer at home, I was really anxious to see him again.

Activities

Activity 1

Every country has different proverbs. In America, we say "Don't bite off more than you can chew," to remind people not to be too ambitious or try to do too many things at once. In Afghanistan, the same idea is expressed by the proverb, "You can't hold two watermelons in one hand."

- Work with a partner from a different cultural background and come up with three pairs of proverbs. Each pair should express the same idea in two different ways.
- Share the messages and the proverbs with the rest of the class.

Activity 2

Describe an object that you found once, and what you did with it. Compare your story with those of other people in the class. Can you devise a proverb that talks about finding objects and what should be done with them?

Activity 3

A time capsule is an airtight box (usually about one cubic meter) that is sometimes built into the foundation of a building. The designers of the time capsule fill it with objects that they think are important, interesting, or characteristic of the time when the building was built.

- Imagine that you are organizing a time capsule to be placed in a skyscraper being built today. The building is expected to remain standing for several hundred years. What objects would you place in the time capsule and why would you choose those particular objects?
- Work with several other people and decide on the contents of a time capsule that will not be opened for at least 500 years. Present your list of items and your reasons for choosing them to the rest of the class.

Activity 4

Write about three discoveries or inventions that have changed the course of history.

Activity 5

What are three things (objects) that everybody needs? Write a short composition describing your three choices and why you think everyone should have them. Start your essay with: **"There are three things everyone needs: . . . ."**

Activity 6

Here are four pictures. What story do you think they tell?

26

Demonstratives in Discourse

Task

Peter Principle and Denise Driven are having an argument. Peter wants to take the afternoon off to watch his youngest son perform in a Christmas pageant at school. Denise feels that he has already taken off too much time from work, and that she needs help in the office.

DD: Mr. Green has informed me that you're not going to be here this afternoon. **That's** outrageous, Peter! What about the Davis contract? **It's** due first thing Monday morning.

PP: Well, my son's in a Christmas play at school. **It's** his first big role. He's one of the Three Wise Men.

DD: He certainly didn't learn **that** role from his father! Is some stupid Christmas play more important than meeting the contract deadline?

PP: You'd better believe **it!** Besides, I spoke with Mr. Green. I told him **it** would get done sooner or later.

DD: If he believes **that**, he'll believe anything. **That's** what makes me so annoyed, Peter. **This** isn't the first time you've bailed out when there was a deadline. You're always asking for permission to take time off, and I get left holding the bag. I'm getting real tired of **it**, Peter. **It's** all I can do to keep this office running professionally!

PP: I'm sure Mr. Green would be happy to give you time off too. Just ask for **it,** Denise. **That's** all you have to do.

DD: **That's** not the point. **It's** true that most of us would probably rather be playing instead of working. But some of us have a sense of responsibility and a respect for hard work.

PP: **That's** true. My responsibility is to my son, and I respect the hard work he's put into learning his lines. **It's** not easy when you're only six years old.

DD: Don't give me **that** nonsense, Peter. I don't much fancy **it.**

PP: **That's** your trouble, Denise. You need a little nonsense in your life.

DD: My personal life is none of your business!

PP: Denise Driven has a personal life? Fancy **that!**

DD: **That's it!** I'm leaving. I'm lodging a formal complaint about **this** with Mr. Green.

PP: Well, **that's that**, then, isn't **it**? I guess there's nothing I can do to calm you down. I may as well leave a little early for the play. **It's** important to get there early, if you want to get a good seat.

- With a partner or in a small group, examine the use of *it, this*, and *that* in the previous dialogue. Important examples are highlighted for you. What is being referred to each time one of these forms is used? Can you substitute other forms? Does this change the meaning?
- What can you say about when native speakers use *it* instead of *that*? Decide on two things you have noticed and report them to the rest of the class.

Focus 1

Form and Meaning of Demonstratives

FORM
MEANING

- You can use demonstratives as determiners or as pronouns.
  (a) Does **this pencil** belong to you?
  (b) Yes, **that's** mine.
- The form of the demonstrative depends on whether the object is singular or plural and near or far.

	Near	Far
singular	(a) You should read **this book**. (c) **This** is delicious.	**(b)** Does **that pencil** belong to you? **(d)** Is **that** yours?
plural	**(e) These problems** aren't so serious. **(g)** If you like peaches, try **these**.	**(f) Those people** live down the street from my parents. **(h) Those** are the cutest puppies I have ever seen!

- Near and far distinctions are determined by
  - physical distance:
    (i) Please sit in **this** chair (**by me**). **That** chair (**over there**) is broken.
  - chronological distance:
    (l) I've been to two parties in the last week, but **this** one (today) is much more enjoyable than **that** party Denise had (a few days ago) at the Gun Club.
  - whether the speaker is involved with the situation or feels distanced from it:
    (m) What are we going to do about **this** budget deficit?
    (n) I don't know. **That's** for you to worry about, not me!

Focus 2

USE

Using Demonstratives, Determiners, and Pronouns

USE

- You can use demonstrative determiners to refer to nouns that have been specified by **prior mention**. (See Unit 25)
  - **(a)** There once was **a** wicked king who lived in **a** castle. Every day **this king** would go to **a** secret room in **the** castle. **This** is where he liked to count his money. **It** was also the place where he kept his beautiful daughter.
- You do not usually repeat a demonstrative to refer to the same item. You should use a personal pronoun or a definite determiner instead.
  - **(b)** Have you tried **these** pears? **They** are quite delicious.
  - **(c)** NOT: Have you tried **these** pears? **These** are quite delicious.
  - **(d)** **This** is the problem Denise was talking about. **It** will continue to get worse, if we don't find a solution.
  - **(e)** NOT: **This** is the problem Denise was talking about. **This** will continue to get worse if we don't find a solution.
  - **(f)** I bought **that** pen and **this** notebook at a drugstore. **The** pen was a little expensive, but **the** notebook was cheap.
  - **(g)** NOT: I bought **that** pen and **this** notebook at the drugstore. **That** pen was a little expensive, but **this** notebook was cheap.

- When you use two demonstratives, they must refer to different items.
  - **(h)** I don't like **these pears**, but **those** (different pears) are delicious.

Exercise 1

Add appropriate demonstratives, pronouns, and determiners to the blanks provided. More than one answer may be possible. The first one has been done for you as an example.

1. When Denise came to Mr. Green with her complaints about Peter, he realized that

   they had talked about ____*these*____ issues before. He told her there was no point in

   discussing ____*them*____ any further.

2. I got these new skirts and blouses on sale. I'd like you to take a look at _____ .

   Which of _____ dresses do you like better, _____ red one or _____

   green one? What about _____ blouses? Which do you prefer? _____ one

   or _____ one?

3. I got a new bike for my birthday. _____ was a gift from my parents. I'm glad they got _____ bike instead of another kind. _____ will be much more practical.

4. The essay that John wrote didn't receive a passing grade. _____ didn't contain any of the guidelines Dr. Montaigne had explained when she had first assigned _____ essay. _____ guidelines were not simple, but _____ had to be followed in order to get a passing grade on _____ essay. _____ grade made John rather upset, but Dr. Montaigne had made _____ guidelines quite clear.

5. Where did you get _____ ring? _____ is really beautiful. _____ looks like _____ came from Mexico. Is _____ silver?

Focus 3

MEANING
Demonstratives for Reference

MEANING

- One very common use of demonstratives is to refer to information in previous sentences. There are two kinds of reference:
  - backward-pointing reference:
    - (a) Everyone started laughing. **This** made John very angry.
    - (b) I knew it was going to rain! **That's** why I didn't want to come to this picnic in the first place.
  - forward-pointing reference:
    - (c) **This** is why I can't come to your party: I don't have the time, I don't have the clothes, and I have no way to get there.
    - (d) I like **these** kinds of Asian food: Chinese, Japanese, Indian, and Thai.
- Using a particular form depends on whether it refers forward or backward in the text:
  - ***This and these*** can be used to point both forward or backward.
  - ***That and those*** can only be used for backward-pointing reference (except with postmodifiers—see Focus 5).
  - Pronouns (such as **it**) almost always refer back to previous elements in a text.

346

Exercise 2

What do the demonstratives refer to in these sentences? Circle the demonstratives in these passages. Then draw an arrow to what each one refers to. Is it an example of forward-pointing or backward-pointing reference? The first passage has been done for you as an example.

1. Most people find it difficult to sleep during the day and work at night. (This) is why people who work "swing shift" (as (that) work schedule is called) are usually paid a higher wage than (those) who work during the day.

2. We hold these truths to be self-evident, that all men are created equal and have a right to life, liberty, and the pursuit of happiness.

3. Let me make this perfectly clear: No new taxes!

4. Frank said that he wanted to leave New York because he was tired of big city life. But I don't think that was the real reason for his move to California. The real reason was that his wife wanted to live in a place with warmer winters. At least, this is what Stuart told me.

5. These soldiers must report immediately to Barracks B: Adams, Collins, and Powell. These men have been assigned to patrol duty: Westmoreland and MacArthur. Those are your orders, men. Troops dismissed!

6. The causes of the American Civil War were not substantially different from those of other wars that have taken place between different regions of any country. This is one of the things that can be learned by studying history.

7. The chemical properties of baking soda are similar to those of any base. This is what allows baking soda to enter into a chemical reaction with any acid, such as that found in vinegar or even orange juice.

8. The management techniques of many American companies now tend to resemble those used in Japan much more closely than they did a few years ago. This is largely attributable to the undeniable success those techniques have had in raising worker productivity.

Focus 4

Using *This / That* versus *It*

USE

- Both demonstrative pronouns (***this / that***) and personal pronouns (***it***) refer back to ideas or items in previous sentences. There is a difference in emphasis.

	Implied Meaning
"Did you hear the news? Scott is in jail." **(a)** "I knew **it**! That boy was always a troublemaker!	I'm not surprised!
(b) "I knew **that**. His mother told me last week."	I'd already heard that news.

- Using ***this/that*** emphasizes that the idea it refers to is the most important information in the new sentence:

  They say that *Mary is getting married to Paul.*
  - **(c)** Does John know **that**?
  - **(d)** Has John heard about **this**?

- Using ***it*** indicates some other part of the new sentence is the most important information. You do not generally use pronouns to talk about significant new information:

They say that *Mary is getting married to Paul.* **(e)** I don't believe **it**! **(f)** I never would have suspected **it**.	***It*** indicates that our emphasis is on the verb—*believing* or *suspecting*.

- In some cases, you **must** use ***that*** instead of ***it***. This is especially true in cases where ***it*** could refer to a physical object rather than an abstract idea or situation.

(g) Don't leave your keys in the car. Someone might steal **it**. **(h)** Don't worry. I'm smarter than **that**.	NOT: Don't worry. I'm smarter than **it**. (This sounds like we are referring to the car.)
Aunt Martha is planning to bring her dog when she visits us. **(i)** I was afraid of **that**! No wonder she was asking if we had cats.	(***That*** indicates we are referring to the situation, not the dog.)

Exercise 3

Choose **this**, **that**, or **it** to put in the blanks of these sentences. Some sentences can use all three with little change of meaning. For some sentences, the choice might indicate a particular emphasis. For some sentences, one form may not be acceptable. Discuss your ideas with other students and your teacher.

1. Someone took your wallet? I was afraid _____ would happen. I told you not to leave your book bag in the library.

2. I'm glad Deborah hasn't had her baby yet. She was afraid _____ would happen while her husband was out of town.

3. I'm sorry you had to spend such a beautiful, sunny day in the library. _____ isn't really fair, is it?

4. I assume you have all heard the news about Arthur. _____ is why I have asked you to come to this meeting.

5. I love the wonderful California climate. _____ is why I moved here.

6. Did you say George's son is involved in another financial scandal? Are you sure of _____ ?

7. I just know Mary's dating someone else. I'm sure of _____ !

8. If you don't take advantage of this great opportunity, I know you'll regret _____ in the future.

9. Don't worry about making such a mess. _____ really doesn't matter.

10. Don't worry about making such a mess. _____ is why I put newspapers over everything.

11. You said "17." Don't you mean "70"? Oh yes, _____ 's what I meant.

12. Don't complain to me. _____ is why we have a complaint department.

Focus 5

That / Those with
Forward-Pointing Reference

USE

- You can use *that* and *those* for forward-pointing reference only when they occur with
  - a relative clause:
    - **(a)** **Those who cannot learn from history** are doomed to repeat it.
    - **(b)** I'm not very fond of dogs, but **those that are well behaved** are OK.
    - **(c)** The boss only gives raises to **those** he really likes. (***whom*** has been omitted)
    - **(d)** This script is really confusing. I can't tell the difference between **that which is supposed to be spoken** and **that which is supposed to be sung**.
  - a prepositional phrase:
    - **(e)** Compare your paragraph to **that of another student** in the class.
    - **(f)** This problem will have to be decided by **those in charge**.

Exercise 4

Identify the demonstratives that are followed by post-modifiers in these passages. Not all sentences contain this structure:

1. There is an old proverb that says God helps those that help themselves.
2. Please put those in the refrigerator.
3. My brother is very fussy about eating certain vegetables. He won't touch these, but those he likes won't stay on his plate for very long.
4. Those in the stock brokerage business think that this is a bad time to invest.
5. One must learn to distinguish between that which is necessary and that which is only desirable.
6. Those who can't tell the difference between teal and aquamarine shouldn't become interior decorators.
7. That is not my responsibility. You'll have to speak to those in charge of that part of the operations.
8. I read about that in the newspapers.

Focus 6

Special Uses of Demonstratives

USE

- In very informal speech or written narratives, people sometimes use *this* and *these* in place of indefinite determiners to introduce nouns for the first time.

  (a) I'm walking down the street, and I see **this** man on the corner. He's talking with **these** two other guys.

- Do not use *that* to refer to humans, except when you are pointing to the person.

  (b) **That** man over there is married to **that** woman in the red dress.

  - When *that* is used in other kinds of reference, it usually indicates the speaker is annoyed, or is insulting the referent.

    (c) Are you talking to **that** boy again? I told you not to speak to him!

    (d) **That's** our brother! He's always trying to tell us younger kids what to do.

    (e) I can't believe you're actually going to marry **that!** (This implies that the person being referred to is considered by the speaker to be a thing, rather than a human being.)

That that is, is. That that is not, is not. Isn't that it? It is!

Answer to Activity 1:

Activities

Activity 1

Here is a puzzle. Can you punctuate this so that it makes sense?

that that is is that that is not is not isn't that it it is

There are four sentences in the correct answer, and that is printed upside down on the previous page.

Activity 2

Write a dialogue like the one in the Task. Work with a partner. First, decide what the argument will be about. Then write your dialogue. Try to use some of the phrases that Peter and Denise used.

• Perform your dialogue for the rest of the class.

Activity 3

Listen to an argument in a television comedy or drama. Write down any examples that you hear using *that* or *it*. Why do you think the speakers used a particular form?

Activity 4

Compare two products from different countries or people from two different settings. For example: How does the coffee of Guatemala differ from that of Sumatra? How do students in high school differ from those in college? Present your comparison in either written or spoken form.

Activity 5

Tell a story in informal spoken English. Use the Present Time Frame and demonstratives (*this* and *these*) instead of indefinite articles. See Focus 6 for an example to get you started.

Possessives

Task

What's wrong with this picture? How observant are you? There are at least 10 rather strange things about this picture. For example, the legs of the table seem to be a person's legs. The child's hair appears to be snakes. Find as many other strange things as you can and describe them.

Focus 1

Possessive Forms

FORM

- There are four kinds of possessive forms:
  - **Possessive determiners** (*my, your, his, her, its, our,* and *their*): Possessive determiners precede the noun.
    (a) Peter, John, and I left **our** shoes on the porch.
  - **Possessive pronouns** (*mine, yours, his, hers, its,* and *theirs*): Possessive pronouns can take the place of the noun phrase.
    (b) Mine were covered with mud.
  - **Possessive phrases** (Formed by adding the prepositional phrase *of*+**noun**): Possessive phrases follow the noun.
    (c) The steps **of the porch** looked like a meeting place for old, dirty shoes.
    the leg **of the chair**
    the end **of the story**
  - **Possessive nouns:** Formed by adding *'s* (pronounced **apostrophe-s**) to a noun, or simply adding an apostrophe to nouns ending in *-s*.
    (d) John's shoes were wet, and **Peter's** were greasy.
    the **student's** answers
    those **babies'** cries
    the **children's** laughter
    Phyllis' cousin

Exercise 1

Underline and identify all the possessive structures in the following passage. Are they *(a)* possessive determiners, *(b)* possessive pronouns, *(c)* possessive nouns, or *(d)* possessive phrases. The first paragraph has been done for you as an example.

Do all the identified structures describe possessive relationships?

(1)Have you ever tested your *(a)* memory? (2)There have been many studies of people's *(c)* ability to remember things. (3)These studies have found that there are two types of memory: *(d)* short-term memory and long-term memory.

(4)Short-term memory depends on the "length" or number of items that someone needs to remember. (5)A person's ability to remember a series of numbers for more than a minute is limited to about 12 or 14 digits. (6)An individual's ability to remember strings of unconnected words seems to average about eight items. (7)Most people's performance on such memory tests will drop quickly if they are tested again, even after only a few hours' time.

(8)Long-term memory seems to be determined by the item's usefulness to the person being tested. (9)For example, people do a better job of remembering one of Shakespeare's sonnets if they can apply the "message" of the poem to some part of their own lives. (10)The more important a piece of information is to a person's life, the longer and more accurately it can be retained.

Focus 2

USE

Possessive Nouns versus Possessive Phrases

USE

- Possessive nouns (*'s*) mean the same thing as nouns with a possessive prepositional phrase (*of...*), but there are guidelines for choosing one form over the other:
  (a) **The tall man's** face appeared in the window.
  (b) The face **of the tall man** appeared in the window.
- Most people prefer possessive nouns (with *'s*) for
  - most animate (living) things:

    the **boy's** cap   NOT: the cap **of the boy**
    the **horse's** mouth   NOT: the mouth **of the horse**

  - double possessives:

    Mary's mother's hat
    John's roommate's sweater
    the **President's secretary's** desk

  - objects that perform an action:
    the **razor's** edge
    the **train's** arrival
    the **rocket's** red glare
  - natural phenomena:
    the **moon's** orbit
    the **river's** mouth
    the **earth's** atmosphere

- Most people prefer possessive phrases (with *of* + noun phrase):
  - for most inanimate (nonliving) things:

    the back **of the chair**   NOT: the **chair's** back

    the roof **of the house**   NOT: the **house's** roof

    the cause **of the problem**   NOT: the **problem's** cause
  - when a possessive noun phrase is very long:

    the daughter **of a well-known local politician**

    NOT: **a well-known local politician's** daughter
  - when a multiple possessive is long:

    the hat of Mary's little, old-fashioned mother

    NOT: **Mary's little, old-fashioned mother's hat**

Exercise 2

For each noun + possessive listed here, write the best possessive form in the blank in the sentence. Add articles where necessary.

EXAMPLES: hat/boy: *The boy's hat* blew into the sea.

cover/ *Time Magazine*: Being on the cover of *Time Magazine* made Elvis Presley even more famous.

1. results/investigation: _____ were reported in the newspaper.

2. restaurant/Alice's mother: We had dinner at _____

3. ability/individual: _____ to remember something depends on how important the information is.

4. rights/women: Suffragettes were early activists in the battle for _____

5. first chapter/novel: _____ begins with the famous words, "Call me Ishmael."

6. take-off/rocket: _____ was quite an amazing spectacle.

7. music/Elvis Presley: _____ has been heard all over the world.

8. discovery/penicillin: Sir Alexander Fleming was responsible for _____ _____.

9. children/a very famous American movie star: I went to school with _____ _____.

10. rotation/earth _____ is what causes night and day.

Exercise 3

Make up five sentences of your own that use the 's possessive form or the *of* possessive form. Explain why you chose the form that you did.

Exercise 4

Change the cues in parentheses to the correct possessive constructions. Add articles where necessary.

Last week Matt went shopping. It was (1)_____ (his roommate Jeff/birthday), and he wanted to buy a really "unusual" gift. He drove (2)_____ (Jeff/car) downtown. When he got there, he realized that the (3)_____ (shopping district/center) was already quite crowded, and most of (4)_____ (stores/ parking lots) were already full. He was in a hurry, so he decided to park in front of a hotel. He thought the (5)_____ (hotel/doorman) looked annoyed, but he was not paying attention. He visited several stores. In (6)_____ (one of the stores/window) he saw the perfect gift: a statue of a cowboy. In (7)_____ (cowboy/hand) there was a container for toothpaste, toothbrush, and a razor. He thought that the statue would look perfect in (8)_____ (their apartment/bathroom). He bought it and hurried back to where he had parked. The car was gone! At first, Matt thought it had been stolen, but then he realized that it had probably been towed away. He called the police, and they verified that the car was at the station. When he got there, he found that (9)_____ (car/front fender) had a dent, and there was a big scratch on (10)_____ (car/side). Matt had to pay for the (11)_____ (repair/cost) and the towing charges. Jeff got a very expensive birthday present, and Matt got a long-overdue lesson about traffic laws and parking regulations.

Exercise 5

Find out some information about the opinions of a classmate on these topics, and his or her reasons for those opinions. Ask questions that determine information about the following things. Report your partner's answers to the rest of the class.

> **EXAMPLE:** best place to sit in a classroom
>> *You: What's the best place to sit in a classroom.*
>> *Your partner: The front of the class is better if you're a good student, but the back of the class is better if you want to sleep.*

1. most important part of the semester (beginning, end, or middle)
2. favorite object that belongs to someone else
3. most important period of history
4. favorite piece of music

Ask two questions of your own that use possessive forms.

Focus 3

MEANING

Other Meanings of Possessive Forms

MEANING

- You can use possessive forms for other kinds of meaning besides **belonging to** someone or something. You can also use possessive forms to indicate
  - amount or quantity:
    - **(a)** Please give me three **dollars'** worth of unleaded gasoline.
    - **(b)** That leather coat cost me a **week's** pay.
    - **(c)** This book represents three **years'** work.
  - part of a whole:
    - **(d)** A **book's index** is a useful place to start when you're looking for specific information.
    - **(e)** John is the most dependable **of all my friends**.
  - a general relationship or association:
    - **(f)** Scientists are still trying to discover **the cause of cancer**.
    - **(g)** **The streets of New York** can be dangerous at night.
  - origin or agent:
    - **(h)** We studied **the sonnets of Shakespeare** in high school.
    - **(i)** **Joan's conversation** with the doctor caused her some concern.
  - identifying a topic:
    - **(j)** *Of Mice and Men* and *Of Human Bondage* are two famous twentieth-century novels.
    - **(k)** He told us **of his experiences in the army**.

Exercise 6

Underline the possessive forms in the following sentences and identify their meaning. Do they indicate

(a) an amount or quantity
(b) a part of a whole
(c) a general relationship/association
(d) an origin or agent
(e) an identified topic
(f) actual possession

                            (b)   *(b)*

EXAMPLE: <u>The streets of San Francisco</u> are famous for <u>their steep hills</u>.

1. Scientists are studying the effects of alcohol on an individual's memory.

2. The wines of France are among the best in the world.

3. The teacher's assistant will hand back the homework.

4. That concept was introduced in the book's first chapter.

5. Chicago is four days' drive from Los Angeles.

6. An investigation of short-term memory has shown that items of personal importance are more easily remembered.

7. The steps of the porch looked like a meeting place of old, dirty shoes.

8. Matt's roommate likes ice cream.

9. Beethoven's symphonies are still thrilling.

Exercise 7

Read the following passage and underline all the possessive structures.

- For each possessive structure you identify, decide on the actual meaning indicated. Mark each structure with a letter to indicate whether the meaning is

  (a) an amount or quantity   **(d)** an origin or agent
  (b) a part of a whole   **(e)** an identified topic
  (c) a general relationship/association   **(f)** actual possession

- Are there other phrases with *of* that are not possessive structures? Mark those structures with an *X*.

- For each possessive noun or possessive phrase you identify, explain why you think the author chose that form instead of another. The first paragraph has been done for you as an example.

(1) The most-visited residence in the United States is, <u>of course</u>, the White House, in Wash-
                                            (x)
ington, DC, the home <u>of the President</u> <u>of the United States</u>. (2) But the second most-visited
                      (f)   *(c)*

residence may surprise you. (3) It is Graceland Mansion in Memphis, Tennessee, the home
                  (f)   *(e)*
<u>of Elvis Presley</u>, the "King" <u>of rock and roll</u>. (4) Presley's influence on the popular music of
                                                    (b)
America was profound. (5) He was one <u>of the first blues artists</u> to make rock and roll popular
                        (b)   *(f)*
with the middle class <u>of the United States</u>. (6) And <u>Elvis's</u> swinging hips and sexy voice made
                        (f)   *(b)*
him the dream boyfriend <u>of an entire generation</u> <u>of teenage girls</u>.

(7) Presley's historic appearance on a 1958 broadcast of the "Ed Sullivan Show" caused

an uproar. (8) His singing could not be heard because of the screams of his adoring fans.

(9) And Presley's famous swinging hips were not seen at all, because of the objections of TV

broadcasters, who felt his wild movements were not suitable for family television. (10) Presley

rapidly became America's most popular male singer of all time. (11) He made hundreds of

records and dozens of films. (12) Everywhere he went crowds of screaming, adoring fans

showered him with gifts, love, and devotion.

(13)But his personal life was marked by tragedy. (14)By the time he died in 1977, everyone had heard the rumors of his troubles with alcohol and drugs. (15)They had read of his failed marriage in the movie magazines. (16)His suspicions about his friends' loyalties and motivations had made a "living nightmare" of his life. (17)He died a prisoner of his own popularity.

(18)In spite of his death, Elvis is still called The King of Rock and Roll. (19)Graceland Mansion is visited by hundreds of adoring fans every day. (20)His records continue to be popular, and there are several radio stations that play nothing but Presley's music.

(21)Some people even believe that he is still alive and living in disguise. (22)There continue to be rumors that his mysterious death was just a trick to allow him to escape from the prison of his fame and his fans' adoration. (23)Many people still believe that he is living a quiet life with a new name and a thick beard to hide his famous face. (24)Today the Memphis post office still receives hundreds of letters addressed to Elvis at Graceland from fans who still await "The King's" return.

Exercise 8

Are the following sentences correct or incorrect? If they are incorrect, identify the problem and correct it.

1. The fame of Elvis Presley spread across America.
2. The table's top was covered with newspapers.
3. The child of Bambang's classmate was sick with the flu.
4. Gladys' well-known next-door neighbor's dog's barking annoyed the entire neighborhood.
5. The scientists' studies' results indicate that memory is affected by such things as weather and time of day.
6. Memory's investigations have shown that the ability of people to remember things declines with age.
7. Rock and roll's king died in 1977.
8. Elvis' death's circumstances are somewhat mysterious.

Activities

Activity 1

Work with a partner to fill in the missing parts of these diagrams. Diagram A contains elements not contained in Diagram B (on the next page). Help your partner complete diagram B correctly. Your partner should help you complete Diagram C, which is incomplete. You should not look at Diagrams B and D. Your partner should not look at Diagrams A and C.

Diagram A (complete)   **Diagram C (incomplete)**

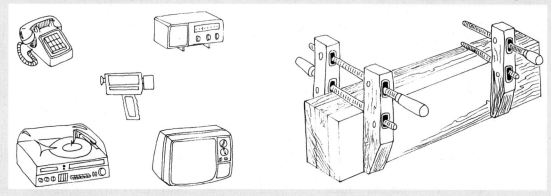

Activity 2

Write a short description of a famous person. What are the things that made him or her famous? Here are some things you might mention in your description: his or her accomplishments, childhood, important experiences, and influence on society.

Activity 3

Check your short-term memory. Study the picture at the beginning of this chapter for 30 seconds. Then close your book and describe it to a partner. Your partner should look at the picture while you describe it and check your description for accuracy.

Activity 1 (Diagrams B and D)

Diagram B (incomplete)   **Diagram D (complete)**

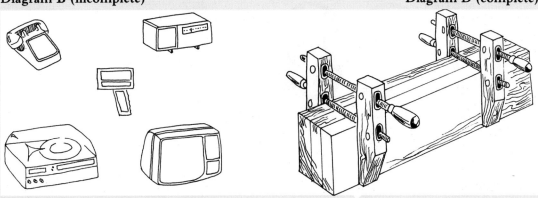

Activity 4

Oh, no! There's been an automobile accident! Look at the picture and describe what has happened to the car and its passengers. After you write your description, check the accuracy of your use of possessive forms.

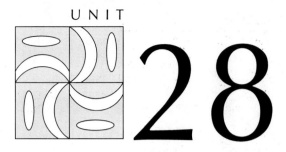

U N I T

28

Quantifiers

Task

Each year the Institute for International Education publishes a statistical profile on international educational exchange. They provide enrollment figures for students who go to another country to study. Examine the following charts on the enrollment of foreign students in educational institutions in the United States.

• Using the information in those charts and your own knowledge, write a brief essay on foreign students in the United States. Talk about general trends and possible exceptions to those trends. Provide information that answers these three questions:

What fields of study do international students pursue in the United States?
How do they finance their education?
Where do most students study?

A. Foreign Students by Field of Study, 1989/90

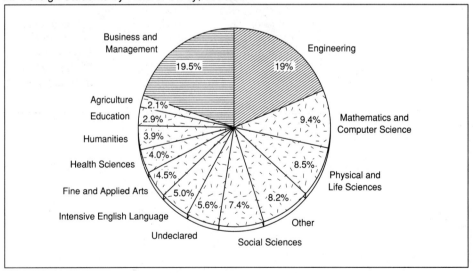

B. Foreign Students by Primary Sources of Funds, 1989/90

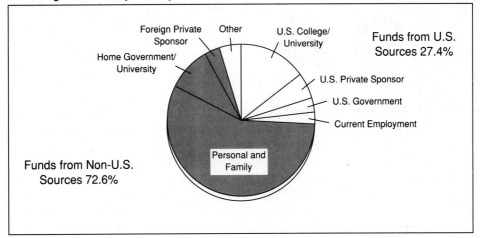

Foreign Private Sponsor

Other

U.S. College/ University

Home Government/ University

Funds from U.S. Sources 27.4%

U.S. Private Sponsor

U.S. Government

Current Employment

Personal and Family

Funds from Non-U.S. Sources 72.6%

C. Foreign Student Enrollment by U.S. State, 1989/90

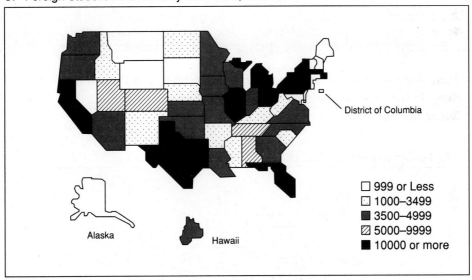

District of Columbia

Alaska

Hawaii

☐ 999 or Less
☐ 1000–3499
■ 3500–4999
▨ 5000–9999
■ 10000 or more

365

MEANING

Quantifiers in English

MEANING

- You can use quantifiers with noun phrases to describe **number** (with count nouns) or **amount** (with non-count nouns). There are two kinds of quantifiers: affirmative quantifiers and negative quantifiers. We have listed quantifiers and phrases with similar meaning in this chart in decreasing order from **all** (100 percent) to **none** (0 percent).

Quantifiers		Phrases of Quantity and Amount With Similar Meaning
Affirmative Quantifiers		
Used with Count Nouns	**Used with Non-Count Nouns**	
all/any each/every	all/any	the total number/amount the entirety
almost all	almost all	the vast majority
most	most	the majority
a great many many lots of/a lot of plenty of	a great deal of much lots of/a lot of plenty of	a large number/amount
a good number of	a good deal of	more than some
quite a few quite a number of	quite a little quite a bit of	more than a few/a little
some/any several a (certain/large/small) number of	some/any a (certain/large/small) amount of	an indeterminate number/amount
a few	a little	a small number/amount
Negative Quantifiers		
Used With Count Nouns	**Used With Non-Count Nouns**	
not all/not every	not all	an unspecified number are/do not
not many	not much	a small number/amount
few	little	an insufficient number/amount
hardly any almost no/none	hardly any almost no/none	the vast majority are/do not
no/none/not any	no/none/not any	the total number/ amount are/do not

Exercise 1

(a) In the following passage, underline the quantifiers and the noun phrases they modify. The first sentence has been done for you as an example.

(b) Are there quantifiers that do not appear with noun phrases? What sentences do they appear in and what do they refer to?

> **EXAMPLE:** *Clause 1 of the first sentence has a quantifier that does not appear with a noun phrase: many. It refers to* **people** *or* **experts.**

MEDICAL EDUCATION IN THE UNITED STATES

(1) Even though American medical education is considered by <u>many</u> to be the best in the world, (2) there are relatively <u>few spaces</u> in American medical schools, and <u>a substantial number of Americans</u> are forced to go overseas to get their basic medical training. (3) As a result, not all the doctors practicing in the United States have received their training from American medical schools. (4) In fact, quite a few have been educated in other countries. (5) However, all physicians must have clinical experience and pass qualifying examinations in order to receive a license to practice in the United States.

(6) Most doctors currently practicing in the United States have completed their practical training in an American hospital or clinic. (7) Every hospital in this country accepts a few recently graduated medical students each year, (8) including graduates from many foreign medical schools. (9) While some popular hospitals receive a great many applications for each available space, (10) a number of hospitals in rural areas may receive only a few. (11) This period of practical training is called a residency, and most last for two years. (12) A few are longer; some are shorter, depending on the specialization of the doctor.

(13) Many doctors study for an extra year before they begin their residency in order to become a specialist in a particular area of medicine. (14) No doctor is an expert in every area of medicine, but some doctors have more than one specialty. (15) Each area of medicine has its own period of residency and its own qualifying examinations.

Exercise 2

Write sentences that describe the training of medical doctors in another country that you are familiar with.

In (country),

1. Most doctors . . . .
2. Not all doctors . . . .
3. All doctors . . . .
4. A few doctors . . . .
5. No doctors . . . .
6. Many doctors . . . .

Focus 2

Affirmative Quantifiers

MEANING
USE

- You can use most affirmative quantifiers in both affirmative and negative statements and questions.
  - **(a) Do most** foreign students have similar educational backgrounds?
  - **(b) Most** graduate schools in the United States **require** an American B.A. degree.
  - **(c) Most** foreign-trained medical students **don't have** clinical experience.
- But some affirmative quantifiers have special meanings or uses.
  - *All* and *almost all*:

(d) Not all graduate students have graduated from American universities. **(e)** AWKWARD: **All** graduate students have**n't** graduated from American universities. **(f)** NOT: **Almost all** graduate students have**n't** graduated from foreign institutions.	Generally *all* and *almost all* do not occur in negative sentences. It is more common to use the negative quantifier *not all* to express those ideas.

- *Any* has two possible meanings.

Some	
(g) Do you have **any** money? **(h)** She doesn't have **any** friends. **(i)** NOT: We ate **any** cookies.	This meaning of **any** is used with plural count nouns and non-count nouns. It is used in questions and negative statements but not in affirmative sentences.
All	
(j) Any American college requires students to be fluent in English.	This meaning of **any** is used with singular count nouns in affirmative sentences, but *any* does **not** mean *all* in questions or negatives.

- *Some* has two possible meanings.

An Unspecified Amount	
(k) Do you want **some** cake? **(l)** I've got **some** questions. **(m)** I **don't** have **any** money. **(n)** NOT: I **don't** have **some** money.	This use occurs only in questions and affirmative statements. In negative statements, the quantifier *any* is used.
A Certain Group or Amount	
(o) Some students came on time, but most of them were late. **(p) Some** students don't like to speak in class.	This use occurs in both affirmative and negative sentences.

• *Much:*

(q) Much of the financial support for study in the United States comes from the students themselves. **(r)** Does it take **much** money to pay for a university education? **(s)** The average foreign student **doesn't have much** money.	**Much** is usually used with specified nouns phrases (noun phrases with *the*), questions, and negative statements.
(t) NOT: I'm having **much** trouble finding a school. **(u)** I'm having **a lot of** trouble finding a school. **(v)** I'm having **a great deal of** trouble finding a school.	*Much* is **not** used with nonspecific noun phrases (noun phrases with *a/an* or no article) in affirmative sentences. *A lot (lots) of* is usually preferred in conversation. *A great deal of, quite a bit of, etc.,* are more common in written contexts.

Exercise 3

Change the following statements concerning number or amount to sentences using quantifiers.

EXAMPLE: The vast majority of students pass their qualifying examination on the first try.

Almost all students pass the exams on their first try.

1. The vast majority of medical students in the United States already have B.A. degrees.
2. An indeterminate number of students have more than one major.
3. There are a small number of scholarships for international students.
4. It takes a large amount of money to fund a university education.
5. A small number of students apply to only one university for admission.
6. An unspecified number of applicants don't pass the qualifying exams such as TOEFL, GRE, or GMAT.
7. The majority of international students apply for admission to more than one university.
8. A large number of students study English before they begin their academic studies.

Exercise 4

What is wrong with these sentences?

1. All doctors don't apply to several hospitals for residency.
2. Some students don't have some trouble passing their exams.
3. Other students have any trouble, but usually pass on the second time.
4. A medical education requires much money.

Exercise 5

Make statements about the statistics you studied in the Task, using each of the quantifiers listed below.

EXAMPLE: *most—Most foreign students in the United States pay for their own education.*

1. all
2. a great many
3. quite a few
4. a lot of
5. a little
6. several

7. some
8. any
9. a few
10. a great deal of
11. much

Focus 3

MEANING ● USE

Negative Quantifiers

MEANING
USE

- Negative quantifiers have a negative meaning and usually do not occur in sentences with negative verbs.

(a) AWKWARD: **Few** doctors **don't** have medical degrees.

(b) BETTER: Almost all doctors have medical degrees.

(c) NOT: **Not all** students **don't** pass the TOEFL on their first try.

(d) BETTER: Some students pass the TOEFL on their first try.

(e) AWKWARD: **None** of the students **didn't** pass the qualifying exams.

(f) BETTER: All the students passed.

- Negative quantifiers often imply that the amount or number is insufficient:

Affirmative Quantifiers (A Small Amount)	Negative Quantifiers (Not Enough)
(g) A few doctors have studied nonwestern medicine. (**Some** doctors have studied it.) **(i)** There's **a little** money left after the bills are paid. (There is still **some** money for other things.)	**(h) Few** doctors have studied nonwestern medicine. (**An insufficient number** have studied it.) **(j)** There's **little** money left after the bills are paid. (There is **not enough** money for other things.)

Exercise 6

Decide whether to use *few* or *a few*, *little* or *a little*. Compare your answers to those of a partner. Prepare to explain why you chose your answer.

1. The students were discouraged because _____ people passed the examination.

2. Even the very best students have _____ difficulty gaining admission to a good university.

3. I can loan you some money, but I've only got _____ dollars.

4. They were working in the laboratory for so long that now there's _____ time to get ready for the quiz.

5. There are _____ scholarships available for first-year medical students, so a medical education is expensive.

6. He put _____ effort into studying for examinations, and as a result didn't pass on the first try.

7. The average medical student usually applies to at least _____ places for residency.

8. Bambang had _____ trouble finding a university. Several schools were willing to accept him.

Exercise 7

Using the following negative quantifiers, make true statements about the statistics on international education that you studied in the Task.

1. few
2. not all
3. little
4. hardly any
5. no

Focus 4

FORM

Each, Every, Any, No: Quantifiers Used with Singular Nouns

FORM

- Most quantifiers are used with plural count nouns and non-count nouns, but there are a few that are used with singular count nouns. Their meaning is the same as that of *all*.
  - *Each, every* and *any*:

(a) The teacher asked **each student** a question. (**All students** were asked.) **(b) Every student** wants to get an *A* in this class. (**All students** want *A*'s.) **(c) Any doctor** knows basic first aid techniques. (All doctors know basic first aid.)	These quantifiers are only used with singular count nouns. **Each** and **any** emphasize individual members of the group. **Every** emphasizes the group as a whole.

- *No*:

(d) No student has ever taken this test more than once. **(e) No doctors** in this country are allowed to practice without a license.	**No** can be used with both singular and plural nouns.

Exercise 8

Change the following statements with plural count nouns to statements with *any, each,* or *every*. Remember to make any other necessary changes to preserve the meaning of the original sentence. More than one answer may be correct, so prepare to explain why you chose the answer you did.

> **EXAMPLE:** All doctors know basic first aid.
> *Every doctor knows basic first aid.*
> *Any doctor knows basic first aid.*

1. All doctors must complete their residencies within two years.
2. All parents want their children to succeed in life.
3. Peter spends all free weekends at the beach.
4. All the people who came to the examination brought calculators.
5. A wise student takes advantage of all opportunities to gain practical experience.

Exercise 9

Complete the following sentences with true information:

1. Each student in this class . . . .
2. Every teacher I have had . . . .
3. Any English class . . . .
4. No student . . . .
5. No teachers . . . .

Focus 5

FORM ● MEANING

Both, Either, and Neither: Fixed-Number Quantifiers

FORM
MEANING

- You can use the quantifiers *both, either,* and *neither* only when you are talking about **two count nouns:**

Form	Meaning	Use
both	**two**	**(a)** Albert and Florence took their medical qualifying exams. **Both students** passed.
neither	**both do not**	**(b) Both** had worried about failing the exams, but **neither student** did.
either	**both** **one or the other**	**(c)** I would trust **either one** to do complex surgery. **(d)** But only one will get the residency. It will be **either** Albert **or** Florence, I'm sure.

- See Unit 8 for more information and practice with *both, either,* and *neither.*

373

Exercise 10

Here is some information about two medical students, Florence Schweitzer and Albert Nightingale:

Florence Schweitzer passed her qualifying exams last week. She has applied for a residency at Providence Hospital. Her specialization is orthopedics. She took the exams last year, but she didn't pass. Providence has only one residency available for this year, but Florence is optimistic. She got very high scores on her specialization exam, and her friend Albert is the only other person who has applied for a residency.

Albert Nightingale passed his qualifying exams last week. He also applied for a residency at Providence. His specialization is pediatrics. This was his second time taking the exams too. He has also applied to Mercy Hospital, and likes the training programs at both hospitals, so he doesn't care which hospital accepts him.

Use each of these quantifiers *(both, neither, either, both of them, and either of them)* in the following blanks so that the statements reflect this information.

1. _____ students took their qualifying exams.

2. _____ student passed the first time, but _____

passed on the second try.

3. Albert will accept a residency at _____ hospital.

4. Albert has applied to two hospitals, and will accept a residency at _____

Exercise 11

Use the quantifiers in **Exercise 10** to make true statements about two students in your class.

Focus 6

FORM

Using Quantifiers with *Of*

FORM

- When using most quantifiers with specific noun phrases, (nouns that use a definite determiner such as **the, this,** or *his*) you must add the preposition **of**. Examine the differences in these two kinds of sentences.

Generic/Nonspecific Reference	Specific Reference
(a) Any bus will take you downtown.	**(b) Any of the buses** that stop here will take you downtown.
(c) Most students want to get good grades.	**(d) Most of the** students who Donna teaches have college degrees.
(e) Several cars have passed.	**(f) Several of the cars** at the police station had been stolen.
(g) Some students never study.	**(h) Some of the students** in this class didn't pass the exam.
(i) Few old-fashioned doctors realize the importance of exercise.	**(j) Few of the doctors** trained in recent years still smoke.
(k) There are **hardly any students** in class today.	**(l) Hardly any of the students** who took the exam yesterday came to school.
(m) I brought **a little wine** to the party.	**(n) A little of the wine** I bought is still left.
(o) Little money is being spent on child-care programs.	**(p) Little of the money** we collected from the book sale is left.
(q) Hardly any time is left to answer questions.	**(r) Hardly any of the time** we spent in class was used for review.

- See Unit 25 for more information and practice with specific and nonspecific nouns.

- **Special cases**
  - You can use **all** with or without *of* in specific reference:

Nonspecific Reference	Specific Reference
(s) All students hate to take tests.	**(t) All the students** in this class hate tests. **(u) All of the students** in this class hate tests.

  - You can use **no** and **almost no** only for nonspecific reference. You must use **none** with specific reference:

Nonspecific Reference	Specific Reference
(v) No buses run after midnight. **(x) Almost no information** was available from the office.	**(w) None of the buses that run after midnight** stop here. **(y) Almost none of the advice he gave me** was very practical.

Exercise 12

Decide whether to use a **quantifier** or **quantifier** + **of** for the following sentences:

1. (All) _____ laboratory equipment on this table should be sterilized before use.

2. (Any) _____ information you provided yesterday will be used to help others.

3. (Almost all) _____ plants require sunlight to survive.

4. (Most) _____ coffee served in restaurants contains caffeine.

5. You won't need (much) _____ your warm clothing if you go to medical school in the Philippines.

6. (A great deal) _____ the population still believes in traditional medicine.

7. (Some) _____ the information in your report was incomplete.

8. I don't need (any) _____ your help.

9. Bob wasted (little) _____ the money he won on frivolous things.

10. (No/None) _____ students came to the party.

376

Focus 7

Using Quantifiers in Place of Noun Phrases

USE

- You can use most quantifiers in place of nonspecific noun phrases if the meaning is clear.

    (a) Many American doctors have studied acupuncture, but only **a few** actually practice it.

    (b) Some Western doctors have been trained in non-Western medicine, but **most** haven't.

    (c) Did **any candidates** fail the qualifying examinations? Yes, **lots.**

    (d) Did Albert have **much trouble** with his car? **Quite a bit.**

- There are certain quantifiers that you cannot use to replace noun phrases:
  - *Much* and *many*:

(e) How much money have you got? I don't have **much.** How about you? **Not much.** We'd better stop at the bank and get a little. Are there any banks around here? **Not many.** I guess we'll have to go downtown.	These forms can only replace nouns in negative sentences, or when used with **not.**

  - *No:*

(f) Is it true that **no students** failed the test? That's correct. **None** did.	*No* cannot be used in place of a noun. *None* is used instead.

  - *Each/every:*

(g) Did **every** candidate pass the exam? Yes, **every one** of them did. NOT: Yes, **every** did.	*Each* and *every* cannot be used to replace a noun phrase. They must be used with *one.*

Exercise 13

Answer the following questions with complete sentences, using quantifiers in place of noun phrases.

> **EXAMPLE:** Where are most doctors trained?
>
> **Most** *are trained here in America, but* **some** *study medicine overseas.*

1. Do all doctors in the United States have to pass qualifying examinations?
2. How many candidates pass the exams on the first try?
3. How many American doctors are well-trained in non-Western medicine?
4. How much money does it take to get a medical education in the United States?
5. How much competition is there for admission to American medical schools?
6. How many doctors have basic training in first aid procedures?
7. How many residency positions do most medical students apply for?
8. How many Americans study at medical schools overseas?
9. How many foreign students are enrolled in United States medical schools?
10. How much persistence does it take to become a doctor in the United States?

Exercise 14

Choose the correct form in these sentences:

1. We don't need (some/any/none of) assistance with our baggage.
2. I feel sorry for Albert. He's so shy and he has (few/a few/quite a few) friends he can talk to if he has problems.
3. Hardly any people (came/didn't come) to the meeting.
4. Albert went to (quite a bit of/a bit of/only a bit of) trouble to get those tickets, so you must remember to thank him.
5. (Not every/Not all/None of)people like to go dancing on Saturday nights.
6. Do you have (many/much/every) time to help me?
7. Sure I do. I've got (a lot/ lots of).
8. Why are Albert and Florence so sad? (Both/Neither/None) passed the chemistry exam.
9. Learning English takes (several/a certain amount of/any) practice.
10. (A great many of/ A great much of/ A great deal of) the time we spent in Hawaii, it was raining.

Exercise 15

Are the following sentences correct or incorrect? If they are incorrect, identify the problem and correct the sentence. There may be more than one problem.

1. None of doctors are allowed to practice without a license.
2. We had much trouble with the examination this morning.
3. A great many of traditional medicines are still used in rural areas.
4. No unlicensed physicians are allowed to practice in the United States.
5. Foreign students need lots of opportunities to get used to American educational techniques.
6. Few students never pass their qualifying exams.
7. Quite a bit of time that Albert spent in his residency was clinical training.
8. Students usually apply to several of universities for admission.
9. A few doctors don't stay up-to-date, but a lot of do.
10. Few students don't take their studies seriously.

Activities

Activity 1

In the Task, you examined some graphs on foreign student enrollment in the United States. Following is some information about foreign student enrollment patterns worldwide. Examine these two graphs and write a brief essay on foreign study throughout the world. Be sure to answer these questions:

• Where do students come from?
• Where do they go?
• What countries have the largest percentage of foreign students in their schools?

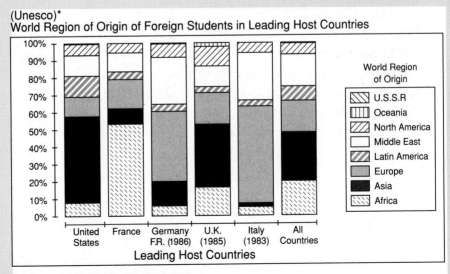

(Unesco)*
World Region of Origin of Foreign Students in Leading Host Countries

* Source: *Unesco Satistical Yearbook,* 1989

(Unesco)
Foreign Student Proportion of Total Enrollment in Leading Host Countries, 1986

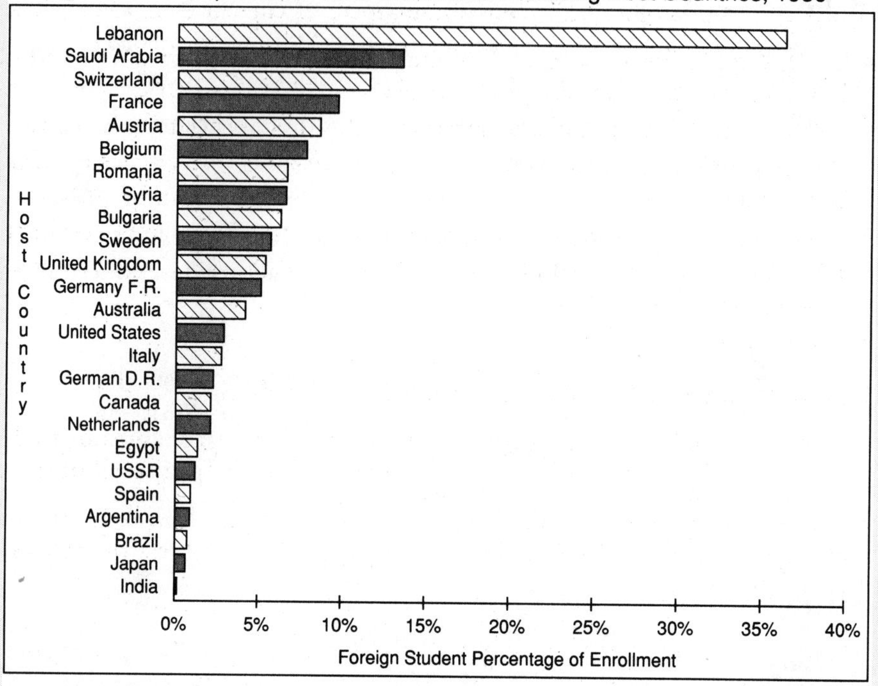
Lebanon
Saudi Arabia
Switzerland
France
Austria
Belgium
Romania
Syria
Bulgaria
Sweden
United Kingdom
Germany F.R.
Australia
United States
Italy
German D.R.
Canada
Netherlands
Egypt
USSR
Spain
Argentina
Brazil
Japan
India
Host Country
0%
5%
10%
15%
20%
25%
30%
35%
40%
Foreign Student Percentage of Enrollment

[1] Source: *Unesco Satistical Yearbook*, 1986
[2] The Vatican City is not included: 99.8% of its total enrollment is foreign.

Activity 2

Conduct a poll of your classmates to find out about their educational backgrounds.

How many years of school do they have?
What subjects have they studied?
Did most of them enjoy school?
Decide on two more questions to ask them.

- Present your information by constructing charts similar to the ones you have been examining in this unit.

Activity 3

In **Exercise 1**, you read about the training of medical doctors in the United States. Describe how people in one of these categories are trained:

traditional artists	farmers	athletes
lawyers	plumbers	English teachers

Activity 4

Conduct a public opinion poll on some aspect of current events.

- In a group, choose some topic of current interest from the news and develop a list of 5–8 questions to determine how people feel about this issue.
- Poll your classmates, and also interview 10–15 people outside of class.
- Devise a graphic representation of your results similar to the charts you have examined in this unit.
- Using your charts, make a presentation of your findings to the rest of the class. Report any interesting differences between the opinions of your classmates and the people you interviewed outside of class.

Activity 5

President Abraham Lincoln was famous for this remark:

"You can fool all of the people some of the time, and you can fool some of the people all of the time. But you can't fool all of the people all of the time."

- Do you think this is true? Think of some examples that support your opinion and explain those examples in a short essay or speech to the rest of the class.

29

Collective Nouns

Task

What is a good way to organize a complicated group project? Business managers have found that certain organizational techniques can make any group or committee run more smoothly and efficiently. Bad organization can result in a few people doing all the work, duplication of effort, or wasted time and energy.

Here is an opportunity for you to explore techniques for streamlining group processes and decision making: Suppose the whole class has decided to take a weekend trip together. In a small group, decide on the best way to organize such a complex project to make sure that work is done efficiently and everyone is involved in the process.

- Decide on the **tasks** that need to be done in order to organize and carry out such a trip.
- Establish a list of **committees** to accomplish these tasks and specify the duties and members of each committee. Make sure that the work is evenly distributed, and that no single committee has too much to do.

When you have decided on your organizational plan, make a report to the rest of the class:

- Describe your organizational plan. Tell what committees you have established, what responsibilities each committee has, and who each committee has as members.
- Report on the decision-making process of your group. Identify any problems you had working as a committee. Present any techniques you used that helped you work together more efficiently.

The class should decide who has the best-organized plan for the project.

Focus 1

Collective Nouns

- There are two kinds of collective nouns: those that refer to groups of things and those that refer to categories. There are some differences in their form and use.
- Some collective nouns refer to groups of things. You can use them to describe groups of collections of

People	Animals	Things
a **troupe** of dancers	a **flock** of birds	a **bunch** of grapes
a **team** of ball players	a **herd** of goats	a **sheaf** of papers
a **committee** of experts	a **pack** of dogs	a **bundle** of letters
a **delegation** of officials	a **gaggle** of geese	a **group** of issues
a **coven** of witches	a **school** of fish	a **flurry** of new
	a **swarm** of insects	developments

- These collective nouns function like other count nouns. You can use them with or without the accompanying noun phrase. They can have both singular or plural forms:

    (a) The **delegation of teachers** left the room.

    (b) The **delegation** left the room.

    (c) The president met with **several delegations** last week.

- The second group of collective nouns refer to categories. These categories are usually social or political categories:

the government	the administration
the middle class	the aristocracy
the media	the clergy
the bourgeoisie	the establishment
the public	the military-industrial complex
the opposition	the arts community

- These collective nouns that refer to categories function differently from collective nouns that refer to groups of things. They always occur with *the*. Their grammatical form is almost always singular.

    NOT: **a** clergy, **a** public, etc.

    NOT: the **publics** of the United States

Exercise 1

Read the following passages. Underline the words and phrases that refer to groups or categories of nouns. The first passage has been done for you as an example.

1. Every year on March 19, <u>a large flock of swallows</u> returns to San Juan Capistrano Mission in Southern California. No one knows how <u>this flock</u> manages to return every year on exactly the same date, but they have been doing just that for more than 200 years. <u>The Chamber of Commerce</u> in San Juan Capistrano has been providing mountains of publicity on the event for many years, and as a result, March 19 is also the day when <u>flocks of tourists</u> arrive at the Mission as well to watch the swallows return.

2. The World Cup Soccer Competition is probably the single most popular athletic event in the world. Teams of athletes from almost every country in the world conduct play-off matches. A team's standing depends on whether it has won or lost the previous game. A team that succeeds in reaching the finals can count on its fans to provide vigorous and energetic support. The young, the enthusiastic, and the dedicated invariably accompany them to the final round of play-offs and cheer them to victory.

3. A committee of scientists has been appointed by the government to look into the effects of acid rain on the forests of North America. They have been asked to present the results of their study to the President by the end of the year. The press and the public will be waiting anxiously for the committee to release its report.

4. There is a very unusual company of actors, which is based in Washington, D.C. Most of the company cannot hear, and many members can only speak by using sign language. The National Theater of the Deaf was founded nearly 30 years ago, and since then they have performed all over the United States and in dozens of foreign countries. The troupe has played an important role in involving the disabled in the arts.

Focus 2

FORM ● MEANING ● USE

Singular and Plural Meaning of Collective Nouns

FORM
MEANING
USE

- Collective nouns can have a singular or plural meaning. You can use them with either singular or plural verbs and pronouns.

(a) The committee of experts **has** decided to release **its** findings next week.	**(b) The committee** of experts **have** decided to release **their** findings next week.
(c) The aristocracy has opposed every challenge to **its** economic privileges.	**(d) The aristocracy have** opposed every challenge to **their** economic privileges.
(e) The middle class in America **has** begun to protest the accelerating decline in **its** standard of living.	**(f) The middle class** in America **have** begun to protest the accelerating decline in **their** standard of living.

- There is a difference in implication. Using singular verbs and pronouns usually implies that the group is operating as a whole. Using plural verbs and pronouns focuses on the individual behavior of the members of the group.

(g) The team **has** just won **its** third championship in a row.	**(h)** The team **are** entering the stadium, waving **their** hands and smiling at the crowd.

- There is also a difference in British and American usage. British English tends to use plural forms with singular collective nouns. American English tends to use singular forms with singular collective nouns:

British Usage	American Usage
(i) The committee **have** made **their** decision **(k)** The aristocracy **were** sometimes cruel to **their** servants.	**(j)** The committee **has** made **its** decision. **(l)** The aristocracy **was** despised for **its** lack of concern for the poor.

- Whichever choice you make, it is usually bad style in written or formal spoken English to change from singular to plural within a single sentence or single reference:

Singular	Plural
(m) The beginning class **likes its** teachers to give **it** lots of homework. **(o)** NOT: The beginning class **likes their** teachers to give **them** lots of homework.	**(n)** The beginning class **like their** teachers to give **them** lots of homework.

Exercise 2

Read the following sentences and underline each collective noun and any pronouns and verbs which refer to it. Decide why the author chose to consider the collective noun singular or plural.

> **EXAMPLE:** The French Revolution was caused in part by the refusal of the aristocracy to give up its social privileges.
>
> Reason: Reference to a single social class, not a collection of individuals.

1. The Roman Catholic clergy will resist any attempt to change its position on abortion.
2. The victorious team all waved to their supporters while the crowd roared its approval.
3. The media is aware of the important role it plays in American Presidential elections.
4. The herd of sheep bleated nervously to their shepherd as a pack of wolves made its way through the forest.
5. The military continues to fight further reductions in its funding.
6. The middle class is facing a greater tax burden than it has ever faced before.
7. A rash of new developments have made a great change on the government's priorities, and it is just beginning to respond to them.

Exercise 3

Decide whether you should use the collective nouns in the following sentences with singular or plural verbs and pronouns and choose the correct form. Although both choices may be grammatical, there may be a clear preference for one form instead of the other, so prepare to explain why you have chosen the forms you did.

1. The staff took a vote on what kind of Christmas party (it/they) (want/wants). (It/They) decided to rent a hall and hire a band.
2. The college administration (want/wants) a basketball team that (is/are) able to win enough games to place (itself/themselves) in the final play-offs.
3. The rowing crew raised (its/their) oars as (its/their) boat crossed the finish line.
4. The advanced grammar class never (like/likes) to turn in (its/their) homework right after a long vacation. (It/They) prefer to finish all assignments before (it/they) leave for vacation.
5. The crowd showed (its/their) approval by letting out a deafening roar.
6. The opposition voiced (its/their) disapproval to the policies the government had released in (its/their) latest report by more than three dozen speeches in Parliament.

Focus 3

MEANING

Singular and Plural Proper Nouns

MEANING

- Many singular proper nouns also describe groups. Most names of such things as organizations and legislative bodies are singular and should be used with singular verbs and pronouns:
  - **(a)** The Supreme Court **has** changed **its** position on several issues.
  - **(b)** The Congress of Deputies **has** requested the release of five political prisoners.
  - **(c)** Parliament **has** adjourned for the summer.
  - **(d)** The House of Representatives **has** begun debate on whether or not to raise the salaries of **its** members.

- Plural proper nouns refer to groups as a whole. Most names of nationalities, families, teams, and so on, are plural and should be used with plural verbs and pronouns:
  - **(e)** **The Russians are** trying to transform **their** economy.
  - **(f)** **The Montagues** and **the Capulets** were the two warring families in Shakespeare's *Romeo and Juliet*.
  - **(g)** **The Democrats** hope to attract **their** supporters from the working class.
  - **(h)** I hope **the Miami Dolphins were** able to win the game yesterday.

Exercise 4

Decide whether the following proper nouns should be considered singular or plural. Write a sentence for each. Be sure the verbs and pronouns in your sentences reflect your choice of whether these proper nouns are singular or plural.

1. The National Assembly
2. The French
3. The Russians
4. The Washington Redskins
5. The government of Brazil
6. The Catholic Church
7. The Chinese
8. The Grateful Dead
9. The Smith Family
10. The Simpsons

Focus 4

FORM ● MEANING

Adjectives Referring to Groups

FORM
MEANING

- Adjectives used with *the* can also refer to a group whose members share a particular characteristic. These constructions are considered to be plural, and the verbs and pronouns reflect this.
  (a) **The rich** get richer and **the poor** get poorer.
  (b) These laws are designed to protect **the young** and **the helpless** from exploitation.
  (c) **The elderly are** making **their** opinions a growing force in American politics.

Exercise 5

For each *the* + **adjective** construction in the following sentences, rewrite the construction as **noun + relative clause**.

> **EXAMPLE:** The French aristocracy did not care about the poor.
> *The poor = people who were poor.*

1. Elvis Presley was very popular with the young.
2. *Dear Abby* is an advice column in the newspaper for the lonely and the confused.
3. Nelson Mandela is an important hero for the oppressed.
4. Albert and Florence became doctors so they could help the sick.
5. The government should establish more comprehensive programs to help the underprivileged.

387

Exercise 6

Circle the collective nouns, proper nouns, and adjectives that refer to groups in the following passage. Decide whether the pronouns and verbs that refer to these constructions should be singular or plural.

(1)The homeless *are/is* an increasing problem in most American cities. (2)The homeless *consist/consists* of several distinct categories of people. (3)The first category *consist/consists* of the mentally disabled. (4)In the early l980s, the Reagan Administration eliminated most of *its/their* funding for treatment programs for the mentally ill. (5)As a result, scores of mental hospitals were closed, and many of the mentally ill *was/were* released, and left to make *its/their* own way. (6)A substantial number *have/has* been unable to establish normal lives, and as a result, *it/they* have ended up living on the streets.

(7)A second category of the homeless *is/are* the unemployed. (8)Typically, the unemployed *is/are* part of the homeless for a relatively short period of time—usually less than a year. (9)Some of *it/them have/has* lost *its/their* jobs; or the factories where *it/they* worked were closed without warning. (10)As a result, *it/they* did not have enough money to pay rent. (11)Many of the unemployed *has/have* also ended up living on the streets or sleeping in *its/their* automobiles. (12)But the majority of the people in this category of the homeless *is/are* able to find housing again, once they have found other jobs.

(13)A third category of the homeless *is/are* the people who *is/are* addicted to drugs or alcohol. (14)Like the mentally ill, this category of homelessness *represent/represents* a persistent social problem. (15)The unemployed can hope for better times, and *is/are* usually able to escape from the terrible cycle of poverty and life on the streets, but the government *has/have* been very slow in committing *its/their* resources to any kind of comprehensive program to help the mentally disabled or the addicted work on *its/their* recovery.

Focus 5

USE

Implications of Collective Nouns

USE

- Like the measure words that you can only use with certain non-count nouns (an **ear** of corn, for example), many collective nouns that refer to groups usually belong only to one particular group. Sometimes a writer will use an inappropriate collective noun to indicate that one group has characteristics common to another group.

As we watched, **a gaggle of schoolgirls** made their way through the mall.	*Gaggle* is the collective noun used for a group of geese. This sentence implies that the girls' activity resembled that of geese in some way.
When the scientists in Antarctica began construction of the research station, they were constantly watched by **a delegation of penguins** which showed no fear of humans.	*Delegation* is the collective used for official groups of representatives or diplomats. This sentence implies that the penguins appeared rather formal and official.

Exercise 7

Read the following sentences. Identify the collective nouns. Discuss with a partner or a small group what the choice of collective nouns implies. Share your ideas with the rest of the class.

1. The mayor was followed by a pack of reporters demanding to know whether he was planning to resign.
2. When herds of tourists filled the gallery, John decided to see the exhibition at another time.
3. A flock of school children filled the air with shouting and laughter.
4. Out of the jungle came a troupe of monkeys which snatched up the food that had been prepared for the picnic.
5. As soon as he stepped out of the limousine, he was surrounded by a swarm of beggars asking for money.

Exercise 8

Are these sentences correct or incorrect? If they are incorrect, identify the problem and correct it.

1. The Supreme Court have decided to reverse its opinion on that issue.
2. I watched the flock of birds as it landed in the field across the road.
3. The rich is always trying to avoid giving its money to pay taxes.
4. The Kremlin are trying to restructure the economy of the USSR.
5. The herd of sheep was frightened by a pack of wolves, and it bleated nervously in their pen.

Activities

Activity 1

English used to have many different collective nouns to refer to specific animals. These nouns sometimes indicated some sort of quality or characteristic that these animals had.

> a pride of lions
> a parliament of owls
> a pod of whales
> an exaltation of larks
> a charm of finches
> a leap of leopards

We rarely use such collective words in modern English. But sometimes for humorous reasons, people will invent collective words to apply to a particular group of people. Here are some examples:

> a sweep of cleaning ladies
> a hustle of salesmen
> a splash of swimmers

389

- Working with a partner, decide on some humorous collective terms for some of these categories of people:

flight attendants	kittens
lawyers	puppies
accountants	computer programmers
English teachers	real-estate salesmen
magicians	

Activity 2

Write a paragraph on one of these topics:

- Compare two athletic teams that play a sport you are familiar with. Why do you think one team is better than the other?
- Discuss one or more famous performing troupes (opera, drama, circus, orchestra). Why are they famous and do you feel that their reputation is justified?
- What lessons can the old teach the young? What lessons can the young teach the old?

Activity 3

There is a joke in American business circles that says, "A camel is a horse that was designed by a committee." Some management experts think that committees result in a better product than a single individual. Others feel that committees tend to be inefficient and badly organized.

- In the Task, you had a firsthand experience with working in a committee. Review your experience with that process. What were the advantages of having a group work together on a single task? What were the disadvantages? Based on your experience, identify the strengths and weaknesses of working on a committee.
- Present your ideas to the rest of the class as a list of **pros** and **cons**. For example, *Pro:* A committee is able to assign tasks to each member, so the work can be divided. *Con:* A committee does not reach decisions quickly, because each member has to agree about the issue before they can take action.
- How are you going to do this activity? By yourself or in a group?

Activity 4

Should the rich pay more taxes or higher penalties (for traffic tickets, for example) than the poor? Why do you think so? Discuss your ideas in a small group and present a report on your group's opinion to the rest of the class. Your report should use phrases like "Our group feels that . . . "

Activity 5

Have you ever seen a political demonstration? Where and when did it occur? What was the demonstration about? What did the crowd do? What did the police do? Write a description of what happened.

UNIT

30

Special Problems
in Past Time Frame:
Choosing Adverbs versus
Aspect Markers to Indicate
Time Relationships

Task

There are certain events that are so important or surprising that they are literally unforgettable. For example, most Americans who were born before 1955 can probably tell you **exactly** what they were doing on November 22, 1963—the day President John F. Kennedy was assassinated—even though that day was more than 25 years ago. It was a day that few people can forget. Anyone living in San Francisco on October 17, 1989, can tell you exactly what he or she was doing when the earthquake occurred at 5:08 P.M.

• Write a paragraph describing a time when you heard some shocking or memorable news or experienced some important event—a time that you will never forget. You can tell about a time when you heard about some important development in world events such as Indira Gandhi's assassination or the tearing down of the Berlin Wall. Or it could be something more personal, such as the day your mother told you that you were going to have a new baby brother or sister. Start your account with: "I will never forget the moment that. . . . " Your description should include what you were doing at the time, what you had been doing, and how you reacted when you heard the news.

Here are two accounts to look at as examples:

EXAMPLE 1:

(1)I will never forget the moment I heard that John F. Kennedy had been assassinated. (2)I was a junior in high school. (3)I was studying in the school library at the time. (4)Ordinarily, I would have been in the music room practicing with the school orchestra. (5)(I used to play the violin when I was in high school.) (6)But our teacher was conducting a special rehearsal for the wind instruments. (7)All of the string players had been excused from the rehearsal, so I had been given a pass to go to the library and do some independent studying.

(8)The library door was open, and I heard a radio playing from one of the classrooms across the hall. (9)At first, I was annoyed by the noise. (10)I wondered why they were playing that radio so loud when people were trying to study. (11)Then all of a sudden, I heard the announcer saying, "We have confirmed that President John F. Kennedy has been shot while traveling through Dallas, and that he is now dead. We repeat: President John F. Kennedy is dead." (12)I was shocked. (13)I could not believe what I had heard, so I listened more carefully. (14)They repeated the information.

391

(15)When I realized it was true, I immediately left the library and returned to the orchestra rehearsal. (16)I had to tell someone! (17)I went back to the orchestra room, where the other students were still rehearsing. (18)Before I had a chance to interrupt the rehearsal, the principal of the school made an announcement on the public address system. (19)Suddenly people began crying, and all normal activities came to a halt. (20)The teacher turned on the television and for the next two hours we watched the news reports of the horrifying developments.

EXAMPLE 2:

(1)I will never forget the moment the earthquake struck San Francisco. (2)I was still in my office. (3)I had been trying to finish a project before I left for the day. (4)Suddenly, the building began to sway. (5)Books fell off their shelves. (6)People were screaming. (7)It seemed like things were moving for several minutes, but I guess the actual time was pretty short. (8)As soon as the building had stopped moving, I tried to get out as quickly as possible. (9)This wasn't easy, because I work on the 17th floor, and of course the electricity went out the moment the earthquake struck, so no elevators were working. (10)I ran down the emergency stairs in darkness and got out to the street. (11)Literally hundreds of people were standing around, wondering what to do. (12)Then someone appeared who had a transistor radio, and we all stood as close as we could to him, while he tried to find a news station that could give us information about what had just happened and about what we should do. (13)After about 20 minutes, I realized that all public transportation had stopped, and if I wanted to go home, I would have to walk. (14)When I finally got home, there was no electricity, but the apartment was OK, and my roommate Matt and the dog were both sitting outside. He was talking to the neighbor, and watching the news broadcasts on a portable battery-operated TV. (15)We all sat around and told each other about our experiences.

- Compare your account to other people's stories. In a group, decide on an answer to this question:

  Are there any common feelings or reactions that all or most people share in situations when they hear about or experience some very important or surprising event?

- Present your list of shared reactions to the rest of the class.

Focus 1

FORM

Irregular Verbs

FORM

- Many of the most common verbs in English are irregular. This means that they have separate forms (rather than just adding **-ed**) when you use them in simple past tense or as past participles (with perfect aspect or with passive voice). Because they are so common, it is important to know these forms well.

Exercise 1

The following is a partially completed chart of the most common irregular verbs in English. Check your knowledge of irregular verbs by filling in the blanks to complete the entire chart. You may work with other students to share your knowledge, or you might want to refer to a dictionary for the forms you are not sure of:

Simple Form	Past Tense Form	Past Participle		Simple Form	Past Tense Form	Past Participle
_____	_____	become		_____	_____	dug
begin	_____	_____		do	_____	_____
_____	bent	_____		_____	drew	_____
_____	_____	bet		_____	_____	drunk
bind	_____	_____		drive	_____	_____
_____	bit	_____		_____	ate	_____
_____	_____	bled		_____	_____	fallen
blow	_____	_____		feed	_____	_____
_____	broke	_____		_____	felt	_____
_____	_____	brought		_____	fought	_____
build	_____	_____		find	_____	_____
_____	_____	bought		_____	fit	_____
catch	_____	_____		fly	_____	_____
_____	chose	_____		forbid	_____	_____
come	_____	_____		forget	_____	_____
_____	cost	_____		_____	forgave	_____
cut	_____	_____		_____	_____	frozen

Simple Form	Past Tense Form	Past Participle
_____	_____	_____
_____	gave	_____
go	_____	_____
_____	_____	ground
_____	grew	_____
hang	_____	_____
_____	had	_____
hear	_____	_____
_____	hid	_____
_____	_____	hit
_____	held	_____
hurt	_____	_____
_____	kept	_____
_____	_____	known
lead	_____	_____
_____	left	_____
lend	_____	_____
_____	_____	let
make	_____	_____
_____	_____	meant
meet	_____	_____
_____	put	_____
_____	_____	quit

Simple Form	Past Tense Form	Past Participle
read	_____	_____
_____	rode	_____
_____	_____	rung
rise	_____	_____
_____	ran	_____
_____	_____	said
see	_____	_____
_____	sought	_____
_____	_____	sold
send	_____	_____
_____	set	_____
_____	_____	shaken
shine	_____	_____
_____	shot	_____
_____	_____	shut
sing	_____	_____
_____	sank	_____
_____	_____	sat
sleep	_____	_____
_____	slid	_____
_____	_____	spoken
speed	_____	_____
_____	spent	_____

Simple Form	Past Tense Form	Past Participle
_____	_____	split
spread	_____	_____
_____	sprang	_____
_____	_____	stood
steal	_____	_____
_____	stuck	_____
_____	_____	stung
strike	_____	_____
swear	_____	_____
_____	swept	_____
_____	swam	_____
_____	_____	swung
take	_____	_____

Simple Form	Past Tense Form	Past Participle
_____	taught	_____
_____	_____	torn
tell	_____	_____
_____	thought	_____
_____	_____	thrown
understand	_____	_____
_____	woke	_____
_____	_____	worn
weave	_____	_____
_____	wept	_____
_____	_____	won
wind	_____	_____
_____	wrote	_____

Focus 2

Indicating Time Relationships in Past Time Frame

USE

- The Past Time Frame is the most frequently used time frame for narratives (telling stories) or talking about past events. In the Past Time Frame, when discussing more than one related action or event, or when two verbs have the same moment of focus, it is necessary to indicate their time relationship. This can be done
  - by sequence: (Things happen in the order in which they are mentioned.)
    - **(a)** He walked up the stairs. He turned the knob and opened the door.
  - by adverbs and adverbial phrases and clauses:
    - **(b) As** he entered the room, he realized something was different. **Before** he had a chance to turn around, he knew something was missing. **In a moment,** he realized what it was.
  - by aspect markers:
    - **(c)** The television **had disappeared.** The antennae wires **were hanging** from the wall. He **had been watching** TV a few hours earlier, but now there **was** nothing there.
- Speakers and writers of English use a mixture of these methods, but in general they are less likely to use aspect to indicate time relationships if the relationship has also been made clear by sequence, by adverbials, or by general context. Students of English sometimes use aspect markers when they don't really need to, because adverbial information has already made the context clear. Knowing when to use (or not use) aspect markers can be difficult, so the first step in learning about this is to notice how native speakers indicate these differences.

Exercise 2

For each of these passages, list the highlighted verbs in the order that the actions occurred. Tell how you think that the order is indicated (by adverb, sequence, or aspect markers).

EXAMPLE: As he **entered the room,** he realized something was different. Before he **had a chance to turn around,** he **knew something was missing.** In a moment, he **realized** what it was. The television **had disappeared.** The antennae wires **were hanging from the wall. He had been watching TV** a few hours earlier, but now **there was nothing there.**

Order of Events	How Indicated
1. he had been watching television	aspect, adverb (a few hours earlier)
2. the television had disappeared	aspect
3. the wires were hanging	aspect
4. there was nothing there	adverb(now)
5. he entered the room	adverb (as)
6. he knew something was missing	sequence
7. he had a chance to turn around	adverb (before)
8. he realized what it was	sequence

1. Police **reported** yesterday that they **had uncovered** a large cache of stolen goods from a warehouse in the southern part of the city. The warehouse **had been** under surveillance for some time. A suspiciously large number of people **had been seen** going in and out of the storage facility. Once the police **had obtained** a search warrant, they **entered** the building in the middle of the night and **discovered** large amounts of electronic equipment and building supplies. Police **announced** that this discovery **might lead** to the solution of a number of robberies.

2. At the time of the earthquake, Jeff **was** still in his office. He **had been trying** to finish a project before he left for the day. Suddenly, the building **began** to sway. Books **fell** off their shelves. People **were screaming.** Although it seemed as if things were moving for several minutes, the actual time was just 15 seconds.

   Even before the building **stopped** moving, people **were trying** to get out as quickly as possible. This wasn't easy for people who **had been working** in the higher floors of the building. The electricity **had gone off** the moment the earthquake struck, so no elevators **were working.** Most people **ran** down emergency stairs in darkness and got out to the street.

Exercise 3

What is the time relationship between the highlighted verbs in each of the numbered sentences in this passage? How is the time relationship indicated? By sequence? By adverbials? By aspect? By both? The first sentence has been done for you as an example.

> EXAMPLE: first action: *had been looking;*
>
> second action: *broke out;*
>
> how indicated: *aspect and adverbial (before)*

(1)Even before the disastrous fire that destroyed large portions of Imperial Rome **broke out,** the Emperor Nero **had been looking** for ways to control or eliminate the growing Christian population in the city. (2)When news of the fire **reached** the emperor's palace, he **became** quite jubilant. (3)He obviously **had been looking** for some excuse, and now he **had** one, made to order. He went immediately to the roof of the palace. The city was a sea of flames all around him. (4)In spite of the fact that people **were screaming** for their lives on the streets below, Nero **ordered** that a lyre be brought to him at once. (5)He **decided** to compose a poem comparing the destruction of Rome to that of Troy in Homer's *Iliad*, and **began** singing.

(6)However, contrary to the common saying, Nero **did not fiddle** while Rome burned, because the fiddle—or violin, as it is more commonly known—**had not yet been invented.** But he did stand on the roof of the palace, and he was heard singing and playing a musical instrument. (7)The actual origins of the fire **were never determined,** but modern scholars agree that the Christian community **had not been** responsible for the destruction of the city. (8)However, the fire **provided** Nero with the excuse he **had been looking for,** and the next day Imperial Troops **began** to round up groups of Christians and take them off to prison.

Focus 3

USE

When, While, and Progressive Aspect

USE

- With most time adverbials, the relationship is clear, but certain adverbs do not give enough information, and you **must** use aspect to express the time relationship.

When indicates that the verb happened **before or at the same time as the moment of focus**.	*While* indicates that the action was **in progress at the moment of focus.**
(a) When Nero heard about the fire, he ran to the roof of the palace.	**(b)** Nero played the violin **while** Rome burned.

- If you use *when* to connect an action that is already in progress with the moment of focus, you **must** use progressive aspect.

	Implied Meaning
When the fire broke out, Nero **persecuted** the Christians.	First the fire happened, then Nero persecuted the Christians.
When the fire broke out, Nero **was persecuting** the Christians.	Nero started persecuting the Christians before the fire happened.

Exercise 6

Work with a partner. Take turns asking and answering these questions about the example passages in the Task. What does this activity tell you about the difference between simple past and past progressive tenses? Present your ideas to the rest of the class.

PASSAGE 1:

1. What was the writer doing when he heard the news about J.F.K.?
2. What did the writer do when he heard the news about J.F.K?
3. What were his classmates in the orchestra doing when they heard the news about J.F.K?
4. What did they do when they heard the news about J.F.K?

PASSAGE 2:

1. What was Jeff doing when the building started to sway?
2. What did Jeff do when the building stopped swaying?
3. What happened to the elevators when the earthquake struck?
4. What was happening when Jeff reached the street?
5. What happened when Jeff reached the street?
6. What was happening when Jeff finally got home?
7. What happened when Jeff finally got home?

Focus 4

Other Uses of Progressive Aspect

USE

- Even though a time relationship is clear, a speaker / writer may decide to also use progressive aspect to indicate these kinds of additional information:
  - to emphasize "in progress" or "uncompleted":
    - **(a)** In 1967, while I **was researching** the economic consequences of the American Civil War, I came upon a fascinating piece of information.
  - repetition or duration:
    - **(b)** During the last few years of his life, Mozart **was constantly trying** to borrow money from anyone who would loan it to him.
  - temporary situation:
    - **(c)** When John first got to Paris, he **was staying for a short while** at the house of a shopkeeper and his family.

Exercise 7

Identify all the past progressive verb forms in the example passages of the Task and tell why you think the author chose to use past progressive.

Exercise 8

Choose the appropriate form of the verbs indicated in the passage below. There may be more than one correct choice, so prepare to explain why you chose the form you did. The first sentence has been done for you as an example.

(1) The St. Lawrence Seaway, the waterway that ((links) / is linking) the Great Lakes of North America with the Atlantic Ocean, was discovered by explorers who (looked / (were looking)) for the Northwest Passage. (2) Geographers at that time (believed / were believing) that there was a water course that (connected / was connecting) the Atlantic and Pacific oceans. (3) Throughout the sixteenth and early seventeenth centuries, both England and France constantly (sent / were sending) one expedition after another to find the passage. (4) Early explorers (investigated / were investigating) virtually every large inlet and river along the entire Eastern coast of North America.

(5) Even though they never (found / were finding) the Northwest Passage, these early explorers (made / were making) a valuable contribution to the knowledge of North American geography. (6) While they (explored / were exploring) the coast, they (made / were making) many other very useful discoveries. (7) Not only the St. Lawrence, but also Hudson Bay, Chesapeake Bay, the Hudson River, and the Delaware River all (were discovered / were being discovered) by explorers who actually (looked / were looking) for something else.

Focus 5

Using Perfect Aspect in Past Time

USE

- You can use both adverbials and aspect markers to indicate that something happened before the moment of focus.

Adverbials	Aspect
Before we left on the trip, we checked the car thoroughly. **After** we checked the oil, we made sure the tires had enough air.	But we **hadn't gotten** more than a few miles when we realized that we **had forgotten** something: We **had left** our suitcases on the front porch. We **had been worrying** so much about the mechanical condition of the car that we left without thinking about its contents.

- However, native speakers do not typically use both. They sometimes tend to avoid the past perfect tense if the time sequence is clear from other information in the passage, and use it only when it is necessary to communicate a logical connection between the two events, to clarify the time relationship, or to change the moment of focus in indirect speech.
- A writer/speaker may decide to use perfect aspect, even when the time relationship is made clear by adverbs or sequence, to indicate
  - the action was fully completed:

    (a) I **had finished** all my homework **before** I went to Jane's party.
  - a strong logical connection:

    (b) He **had seen** the movie, and **therefore** didn't want to go with us.

Exercise 9

Examine how adverbials and aspect are used to indicate time relationships. For each sentence in these passages, identify the moment of focus and list the verbs that happened before the moment of focus in the order that they occurred. Are the time relationships indicated by adverbials, by aspect, or by both? The first two sentences in each passage have been done for you as an example.

(1)Before we left on the trip, we checked the car thoroughly. (2)After we checked the oil, we made sure the tires had enough air. (3)But we hadn't gotten more than a few miles when we realized that we had forgotten something: We had left our suitcases on the front porch. (4)We had been worrying so much about the mechanical condition of the car that we left without thinking about its contents.

Moment of Focus	Time Before	How Indicated
1) we left on the trip	we checked the car	adverb(before)
2) we made sure the tires had enough air	we checked the oil	adverb(after)

The fifteenth century saw the emergence of a new social and economic order in Europe. (1)By the end of the fourteenth century, the population of Europe was about a third smaller than it had been at the beginning. (2)It was one of the few times in history when the population had not only stopped growing but had actually decreased. (3)This smaller population was caused by repeated outbreaks of bubonic plague that had swept through the continent several times during the century, (4)and when the century ended, this had resulted in some fundamental changes in society. (5)So many people had died that the traditional feudal landlords were forced to intermarry with wealthy merchant families, rather than aristocratic ones. (6)People who had previously only had the opportunity to make a living as farmers or serfs were able to become craftsmen and artisans. (7)The plague had killed so many people that the traditional social boundaries were wiped out, and this created a period of great social mobility and economic change.

Moment of Focus	Time Before	How Indicated
1) the population was one-third smaller	than it had been	adverbial (by the end of the fourteenth-century)
2) It was one of the few times in history	the population had stopped growing / had decreased	aspect

402

Exercise 10

Use the **past perfect** in the following sentences only if it is necessary to the meaning of the sentence. Otherwise use the **simple past** or **past progressive.**

1. Because Nero _____ (want) an excuse to persecute the Christians, he told everyone that they _____ (start) the fire.

2. Peter _____ (go) to talk with Mr. Green about the fight he _____ (have) with Denise earlier in the day.

3. As soon as the building _____ (stop moving), Jeff _____ (try) to call Matt, but the telephones _____ (stop working).

4. It was too late to put out the fire because it _____ (grow) too big for anything to control.

5. I _____ (look) everywhere for my wallet, but I _____ (not find) it anywhere. It _____ (disappear).

6. When the radio _____ (announce) that President Kennedy _____ (be shot), all normal activities _____ (come) to a halt.

7. Denise _____ (go) to Peter's office to complain about his attitude, but he _____ (leave) early to take his children to the circus.

8. Mary _____ (be) extremely worried about John since she _____ (not receive) any letters from him in over a month.

Focus 6

USE

Perfect Progressive Aspect in Past Time

USE

- An author may decide to use perfect progressive aspect in addition to adverbs or where the time sequence is already clear to give additional information about the verb:
  - continuous action rather than repeated action:

(a) It **had been snowing for three hours.** Unless they cleared the roads soon, it was likely that we would have to spend the night in our car.	**(b)** It **had snowed several times** since we arrived, but there still wasn't enough snow to ski.

  - uncompleted action rather than completed action:

(c) I **had been visiting** my aunt, when she suddenly became quite ill and asked me to drive her to the hospital.	**(d)** I **had visited** my aunt, so I was free to spend the rest of the afternoon at the museum.

Exercise 11

Decide whether **past perfect** or **past perfect progressive** is the appropriate tense for the verbs in the blanks.

1. When the earthquake struck, Jeff was still in the office because he _____ (try) to finish a project before he left for the day.

2. Emperor Nero _____ (look) for a reason to arrest Christians even before the fire that destroyed much of Rome.

3. By the beginning of the 15th Century, the Bubonic Plague _____ (cause) some fundamental social and political changes.

4. The police _____ (keep) the warehouse under surveillance for some time when they finally obtain a search warrant and investigated.

5. They first became suspicious because so many people _____ (go) in and out of the warehouse at strange hours of the day and night.

Exercise 12

Decide whether the verbs below should be in past tense, past perfect, or past perfect progressive. More than one answer may be correct, so prepare to explain why you chose the tense you did.

1. I _____ (work) in the library for about 20 minutes when I _____ (over-

   hear) the radio broadcast announcing Kennedy's assassination.

2. Jeff _____ (experience) several minor earthquakes, but he _____ (be) still

   surprised by the strength of this one.

3. Bob _____ (be) not really happy with what he _____ (do), so he

   _____ (decide) to look for another job.

4. European explorers _____ (try) to reach Asia when they _____ (land) in

   the New World "by accident."

5. When Jeff _____ (get) to the street, he _____ (see) that hundreds of other

   people _____ (leave) their offices and _____ (stand) out on the street

   wondering what to do.

Exercise 13

Decide on the correct verb tense (present, present perfect, simple past, past perfect, past progressive, or past perfect progressive) for the verbs in the blanks. There may be more than one correct answer, so prepare to explain why you made the choice you did.

(1)George Washington _____ (be) the first President of the United States, and _____ (serve) as the leader of American troops during the War of Independence. (2)According to a famous story, one year, when George _____ (be) a young boy, and _____ (learn) how to use farming tools, his father _____ (give) him a hatchet for his birthday. (3)George _____ (be) anxious to use the hatchet, so he _____ (run) out of the house and _____ (chop) down a cherry tree in his father's garden. (4)When his father _____ (discover) that someone _____ (chop) down the tree, he _____ (be) furious. (5)He _____ (demand) to know who _____ (chop) down his cherry tree. (6)When Little George _____ (hear) his father's angry shouting, he _____ (go) to his father and _____ (tell) him that he _____ (do) it with his new hatchet. (7)He said, "I _____ (be) sorry you _____ (are) angry, and I _____ (know) you will punish me, but I must admit my crime, because I cannot tell a lie." (8)George's father _____ (be) so impressed with his honesty, that he _____ (decide) not to punish the boy after all, and, in fact,_____ (reward) him, by giving him a silver dollar.

(9)This story actually never _____ (happen), but millions of American children _____ (read) this story in school. (10)Parents and teachers _____ (think) that it is a good way to teach children to be honest and to always tell the truth.

Activities

Activity 1

Write a paragraph that tells about a personal experience that happened to you or to someone you know which supports the truth of one of the following proverbs.

> An idle mind is the devil's playground.
> Too many cooks spoil the broth.
> Two heads are better than one.
> If at first you don't succeed, try, try again.
> Never count your chickens before they have hatched.

Activity 2

Form groups of three to five people. You are going to write a group story—but in a special way. Each person should take a piece of paper and start a story with this sentence:

> "It was a dark and stormy night. Suddenly, (your teacher's name) heard a terrible scream."

Then each person in the group should write for three minutes. When the three minutes are up, fold the paper so that only the last sentence or two can be read. Pass your story to the person on your right, and take the paper of the person on your left. Then each person should write for three minutes to continue that person's story. Repeat the process until the papers have gone completely around the group. Unfold the papers and read the resulting stories to each other.

- Which story has the funniest combination of sentences? Which story has the clearest sequence of activities? Choose the story you like best to read aloud to the rest of the class.

Activity 3

Every country has famous stories in its history that all children learn about when they are growing up. The interesting thing about such stories is that often they are not actually true. In the United States, for example, all schoolchildren have heard the story of George Washington and the Cherry Tree (Exercise 12).

Do you know any similar kinds of famous stories about real people that actually never happened? Write an essay that tells such a story, and why you think the story is told, even though it never happened.

Activity 4

Some historians feel that specific individual people and events do not actually change history but only reflect existing social or political trends. Do you agree or disagree with this theory?

- In a brief essay or oral presentation, choose a famous moment in history (such as Kennedy's assassination, the burning of Rome, or some other event) and describe what happened. Then explain why you think that the incident did or did not actually **cause** the historical developments that followed.

407

31

Modals in Past Time Frame

Task

How has your personality changed as you have grown older? In what ways are you different than you were in the past?

- Identify some things that you used to do five or ten years ago but don't do anymore. Then identify some things that you do now, but couldn't or wouldn't do five or ten years ago. Compare your list of activities with those of other students in the class.
- Based on the changes you thought of, and those of other students in the class, decide on two general ways that people's lives change for the better as they grow older. Write a brief essay about each area. Use the lists of your previous and current activities to provide examples to support your opinions. Here are two examples (which will also be used in Exercise 2):

EXAMPLE 1:

Growing older makes people more careful about their health. That is certainly true for me. I used to smoke three packs of cigarettes a day. I would start every morning by lighting a cigarette and coughing for five minutes. Whenever I walked up a flight of stairs, I would have to stop halfway up to take a rest. I knew smoking would eventually do serious damage to my lungs, but I didn't care. I was going to live forever. Besides, I used to think that smoking made me look sophisticated and mature.

But then I got married, and I had to think about my family. I wasn't going to let cigarettes make my wife a widow! I was afraid I wouldn't live long enough to see my grandchildren grow up. So I quit smoking and took up running. When I first started, I couldn't run more than a few hundred yards before I had to rest. But I knew it would only get easier, and the longer I quit smoking the faster I was able to run. Now I can run a mile in eight minutes. I'm in much better shape now than I used to be.

EXAMPLE 2:

Growing older makes people less worried about what other people think. In high school, I used to be really shy. I would avoid talking to people and I couldn't express my ideas in class without feeling very uncomfortable. I guess I was afraid that people were going to laugh at me, or that they would think I was strange. In high school, people were supposed to "fit in." They weren't allowed to be different. So I used to wear the same kind of clothes and try to behave the same way as everybody else. I felt I had to be "one of the crowd."

Now that I am older, I can stand up in front of other people and tell them what I think. I certainly couldn't do that in high school. I wear clothes because I like them, not because other people like them. I think I'm much more independent and self-confident than I used to be in high school.

Focus 1

FORM ● MEANING

Overview of Modals in Past Time Frame

FORM
MEANING

- The use of one-word and phrasal modals in the Past Time Frame is similar to their use in the Present and Future Time Frames, but there are some different uses and possible forms. This chart shows common modal meanings and forms in Past Time Frame.

MODALS IN PAST TIME

Meaning	One Word Modals	Examples	Phrasal Modals	Examples
necessity	*(No one-word modals for these uses)*		*had to*	**(a)** I **had to** do my homework before we went to the movies.
permission			*was allowed to*	**(b)** John **was allowed to** bring a guest.
advisability/ obligation			*was supposed to*	**(c)** You **were supposed to be** at the doctor's office at 2:00.
ability	*could/couldn't*	**(d)** John **could** speak French when he was younger.	*was able to*	**(e)** I **was able to** get tickets to the concert.
habitual actions	*would/wouldn't*	**(f)** When he lived in France, he **would** always have wine with his meals.	*used to*	**(g)** He **used to** play tennis, but he doesn't anymore.
future events in past time	*would/wouldn't* *might/might not*	**(h)** Naomi hoped that she **would** have the kind of vacation where she **might** meet someone and fall in love.	*was going to/ was about to/ was to*	**(i)** Nora **was about to** leave for the airport. She **was going to** spend a couple of months in Japan.

410

Exercise 1

It is important to be able to recognize when modals refer to the Present or Future Time Frame and when they refer to the Past Time Frame. Decide whether the following sentences are **a)** requests or **b)** questions about past habits and abilities.

1. Could you tell me how to get to Carnegie Hall?
2. Would you cry when your mother punished you?
3. Could you ride your bicycle to work last week?
4. Would you mind putting out that cigar?
5. Do you think you could tell that joke without laughing?
6. Would you pretend you could fly when you were a child?

Exercise 2

Underline modal forms in the example paragraphs in the Task. Identify the meaning by writing a letter: *(a)* necessity; *(b)* permission; *(c)* advisability; *(d)* ability; *(e)* habitual action; *(f)* future event over each one-word or phrasal modal you have underlined.

Focus 2

MEANING

Permission, Necessity, and Advisability

MEANING

- You cannot use one-word modals to talk about **permission, necessity,** or **advisability** in the Past Time Frame. You must use phrasal modals to express those meanings.

    When I was a child, my brothers and sisters and I **had to** do a number of routine chores. We **were supposed to** keep our rooms clean, and if we didn't, we **weren't allowed to** watch TV until everything was clean and orderly. We **had to** wash the dishes. I **was supposed** to wash them on Mondays, but sometimes I **was allowed** to switch nights with my sister when I **had to** do a lot of homework.

Exercise 3

Write five statements about things you **were allowed to do** when you were a child. Write five statements about things you **were not allowed to do.**

Exercise 4

Find a partner and ask if he or she was allowed to do the things you wrote about in Exercise 3.

> **EXAMPLE:** *When you were a child, were you allowed to stay out after dark?*

Identify some privileges that were the same for both of you, and some that were different. Report your findings to the rest of the class.

Exercise 5

Make five statements about things that you **had to do** when you were a child. Make five statements about things that you **were supposed to do** when you were a child but did not always do.

Exercise 6

Follow the same process in working with a partner that you used in Exercise 4.

Focus 3

MEANING

Ability in Past Time Frame
Could versus *Was Able To*

MEANING

- You can use both *could* and *was/were able to* to talk about abilities in Past Time Frame.

(a) When Jeanne was a child, she **could** speak excellent French, but she **couldn't** speak English. **Could** you speak any other languages as a child? Yes, I **could** speak a little Italian.	**(b) Were** you **able to** go to Joan's party? No, I **wasn't.** But I **was able to** send her a birthday card.

- Their use depends on whether they refer to a general ability or a specific ability.

General Ability (skills that exist over time)	**Specific Ability** (specific events or actions)
(c) John **could speak** French,	so he **was able to find** us a hotel in Paris.
(d) John **was able to speak** French,	but he **couldn't find** us a hotel anywhere.
(e) John **couldn't ride** a bike,	so he **wasn't able to join** us on our ride.
(f) John **wasn't able to ride a bike,**	but he **was able to enjoy** the picnic anyway.

- In statements of general ability, there is no difference in meaning or use between *could* and *was able to*. In statements of specific ability, you must use *could* with negative sentences.

    (g) AWKWARD: **Could** you get tickets for the concert? (This sounds like a request in Present Time.)

    (h) NOT: I **could** get two tickets to the concert.

    (i) OK: I stood in line for over an hour, but I **couldn't** get any.

Exercise 7

Decide whether the following statements refer to general ability or specific ability.

1. George was able to get tickets to the play.
2. However, he couldn't find them when it was time to go to the theater.
3. Peter could convince his boss to let him do anything he wanted.
4. As a result, he was able to stay home from work last week.
5. Professor Smith could speak Russian.
6. Because of this, she was able to translate Gorbachev's speech to the U.N.
7. Bambang couldn't pass the TOEFL, so he enrolled in an English course.
8. Bambang wasn't able to pass the TOEFL last semester, but he succeeded this semester.

Exercise 8

Here is a list of activities. From this list, identify things that you were able to do ten years ago. Write complete sentences that describe those abilities. Identify things that you couldn't do ten years ago and write complete sentences about them.

Think of three to five other original things for each category and write sentences about them. You should have a total of eight sentences that describe things you could do ten years ago, and eight sentences about things you couldn't do ten years ago.

ride a bike	buy alcoholic beverages
speak fluent English	run a mile in eight minutes
understand American films	drive a truck
play a musical instrument	live independently away from home
read and write English	attend university classes
speak a second language	swim
read and write a second language	play American football
drive a car	translate things into English

Exercise 9

Underline the structures that refer to past abilities in these short passages. Why do you think the author decided to use the particular form he did?

1. Matt stood in line for four hours, but he wasn't able to get tickets for the Grateful Dead concert. When he got home, Jeff could tell that he was frustrated and a little angry. He wanted to cheer Matt up, but he couldn't do much to improve Matt's mood.

2. Billy was a genius. He was able to do many things that other children his age couldn't do. He could solve complicated mathematical equations. He could write poetry and quote Shakespeare. He was even able to get into college when he was only 14 years old. But he couldn't make friends with other children his own age.

Focus 4

MEANING

Habitual Actions: *Would* versus *Used To*

MEANING

- You can use ***would*** and ***used to*** to describe habits and regular activities in the past.
    - (a) I **used to** live in Washington, D.C. Every day I **would** go jogging past all the famous monuments. No matter how hot or cold it was, I **would** run around the Tidal Basin and along the Mall.
- Use of these forms depends on whether they describe a habitual **activity** or a habitual **state**.

Activities can be expressed by both ***would*** and ***used to***.	**States** must be expressed by **used to** or simple past tense. We do not use ***would***.
(b) When I was a child, I **would wait** at the bus stop for my father to come home. **(c)** When I was a child, I **used to wait** at the bus stop.	**(d)** When I was a child, I **used to have** lots of toys. **(e)** When I was a child, I **had** lots of toys. **(f)** NOT: When I was a child, I **would have** lots of toys.

414

Exercise 10

Here is a list of things many children do:

believe in ghosts

be afraid of the dark

eat vegetables

play Cowboys and Indians

pretend to be able to fly

ride a bicycle

spend the night at a friend's house

have a secret hiding place

play with dolls

like going to the doctor

enjoy going to school

obey older brothers or sisters

cry when hurt

1. From this list choose five things that you used to do when you were a child.
2. Choose five things that you did not do.
3. Think of three original things for each category.
4. Write complete sentences describing those activities. Be sure to use the correct form for all stative verbs. You should have eight sentences describing things you used to do as a child and eight sentences about things you did not do.

Exercise 11

Ask a partner questions about the things you wrote about in Exercise 11.

EXAMPLE: *When you were a child, did you ever pretend that you could fly?*

Report some of your partner's answers to the rest of the class.

Focus 5

FORM ● USE

Future in Past Time

FORM
USE

- The Past Time Frame can include references to future events. The actual time of these events may be in the past in relation to *now* (the moment of speaking or writing), but it is in the future in relation to our moment of focus.

    (a) My parents **got married** almost 50 years ago. **In 1937,** my father first met the woman that he **would** marry a few years later. From that very first day, my father knew that he **was** eventually **going to** marry her.

    (b) Although Lincoln **wasn't to become** President until 1860, he started running for political offices quite early in his career. He **would have** three unsuccessful tries at public office before he finally won his first election.

Exercise 12

Underline all the modal structures that refer to future events or intentions in these paragraphs.

(1)When I was a child, I used to dream about my future. (2)I thought I was going to be a doctor or a movie star. (3)I would have a university medical degree. (4)I would have a job where I could do what I wanted, and I wouldn't have to go to an office every day. (5)I was going to be famous, and I was definitely going to have lots of money. (6)I would have a big house in Hollywood and ten children.

(1)Nora was going to spend a month in Japan before she started her new job, which was to begin in six weeks. (2)She was going to fly to Japan last Monday, but a strange thing happened as she was about to leave for the airport. (3)Suddenly she had a strong sensation that she shouldn't get on the plane. (4)She had a strange feeling that there might be an accident, or that there would be some other mishap. (5)She knew that she could take a flight later in the week, so that's what she decided to do.

Focus 6

Was Going To versus Would

USE

- You should use **was going to** instead of **would**
  - to introduce a topic:
    - **(a)** Elizabeth didn't have much time to get ready for the prom. She **was going to** do all her errands in a single afternoon. First she **would** pick up her dress. Then she **would** get her hair done. That **would** leave her the rest of the afternoon to get ready.
  - to indicate immediate future:
    - **(b)** John didn't want to leave the house. It **was going to** rain any minute.
  - to describe unfulfilled intentions (intended actions that did not actually take place):
    - **(c)** At first, my parents **weren't going to** let me stay up late, but I convinced them to let me do it.
    - **(d)** Oh, here you are! I **was going to** call you, but now I don't have to.
    - **(e)** We **were going to** go skiing tomorrow, but there's no snow, so we'll just stay home instead.

Exercise 13

Do the following sentences describe **a)** unfulfilled intentions or **b)** future activities? In sentences that describe future activities, substitute *would* for *was/were going to*.

> **EXAMPLE:** Nora and Jim aren't here right now. They said they **were going to** be studying at the library.
>
> *It describes future activity: They said they would be studying at the library.*

1. I **wasn't going to** mention the money you owe me. But since you brought it up, I guess we should talk about it.
2. My teacher **wasn't going to** postpone the test, so we studied for the entire weekend.
3. The committee organized the refreshments for the party. Mary **was going to** bring cookies. John **was going to** take care of beverages.
4. I'm not finished painting the house. Jim **was going to help,** but I guess he had something else to do.
5. **Were you going to** send me a check? I haven't received it yet.
6. I never thought the party **was going to** be this much fun.
7. We **weren't going to** extend our vacation, but the weather was so nice that we decided to stay for a few more days.

Exercise 14

Decide which form, *would* or *was/were going to,* you should use in the following sentences. In some cases, both answers may be correct.

1. As soon as Charley heard about Rebecca's party, he decided that he _____ (not go). Gladys _____ (be) there, and she and Charley didn't get along. He was afraid that she _____ (probably drink) too much and then she _____ (want) to tell everyone about how they used to be engaged to be married.

2. Last week Jeff stood in line for five hours to get a ticket to the opera, but he knew it was worth the long wait. It _____ (be) a great performance. Pavarotti _____ (sing) the part of Falstaff. Jeff had heard him before, so he was sure it _____ (be) wonderful.

3. Naomi didn't know what to do for her vacation. Perhaps she _____ (go) to Mexico. The plane ticket _____ (be) expensive, but she didn't want to travel by herself on the bus.

4. When I talked to Janet last Sunday night, she wasn't planning on getting much sleep. Her project was already a week late, and she couldn't ask the professor for another extension. She _____ (finish) her assignment, even if she had to stay up until dawn. It _____ (not be) easy. She had to finish reading *War and Peace,* and then write a ten-page paper. She _____ (probably be) up all night.

5. We performed a very difficult experiment in our chemistry class the other day. I was very nervous because we had to put just the right amount of chemicals into a solution in order for the reaction to occur. Too much phosphorous _____ (cause) the wrong reaction. If there was too little, nothing _____ (happen) at all. If I _____ (do) the experiment correctly, it _____ (be) necessary to measure very, very carefully.

Exercise 15

For the expressions of Future in Past Time Frame that you found in the passage in Exercise 13, decide why you think the author used one form rather than another.

Activities

Activity 1

In the introductory Task, you talked about ways in which people change for the better as they grow older. Now think about ways that people change for the worse.

- Make a list of things that you can no longer do that you used to be able to do. These may be activities or privileges. If you wish, compare your list to those of other students in the class.
- Write a paragraph describing one general way that people's lives change for the worse as they grow older. Use the list of things you can no longer do to help you organize your thoughts and provide examples for you to support your ideas.

Activity 2

In 1989, important political changes in Eastern Europe resulted in important changes in worldwide economics, politics, and military alliances. In 1991, the outbreak of war in the Middle East caused similar unexpected changes in world affairs.

- What predictions did people make about world events before these changes occurred? What things are happening now that seemed impossible a few years ago? With other students, develop two lists:

    1. things people thought were going to happen that no longer seem likely to happen
    2. things that are happening now that people never thought would happen

    Make a presentation to the rest of the class about great surprises in history or unforseen developments in world affairs.

Activity 3

Write a short paragraph about one or more of these topics:

- bad habits that you used to have but do not have anymore.
- things you would do as a child when you were unhappy.
- a time when you were going to do something but were not allowed or were not able to do so.
- how your life has turned out differently from your expectations (things you thought were going to happen that did not and vice versa).

Activity 4

Science Fiction is a kind of literature that describes how things will be in the future. Writers of science fiction have been making predictions about the future for many years. Jules Verne, H. G. Wells, George Orwell, and Aldous Huxley were all famous writers who wrote novels describing life at the end of the twentieth century. Compare their visions of the future with the way things actually are. Were the writers right or wrong in their portrayals of the future?

- Jules Verne's predictions in *From the Earth to the Moon* and *Twenty Thousand Leagues Under the Sea:*

    Everyone will own an airplane.

    There will be colonies on the moon.

    There will be a single world language.

    People will use solar power to get energy.

- H. G. Wells' predictions in *The War of the Worlds* and other novels:

    Aliens from Mars will invade the earth.

    The aliens will conquer the earth.

    The aliens will succumb to bacterial infections.

    People will be able to travel through time.

    Scientists will discover a chemical that will make people invisible.

- George Orwell's predictions in *1984:*

    The government will control all aspects of people's lives.

    There will only be three or four huge governments, and they will constantly be at war with each other.

    People will be watched by police, by hidden cameras, and microphones.

    Anyone who tries to disagree with the government will be put in prison.

- Aldous Huxley's predictions in *Brave New World:*

    Children will be born through artificial means.

    They will be raised in state-run nurseries, instead of in individual families.

    There will be movies that are so realistic that people will think they are actually happening.

    The use of mind-altering drugs will be widespread, and encouraged by the government.

- Which writer did the most accurate job of predicting the future? Write an essay or make a presentation to the rest of the class on the accurate and mistaken predictions of these famous writers.

Activity 5

How has the social role of women changed in the last 50 years? What things were your grandmothers not allowed to do, simply because they were women? What things would women never consider doing 50 years ago that are commonplace today? Write a paragraph or make a presentation to the rest of the class discussing the five biggest differences between women's lives 50 years ago as compared with today.

32

Reported Speech

Task

Look at the following series of pictures. It is the photographic record of a conversation between Jack and Jean.

• What do you think these people are talking about? Write down the exact conversation that you think occurred between them.

PHOTO 1:

Jack:

Jean:

Jack:

Jean:

PHOTO 2:

Jack:

Jean:

Jack:

PHOTO 3:

Jean:

Jack:

Jean:

PHOTO 4:

Jack:

Jean:

Jack:

Jean:

- Now compare your conversation with that of another student in the class. Discuss what you thought they were talking about in each picture and why you thought that. Your discussion might be something like this:

    You: In the first picture, I thought that Jack was telling Jean that he had something important to tell her.

    Your partner: Oh, really? I thought that he was trying to introduce himself for the first time. Why did you think he already knew her?

    You: Because they're sitting rather close together.

- Report the three most interesting differences between your two conversations (and your reasons for thinking so) to the rest of the class.

Focus 1

Basic Time Frame in Direct Quotation and Reported Speech

MEANING

- When people describe a conversation that happened in the past, they often use reported speech rather than direct quotation. **Direct quotation** is the **actual words that were spoken** in the conversation. **Reported speech** expresses the **meaning** of what was said.

Direct Quotation	Reported Speech
present time frame: **now:** the conversation itself **then:** things that happen before the conversation use past tense. **I/My** = Jack	**past time frame:** **now:** the report of the conversation **then:** the conversation itself **time before then:** Things that happened before the conversation use perfect aspect. **I/My** = Jean **He/his** = Jack
Jack is speaking at this moment: "I'm really sick. I am having terrible headaches. I'm going to try to see my doctor this afternoon, if I can get someone to drive me to his office."	Jean is reporting a conversation with Jack: "I'm worried about Jack. I saw him yesterday. He said that he was really sick. He was having terrible headaches. He was going to try to see his doctor yesterday afternoon, if he could get someone to drive him to the doctor's office. I hope he's O.K.!"
"My headache was getting worse all the time, so I went to the doctor yesterday. She took my temperature. She prescribed some pills. My condition has improved, but I still haven't gone back to work yet."	"I saw Jack yesterday. He's a little better. He said that his headache had been getting worse, so he had gone to the doctor the day before yesterday. She had taken his temperature. She had prescribed some pills. Jack felt that his condition had improved, but he still hadn't gone back to work."

Focus 2

FORM

Tense Change in Reported Speech

FORM

- The change in the frame of reference requires changes in form. You need to make changes in verb tenses
  - to refer to the Present Time Frame:

Direct Quotation: Moment of Focus: now Form: present tenses	Reported Speech: Moment of Focus: then Form: past tenses
I'**m** really sick. I **am having** terrible headaches. I'**m going to try** to see my doctor this afternoon, if I **can get** someone to drive me to his office."	He **was** really sick. He **was having** terrible headaches. He **was going to try** to see his doctor yesterday afternoon, if he **could get** someone to drive him to the doctor's office.

  - to refer to the Past Time Frame:

Moment of Focus: time before now Form: past tense/present perfect	Moment of Focus: time before then Form: past perfect tenses
My headache **was getting** worse all the time, so I **went** to the doctor yesterday. She **took** my temperature. She **prescribed** some pills. My condition **has improved,** but I still **haven't gone** back to work yet.	His headache **had been getting** worse, so he **had gone** to the doctor the day before yesterday. She **had taken** his temperature. She **had prescribed** some pills. Jack felt that his condition **had improved** but when I spoke to him he still **hadn't gone** back to work.

Exercise 1

Denise Driven had a meeting with her boss, Mr. Green, to complain about some of the things that Peter Principle was or was not doing in the office. Listed below are some of the complaints that Denise made about Peter. Change these direct quotations to reported speech, using the cue given:

EXAMPLE: "I've been getting more and more annoyed by Peter's behavior." Denise reported that. . . .

Denise reported that she had been getting more and more annoyed by Peter's behavior.

1. "Peter needs to be more serious about work." Denise felt that. . . .
2. "Peter came to work 15 minutes late for the second time in a month." Denise was angry that. . . .
3. "Peter is going to leave the office early to see his child perform in a school play." She complained that. . . .
4. "He is always whistling in the office." She didn't like the fact that. . . .
5. "He has made rude comments about my personal life." She was upset that. . . .

Exercise 2

Listed below are other complaints Denise had about Peter. How do you think she stated her complaints? Restate them as direct quotations, using **"Denise said. . . ."**

EXAMPLE: She reported that she had been getting more and more annoyed by Peter's behavior.

Denise said, "I have been getting more and more annoyed by Peter's behavior."

1. She was annoyed that he didn't always finish projects on time.
2. She was unhappy that he told too many jokes at staff meetings.
3. She didn't like the fact that he refused to come into the office on Saturdays.
4. She was upset that he was going to miss an important meeting because he had promised to take his children to the circus.
5. She was angry that he constantly allowed his personal life to interfere with his work obligations.

Focus 3

Modal Changes in Reported Speech

- You need to change present modals to past modals in reported speech:

Direct Quotation	Reported Speech
(a) "I **will try** to see my doctor this afternoon, if I **can** get someone to drive me to his office."	**(b)** He said that he **would try** to see his doctor yesterday afternoon, if he **could** get someone to drive him to the doctor's office.
may changes to	*might*
can	*could*
shall	*should*
will	*would*

- But do not change past modals to perfect modals:

Direct Quotation	Reported Speech
(c) "I **couldn't** get tickets."	**(d)** Jack said that he **couldn't** get tickets.
	(e) NOT: Jack said that he **couldn't have gotten** tickets.

Exercise 3

The following is the response Mr. Green made when he talked with Denise. Change his direct quotation to reported speech. Start your paragraph with: *Mr. Green said that.* . . . Add *Mr. Green suggested that* . . . and *Mr. Green thought that* . . . in other places in the paragraph.

> Mr. Green said, "The personnel officer will be asked to speak to Peter. If Peter can't get to the office on time, he will just have to take an earlier bus. He may not be crazy about getting up at 5:30, but he will have to do it if he wants to keep his job. Personnel won't talk to Peter about the other problems he may be having, though. One of Peter's friends in the office can deal with him directly about his lack of responsibility. Peter probably won't change much, but he may be more willing to listen to the complaints if he can get the information from someone he likes and respects."

Focus 4

Changes in Pronouns and Possessive Determiners

FORM

- In reported speech, you must change pronoun and possessive determiners in order to maintain meaning:

	Implied Meaning
(a) Jack said,"**I** am sick."	Jack is sick.
(b) Jack told me that **I** was sick.	I am sick, not Jack.
(c) Jack told me that **he** was sick.	Jack is sick.
Direct Quotation	**Reported Speech**
(d) "**You** will be happy to know that **my** condition has improved, but **I** still haven't gone back to **my** office yet."	**(e)** He said that **I** would be happy to know that **his** condition had improved, but **he** still hadn't gone back to **his** office yet.

- If there is some confusion about what a pronoun or possessive determiner refers to, it may be necessary to substitute the actual noun:

Direct Quotation	**Reported Speech**
(f) "I asked my brother Peter to bring **his** wife to the party."	**(g)** Jack asked his brother to bring his— **Peter's**—wife to the party.

427

Focus 5

Changes in Demonstratives and Adverbials

FORM

- You may also need to change demonstratives and adverbials to maintain meaning:

	Implied Meaning
(a) On Saturday, Jack said, "Please come **here** for dinner **tonight**." **(b)** On Saturday, Jack asked me to go **there** for dinner **that night**.	Jack wants the speaker to arrive at his house on Saturday.
(c) On Saturday, Jack asked me to come **here** for dinner **tonight**.	Jack wants the speaker to arrive at the place and time of the second conversation—not Jack's house, not Saturday.
Direct Quotation	**Reported Speech**
(d) "I went to the doctor **yesterday**."	**(e)** Jack told me that he had gone to the doctor **on the previous day**.

- Here are some examples of common changes in reference that reported speech requires:

this/these	changes to	that/those
here		there
today/tonight		the day/that night
yesterday		the day before/the previous day
tomorrow		the next day
two days from today		two days from then
two days ago		two days earlier

Exercise 4

Change the following statements into reported speech:

> **EXAMPLE:** Jack said, "I came here to see my doctor, but she's on vacation until tomorrow."
>
> *Jack said that he had gone there to see his doctor, but she was on vacation until the next day.*

1. Yesterday morning Peter said, "I am coming to the meeting this afternoon."
2. When I saw Mary last week she told me, "My father may be able to take this letter directly to the Immigration Office later today."
3. Last week my brother told me, "I have already completed all the assignments I have for my classes this week."
4. Two days ago I spoke to the doctor, and she said, "The results of your test will be here by tomorrow morning."
5. Yesterday my mother promised me, "Tomorrow when you come here, I'll give you some of my delicious fudge."

Focus 6

FORM

Statements in Reported Speech

FORM

- In direct quotation, you use the same markers, **quotation marks ("...")**, for statements, questions, and imperatives.
  - **(a)** The doctor told me, "I'm afraid we'll have to do more tests."
  - **(b)** The doctor asked me, "Have you been having these headaches for a long time?"

  In reported speech, different markers are used for statements, questions, and imperatives.
- **That** introduces reported statements. In informal contexts and conversation, **that** is often omitted.
  - **(c)** The doctor told me **that** he was afraid we would have to do more tests.
  - **(d)** The doctor told me he was afraid we would have to do more tests.

Exercise 5

Underline the reported statements in the following passage. Restate each one as direct quotation. Be sure to make the other necessary changes of tense and reference to reflect how the original statements were actually produced. The first one has been done for you as an example.

> **EXAMPLE:** *The representatives announced, "The rate of violent crime has decreased significantly over the last five months."*

(1) At last month's press conference, representatives of the Metropolitan Police Department announced <u>the rate of violent crime had decreased significantly over the last five months.</u> (2) They admitted there had been a slight increase in thefts and burglaries, and that the Department would continue frequent patrols in all neighborhoods. (3) When asked about the budget being discussed with the Mayor's office, they predicted that it would be finalized by the end of that week and that the accelerated hiring program might begin as soon as the following Wednesday.

Exercise 6

Underline the reported statements in the following passage. Restate each one as a direct quotation. Be sure to make the other necessary changes of tense and reference to reflect the exact words that the child actually heard or thought. The first one has been done for you as an example.

> **EXAMPLE:** *His parents told him, "We found you under a cabbage leaf."*

(1) When I was a child, I had some very strange ideas about where babies come from. (2) My parents always told me <u>that they had found me under a cabbage leaf.</u> (3) I knew that probably wasn't true, since I realized there were lots of new babies in my neighborhood and no cabbage plants at all. (4) For several years, I thought my parents had actually bought my younger sister at the hospital. (5) I figured hospitals were places that sold babies to any couple that wanted one. (6) This was because when my mother came back from the hospital after giving birth to my sister, I heard her remind my father that he had to be sure to pay the bill before that week was over. (7) I was a little jealous of my new sister, and I hoped that my father would forget to pay and that the hospital would decide to take her back and sell her to someone else. (8) It wasn't until several years later that I found out that babies were neither bought nor found.

Focus 7

Questions in Reported Speech

FORM

- You need to mark questions in reported speech with two kinds of changes:
  - Changes in word order: All reported speech occurs in statement word order, whether it is a statement or a question.

Direct Quotation:	Reported Speech:
(a) "Am I late?"	(b) Jack asked **if he was late.**
(c) "Do you need money?"	(d) Jack wanted to know **whether I needed money.**
(e) "How much do you need?"	(f) He asked **how much I needed.**

- Addition of question markers:

Yes/no Questions:	
(g) He wanted to know **if** I could bring my notes to the meeting. (h) He wanted to know **whether** I could bring my notes to the meeting. (i) He wanted to know **whether or not** I could bring my notes to the meeting.	We use **if/whether(or not)** to report "**yes/no**" and "**either/or**" questions. **If** is preferred for "**yes/no**" questions. **Whether(or not)** is preferred for "**either/or**" questions, but both forms can be used in both kinds of questions.

Wh-Questions:	
(j) I applied for a job. They wanted to know **where I lived, when I was born, how many brothers and sisters I had,** and **what kind of previous experience I had had in sales.**	We use a **wh-question word** to report **wh- questions.**

431

Exercise 7

Below is a list of interview questions that were common in American businesses 30 or 40 years ago. Employers these days no longer ask some of these questions. In other cases, the law prohibits asking such questions.

1. Are you married or single?
2. Does your wife work outside the home?
3. How many children do you have?
4. Are you a Communist?
5. Do you go to church?
6. How old are you?
7. Why do you want to work for this company?
8. Do you use drugs?
9. What is your racial background?
10. How much experience do you have?

Restate these questions as statements about old-fashioned hiring practices by adding such reporting phrases as, "A number of years ago employers used to ask, . . . " "They wanted to know, . . . " "They often asked prospective employees to tell them, . . . " and other similar phrases you can think of. Which questions do you think are still in use today?

Exercise 8

Read the following report of a job interview. Then write the list of questions the interviewer actually asked.

EXAMPLE: *Where did you go to high school?*

(1)Bob applied for a summer job as a computer programmer in a large company. (2)The head of the Personnel Office interviewed him. (3)She wanted to know where he had graduated from high school, and if he had ever studied in a college or university. (4)She wanted to know if he had ever been arrested, or whether he had ever needed to borrow money in order to pay off credit card purchases. (5)She wanted to know how fast he could type and what kind of experience he had had with computers, and whether he was more proficient in COBOL or BASIC. (6)She asked him what companies he had worked for in the past. (7)She wanted to know what his previous salary had been. (8)She wanted to know why he was no longer working at his previous job. (9)She asked him if he would voluntarily take a drug test. (10)He began to wonder if he really wanted to work for a company that wanted to know so much about his private life.

Focus 8

Commands and Requests in Reported Speech

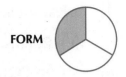

FORM

- Use indirect objects and infinitive complements to report commands and requests.
  - To report **commands**, use verbs like *tell, order*, etc. To report **requests**, use verbs such as *ask, request*, etc.
    - **(a)** The teacher **told me to do** the homework.
    - **(b)** My roommate **asked me to help** with the dishes.
  - Report negative commands and requests with **not + infinitive**.
    - **(c)** The teacher told me **not to joke** with other students.
    - **(d)** My roommate asked me **not to play** my stereo too loud.

Exercise 9

Rewrite the following indirect commands and requests as direct quotations.

> **EXAMPLE:** On his first day in the Army, Kilroy was told to report to the drill field by the master sergeant.
> *The master sergeant told Kilroy, "Report to the drill field."*

1. Another officer assigned him to clean the area for nearly an hour.
2. The officers ordered all the new recruits not to talk to each other.
3. They were told to stand at attention until their papers had been processed.
4. Kilroy asked to go to the bathroom, but this request was denied.
5. Finally the processing was over, and they were ordered to return to their barracks.
6. Several other recruits invited Kilroy to join them in a game of cards.
7. He told them he was too tired, and asked them not to be too noisy, since he wanted to sleep.

Focus 9

When No Tense Changes Are Required

FORM

- You do not need to make the tense and modal changes if you are reporting
  - things that are always true:

(a) My father always told me, "Time **is** money."	**(b)** My father always told me that time **is** money.

- things that are still true:

(c) Jean told me, "Jack **is still living** with his parents after all these years."	**(d)** Jean told me (that) Jack **is still living** with his parents after all these years.

- hypothetical statements:

(e) Peter said, "If I **had** the money, I **would make** a donation to the club, but I **am** a little short on cash this month."	**(f)** Peter said that if he **had** the money, he **would make** a donation to the club, but that he **was** a little short on cash this (last) month.

- statements that occurred only a very short time ago:

(g) Bambang told me, "I **can't** understand a word you're saying."	**(h)** He **just** said that he **can't** understand a word **you're** saying.

- statements where such a change would alter the meaning:

(i) Jack said, "I **could** speak Spanish when I was a child."	**(j)** Jack said that he **could** speak Spanish when he was a child.
	(k) NOT: Jack said that he **could have** spoken Spanish. (This means he had the ability but didn't do it.)

434

Exercise 10

Decide whether tense changes are required for all the verb phrases in the following sentences, if they are changed to reported speech. If a tense change is not required, state the reason why.

EXAMPLE: Shakespeare once observed, "Love is blind."

No change. Timeless truth—still true.

Last week our teacher reminded us, "You should do your homework before you come to class tomorrow."

Last week our teacher reminded us to do our homework before we came to class the next day.

1. A student in my geography class reported, "Not all the people who live in China speak Chinese as their first language."
2. My brother told me, "I wouldn't need to borrow money from you all the time if I had a better-paying job."
3. It was only a minute ago that I asked, "Are you paying attention?"
4. John told me, "I couldn't get any tickets for the concert."
5. Yesterday Denise said "If I were you, I would plan things a little more completely before you leave for vacation next week."
6. This morning Peter told me, "I'm still having problems with Denise, but I'm trying extra hard to get along with her."

Focus 10

USE

Using Reported Speech versus Direct Quotation

USE

- You can use reported speech patterns
  - when you report conversations held earlier:
    - **(a)** No wonder Denise looks sad. I heard that she wouldn't be taking a vacation after all. Apparently, something has come up that makes it impossible for her to leave.
  - when you report things that were thought or believed but not necessarily spoken:
    - **(b)** When he reached the New World, Christopher Columbus **thought** that he had reached Asia, so he called the inhabitants he found there "Indians."
    - **(c)** When I was a little boy, I **was very curious about** whether or not there were dogs in heaven.
  - to make questions or requests more polite:
    - **(d)** Can you tell me **what your ZIP code is?**
    - **(e)** Do you know **what time the store opens?**
    - **(f)** I wonder **if Dr. Jones is able to come to the phone.**

435

To most native speakers, *yes/no* and *Wh-*questions sound more polite if they are embedded in a conversational frame such as, "Do you know," "Can you tell me," or "I wonder. . . ." Such embedded questions usually have a present time frame, and so the tense of the embedded question does not need to be changed.

- in most formal expository prose:

  (g) I will never forget the day my father told me that the family had decided that I could go to the United States to complete my studies.

  (h) AWKWARD: I will never forget the day my father said, "The family has decided that you can go to the United States to complete your studies."

- You will find direct quotation primarily in narrative fiction and popular non-fiction such as magazine articles, where the author uses quotations of experts to support a point. For most story-telling, direct quotation is more acceptable.

Exercise 11

Identify the examples of reported speech in the following passages and tell why you think the author chose to use (or not to use) reported speech. Discuss your ideas with a partner and present them to the rest of the class.

1. Shakespeare once observed that love is blind. My friend Charley is certainly living proof of that. Six months ago he told me that he had finally met the woman of his dreams. But she doesn't appear to be interested in any of the things that he likes to do. He still comes alone to the bowling club and the soup kitchen. All his friends have noticed that he still seems single on Saturday nights. I thought people who are in love were supposed to enjoy being together.

2. I wonder if you know how I can get in touch with Mona. Do you happen to know where she is living these days? She's moved, and I don't have her new address.

3. People used to think that breathing night air was very unhealthy. Doctors in the Middle Ages actually recommended that people should close all windows when they slept, even in the hottest weather.

4. It was a dark and stormy night. Jason heard a voice whispering on the steps outside. "Your life is in greatest peril," said the voice. But when he looked out the window, there was no one there.

5. I got some rather shocking news yesterday. I heard that a friend of mine had been put in jail for stealing money from her office. She had apparently embezzled thousands of dollars. Of course, I wondered whether she was guilty or not. I still do. I suppose that it could be possible. But I don't really think Denise would do such a thing.

Activities

Activity 1

Work with a different partner from the one with whom you worked on the Task. Together write a conversation that matches the photos in the Task. Act out your conversation for the rest of the class. Other students should write a paraphrase of your conversation.

Activity 2

To *eavesdrop* means to listen secretly to someone else's conversation. Go to a public place, like a restaurant, a shopping mall, or a bus station, and eavesdrop on someone's conversation. It is important not to let people know what you are doing, so pretend to read a book, study your English grammar, read a magazine in another language (people might think that you don't understand English), or pretend to write a letter.

Afterward, try to remember what the people were talking about, and what they said to each other. Did you learn anything interesting about their lives, or about English, as a result of this experience?

Activity 3

Listen to a news broadcast on television. Report one story that you heard on that broadcast to the rest of the class. Start with some sort of statement like this: I heard on the news that . . . , It was announced that . . . , and so on.

Activity 4

Play a game of Telephone. Form two or more teams of ten people each. Student 1 should make a statement to Student 2 very quietly so that only Student 2 can hear what was said. Student 2 then reports what was said to Student 3, using indirect speech ("Student 1 told me that . . . "). Student 3 tells Student 4, and so forth. When the last student receives the report, he or she should announce the message to the rest of the class. Compare how close that message is with what was originally said by Student 1. The team that has the closest, most accurate report wins a point. Student 2 starts the next round.

Activity 5

Write a paragraph discussing some of the misconceptions about life that you had when you were a child. Describe what you thought, and why you thought it. See Exercise 6 for an example.

Activity 6

Tell about a time when you had an important conversation with someone. Perhaps you learned some important information about yourself or someone else. Perhaps you found out about a decision that had a big effect on your life in some way. Perhaps you got some valuable advice.

- First, tell the **story** of the conversation. Write down who it was with and where, and when it took place. Then try to write the conversation word for word.
- Next, write a paragraph telling what you learned from this conversation and why it was important for you. You may want to begin your paragraph with, **"When I was . . . , I learned that. . . . "**

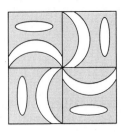

Index